Morality

AN INVITATION TO CHRISTIAN LIVING

Harcourt
Religion Publishers

JOSEPH STOUTZENBERGER

Our Mission

The primary mission of Harcourt Religion Publishers is to provide the Catholic and Christian educational markets with the highest quality catechetical print and media resources. The content of these resources reflects the best insights of current theology, methodology, and pedagogical research. The resources are practical and easy to use, designed to meet expressed market needs, and written to reflect the teachings of the Catholic Church.

Nihil Obstat
Rev. Richard L. Schaefer

Imprimatur
✠ Most Rev. Jerome Hanus OSB
Archbishop of Dubuque
June 25, 1999

The Imprimatur is an official declaration that a book or pamphlet is free of doctrinal or moral error. No implication is contained therein that anyone who granted the Imprimatur agrees with the contents, opinions, or statements expressed.

Copyright © 2001 by Harcourt Religion Publishers. All rights reserved. No part of this publication may be reproduced or transmitted in any form or by any means, electronic or mechanical, including photocopy, recording, or any information storage and retrieval system, without permission in writing from the publisher.

Requests for permission to make copies of any part of the work should be mailed to: Permissions Department, Harcourt, Inc., 6277 Sea Harbor Drive, Orlando, Florida 32887-6777.

For permission to reprint copyrighted material, grateful acknowledgement is made to the following sources:

New Revised Standard Version Bible: Catholic Edition copyright © 1993 and 1989 by the Division of Christian Education of the National Council of the Churches of Christ in the U.S.A. Used by permission. All rights reserved.

American Bible Society: Scripture selections from THE HOLY BIBLE: Contemporary English Version. Text copyright © 1995 by American Bible Society.

Excerpts from the English translation of the *Catechism of the Catholic Church* for use in the United States of America Copyright © 1993, United States Catholic Conference, Inc.—Libreria Editrice Vaticana. Used with permission.

Excerpts from the Vatican documents are used with permission from Libreria Editrice Vaticana.

Excerpts from *Economic Justice For All* Copyright © 1986 United States Catholic Conference, Inc. (USCC), Washington, DC; *The Challenge of Peace: God's Promise, Our Response* © 1983, USCC; *Summary of "The Challenge of Peace"* © 1983 USCC; *Statement on Capital Punishment* © 1980, USCC; and *To Live in Christ Jesus* © 1976, USCC. Reprinted with permission. All rights reserved.

Printed in the United States of America

ISBN 0-15-950644-1

Chapter 8

Moral Decision Making: A Process   42

Part 2:   Christian Morality Applied

Chapter 9

Sex and Morality: Caring for Our Bodies, Ourselves, and Others   164

Chapter 14

Violence and Peace: Respect for Life at Home and Abroad — 260

Chapter 15

Justice: The Moral Character of Society — 280

To Katie and Josh, Pat, and Tim

We are God's work of art, created in Christ Jesus to live the good life . . .
Ephesians 2:10 (NJB)

CHAPTER 1

Morality
An Invitation to Life in Christ

Welcome to your morality course. During this course you will be discussing issues and concerns that you already think about. You will have an opportunity to explore your decisions, your behaviors, and the values of society. Your active participation in reading and reflecting on the many topics under discussion can help you become more conscious of the world you live in and more conscientious, caring, and honest in your decision making. In particular, the course invites you to look at morality from a Christian perspective and in light of Catholic teaching. This course presumes that it makes all the difference in the world if you view yourself and other people as Jesus does. Use the course to help you grow toward becoming yourself, living a life worthy of who you are— a child of God.

Chapter Overview

• Moral decision making in large measure defines who we are.

• Christian morality is our response to Jesus.

• "God loves us" represents the starting point of Christian morality.

• Grace as sharing in God's life is both a comfort and a challenge.

• Moral decision making is both an art and a science.

Before we begin. . .

1. Think about situations that call for moral decision making. Describe three such situations.

2. What would your life be like if you did not have to consider the moral implications of your actions? Would you prefer life to be like that?

Let us pray . . .

Jesus, savior and brother, you have told us that you are never far from us. Throughout our moral life—the choices we make day by day and moment by moment—may we always seek to walk with you as we face the challenges that come our way. Send your Holy Spirit to guide us on our journey. Amen.

Morality
Our Capacity to Choose Good or Evil

morality—our decision-making capacity as it affects ourselves and others

We humans possess a special capacity for decision making. **Morality** refers to decision making that deliberately affects ourselves or others in either positive or negative ways. Thus, morality represents a uniquely human activity.

The Blessing and the Burden of Decision Making

- You are at a dance with some classmates. A boy with whom you were friends in grade school comes into the room, and someone in your group says, "Look at that guy. What a loser!" The others laugh. How do you respond?

- You are a girl who has been going out with a certain boy for a few weeks. You go out with him only because you want to have someone to talk to on the phone and to do things with on weekends. He starts to end all of his conversations with you by saying, "I love you." You're uncomfortable about this, but you don't want to hurt his feelings. What do you do?

- Your parents are going away for the weekend, leaving you and your brother in charge of the house. Your brother, a high school senior, invites some of his friends over on Friday night. They bring a case of beer with them. What do you do?

- You are walking along a downtown street in a large city. A poorly clad older woman comes up to you and asks, "Can you spare some

change so I can get something to eat?" How do you respond?

- You are about to go to a party when a friend who has been having family problems calls and asks if she can come over to talk to you. She sounds upset. What do you do?

- One day your math teacher leaves the classroom for a moment, and a student takes a copy of an upcoming test from the teacher's desk. When the teacher returns he notices that a test is missing. After the period he calls you aside and

asks you if you know what happened to the missing test. What do you say to him?

- You finish drinking from an aluminum can. You recall the messages you've heard about recycling, but no one who is with you keeps their cans separate from the rest of the trash. What do you do with the can?

- The school's chaplain invites students to spend part of their Christmas vacation collecting and delivering toys to children in poor families. How do you respond?

To Be Moral Is to Be Human

Many traditional moral philosophers highlighted the link between being moral and being human. They proposed that moral behavior is acting in a human way while immoral behavior distorts or falls short of acting in a human fashion. (We will further explore this link in chapter seven under the topic "natural law.") During this course we will be struggling to determine the difference between right and wrong behavior, good and bad decisions—in other words, between humane and inhumane responses to problems that come our way. In a sense, a term for this struggle itself is *morality* or *moral decision making*.

The following distinctions are basic to our study. Decisions are *moral* in a positive sense when we use our decision-making capacity—as best we can—to promote human welfare, our own and that of others. Decisions are *immoral* that are deliberately harmful and destructive, of ourselves or others. *Nonmoral* decisions are neutral; such decisions have neither a positive nor a negative effect on people. Amorality refers to disregarding the fact that our decisions can either promote our welfare and that of others or prove to be harmful. People who are *amoral* have no sense of right or wrong and thus display no sensitivity to the moral dimensions of their actions. **A**

Moral Distinctions	
Moral	positive; promotes human welfare
Immoral	negative; harmful and destructive
Nonmoral	neutral; neither harms nor hurts
Amoral	no sense of right or wrong; insensitive to moral effects of actions

Morality Requires a Sense of Responsibility

The above terms flow from the definition of morality, that our decisions are moral ones when they deliberately affect ourselves and others in positive or negative ways. For example, walking down a street is not of itself an action that has moral implications; we would call such action nonmoral behavior. Similarly, accidentally falling into a pothole and breaking the expensive watch our mother just gave us is not a moral matter—unless, of course, we display no concern about whether or not we break the watch or hurt our mother's feelings, in which case we would be acting amorally. However, walking down a street while throwing stones at passing cars or tripping passing in-line skaters does have moral implications. Likewise, walking down a street as part of an event designed to raise funds for fighting hunger has moral implications. Morality reminds us that much—and quite possibly most—of our behavior does not concern ourselves alone. Whether we like it or not, we live our lives as part of an ever-expanding circle of people. That is, we live in a world where people are responsible for one another. We might prefer not to bother with all the moral implications of our actions. However, our actions or inactions can affect other people; therefore, a moral sense reminds us to recognize and accept responsibility for our actions.

Activity A

Do you agree with the traditional philosophical position that acting morally is acting humanly but that acting immorally distorts one's humanity and falls short of being human? Use examples to defend your answer.

Moral Decision Making—
An Everyday Thing

We are constantly making choices—this fact comes with being human. (Remember the old saying, that even "not to decide is to decide.") Morality, therefore, is an everyday thing. It has to do with how we spend our money, our time, and our talents; how we treat our parents, our friends, people we don't like, and the environment; how we respond to our neighbor in need; and how we attempt to resolve conflicts. Our moral viewpoints guide what we do with the many decisions that come our way over a lifetime.

The brief sketches opening this chapter represent a mere sampling of the types of decisions that all of us must face. Each new day greets us with the challenge of making decisions that have an impact on ourselves or others in positive or negative ways. Each new encounter with another calls us to respond—pleasantly or angrily, honestly or deceptively, encouragingly or cuttingly. With each new piece of information that enters our consciousness, with each new experience that we have, with each "yes" or "no" that we say to those around us, we are shaping our moral viewpoints and ourselves as decision makers.

Even if you have been an adolescent for only a short time, no doubt you are experiencing the blessings and the burdens of decision making. Not too long ago your choices were simpler: Do I accept the demands of my parents and other adults, or do I act counter to them? Now you are being met with so many more decisions—decisions that you never had to face before, and with decisions for which you alone will be held responsible. You are expected to take charge of your life, to use your talents wisely, to act responsibly, and to consider the welfare of others—without always having someone tell you the right thing to do. How you will use this new power now will play a large role in determining who you will become.

Consider just two of the many examples illustrating this blessing and burden of decision making. You either are or will soon arrive at an age when you can legally drive a car. This "license" symbolizes the excitement of increasing freedom. It also represents the accountability that faces you as a maturing young person. Moreover, with or without the independence afforded by a car, you will more often find yourself in circumstances where you are not under adult supervision. You are expected to act in ways that demonstrate greater and greater personal authority.

Similarly, in recent years your sexuality has blossomed into a wonderful gift. You will want to share yourself, physically, with another. This developing dimension of yourself certainly makes an important statement about who you are. However, your decision making about right and wrong in regard to your sexuality makes an even greater statement about who you are.

Moral decision making contributes greatly to defining who you are. Your identity takes shape as you bump up against family members, peers, teachers, and even strangers. Constantly, you are called upon to make choices that affect yourself and others. When your conscious choices help or harm someone, then you have entered into the realm of moral decision making.

Moral decision making, then, is a very important dimension of your life right now. It brings joys and demands, challenges and opportunities. Through this capacity, you participate in shaping both yourself and, at least in a small way, your world. To exercise this capacity is to be human; to shirk from making decisions is to diminish your humanity. A course on morality is designed to help you develop the skill of decision making in light of Catholic teaching. **B** **C**

For review . . .

1. Why is morality so closely associated with being human? Give an example to illustrate that moral decision making is both a blessing and a burden.

2. Explain the difference among the following terms: moral, immoral, nonmoral, and amoral.

3. Why does being moral require a sense of responsibility?

4. What does it mean to say that morality is an everyday occurrence?

Activity B

Morality cannot be reduced to our individual perception about right and wrong. However, it is important to realize that each person has his or her own sense of what is moral and what is not. It's helpful to know what our own sense of morality is and then to check out our sense of morality over and against that of friends, experts in certain areas of thought, people with other experiences, and Church leaders. (Again, this is the purpose of our course.) With that in mind, consider the following twelve actions.

1. Rank these actions in terms of the degree to which you consider them to be more or less moral. (1 = "It's not particularly wrong; it wouldn't bother me at all." 12 = "This is seriously wrong; it would bother me a great deal.")

2. When finished, ask yourself: What might others conclude about me based on my ranking? Compare your rankings with those of others and discuss your reasoning.

_____ a. I started a fight with a smaller, younger student whom I simply "didn't like."

_____ b. My former boyfriend/girlfriend rejected me. I spread unkind stories about him or her.

_____ c. I helped a friend pay for an abortion.

_____ d. A student who just doesn't fit in was being mocked, and I joined in.

_____ e. I lied to my parents about where I was on Friday night. I was out drinking with friends.

_____ f. I saw a student drop ten dollars in the cafeteria. I kept it.

_____ g. I sold a car stereo system when I knew the system didn't work properly. I lied about it and made money on the deal.

_____ h. I am a boy who fathered a child and then denied that the child was mine.

_____ i. I saw a student drop an envelope containing $200. It was marked "tuition." I kept it.

_____ j. I looked at another student's answers during a test.

_____ k. I saw a traffic accident occur. I knew some people were hurt. I ignored it because I was late for practice and I might have been cut from the team.

_____ l. I was baby-sitting my younger brother and sister. Against my parents' wishes, I let my siblings watch a violent and sexually explicit movie on cable because I wanted to see it.

Activity C

1. Write down three types of moral decisions that were important to you four years ago.

2. Write about three areas of moral decision making that you are now being called upon to address that you didn't have to face before.

3. Based on this information, make a case that moral decision making has or has not recently become a more significant dimension of your life.

Christian Morality
Our Response to Jesus

Christian morality— the way that we live our lives in response to Jesus

Strictly on a human level, a sense of morality pushes us to use our decision-making capacity in positive ways. Christian morality adds a very important dimension to moral discussion. **Christian morality** refers to the way that we live our lives in response to Jesus. Because of Jesus, we are not alone when faced with the awesome responsibility of moral decision making. Looking to Jesus does not do away with our own need to make honest, caring, and thoughtful choices. Nonetheless, we find in Jesus the primary focus for addressing the question, "What should I do?"

Morality includes many facets. Just as an orchestra blends together many different instruments to create beautiful music, so we tap many different resources to create something beautiful out of our moral decision making. For Christians, every facet of decision making takes on new meaning viewed in light of Jesus Christ, the first and last reference point for Christian morality. The *Catechism of the Catholic Church*, currently a very important sourcebook for official Catholic teaching, describes the process of Christian moral decision making in these words:

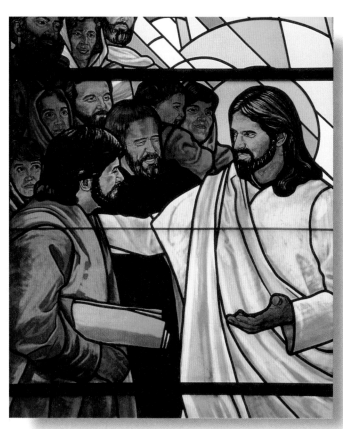

It is by looking to him in faith that Christ's faithful can hope that he himself fulfills his promises in them, and that, by loving him with the same love with which he has loved them, they may perform works in keeping with their dignity (1698). **D** **E**

Activity D

Read over again the stories on page 2 of this chapter. Now put Jesus into each situation. Would your response change? If yes, how?

Activity E

1. Draw a picture, create a collage, or write a song or poem whose theme is "Morality—responding to Jesus."

2. Explain why you chose the words or images that you used.

"Christian, Recognize Your Dignity . . ."

The Catechism begins its discussion of the moral life with the words: "Christian, recognize your dignity" (1691). Why is this simple but fundamental recognition key to Christian morality? One version of a popular fairy tale can shed some light on that question.

Like Rapunzel we can easily lose sight of our true dignity, even without a witch's spell being cast upon us. Like Rapunzel, only when we see ourselves in the eyes of the one who loves us completely do we truly see ourselves.

Rapunzel and the Prince

Rapunzel was admired for her good cheer and kindness by all who knew her. Her grace and beauty were obvious to everyone who was fortunate enough to cross her path. Rapunzel often visited those in her village who were sick or who felt lonely. She never failed to bring some cheer to their lives, and in return she felt their love and appreciation.

One day, however, Rapunzel met a witch who cast a spell upon her. From that day on, Rapunzel believed that she was ugly and unlovable. The witch carried her away and kept her imprisoned in a desolate tower. The witch removed from the tower all mirrors and shiny objects that might serve as a mirror. And everyone knows that you cannot see yourself in a witch's eyes!

Thereafter, Rapunzel never saw herself for who she truly was. Because of the witch's spell, she saw only repulsiveness in herself; and when anyone wandered near the tower, Rapunzel hid in a dark corner where she could not be seen.

Years after this change in Rapunzel, a prince traveling nearby caught a glimpse of Rapunzel before she cowered into the darkness. Captivated by her beauty, the prince made his way toward the tower. He watched as the witch climbed Rapunzel's hair to scale the tower wall. Later the prince gained entrance into Rapunzel's hideaway in the same way. The prince calmed the frightened Rapunzel and slowly moved toward her. Eventually, the prince was close enough for Rapunzel to look into his eyes. Gazing at him Rapunzel saw herself reflected in his eyes. She saw her true self for the first time since the evil spell had been cast upon her. Instead of ugliness and repulsiveness, Rapunzel saw beauty and goodness.

She felt herself being transformed, and the power of the spell was broken. Rapunzel was so transformed by this renewed vision of herself that she rejoined those in her village whom she had shunned. She vowed to live the rest of her life sharing with others the beauty and goodness she had rediscovered in herself.

ADAPTED FROM *GRIMM'S FAIRY TALES*

God Loves Us—The Starting Point of Christian Morality

The starting point of Christian moral decision making is not "What should we do?" nor even "What do we do?" but rather "Who are we?"

In the Christian vision we are children of God, a God who loves us. We are beloved of God, made in God's image and, therefore, called to be lovers as well.

In his message and, more importantly, in his very life, Jesus reveals the scope and the depth of God's love for us. *Only when we see ourselves in the eyes of Jesus do we truly see ourselves.* The gaze of Jesus, always a loving gaze, is the gaze of one who shares our humanity as well as the gaze of one who knows our deepest core. In Jesus we discover the beauty, the glory, and the power of who we are. The Gospels tell the story of true human dignity better than any fairy tale. **F**

*Every **blade of grass** has its **angel** that bends over it and whispers, "**Grow**, grow."*

—THE TALMUD

For review . . .

5. Define Christian morality.

6. With what statement does the Catechism begin its discussion of the moral life?

7. What realization is the starting point for Christian moral decision making?

Activity F

Answer **agree, disagree,** or **uncertain** to the following statements. Explain your choices. If possible, use an example to support your response.

1. Having a strong sense of personal dignity helps people act morally.

2. Experiencing love helps people love others.

3. I can honestly say that I have experienced God's love in my life.

4. "Living my life in response to Jesus" is a good definition of morality for me.

5. When faced with important moral decisions, I have asked myself, "What would Jesus do?"

Grace
Sharing in God's Life

grace—God's love and life in us, God's help

Our justification comes from the grace of God. Grace is favor, *the free and undeserved help that God gives us to respond to his call to become children of God, adoptive sons, partakers of the divine nature and of eternal life [Cf. Jn 1:12–18; 17:3; Rom 8:14–17; 2 Pet 1:3–4].*

CATECHISM, #1996

In the Christian worldview we humans live always in the sight of God. Thanks to Jesus we know that God does not look down upon us like a guard in a tower looking down on prisoners in a prison yard. Instead, through Christ we share in God's life. The term for our participation in the life of God is **grace** (Catechism, #1997). Grace is an *awesome* Christian concept. More accurately, grace is a powerful statement about how awesome we humans truly are and are called to be. Christian morality is our response to Christ's invitation to live life in the light of grace.

All of us need the transformation that the gift of grace brings. All of us could use greater freedom, wisdom, courage, and compassion— qualities that come only with God's help. Here are the stories of two young people in need of grace in their lives.

Amy's Dream World

Amy is a sophomore in high school. Whenever she goes to a party or any other social gathering, Amy clings desperately to her friends, Lauren and Ashley. If Lauren talks to someone else, there is Amy, always right beside her. If Ashley goes to the bathroom, Amy goes to the bathroom. If Lauren and Ashley are talking to boys, Amy nervously joins in.

Recently, Amy has begun to make up stories about the things she has done, the places she has been, and the people with whom she is friends. In fact, she spends more time talking about imaginary exploits than in actually living life. Her few friends continue to include her in their activities, although with less enthusiasm as time goes by.

Dave and His Mother

Dave is a freshman in high school. He has always been close to his mother. Now that he has entered high school, however, he notices he no longer has an easy relationship with her. Dave no longer confides in his mother about what he is doing, where he is going, and who his friends are. He resents her questioning him about these areas of his life.

The family table at mealtime has become a battleground. His mom asks, "What did you do in school today?" "Oh, nothing," Dave always answers. Whenever his mother probes for more details, Dave tightens his shoulders and gives her a look that begins the next battle between them. **G**

Activity G

1. If you were Amy or Dave, what would you need to hear about yourself and your actions?

2. If Amy and Dave were your friends and sought you out for help, what message would you want to convey to them?

3. If Jesus were physically present today, what do you imagine he would say to Amy and Dave? Would the message of Jesus to Amy and Dave parallel your own message to them?

Grace Brings Comfort

Like all of us, Amy is not all that she would like to be. She is not as comfortable with herself in social situations as she desperately wants to be; she does not have a life that comes close to that of her dreams. Like all of us, Dave is stretching to be himself; but with his mother, Dave asserts his independence too aggressively and thus hurtfully.

One message of Jesus' that both Amy and Dave need to hear is the following:

> *Are not two sparrows sold for a penny? Yet not one of them will fall to the ground apart from your Father. And even the hairs of your head are all counted. So do not be afraid; you are of more value than many sparrows.*
>
> MATTHEW 10:29–31

That is, like all of us, Amy and Dave need to hear that they are so loved by God that the very hairs on their heads have been counted and that they are indeed worth more than many sparrows. Jesus' gift of God's loving presence and activity in our lives is what we mean by grace.

The prophet Isaiah uses the image of a mother caring for her children to describe how much greater than any human experience is God's love for us. Such is the intimacy with God that the concept of grace conveys. **H**

> *Can a woman forget her nursing child,*
>
> *or show no compassion for the child of her womb?*
>
> *Even these may forget,*
>
> *yet I will not forget you.*
>
> *See, I have inscribed you on the palms of my hands . . .*
>
> ISAIAH 49:15–16

Grace Brings Challenge: "Cheap Grace" Versus "Costly Grace"

World War II had a profound impact on modern discussion's about morality. Those who have tried to make sense of moral and immoral behavior during that era have come to a disturbing realization. Some people in Germany and other countries contributed to the deaths of millions of people either by simply doing what they were told to do or by not taking steps to confront evil.

In contrast to such people, Dietrich Bonhoeffer, a German Lutheran pastor, actively protested the Nazi regime's policies in his country before and during the war. In the 1930s Bonhoeffer spent some time in the United States where he held a comfortable and prestigious teaching position. However, at the risk of his life he returned to Germany. He felt that during this troubled time he could influence his country's policies more by living in Germany. As a result of his anti-Nazi activities, he was imprisoned and then executed by hanging just before the war ended.

Bonhoeffer was concerned that many of his fellow Christians found the message of Jesus to be comforting but not personally challenging. He believed that faith in Jesus should lead Christians to resist actively the inhumanity that they saw around them. To describe his concern Bonhoeffer distinguished between what he called *cheap grace* and *costly grace*.

Activity H

Without naming names, tell the story of someone, real or fictional, who could benefit from hearing Jesus' message that God loves her or him.

Bonhoeffer warned his fellow Christians not to settle for grace that is cheap. As stated earlier, grace names God's presence and help in our lives, nurturing a relationship marked by God's enduring love for us. For Bonhoeffer, **cheap grace** denotes a relationship with God that we take for granted—God loves us no matter what, so it doesn't matter what we do. In other words, cheap grace is a one-way love relationship.

On the other hand, **costly grace** denotes a relationship with God that involves a response on our part. It is a two-way love relationship. We experience God's love so deeply that we are moved to love others in return. Bonhoeffer called this type of grace costly because there is a cost involved. For Bonhoeffer, the cost was death by hanging.

cheap grace— believing "God loves me no matter what; therefore I can do whatever I want"

costly grace— a relationship with God that involves a challenge and a response on our part

Bonhoeffer's distinction between cheap grace and costly grace helps us better understand the calling of the Christian life: God's love, like all true love, empowers us. Of course, choosing to do the right thing requires personal courage. God's grace, the source of courage, is there for us every step of the way. Remember that Jesus himself modeled costly grace most forcefully through his death on the cross. Christians who seek to follow Jesus will certainly find their dedication to him costly. They will also find support and inspiration leading to empowerment. As Bonhoeffer discovered, grace—costly grace—challenges but also strengthens us. **1**

Cheap grace is the deadly enemy of our Church. We are fighting today for costly grace. . . . Cheap grace means the justification of sin without the justification of the sinner. Grace alone does everything, they say, and so everything can remain as it was before. . . . let the Christian live like the rest of the world, let him model himself on the world's standards in every sphere of life, and not presumptuously aspire to live a different life. . . .

Costly grace is the treasure hidden in the field; for the sake of it a man will gladly go and sell all that he has. . . . Such grace is costly because it calls us to follow, and it is grace because it calls us to follow Jesus Christ. . . . Above all, it is costly because it cost God the life of his Son. . . .

DIETRICH BONHOEFFER, *THE COST OF DISCIPLESHIP* [NEW YORK: THE MACMILLAN COMPANY, 1963].

Activity I

Has being a Christian ever been a challenge for you? If so, describe the situation.
Do you think that for most people today being a Christian is viewed as a challenge? Why or why not?

Costly Grace Is Not a Contradiction

How can Bonhoeffer's insight about costly grace help Amy and Dave—and us? Both of these young people are faced with their own personal problems. We have difficulty imagining Amy and Dave dedicating themselves to others as Bonhoeffer envisioned Christians doing. But actually, it is people exactly like Amy and Dave who make up the Church. They are, in fact, *saints in the making*. It is people exactly like Amy and Dave who have become the great heroines and heroes, the great saints, throughout Christian history. That is, people don't become heroes and then act heroically. Rather, people struggle to do the right thing and in so doing shape themselves little by little into being holy and heroic persons.

Jesus' words of comfort and his words of challenge are not contradictory messages. Actually, they represent two sides of the same message. Amy and Dave need a breakthrough in their lives, a sense of being loved, a burst of courage, and an experience of grace. In other words, Amy and Dave need to hear Jesus' words of comfort which say that God lives in them and that God loves them as they are. Such an experience of the presence of God and of being loved can free them to explore new patterns of behavior. This is always challenging and often painful. Amy's struggle is to love herself more; Dave's struggle is to practice greater sensitivity toward his mother.

For ourselves, Bonhoeffer's insight about costly grace reminds us that grace—God's life within us and God's love for us—is a gift to be shared. We honor Mary, the Blessed Mother, as being "full of grace" because she opened herself to the joy and sorrow of becoming the Mother of the Savior of the world. Likewise, we live our lives "full of grace" when we open ourselves to the joy and pain of others. When we notice that someone is being left out and we take the initiative to include that person in our group, then we are accepting and sharing the gift of grace. When we volunteer to participate in a community-service activity at the cost of sacrificing our time, then we are sharing grace. When we risk going against the crowd because we realize that if we don't someone might get hurt, then we are living out the grace that is costly.

As we will see later on, Jesus sums up his moral teaching in one word—love (Matthew 22:37–40). However, in our culture love often means no more than a message on a greeting card—cozy, comforting, and not very demanding. In this climate, just as during the World War II era, we need to remember Bonhoeffer's insistence on costly grace. We must remember that the message of Jesus is not just consoling and comforting but is also very challenging. That is, the grace of Jesus is often demanding and unsettling—a costly grace. **J**

For review . . .

8. Define grace.
9. Who was Dietrich Bonhoeffer?
10. What is the difference between cheap grace and costly grace?
11. How did Bonhoeffer live out his message of costly grace?
12. What does it mean to live our lives "full of grace"?

Activity J

Describe possible responses to the following situations. How might the concept costly grace be applied to each?

1. Your religion teacher, whom you like, announces that a service club is having its first meeting today after school. You enjoyed doing a service project over the summer, so you think you'll attend the meeting to find out what's involved. When you arrive you discover that none of your friends have come and that all the others in the room are students who are looked down upon by most of your classmates.

2. You invite a friend over to your house for the evening. The two of you go to a local video store. You warn your friend that your parents strictly forbid you from watching excessively violent films or ones that contain strong sexual content. There's one last copy of a newly released video that you know your parents would not approve of. Your friend grabs the video and says, "This movie is supposed to be great. Don't listen to your parents. Let's get this one. They'll never know the difference." What do you do?

3. You're out on a Friday night with a crowd that you don't normally hang out with. They end up drinking in the basement of one boy's house. Sometime after midnight the party breaks up, and you head back to your neighborhood. Along the way, some of the boys decide to vandalize a few cars. The police come and stop you and one other person. A police officer asks you, "Who did this?"

4. Administrators at your school recently approved use of the auditorium for a "battle of the bands" program. A friend confides to you that one band planned to use the event to showcase a performance that would clearly embarrass the school. Your friend says, "If school officials find out, the band members will know that I told them, so make sure you don't tell anyone."

Morality
An Art and a Science

To act morally it is first necessary that a person desire to do what is right. What type of thinking can help a person who desires to live a good life actually make good moral decisions? That is, is morality more a matter of knowing what to do or of knowing how to do it? As you might imagine, the answer given by traditional moral philosophers is: both. In actuality, two kinds of thinking come into play in moral decision making. First, the science of morality refers to thoughtfully determining what is right. Secondly, the art of morality refers to practical reasoning, having the ability to see things through and to do what is right.

> *I came that they may have life, and have it abundantly.*
>
> JOHN 10:10

Critical Thinking—The Science of Morality

As a science, moral decision making requires systematic thought and analysis. When we deepen our knowledge and understanding about ourselves and about our world, we are developing the science of morality. One dimension of the science of morality is **critical thinking**, examining with an open mind what we normally take for granted. We are frequently presented with questionable propositions in the form of unquestionable truths. For instance, we can easily be deceived that the world's hungry masses are simply meant to be that way, that the accumulation of wealth is an unrestricted right, or that the unborn are nobodies undeserving of our consideration. Likewise, we might hear the following statements presented as truths with no room for criticism or disagreement:

critical thinking— using systematic thinking and analysis in our lives

- People have a constitutional right to bear arms. Sale of guns should not be restricted in any way.

- "An eye for an eye, a tooth for a tooth"— even the Bible says that capital punishment is giving wrongdoers what they deserve.

- Most stores charge outrageous prices. Stealing from them is okay as long as you don't get caught.

- It's a free country. People should be able to say anything they want to over the Internet.

- Poor people are lazy. Anyone willing to work hard can make a decent living.

- People who are wealthy have a right to do whatever they want with their money. They've earned it.

As a science, moral decision making means employing our thinking and reasoning capacity in the decisions that we make. It involves being attentive to the world around us, seeking out knowledge and understanding, and critically analyzing all information that comes our way. Being critical of our culture does not imply a total rejection of it. Within our culture we find many expressions of beauty, truth, and holiness. For instance, popular music, movies, books, and even comic strips can possibly help us be attentive to the world around us. They can offer us an honest and critical look at the very culture of which they are a part. Critical thinking implies a thoughtful evaluation of both the positive and the negative dimensions of our culture.

> *I am* **sending** *you out like* **sheep** *into the midst of wolves; so* **be wise** *as serpents and* **innocent** *as doves.*
>
> MATTHEW 10:16

In the Christian vision, Scripture, Church teaching, and people in our community who have experience and knowledge can serve as valuable resources for us in our attempts to make thoughtful decisions. **K**

Activity K

List as many examples as possible of the following.

1. Elements in our society that contribute positively to a sense of morality.

2. Elements in our culture that do not contribute positively to a sense of morality.

3. Examples of popular music that contribute positively to a sense of morality.

4. Television shows that consistently demonstrate positive moral messages.

5. Movies that have a positive moral message.

6. Books that examine positive moral themes.

7. Comic strips, comic books, or cartoons that contribute positively to a sense of morality in our society.

Creativity and Imagination— The Art of Morality

Morality is also an art. It is not simply a matter of thinking but also of doing. As an art, morality represents the practical dimension of our life with God and with one another. It requires know-how, skill, and practice. By practicing the art of morality we are constantly fashioning ourselves and our world, which calls for creativity and imagination. Since morality is an art, we are called upon to use our abilities to enhance ourselves and the lives of those around us, just like the servants who are given talents in the following story told by Jesus.

Using the Master's Talents

For it is as if a man, going on a journey, summoned his slaves and entrusted his property to them; to one he gave five talents, to another two, to another one, to each according to his ability. Then he went away. The one who had received the five talents went off at once and traded with them, and made five more talents. In the same way, the one who had the two talents made two more talents. But the one who had received the one talent went off and dug a hole in the ground and hid his master's money. After a long time the master of those slaves came and settled accounts with them. Then the one who had received the five talents came forward, bringing five more talents, saying, "Master, you handed over to me five talents; see, I have made five more talents." His master said to him, "Well done, good and trustworthy slave; you have been trustworthy in a few things, I will put you in charge of many things; enter into the joy of your master." And the one with the two talents also came forward, saying, "Master, you handed over to me two talents; see, I have made two more talents." His master said to him, "Well done, good and trustworthy slave; you have been trustworthy in a few things, I will put you in charge of many things; enter into the joy of your master." Then the one who had received the one talent also came forward, saying, "Master, I knew that you were a harsh man, reaping where you did not sow, and gathering where you did not scatter seed; so I was afraid, and I went and hid your talent in the ground. Here you have what is yours." But his master replied, "You wicked and lazy slave! You knew, did you, that I reap where I did not sow, and gather where I did not scatter? Then you ought to have invested my money with the bankers and on my return I would have received what was my own with interest. . . ."

MATTHEW 25:14–27

talent—a unit of money in Jesus' time; in current usage it designates a natural endowment with which we are born

Did you know that the English word *talent* comes from the word used in the Gospel story about the servants who are given talents by their master? In the story the **talent** actually refers to a unit of money in use at the time; but it later came to designate all the natural endowments with which we are born.

All of us have been given many talents. As the above story indicates, according to the Christian vision we are to make something beautiful out of the talents that we have received. We are not to stand idly by and simply

*I will always **love** you; that's why I've been so **patient** and **kind**. You are **precious** to me, and so I will **rebuild** your **nation**. Once again you will **dance** for joy and **play** your tambourines.*

Jeremiah 31:3–4 (CEV)

stay out of trouble. Rather, we are to invest our talents in the troubling situations surrounding us. We are not simply to keep our hands clean; instead we are to dirty our hands in the muddy business of helping to fashion the world to be the way God intends it to be.

At times morality is presented in terms of negatives—a long series of "thou shalt nots." In recent years Church teaching has reemphasized the more essential, positive dimension of morality. Morality understood positively results in people working together with the Spirit to transform the world into a shining reflection of God's love. This Christian vision calls for imagination—the ability to see beyond the way things are. It also calls for actions and decisions that are *creative* in the best sense of the word. The Catechism calls for the creative use of our talents in these simple words: "God put us in the world to know, to love, and to serve him, and so to come to paradise" (1721). **L**

Activity L

Violence, drug abuse, homelessness, poor eating habits—the list of societal problems is endless. As a group, describe three problems that currently exist at your school, in your community, or in the nation. For each problem, describe a creative way that it could be addressed. If possible, determine a role that you might play in solving the problem.

Imagining the World Differently

The sun beams down rays of light and heat. For the most part, we ignore its potential as a source of energy and instead use up the limited supplies of oil and coal found in the earth. Imagine creating practical, efficient means to harness the sun's energy!

You notice more and more older people living alone in your community. You find that many of them could use help with shopping, yard work, and other odd jobs. For their part, the older local citizens have a great deal to offer by volunteering in libraries and hospitals or in teaching about "living history." Imagine creating an exchange program between old and young in a community!

What is more human than our ability to imagine? We are blessed with a marvelous capacity to wonder and to dream. We stand in awe of a Leonardo da Vinci who imagined a flying machine centuries before the first plane, a Katherine Drexel who founded an order of sisters to work with Native Americans because she could see in them a beauty that narrow-minded white people missed, or the early explorers who imagined that the earth was round. And yet we share their ability to dream dreams.

In a sense, every moral decision that we make is an act of imagination. Conversely, every moral failure is a failure of imagination. The Christian vision of morality calls for us to dream dreams of how the world can be and to participate in making those dreams come true. **M**

Being Co-Workers and Co-Creators with God

In the classic Christmas movie, "It's a Wonderful Life," George Bailey has the opportunity to see what life would be like if he had never existed. With the help of his guardian angel, he discovers how much of a difference he has actually made in many people's lives.

According to Christian teaching, we are created in God's image. Therefore, like George Bailey, we are co-creators with God in the continuing story of creation. Humans are **co-creators** when they help transform the world and the human community into what God intends these to be. We have been given the responsibility to help move the world and the human community along toward becoming more and more what God envisions them to be. We should not make too much of our power to shape ourselves and our world, but we should not minimize our potential as co-creators either. Our aim should be to "fully become 'God's fellow workers' and co-workers for his kingdom" [1 Cor 3:9; 1 Thess 3:2; Col 4:11] (Catechism, #307). That is, the talents that we have been given are to be used to carry on the Master-Creator's work.

We admire those who make beautiful music, who create stirring portrayals in movies and plays, or who make us laugh with their creative humor. The great composer Beethoven continued to create beautiful music even though he himself had become deaf!

co-creators—people who help transform the world and the human community into what God intends them to be

Activity M

Use examples to illustrate the following:

- A moral decision as an act of imagination
- A moral decision as a failure of imagination

Applied to morality, the spirit of creativity asks: How can we create something beautiful out of ourselves and our relationships? In other words, how can we be morally creative with our thinking and feeling, our sexuality, our unique personality, our family situation and community? In this endeavor it is important to remember: If you have been given lemons, make lemonade! **N**

For review . . .

13. In what sense is moral decision making a science?

14. What is critical thinking?

15. In what sense is moral decision making an art?

16. What did the word *talent* mean in biblical times? What does the word mean now?

17. According to the Christian vision, what are we asked to do with our talents?

18. What does it mean to be a co-creator with God?

Activity N

Instead of asking, "what is God doing for me," we should ask, "what might God do with me?" Think about your life—past, present, and future. What do you envision that God has done with you, is doing with you, or will do with you? Write a response to this question in your journal or notebook.

Conclusion
Morality—Christian Vision in Practice

As Christians we have a vision that we bring to our moral decision making. That vision reminds us first of all of Jesus' good news that God loves us. We, in turn, practice the art of Christian moral decision making in all of our attempts to love others and to live life to the fullest. We do not make decisions in isolation but within a community. We also look thoughtfully and critically at ourselves and our world to uncover the truth and beauty that might otherwise lie hidden. Finally, in the Christian vision we are invited to apply our creative imagination to our moral decision making as co-workers with God.

Let us pray . . .

. . . put on the Lord Jesus Christ . . .
ROMANS 13:14

Lord Jesus Christ, may we live our lives seeking always to follow you. May your Spirit come upon us: to inspire us, to guide us, to set us free to live a life filled with grace. We pray that we may praise you with every word we say. With wonder and awe, we rejoice that you are always nearer to us than we could ever know. Amen.

CHAPTER 2

The Virtues
Cultivating Character

We make the majority of our decisions without a great deal of thought. Mostly, we act according to our upbringing and the norms of the society of which we are a part. This chapter explores more closely the link between our "being" and our "doing." On the one hand, "who we are" precedes and shapes "what we do." On the other hand, as the first chapter suggests, our actions shape who we are. In its long tradition, Christianity has proposed cultivating character traits that lay the foundations for us to act in line with our best selves. Such character traits are called virtues.

Chapter Overview

- Virtues are character strengths that we develop over time and through consistent use.

- The theological virtues are faith, hope, and love.

- The cardinal virtues are prudence, justice, fortitude, and temperance.

- A virtuous person is a person of integrity.

- An important aspect of the moral life is creating communities of character.

Review the following scenarios. Select the one that you feel most closely relates to an experience that you have had. What does that experience say about your understanding of moral character?

- Walking alone down a school corridor, you spot an open locker. A few dollars and some change are clearly visible in the locker. Is your immediate response, "I should close this locker so that nothing is stolen," or "I wonder if I could take the money and get away with it"?

- Your parent asks you to help with some work around the house. Are you thinking, "What excuse can I come up with to get out of this," or "I'm happy to do my part"?

- Because of an accident that just occurred ahead of you, you are one of many drivers caught in traffic on a busy freeway. Do you think, "I can't believe I'll be delayed for hours now," or "I sure hope nobody is seriously hurt"?

- When a new student arrives at your school, do you say, "I'll try to make her feel welcome," or "She'd better not try to move in on my friends"?

- Your parents work late. They ask you not to have friends over until they get home. Since they will have no way of checking on you, do you plan on ignoring their request?

- You are attending a family wedding at a country club when two of your cousins drive by in a golf cart which they "borrowed" from the clubhouse. They intend to ride around the course for a while and then to drive the cart into a lake on the property. They invite you to go with them. Do you say, "Let's go," or "I don't think you should do that"?

Let us pray . . .

God our Father, you give us the grace we need to form ourselves and our world into persons and communities of good character. Give us the courage to accept this grace. We ask for strength to develop positive patterns of behavior and the courage to avoid negative acts. As you see us, at the core of our being where we are one with you, may we see others. You treat us with love and forgiveness. May we strive to treat others in a similar way. We ask this through Christ our Lord. Amen.

Virtues
Habits of the Heart

character—
the inclinations toward goodness or evil that are part of the fabric of a person's being

In each of the scenarios on the previous page, you would have little time to think through any decision that you make. What you end up doing would depend greatly on the values and inclinations that you have internalized over the years. **Character** refers to the inclinations toward goodness or evil that are part of the fabric of a person's being.

If we remarked about a friend of ours, "She's a real character!" we would probably mean that she exhibits certain clearly distinctive characteristics that set her apart from other people. However, the more accurate term for our mixture of unique qualities is *personality*. We all have a personality, regardless of whether or not we do anything positive with it. Character is different from personality.

Good character results when we cultivate our unique traits and use them in positive ways. Virtues are character strengths applied consistently throughout moral decision making. **Virtues**, then, are positive patterns of behavior. (On the other hand, **vices** are negative behavior patterns.) Even though our character is uniquely ours and we in fact shape and sustain it, it's important to keep in mind that the source of our unique power to do good is a gift of God's grace. With God's help, virtues help us in building our character, as well as in doing good. We should always keep in mind that Jesus' free gift of salvation offers us the grace necessary to persevere in virtuous living (Catechism, #s 1810–1811).

The word *virtue* comes from a Latin root meaning strength or power. Virtues are character strengths, given by God but cultivated by those who exhibit them. In a sense, virtues are habits—habits of the heart. Sometimes we think of habits as actions that we do unthinkingly, as if we had no control over them. In fact, good habits and good character do not take away our freedom but instead channel our freedom toward positive ends. Like becoming a good swimmer or learning to speak a foreign language, cultivating virtues is a matter of hard work and practice.

Virtuous living resembles correct eating habits. In the long run, programs for quick weight loss seldom work. Cultivating healthy eating, sleeping, and exercise habits is the only way to maintain good health. Similarly in the face of internal and external pressures, a virtuous person tends to make wholesome choices. Why? The reason is that virtue is not a one-time event; it is an ongoing pattern of behavior. Of course, our patterns of behavior are influenced strongly by the important people in our lives. Again, this does not take away from the fact that we develop our particular virtues through years of practice. Virtuous persons—persons of good character—cultivate fundamental values, convictions, and behavior patterns that become almost second nature to them. These virtues serve as the basis for consistent responses to the many moral decisions that come their way. **A**

> A **virtue** *is an habitual and firm disposition to* **do the good.**
>
> CATECHISM, #1803

virtues—character strengths manifested on a consistent basis in decision making

vices—patterns of behavior that are harmful to one's self or others

Activity A

Select one of the following behaviors that you would consider to be a virtue you would want to cultivate more in yourself. Explain your choice.

- Saying "no" when I really do not want to do something
- Demonstrating concern for the environment
- Developing enthusiasm for learning
- Showing patience with my friends
- Speaking more positively about myself
- Taking better care of my body

Authentic Freedom: Freedom Versus License

Character development leads to *authentic* freedom. It's important to speak about authentic freedom since today so many imitations are passed off as the genuine article. As the Catechism states: "Freedom is the power to act or not to act, and so to perform deliberate acts of one's own. Freedom attains perfection in its acts when directed toward God" (1744). Put simply, authentic freedom means having a sense of who you truly want to be, working at expanding skills that would move you along toward this identity, and having the courage to take whatever steps are necessary to attain your goal of being a follower of Christ.

If we think that freedom sounds simple or easy, we are highly mistaken. The above notion of freedom takes guts, bravery, and courage—in short, strength of character. It is an overwhelming task, and we can't help but fall short of being free. Authentic freedom is so challenging that many people settle for a distorted version of freedom—*license*. License is a permission slip, granting us approval to do whatever we want. License lets us off the hook; authentic freedom challenges us to strive to be more and better than we ever imagined. **B**

For review . . .

1. Define the terms character and virtue.

2. What is the root meaning of the word virtue?

3. What is the relationship between good character and freedom?

4. In what way does virtue affect behavior patterns?

5. What is authentic freedom? How is it different from license?

Activity B

Write a response to the following questions:

- Do you agree or disagree with the above definition of authentic freedom? If not, how would you define freedom?

- Do you believe that many people mean *license* when they talk about *freedom*? Give examples.

- On a scale of one to ten, how free do you think you are? Explain.

- Would you like to become more free as defined in the text? What would it take to increase your freedom?

- What do you think the Catechism means by the following statement: "The more one does what is good, the freer one becomes" (1733)? Do you agree?

The Theological Virtues
Faith, Hope, and Charity

Three pivotal virtues identified in the Christian tradition are faith, hope, and charity. (Charity is the traditional biblical word meaning love; for ease of understanding, we will primarily use the word *love* throughout the remainder of our discussion unless doing so compromises our meaning.) These three are known as **theological virtues** because they are rooted in God and reflect God's presence in our lives. (In Greek, *theos* means god.) Like grace, they are gifts from God but also call for a response on our part. Virtues are identifying marks—positive character traits—which show themselves in patterns of behavior that are found in people over a long period of time. That is, by living faithfully, hopefully, and lovingly, we are reflecting and cooperating with God's gifts of faith, hope, and love. Because our focus is morality, let's look at these three virtues as they might be demonstrated in decisions that we make.

theological virtues— faith, hope, and love, the foundations of the Christian moral life

Faith—Seeking to Do God's Will

Faith is the virtue by which we recognize that God exists and that God's very existence holds moral implications for us. That is, a faithful person seeks to know and to do God's will. For example, when frightened in the middle of the night, Mark Twain's Tom Sawyer would promise God that he would always be a good Christian and never do wrong. Once daylight appeared and he was no longer frightened, however, Tom always returned to being his usual mischievous self. As a virtue, **faith**—believing in God and being faithful to God—means responding courageously during the many times when our faith is on the line.

faith— belief in God; the theological virtue of seeking to know and to do God's will

Jesus models such faithfulness when he prays in the Garden of Gethsemane the night before his death: "Abba, Father, for you all things are possible; remove this cup from me; yet, not what I want, but what you want" (Mark 14:36).

Jesus is alone in the garden. His disciples are off sleeping. He has one last chance to abandon the message to which he had committed himself. Instead, no doubt knowing that dire consequences would result, he prays to his Father: "not what I want, but what you want."

A Test of Faith

Here's the story of someone whose faith is also being tested in a way which might be more familiar to you.

Jana wants desperately to make the soccer team this year. Playing around before regular practice sessions begin, she shows herself to be a strong candidate to make the team and contribute. She definitely is becoming part of the "in" group among the best players.

However, Jana notices that a number of players, ones who undoubtedly will be the mainstay of the team, constantly make cutting remarks about a girl name Rhea who also shows some talent. As time goes by the badgering worsens. Jana doesn't join in. She keeps quiet and concentrates on her game. But even by not participating in the jokes, Jana realizes that she is distancing herself from the better players and not helping Rhea from suffering their taunts. Feeling more and more uncomfortable, she wants to yell,

"Leave her alone!" Instead, she hopes that Rhea realizes that she isn't wanted and just goes away. **C**

Activity C

Rewrite Jana's story so that her action reflects being a person of faith. Based on your rewrite, make up a slogan that could serve as a brief description of the virtue of faith.

In the story, Jana is being challenged to be faithful both to her God and to who she is. Like Jesus praying in the garden, she desperately wants not to be in this situation. However, the problem doesn't go away. If she is to be a person of faith, she will search to find the strength of character within herself to be faithful to what she knows is right.

The virtue of faith includes many dimensions. To begin with, faith requires openness and trust. Acting in faith means that we seek to allow God's Spirit to operate throughout our lives. Put simply, faith-in-action involves trying to discover what is God's will and then acting accordingly.

Richie Fernando

A Model of Faith

In 1996 twenty-six-year-old Richie Fernando was a Filipino Jesuit working in Cambodia at a center for persons with disabilities—most of whom were maimed by land mines remaining from the years of civil war that had ravaged the country. One night an incident occurred that led to his death but also showed him to be a person of deep faith. Here is his story as told by a fellow Jesuit.

On the night of October 16, several students were reprimanded for gambling, an activity that is strictly forbidden because a month's wages can be lost in an evening. The staff met the following day and decided that the ringleader, a former soldier, would be suspended from school but be allowed to graduate. In retaliation the man appeared at school with a hand grenade and threatened to throw it into the midst of the staff and students. He was restrained by a Thai volunteer, who held the man's hands behind his back while Richie helped get the handicapped students to safety. When all were at a safe distance, the volunteer released the man and dashed out of the building.

But Richie saw the armed man move toward a classroom where the director was teaching another group of disabled students. He rushed back into the building and tried to restrain and disarm the man. As the man with the grenade struggled to free himself, the grenade got tossed or dropped— no one is quite sure—behind Richie. It exploded, and the impact struck Richie in the head and back. He died on the way to the hospital.

This most uncontroversial and fun-loving of young men, with a sunny, optimistic personality, belied the cynical suspicion that martyrs are gloomy fanatics who somehow "bring it on themselves." He explained his desire to commit himself to the Cambodia mission by simply stating: "Jesus came to be good news to the poorest. I want to be with Cambodian people and work with them to rebuild their country after the years of killing and war." After his death Richie's retreat diary was found. On January 3, nine months before his death, he had written:

I wish, when I die, that people remember

not how great, powerful, or talented I was,

but that I served and spoke for the truth.

I gave witness to what is right.

I was sincere with all my words and actions.

In other words, I loved and I followed Christ. **D**

REPRINTED WITH THE PERMISSION OF THOMAS MICHEL SJ AND AMERICA PRESS, INC., 106 WEST 56TH STREET, NEW YORK, NY. ORIGINALLY PUBLISHED IN AMERICA, 177:2, JULY 19–26, 1997.

Activity D

Think about another person who models the virtue of faith. Write a story about the person. Illustrate the story with an appropriate drawing.

Hope—A Virtue of Responsibility

On a class trip, Suzie joins a large group of students in a crowded restaurant. After the meal, a friend suggests that they leave the restaurant without paying the bill. "Let's take a chance and hope that we don't get caught," the friend whispers to Suzie.

Tim is prodded by his parents to get involved in school activities. A service club looks for help with a variety of activities aimed at assisting poor people. "Why don't you volunteer some time in the service club?" Tim's father asks. "You can help other people, and it also might be interesting." "It wouldn't do any good, so why should I bother?" Tim responds. "Besides, after school is the only time I get to watch TV and relax."

hope—trusting in God, in everything that Christ has promised, and in the help of the Holy Spirit

In these brief stories, Suzie's friend, who considers walking out of the restaurant without paying the bill, *hopes* that she won't get caught, and Tim has little *hope* that he can influence the future. In these instances hope obviously does not reflect the virtue that it is meant to be.

In popular usage the word ***hope*** often describes a passive quality and not an active virtue. For instance, in the following popular uses, hope implies passivity—standing by, letting things happen, and not taking charge of the situation:

- I hope it doesn't rain today. I didn't bring a raincoat.

- I hope we don't have a test today. I didn't study.

- I hope my parents don't notice the scrape on the car.

In these uses of the word, hope really means "wish," since none of the statements imply any sense of taking action or taking responsibility. By contrast, hope as a virtue does not comprise a "wish list" of things that we would like to see happen apart from our involvement in them. Rather, our hopes are those things to which we are willing to dedicate ourselves; instead of passivity, hope implies activity in cooperation with God's grace. Hope is intimately tied to responsibility. It is future oriented and means taking seriously the consequences of our actions.

Hope means having the vision to see things differently from the way they are and being so involved with that vision that we take steps to try to bring it about. In that sense, hope is an important motivator for moral behavior. And, of course, what better vision of the world exists than the vision that Jesus provides us—the vision of God's kingdom? Jesus provides hope that, no matter how hopeless our current circumstances appear and despite trials and setbacks, in the end all will be well. This message of hope frees us to act with an heroic "never give up" enthusiasm for life and goodness.

If hope became an active force in their lives, both Suzie and Tim would choose behaviors that are far sighted and filled with promise. As with the virtue of faith, it is through their actions that people demonstrate their hope. Also, hope is not an isolating, individualistic virtue. Hope is contagious. As such, an important dimension of hope is living in ways that give hope to others. **E**

Activity E

1. The Catechism uses the following terms to help us appreciate how hope can motivate us to act morally: desire, trust, response, inspiration, a cure for discouragement, and expectation. Write your own description of hope, using four of these terms.

2. Hope inspires us with a vision of how things can be. Give one example of each of the following: How you would like teenagers to be perceived? Women? Men?

Love—The Cornerstone of Virtues

Antoinette recently broke up with her boyfriend, Doug. Through friends she discovers that Doug has been telling negative stories and making insulting sexual comments about her. Angry and hurt, Antoinette wonders how best to respond to Doug's accusations.

Since her grandmother had a stroke, Kathleen's family life has been greatly disrupted. Her grandmother now needs constant attention. Kathleen tells her mother that she wants to help out in whatever way she can, so she begins spending quite a bit of her free time by her grandmother's side. Consequently, she ends up missing out on some social activities in which she normally would participate. When her mother asks her if she feels that her social life is being neglected, Kathleen tells her that she is happy to give back this gift of her time to her grandmother.

love—the theological virtue representing the core of the Christian moral life. Love is the virtue that places concern for God, manifest especially through concern for others, above everything else.

Love is the cornerstone of all virtues. One of the most beautiful descriptions ever written about love is found in the thirteenth chapter of Paul's first letter to the Church at Corinth:

> *Love is patient; love is kind; love is not envious or boastful or arrogant or rude. It does not insist on its own way; it is not irritable or resentful; it does not rejoice in wrongdoing, but rejoices in the truth. It bears all things, believes all things, hopes all things, endures all things. Love never ends. And now faith, hope, and love abide, these three; and the greatest of these is love.*
>
> 1 Corinthians 13:4–7, 13

Every other virtue that we might practice represents some dimension of love; every time we practice any virtue, we are giving expression to love. In the above stories Kathleen practices love when she spends time with her grandmother at personal sacrifice to herself. Doug violates love when he spreads stories about his former girlfriend, Antoinette.

Love, like hope, can be misunderstood. As with hope sometimes we consider love to be only a passive quality. We might emphasize a passive "being lovable" rather than actively loving. Also, people sometimes suggest that selfish and possessive behaviors are motivated by "love." (For instance, Doug might claim that he is really demeaning Antoinette because he loves her so much and is angry that she broke up with him.) In fact, "selfish love" is a contradiction in terms. The Catechism defines love in the words of the medieval theologian Saint Thomas Aquinas: "To love is to will the good of another" (1766). **F**

Activity F

1. Give three examples of misusing or misinterpreting the concept love, examples that you might find in popular culture.

2. Describe three specific situations when the Catechism's definition of love—to will the good of another—might be a real challenge for those involved.

The Art of Loving—Five Characteristics of Love

"Love" sounds so idealistic, while the problems we face with love are so real and so complex. Like all virtues, love is an art. As best we can we apply the art of loving to the concrete situations in which we find ourselves. But what does the art of loving look like? For instance:

- What is the best way to show love when another student is copying our test answers?

- What specifically does it mean to love a group of students who act like snobs and exclude us from their activities?

- How can we feel free to love the people we meet on a day when a few extra pimples or some added weight make us feel anything but lovable?

- How do we love the boy or girl who pledges loyalty to us over the weekend and then on Monday tells us that he or she still cares for an old girlfriend or boyfriend?

- How do we love when we discover that some people from our old crowd are now involved in organized shoplifting and invite us to join them on a "shopping spree"?

- What is the best way for us to give at least some expression of love to the multitude of hungry people whom we hear about in the news or in religion class?

Like every art, love—and moral decision making—is not an exact science. As new parents soon discover, sometimes love means hugs and kisses; at other times "tough love" is called for. For instance, in many of the above situations, the art of loving clearly requires saying "no" rather than complacently complying with another's wishes. In other situations the art of loving involves the art of honest confrontation and of being assertive. Despite our possible reluctance to act on our negative feelings toward others, the art of loving suggests that we should respond with care and respect for ourselves and for whoever else is involved.

In his classic work called *The Art of Loving*, psychoanalyst Erich Fromm suggests the following five characteristics common to the practice of loving:

Characteristics of Love

Giving—sharing oneself with another

Caring—concern for the life and the growth of another

Responsibility—the readiness and the ability to respond to another

Respect—taking time to see another as he or she truly is

Knowledge—knowing the inner core, not merely the outward appearance, of another

Fromm's list of characteristics can help us as we seek to practice "the art of loving" in our moral decision making. All dimensions of morality make sense only in relation to the art of loving. That is, moral laws are norms for love; moral principles are the principles of love. Sin indicates a failure to love. In short, moral decision making is the process of practicing the art of loving. **G**

For review . . .

6. Name and define the theological virtues.
7. Describe faith-in-action as it applies to moral decision making.
8. What is the difference between a *hope* and a *wish*?
9. What is the cornerstone of all virtues?
10. How does Saint Thomas Aquinas define love?
11. According to Erich Fromm, what are the five characteristics of the art of loving?

Activity G

"Tough love" means challenging or confronting another person for his or her own benefit. Have you ever attempted "tough love" or been on the receiving end of "tough love"? Describe the experience.

The Cardinal Virtues
Hinges Holding Together the Moral Life

cardinal virtues—
prudence, justice, fortitude, and temperance

During the Middle Ages theater troupes traveled throughout Europe putting on morality plays in which performers would portray various virtues and vices. Just as in today's television sitcoms, the vices—gluttony, lust, envy, and laziness—always received more play time. The reason for this is obvious—virtuous people get into less trouble than those who live a life of vice. Repeating a line from the beginning of this chapter, a *virtuous person tends to make wholesome choices.* Most of the people portrayed in TV sitcoms are making unwholesome choices. TV plots consist of these characters trying to correct or cover the problems their bad choices have caused.

What are the key Christian virtues? Even though they have ancient-sounding names, they still hold an appeal and serve a purpose in today's television-saturated world. Four pivotal virtues traditionally advocated in Christianity are prudence, justice, fortitude, and temperance. They are called the **cardinal virtues** based on the Latin root of the word—*cardo,* which means hinge. The Christian moral life hinges on these four virtues working together smoothly, just as the hinges of a door keep it centered, stable, and workable. Not as abstract and lofty as faith, hope, and love may appear to be, the cardinal virtues are practical, common-sense virtues. If we neglect them, we weaken our character. Used consistently, they support all of our endeavors to live a good life. **H**

Activity H

1. Make a list of vices (negative behavior patterns) and virtues (positive behavior patterns).

2. Find out what you can about how certain vices and virtues were traditionally portrayed. Either pantomime or draw a picture of one vice and one virtue. (Try to make the virtue at least as exciting as the vice.)

3. Name some television characters who exhibit a particular vice. Describe an incident when they exhibited that vice.

4. Name some television characters who exhibit a particular virtue. Describe an incident when they exhibited that virtue.

Prudence—Practical Judgment

prudence—
practical judgment

Driving onto train tracks when red lights are flashing at a railroad crossing is *not* prudent. Talking on a cell phone outdoors during a thunderstorm is *not* prudent. Organizing your study time during exams *is* prudent. Staying home the night before a big test or a big game is prudent behavior. **Prudence** is practical judgment. It asks the question: "What is the right thing to do in this particular situation?" Prudence operates a lot like common sense. It is the art of making sensible choices in spur-of-the-moment decisions. The Book of Proverbs describes prudence concisely in these words: "the prudent man looks where he is going" [Proverbs 14:15] (Catechism, #1806). The Catechism goes on to say that "prudence disposes the practical reason to discern, in every circumstance, our true good and to choose the right means for achieving it" (1835).

Justice—The Virtue of Rights and Responsibilities

justice—the virtue
that reminds us that
the people with whom
we share our world
have rights and that,
as much as possible,
all people deserve to
have basic needs met

We are social beings. **Justice** is the virtue that reminds us that the people with whom we share our world have rights and that, as much as possible, all people deserve to have basic needs met. Justice is a great challenge. It is the subject of much discussion throughout Scripture and remains as relevant as today's newspaper headlines. For instance, a just person strives to treat rich and poor, friends and strangers, those like us and those unlike us, with equal dignity. Developing a sense of justice insures that morality does not remain individualized. Indeed, morality is always a social affair. However, justice is the virtue that explicitly ranks our own good as equal to the common good, the good of all people. Since matters of justice are such an important aspect of morality, we will examine them more closely in a later chapter.

Fortitude—The Courage to Act

fortitude—a fancy
term for courage

Fortitude is simply a fancy term for the virtue that the cowardly lion requests from the Wizard of Oz—courage. It "ensures firmness in difficulties and constancy in the pursuit of the good" (Catechism, #1837). "Being good" is easy when everyone else is. The challenge is to stand up for what is right in the face of peer pressure or in circumstances when we are being called upon to step out of our usual patterns of behavior. Without the courage to act, all the other virtues are useless. In an atmosphere where walking out the door with the wrong brand of sneakers takes great courage and opens us up to ridicule, how much more courage is required to follow our beliefs when it really means going against the grain of the society in which we live.

Temperance—The Virtue of Self-Control

temperance—refers to self-control in general

North Americans know the word "temperance" from the movement to ban alcohol that resulted in Prohibition in the United States. The temperance movement was made up mostly of women. The image they promoted was that of a male factory worker receiving his pay on Friday and heading straight for the nearest bar where he spent a large chunk of his paycheck on whiskey and beer. Meanwhile, his poor wife was home trying to figure out how to feed the kids.

As the temperance movement called for control over the consumption of alcohol, so **temperance** the virtue refers to self-control in general. Interestingly, "self-control" has taken on a negative connotation in some circles—as if self-control were an affront to our freedom. In fact, freedom requires self-control. If we are incapable of regulating the amount of food we eat or the amount of alcohol we consume, we're not very free. Being addicted to drugs or to cigarettes is not freedom. Being consumed with possessing the latest clothes, styles, or gadgets is not freedom. As justice is the virtue of social harmony and balance, so temperance is the virtue of personal harmony and balance. As justice advocates wholesome ordering of social resources, so temperance advocates a wholesome personal lifestyle.

The American temperance movement led to making all alcohol consumption illegal. As a virtue, temperance need not eliminate pleasure, partying, sensual experiences, and even wild times. Instead, temperance reminds us that even good things turn sour when they control us. A life of harmony and wholeness is not a life devoid of pleasure. It is one that aims to keep things in balance. As the Catechism reminds us, "temperance moderates the attraction of the pleasures of the senses and provides balance in the use of created goods" (1838). ∎

For review . . .

12. Name the four cardinal virtues.
13. What is the root meaning of the word *cardinal*? How does this root meaning explain the role of the cardinal virtues in the Christian moral life?
14. Define prudence.
15. What does justice emphasize about virtuous living?
16. Define fortitude.
17. What social problem did the American temperance movement address?
18. Define temperance.

Activity I

In a journal or notebook, use the following questions to do a self-assessment of what you typically bring to your decision making.

1. If you were to receive an award today for a virtue that you exhibit, what would the award be for? Describe how you think you came to possess this virtue.

2. What personal character strengths do you believe are most important in shaping your style of decision making? Tell the story of a time when these strengths manifested themselves in a decision you made.

3. If you had an opportunity to make a request of the Wizard of Oz, what character strengths would you ask for? Describe how you would like to make use of these in your future decision making.

4. If you were to die in five years, what do you hope people would say about you?

A Virtuous Person
A Person of Integrity

The anonymous poem on the right is worth thinking about. It attests to how our being shapes our actions and how our actions shape our being. We form our character through what we think, what we say, and what we do. In turn, our character sustains us during the many circumstances in which we find ourselves in our quest to lead a life that is good and true.

Character does not manifest itself only when we are at home, at school, when we are with our friends or with our family, when we are at work or at play. Character implies that we operate in an overall consistent pattern. A term for such consistency, such unity of character, is **integrity**. (As an integer is a whole number, so persons of integrity manifest wholeness in their behavior.) Integrity is a synonym for honesty and genuineness. Its opposite is being untruthful and phony. For a number of decades now, each new generation of American youth has echoed *Catcher in the Rye*'s Holden Caulfield's criticism of anything or anyone "phony." Salinger's book is an excellent chronicle of how difficult it is to act with integrity on a consistent basis.

> Watch your thoughts;
> they become your words.
> Watch your words;
> they become actions.
> Watch your actions;
> they become habits.
> Watch your habits;
> they become character.
> Watch your character;
> it becomes your destiny.

AN ANONYMOUS POEM QUOTED BY RICHARD M. GULA, *MORAL DISCERNMENT* [NEW YORK: PAULIST PRESS, 1997].

Integrity means being true to oneself. What could be more natural, you might ask? In fact, if you are like most of us, when you look back over your actions for the past week or so you quite likely could name numerous times when you weren't true to yourself. Are there guidelines that can help us in our struggles to be persons of integrity? Here are some to consider.

integrity—honesty, genuineness, and consistency in behavior patterns

Genuineness

genuine—not hiding behind a role or image; seeking honest communication with others

Persons of integrity try to be spontaneous and honest. Spontaneity does not mean "letting it all hang out" or being impulsive. (Keep in mind the virtue of prudence.) A **genuine** person does not hide behind a role or an image—being cute, being the rebel or the misfit, acting like the class clown—but allows multiple dimensions of her or his personality to come out. A genuine person tries not to play games or manipulate people but instead seeks to make honest connections with people. **J**

Consistency

lived values—qualities and concerns that we demonstrate as being important through our actions

stated values—qualities and concerns that we claim are important to us

We can say that we care about the environment, but do we show that care in our actions? We can say that we take our education seriously, but do the choices we make back that up? We can say that family is important to us, but if we complain every time our parents ask us to join them on a family outing, then we are not living that value. It is important to distinguish between our stated values and our lived values. **Stated values** are those values that we claim are important to us. **Lived values** are the values that we demonstrate in our actions. Persons of integrity investigate their stated values and seek to determine whether or not there is a gap between what they claim to be a value and the values that they consistently act upon. If they discover that their lived values are not in line with their stated values, then narrowing the gap between the two is an important step toward personal integrity.

Stated and Lived Values

Based on how important you think each item is to you, rank the following from 1 (of little value) to 10 (of great value). Write the appropriate number in the left-hand column.

Then, in the column on the right, rank items in terms of the amount of time, thought, and energy you give to each, from 1 (very little) to 10 (a great deal).

_____	watching television	_____
_____	listening to music	_____
_____	doing well in school	_____
_____	keeping physically fit	_____
_____	career goals	_____
_____	religion	_____
_____	sports	_____
_____	friendships	_____

When finished, explain what your rankings say about your stated and lived values.

Activity J

Write about an incident when you or someone you know was treated in a manipulative way. (We are manipulative when we treat people for what they can do for us rather than out of a sense of care and mutual respect.) Then write about an incident when you or someone you know was treated with genuineness. Describe the difference between the two experiences.

Selfishness is not identical with self-love but its very opposite.

Erich Fromm

Openness

Being true to oneself is not the same as not being open to change. In fact, persons of integrity can admit mistakes and can alter behavior patterns when they realize that they are ineffective or harmful. When we are at home with ourselves, relatively comfortable with who we are, we are less likely to be devastated by criticism and more apt to engage in honest self-exploration.

Empathy

empathy—
identifying the joys and sorrows of others as our own

Heaven has been described as the ability to rejoice in another's good fortune. If that's the case, then integrity is a roadmap to heaven. Persons of integrity seek to get beyond narrow viewpoints, especially their own. Being true to oneself is not the same as being self-centered. When we are free enough to try overcoming barriers between ourselves and others, then we start to identify their joys and sorrows as our own. Such **empathy** for others is not a belittling of self but an expansion of self. Empathy is the ability to identify with others, to feel their joys and sorrows as one's own. **K**

Activity K

Place a + next to the following terms that you associate with integrity. Place a 0 next to the terms that you do not associate with integrity. If a particular term sometimes may and sometimes may not reflect integrity, put +0. When finished, use a few of the terms to describe integrity or lack of integrity displayed in a specific way.

_____ judgmental	_____ self-accepting	_____ critical
_____ spontaneous	_____ expressive of feelings	_____ defensive
_____ straightforward	_____ manipulative	_____ truthful
_____ selfish	_____ fair	_____ open-minded
_____ aggressive	_____ involved	_____ conscientious

Creating Communities of Character

How do we see the world? The communities to which we belong determine, for the most part, how we view the world. Even though morality has to do with our personal decision making, isn't it true that we generally act in line with the norms of our particular community? Therefore, in addition to trying to act virtuously as an individual, a Christian who is concerned about moral behavior should also think about how to create an environment where virtue is the norm. That is, *an important goal of the moral life is creating communities of good character.*

Taking a Risk

• Antonio arrives at a movie theater early and buys five tickets for a later show that is close to being sold out. When his friends finally get there, he discovers that one person for whom he bought a ticket isn't coming. Not wanting to waste the ticket, he offers it to a group of girls standing in line at the box office. They look upon him suspiciously and say, "No thanks." Antonio then approaches an older woman and tells her, "I have an extra ticket for the eight o'clock show. You can have it if you want." The woman ignores him. Antonio realizes that, in today's tense atmosphere, his gesture of friendship could be perceived by some people as a threat. He decides to stop offering the ticket to people before his offer backfires and he gets in serious trouble.

• The engine of Joe's car starts to sputter, and then he hears a loud "ping." The engine is still running but with little power. Joe spots an exit off of the expressway and decides to take it. He pulls into a mini-mart and calls home to explain the situation. As he leaves a message on the answering machine, he realizes that he may be stuck here in the middle of nowhere for a long time. When he gets off the phone, an older man fixing a cup of coffee next to him says, "Excuse me. I couldn't help but overhear your conversation. I used to be a truck driver, so I know what it's like to be in your situation. Sounds like one of your cylinders is gone. If you can get your car running even slowly, I could guide you to a local gas station. They're very honest and could take a look at it for you. Then, if you want, I could drive you into town where you could get a bus."

Joe ponders this offer. Not knowing what else to do, he follows the man to the gas station where the mechanic assures him that he'll take a look at it tomorrow and give him a call assessing the damage. As the older man is driving Joe into town, he tells Joe that he has two sons about Joe's age and he would hope that someone would help them if they were ever in trouble. When they arrive at the bus station, Joe thanks the man and catches a bus home. During the ride, Joe thinks about the fact that so many people are actually amazingly kind and generous. He hopes to remember this incident when he sees someone in trouble. **L**

Activity L

1. Joe claims that, "most people are actually amazingly kind and generous." Regardless of whether or not you agree with him, give examples to support his claim.

2. What situations tend to bring out virtue and good behavior in people? What situations tend to hinder virtue and good behavior in people?

3. What virtues do you believe are particularly strong in our society? Which virtues tend to be lacking in our society?

A **community of good character** is one in which commonly accepted behavior patterns lean toward honesty and empathy. Christians often repeat stories such as the Good Samaritan story in order to foster patterns of generosity and to counteract patterns of selfishness and fear. As we will see in the next chapter, Jesus did not simply call individuals to be persons of virtuous character. Rather, he wanted to form a community where living in the spirit in which he lived would become a way of life. In other words, Christian morality does not simply ask, "What ought I to do to be good?" It also asks, "What ought I to do to help others be good as well?" To live a consistent moral life we ask ourselves, "How can I develop virtues in myself?" In addition we also ask, "How can I help create virtuous living as the standard in my community?" Obviously, the first question supports the second; but the second question must not be overlooked.

> Human **interdependence** is increasing and gradually **spreading** throughout the world. The **unity** of the human **family**, embracing people who enjoy equal natural **dignity**, implies a universal **common good**.
>
> CATECHISM, #1911

For review . . .

19. Define integrity. What would its opposite be?

20. Name and explain the guidelines that help us to be persons of integrity.

21. What is the difference between stated values and lived values?

22. What is the relationship between lived values and being a person of integrity?

23. What does it mean to say that a goal of the Christian moral life is to create communities of character?

Conclusion
Become a Person of Integrity—Cultivate Character

Virtue, character, and integrity are formidable-sounding words. An important part of Christian tradition, they still call us to think about how our lives and our communities foster goodness. They lay before us the question: Do we want to be known simply as a "character" or as a person of good character? Only by living a life of integrity, a virtuous life, do we become persons of good character. As we struggle to live lives of faith, hope, and love, we are shaping our identity. The identity we cultivate today in large measure stays with us over a lifetime.

Let us pray . . .

Kindness is rewarded—
but if you are cruel,
you hurt yourself.
Meanness gets you nowhere,
but goodness is rewarded.

Always do the right thing,
and you will live;
keep on doing wrong,
and you will die. Amen.

PROVERBS 11:17–19 [CEV]

CHAPTER 3

Conscience
Being True to Our Deepest Self

The Christian moral vision takes heart and flesh in the day-to-day decisions we make. Conscience has come to be identified both with our capacity for right judgment in making decisions and with our faithfulness to that judgment. In this chapter we will look at popular uses of the term *conscience* and then define it in a way that reflects its original meaning. We will summarize recent Church teaching on conscience and finally relate the term to current discussion about moral maturity.

Chapter Overview

- Popular uses of the word *conscience* are frequently inadequate to describe all that the term involves.

- A fuller understanding of conscience includes three dimensions: awareness, development, and judgment.

- In Scripture the image most closely akin to conscience is "heart."

- Church teaching emphasizes the importance of using our conscience to make informed moral decisions.

- Pope John Paul II cautions against misinterpreting the meaning of conscience.

- To follow your conscience requires a high degree of moral maturity.

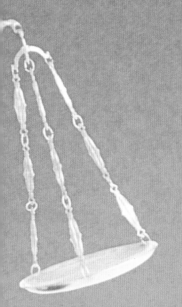

Before we begin . . .

1. Take a few minutes to draw a symbolic representation of conscience.

2. What does your drawing say about conscience?

Let us pray . . .

Gracious God, you have blessed us with the awesome power of conscience. Gazing inward, we search our hearts and ask: How are my decisions shaping who I will become? How are my actions affecting others? What is your will for me? You entrusted us with freedom and the power of choice. In our moral decision making, make us worthy by the power of your Holy Spirit of the trust you have placed in us. Amen.

The Nature of Conscience

Both in fictional and in real-life dramas, we often encounter the theme of being true to conscience. The theme deserves frequent treatment. Being true to conscience is an important sign of living an authentic human existence. Conscience represents our dignity and integrity as persons. We recognize as **heroes** those who follow conscience in the face of difficulties, sometimes even in the face of losing their lives.

hero—someone who follows her or his conscience in the face of difficulties

For instance, during World War II, a young Austrian Catholic named Franz Jagerstatter believed in his conscience that the war his country—at the time part of Nazi Germany—was fighting was wrong. Therefore, he refused to be drafted into his country's army. He found no support for his conscientious stand—not even from his parish priest. For being true to his conscience, Jagerstatter was executed by the Nazi leaders of his country.

The Heroism of Being True to Conscience

The movie's theme is a familiar one. A tough but honest cop faces a dilemma: Should he take the payoff or try to bring the wrongdoers to justice? Many of his fellow police officers and many public officials already close their eyes to crime in their city. If he merely remains silent about certain criminal activity, he receives a great deal of money and stays out of trouble. If he refuses the payoff, he endangers himself and his family.

As the movie's hero, he of course follows his conscience under trying circumstances. He fights crime while others are complacent about it, triumphs over evil, and emerges as a shining beacon of morality in a corrupt and grimy world.

During the late 1960s and the 1970s, Cesar Chavez, founder of the United Farm Workers Union, led a variety of protest actions to draw attention to the suffering of migrant farmworkers in California and elsewhere. Largely through his efforts, poorly paid migrant farmworkers gained a union. Even after achieving unionization for the farmworkers, Chavez continued his heroic struggle. He fought against the use of cancer-causing pesticides in the growing of fruit and against other dangers faced by farmworkers.

The challenge to be true to our conscience flows naturally from the Christian vision of morality. Throughout history and in our present day, we find many real-life reminders that the call to be persons of conscience is a call to be heroic. **A**

Activity A

Many critics of our contemporary culture lament that we have few heroes to imitate and inspire us. However, heroes need not be celebrities—people who make the cover of *People* or *Sports Illustrated*. Rank the following people from "1," most heroic, to "10," least heroic. Then defend your top choices and explain what you believe it means to be a hero.

_____ Two boys ride an amusement park ride in a dangerous fashion.

_____ A young girl volunteers one evening a week at a convalescent home.

_____ A boy whose family is poor attends high school and also works to help support his family.

_____ A tenth-grade girl attends a basketball camp where all other participants are boys.

_____ A junior in high school works at two jobs during the summer to raise money in order to attend her school band's trip to Europe.

_____ Even though cheating would be easy and other students around him are cheating, a boy with poor grades does his own work during a science test.

_____ A girl whose eyesight is very poor enrolls in a special program for blind skiers.

_____ A boy who believes strongly that abortion should be illegal is arrested while participating in an anti-abortion protest.

_____ A Mexican American girl who speaks little English attends a school where everyone else is English-speaking, because she feels that she can get a better education there.

The Question of Conscience

conscience—moral decision making involving awareness that there is right and wrong, a process of discernment, and finally judgment

In any discussion about morality, we cannot ignore the question of **conscience**. However, the word is used without much precision. It means somewhat different things to different people. In order to have a fruitful discussion about conscience, it is necessary to define the term much more precisely than the way it is commonly used. How we define the term makes all the difference when we try to answer the following questions: "Do I follow my conscience?" and "What does it mean to follow my conscience?"

Conscience

A Term with Many Meanings

In popular usage conscience has developed a number of similar meanings. For instance, the following three cases emphasize different aspects of conscience. In each incident conscience actually means something slightly different from its meaning in the other examples.

- Jen saw the makeup on the drugstore display rack. It was a brand that she had been wanting to try, but she had no money. The only person nearby was a young clerk reading a magazine behind a counter. Jen picked up the makeup and examined it. It was small enough to slip into her pocket. She wanted desperately to walk out of the store with it, but a little voice inside her—her conscience—gnawed at her to put the makeup back.

- Mick knew Andrea planned to invite him to her prom. He didn't want to go with her, but his mother had drummed it into him: Never hurt a girl's feelings! That saying, like many others repeated over and over again by his parents (Always clean your plate. Be polite to your elders.), made it difficult for Mick to go against his upbringing which had molded his conscience.

- With the end of the game near, emotions were at a fever pitch. Defensive captains exhorted their teammates, "If we stop them here, we win the game! Let's hit 'em and hit 'em hard!" Darrell dug in at his defensive-end position. When the ball was snapped, he rushed uncontested toward the quarterback and threw him fiercely to the ground. For what seemed like an eternity to Darrell, the quarterback lay unconscious in the middle of the football field. Darrell began to feel bad that he had attacked him so savagely. For weeks thereafter Darrell was racked with guilt feelings, which caused him bad dreams and anxious moments. Constantly, he replayed the scene in his mind, and each time he felt terrible about what he had done. **B**

Activity B

Describe a television show, movie, or novel that depicts a person facing a crisis of conscience. In response to the crisis, what choices does the person make? Does the person define conscience in a way similar or different from any of the three people in the above scenarios?

Conscience in Popular Usage

The stories of Jen, Mick, and Darrell point out some of the confusion surrounding the term conscience. Each example describes one aspect of *conscience*. However, if misinterpreted, each usage can actually distort conscience's true meaning and function. Therefore, we need to define the term more precisely. Let's look at each incident to see what conscience means in each case.

An "Inner Voice"

Is conscience an "inner voice" such as Jen experienced in the drugstore? Do we carry around within us—whether we like it or not—someone or something that tells us to "Do this" and "Don't do that"? In the children's story of *Pinocchio*, Jiminy Cricket is assigned to be Pinocchio's "conscience." Have we been assigned a conscience whose voice speaks to us when we face troubling moral decisions?

If these questions suggest that we have a conscience the way we *have* a watch or a car, then the answer to these questions is "no." Conscience is not a voice within us, separate from who we are. Rather, it is a reflection of our very being: Conscience is not something we have; it is something we are. Conscience refers to our entire being as valuing creatures who desire to turn toward goodness and truth.

Certainly Jen would do well to listen to the voice within reminding her that what she wants to do is not necessarily what is good to do. However, in another situation Jen might find that she should not follow the initial directive of her inner voice. For instance, Jen might hear her inner voice suggesting, "Always obey those in authority." Upon reflection she might decide that obeying this particular person in an authority position would not be a good thing to do. In other words, conscience should not be viewed as an "inner voice" that we leave untouched, unexamined, and undeveloped.

Our Upbringing

Let us consider the second incident described: Can conscience be equated with our upbringing? Like Mick in the story, all of us were told many things as we were growing up about what is right or proper and about what is wrong or inappropriate. As a result we walk around as if we have tapes ingrained into us, ready to play a message from our parents or others in authority who have given us advice. A number of years ago author Robert Fulghum wrote *All I Really Need to Know I Learned in Kindergarten*. The book's title struck a chord with many people. Consciously or unconsciously we carry within us the messages from our early years. Violating those messages is psychologically jarring.

Equating conscience with our upbringing serves to remind us that, like morality itself, conscience has a cultural and a community dimension. While we retain uniqueness and freedom, nevertheless our conscience is formed and molded—cultivated—by our culture and our community. Significant people in our lives, especially in our early lives, shape our sense of right and wrong. **C**

The same reservations apply to this understanding of conscience as apply to the "inner voice" notion. In the story, Mick should take seriously his parent's advice about not hurting someone's feelings. However, he also needs to examine critically all the taped messages that he carries around within himself. Likewise, we need to take what has been given to us by those who went before us and build on that. For instance, in 1947, Brooklyn Dodgers owner Branch Rickey signed Jackie Robinson as the first African American person to play major league baseball. Rickey acted as the conscience of the nation by going against commonly accepted beliefs of the time, reminding the country that racial discrimination is wrong in all areas of life. In terms of conscience we have received valuable lessons from the authority figures of our past, but there are more lessons to learn.

Activity C

Significant persons from our childhood can also be characters in books, television shows, or movies. Name three such characters who helped to shape your conscience. What positive messages did you receive from each?

A Feeling

If we were asked to write a sentence with the word "conscience" in it, many of us would include the phrase "guilty conscience." Guilty conscience means feeling bad about something we did. On the other hand, a "good conscience" also refers to a feeling—the positive feeling that results when we do something good. And a "clear conscience" means not feeling responsible for any wrongdoing in a particular situation. ("Yes, I was at the party, but I wasn't drinking. My conscience is clear.")

In the third example presented, Darrell feels guilty about hurting an opposing player during a football game. Is such a feeling the work of conscience? Actually, people can feel guilty about their actions even though they are not clearly responsible for the consequences of those actions. For that reason Darrell's "feeling guilty" is not an adequate explanation for what we mean by conscience.

Our feelings of guilt and of lack of guilt certainly are related to conscience. However, just as with "inner voice" and "upbringing" as descriptions of conscience, our feelings are only one dimension of what conscience involves.

Looking at our own lives we might discover times when we felt guilty, even though closer examination indicates that we did nothing wrong. For instance, as children, perhaps we felt guilty when we broke something valuable belonging to someone else, even though we were actually trying to help. Or we might feel guilty about making an unkind remark that we did not intend to cause harm. If conscience is to be the over-arching guide for moral decision making, then it does not refer only to a feeling. Feelings are significant and need to be respected and taken seriously. However, of themselves, good or bad feelings are not what we mean by conscience. **D**

Root Meaning of Conscience: An Action, Not a Thing

Sometimes knowing the origin of a word helps us clarify its meaning. The Latin root of our English word *conscience* is the active verb *to know*. From this root meaning we discover two things: Originally, conscience had to do with knowing; and conscience referred to an action rather than a thing. Conscience, therefore, originally meant our acts of *judging* based on our *knowledge* of right and wrong. If

we are to crown conscience as central to moral decision making, then we need to retrieve this older sense of the term. The Catechism's definition of conscience does just that when it states:

> *Conscience is a judgment of reason by which the human person recognizes the moral quality of a concrete act* (1796).

Activity D

1. Have you ever felt guilty for an action that harmed another even though you did not intend to cause harm? If so, explain the situation.

2. Have you ever not felt guilty when doing something that turned out to be wrong or hurtful? If so, explain the situation.

3. Have you ever felt guilty when you knowingly did something wrong or hurtful? If so, explain the situation. What did you do about the feelings? (For instance, did you use the guilt feelings as the motivation to make amends?)

consciousness—
awareness of
oneself and one's
surroundings

As an activity involving knowing, conscience is related to **consciousness**. Consciousness refers to a general awareness of ourselves, other people, and our surroundings. Conscience refers to our awareness—our consciousness—of right and wrong. Therefore, conscience and consciousness cannot be separated. To the degree that we are conscious, we are aware of ourselves, of others, of our personal values, of our society's values, and of Church teaching about morality. When we "follow our conscience," we are acting out of that awareness. When we act in a conscientious manner, we make moral choices consistent with our consciousness of good and bad. As you can see, *conscience* and *consciousness* are interrelated terms.

And so the root meaning of conscience helps us to appreciate how this important capacity serves us in our decision making. None of the popular applications of the term comprises all that conscience is, for it is more than just an inner voice, more than just a feeling, and more than all the messages about right and wrong that we have accumulated over the years. These popular notions present us with aspects of conscience—or, more accurately, with material for us to consider in acting conscientiously. However, they are incomplete descriptions of conscience. **E**

A fuller definition of conscience includes three interrelated dimensions:

1. Conscience begins with our basic, underlying awareness that there is right and wrong.

2. Conscience includes everything we do to develop our awareness of truth and goodness.

3. Finally, conscience refers to the judgment that we make about right and wrong.

For review . . .

1. Who were Franz Jagerstatter and Cesar Chavez?

2. Name three ways that conscience is understood in popular usage. Why is each usage insufficient to express all that conscience involves?

3. Who were Branch Rickey and Jackie Robinson?

4. What does the Latin root of the word *conscience* mean? What does this root meaning tell us about conscience?

Activity E

Conscience is related to consciousness, awareness. Therefore, to "raise consciousness" or to "deepen consciousness" means to increase our awareness of right and wrong.

• Name some areas in which your consciousness concerning right and wrong has been raised or deepened in recent years.

• Name some areas in which the general consciousness of our society has been raised over time.

• Name some areas of moral inquiry about which you would like to gain greater knowledge so that you may make more thoughtful decisions.

Three Dimensions of Conscience

In the story below, Jerry faces a painful dilemma filled with many possible moral decisions. He is faced with making decisions at home that affect his parents. He also recognizes that the tension in his home could influence him to "act out" in negative ways outside of his home, perhaps even to imitate his father's destructive behavior. In the face of this moral—not to mention psychological—powder keg, Jerry acts in a very conscientious way.

Let's take apart Jerry's decision to seek help from a counselor. In doing so we will uncover the three dimensions of conscience at work here. First, Jerry has a basic *awareness* that he is faced with decisions that could lead to good or bad results. Jerry is drawn to the good. At its most primitive level, "the good" could be more or less selfish, more or less selfless. Nevertheless, Jerry is motivated by an underlying orientation toward goodness and away from evil. This represents the basic groundwork of conscience.

Second, Jerry *develops* his awareness through self-examination. He is being conscientious insofar as he thinks about the options that are available to him.

Third, Jerry makes a *judgment:* Get help. So he decides to see a counselor who will help him decide on a course of action. Looking closely at Jerry's decision making in this instance, we can distinguish the three dimensions of conscience that are named above.

Jerry's Problem

Even as a young child, Jerry knew there was an abnormal amount of tension in his family. As he grew older Jerry realized that the tension arose because of his father's drinking problem. Recently, his mother has been confiding in him her feelings and concerns about Jerry and his father. She has even started asking him questions: "Have you seen Dad drinking lately?" "Has Dad ever talked to you about his drinking?" "You don't drink, do you? You don't want to end up like your father!"

His father, too, has been confiding in Jerry. On a number of Saturday afternoons, his father has told him, "I'm going down to the bar to watch some of the ballgame, Jerry. Don't tell your mother where I went; she'll just get upset."

Jerry doesn't know what to say or do. He finds that he has been

lying to his parents quite a bit lately and spending more and more time with a crowd known for getting into trouble. Jerry wants to do what is right, which for him means especially that he doesn't want to hurt either his mother or his father. After some thought, Jerry decides this problem is too big to handle by himself and so he seeks help. He decides to approach a school counselor. He hopes that with her help, he can unravel some of his own thoughts and feelings and devise some plan to deal with both of his parents as best he can. **F**

Activity F

If you were a member of a peer-counseling team at Jerry's school and he came to you for help, what advice would you give him?

Awareness: Taking Seriously Our Capacity to Seek the Good

Deep within his conscience man discovers a law which he has not laid upon himself but which he must obey.

CATECHISM, #1776

On its most elementary level, conscience refers to a basic recognition that our actions have good or bad results. **Consequences** are the outcomes of our actions. In moral decision making, conscience can come into play only when people admit that there is right and wrong and that they can choose between the two. We might question the existence of a basic awareness of good and evil in humans. Surely, some people seemingly exhibit no such sense of right and wrong. While this may be true, it does not deny the existence of such a capacity as an essential human trait. A person who takes no responsibility for his or her actions we label as mentally ill—in psychological parlance, a **psychopath**. In other words, to be human means to have a sense of right and wrong; not to have such an awareness is a sickness, a pathology, a distortion of one's humanity. **G**

If we deny the capacity to evaluate right from wrong as a natural human trait, then we are saying that moral discussion is fruitless. In fact humans have discussed, debated, and struggled over morality for many centuries. Many people have even chosen to die for what they believe is right.

If we possess a capacity for awareness of right and wrong, does it mean that we normally act on that awareness in our choices? Not necessarily. We possess many untapped capabilities, and conscience may be one that a person leaves untapped. However, nonuse does not equal nonexistence. Just as we have a capacity for learning that may go untapped, so we possess a basic capacity to recognize goodness that may shrivel up from lack of use. The term for conscience when it is either ignored or underemployed is **lax conscience**. A lax conscience is a lazy conscience. A person with a lax conscience chooses not to face or to think about possible decisions that he or she has to make, thereby also making a judgment not to act upon the possible good.

*Not to **decide** is to decide.*

consequences— the outcome of our actions

psychopath— a person lacking any sense of right and wrong

lax conscience— when a person does not employ a process of conscientious decision making, therefore, a "lazy conscience"

Activity G

In a psychology book or other reference source, look up the word *psychopath*. What does it mean? What factors in society could lead a person to develop a psychopathic personality?

Development: Enhancing Our Capacity to Know and to Choose the Good

informed conscience— a conscience that is educated and developed through constant use and examination

Our basic orientation toward goodness is not all that there is to conscience. We must build on and develop this orientation. Therefore, when we speak about following our conscience, we are referring to an **informed conscience**: a conscience that is educated and developed through constant use and examination. **H**

For instance, look at the brief anecdote in the activity below. We may find Jim's remark to be comical. Certainly, his logic goes counter to what it means to be conscientious. The second dimension of conscience operates against any such "ignorance is bliss" stance. At its very root, conscience seeks more knowledge, greater refinement, and deeper sensitivity. Therefore, the second aspect of conscience refers to all those steps that we take to form and develop our capacity to know right from wrong.

The Catechism expresses concisely what this dimension of conscience requires:

> *Beloved, do **not believe** every **spirit**, but **test** the **spirits** to see whether they are from God . . .*
>
> 1 JOHN 4:1

In the formation of conscience the Word of God is the light for our path [Cf. Ps 119:105]; we must assimilate it in faith and prayer and put it into practice. We must also examine our conscience before the Lord's Cross. We are assisted by the gifts of the Holy Spirit, aided by the witness or advice of others and guided by the authoritative teaching of the Church [Cf. DH 14] (1785).

In other words, when we read about Jesus and about his words and deeds, when we study Church teaching on morality, when we seek advice from others, we are using the gifts of the Spirit to develop our conscience and to move ourselves along to becoming more refined instruments for informed moral decision making.

If we make this course a process for deepening our consciousness of ourselves and others and a study of how our actions impact on ourselves and others, then the course itself will be the work of developing an informed conscience. As the first level of conscience exemplifies our dignity as human persons, so the second level nurtures and furthers that dignity.

Activity H

1. Read over the following scenario. Evaluate Jim's response in terms of the second dimension of conscience. What would a conscientious response on his part entail?

   One day a group of ninth-grade boys was gathered for a talk on moral issues related to sex. Jim remarked to his friend, "I don't want to hear about what I shouldn't do. If I don't know something is wrong, I can't be held responsible."

2. When college seniors have a morality course, they often say, "This course should be taken in freshman year. By senior year my morality and values are already set."

   State your opinion on the following questions. Give reasons to support your opinions.
   • Are a person's values ever completely set? Is moral development ever finished?

   • Is junior or senior year of high school too late for a morality course to have an impact on the values and moral decision making of students?

   • During which year or years of schooling would you recommend a morality course be given?

Judgment: Making Choices Based on Our Awareness of the Good

*Little **children**, let us **love**, not in word or speech, but in **truth** and **action**.*

1 JOHN 3:18

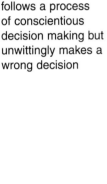

erroneous conscience— when a person follows a process of conscientious decision making but unwittingly makes a wrong decision

When it comes right down to it, morality involves decisions and acting upon those decisions. Likewise, conscience is not a drama played out endlessly in our mind. It is meant to result in judgments. Therefore, the message of conscience will lead us to be a certain kind of person or to perform a particular kind of action. Seeking to be sensitive to our evaluation of goodness and truth, and using as a guide all the information and awareness that our informed conscience can provide, we then choose the best course of action known to us. At this point, conscience refers to our moral judgment.

An important question related to this third aspect of conscience is: Even though we seek to be as conscientious as possible, can we judge wrongly? The answer to that question is "yes." We are imperfect creatures subject to mistakes and misguided judgments. Church teaching speaks of a conscience that judges wrongly even after a period of conscientious decision making as an **erroneous conscience**, a conscience in error.

Yet it can happen that moral conscience remains in ignorance and makes erroneous judgments about acts to be performed or already committed. (Catechism, #1790)

Of course, when we follow the directives of our conscience we cannot know that we are wrong. Other people may "know better" than we that we are wrong. Likewise, hindsight—looking back after we have acted—might convince us that we were wrong. However, being conscientious means that we make judgments based on our awareness of good and bad. We are responsible for seeking truth—especially as Catholics the truths found in Church teaching—and for acting accordingly.

SCULPTURE / MONUMENT TO HOLOCAUST VICTIMS OF WORLD WAR II. AUSCHWITZ, GERMANY.

BAGHDAD SKIES ERUPT WITH ANTI-AIRCRAFT FIRE AS U.S. WARPLANES STRIKE TARGETS IN THE IRAQI CAPITAL EARLY THURSDAY MORNING, JANUARY 18, 1991

reasons. Moreover, many slave owners hardened their hearts and closed their minds to developing their consciences on this particular issue. Nonetheless, at the time some people apparently adopted slavery in good conscience. That is, they made what we today would consider mistaken judgments with their consciences and then followed their erroneous consciences.

In similar fashion in the early 1990s, the United States engaged in a military action against the country of Iraq, which came to be known as the Gulf War. At the time people in good conscience both applauded and denounced U.S. bombing of Iraq. Some U.S. Catholics made conscientious decisions to support or participate in the war, while Church leaders generally condemned the action.

Whether or not we follow our conscience, we remain subject to the limitations of our human condition. While we must keep this caution in mind, a person striving for the good, seeking truth, and acting conscientiously represents the glory and the grandeur of being created in God's image.

sin—when people act contrary to their conscience and purposely choose to do wrong

A second important question regarding conscience as judgment is: Do people always act according to their best judgment? The answer to this question is clearly "no." When people do not follow their conscience—their best judgment—and when their actions are wrong, then Church teaching labels those actions **sin**.

Admittedly, since development of conscience differs somewhat with each individual, one person might conscientiously perform actions that another would find evil. For instance, in pre-Civil War United States, conscientious people stood on both sides of the slavery question. Of course, many people advocated slavery for selfish rather than for conscientious

For review . . .

5. An accurate definition of conscience includes three interrelated dimensions. What are they?

6. What is the relationship between consciousness and conscience?

7. Define psychopath.

8. What is a lax conscience?

9. What does developing an informed conscience involve?

10. Define erroneous conscience.

11. What term is used in Church teaching for not following one's conscience?

Activity I

Describe a moral dilemma that you or someone you know has faced. Evaluate the process used to arrive at a decision in terms of the three dimensions of conscience described above.

Conscience in Christian Tradition

To fully understand the term *conscience*, we must look at it through the double lens of Scripture and Church teachings. For as previously mentioned, we need the wisdom of others—the collected wisdom of the ages—to know truth and act accordingly.

Conscience in Scripture—Knowing of the Heart

The Bible seldom uses the word *conscience*. (In the *New Revised Standard Version* the term is used once in the Old Testament, never in the Gospels, and only twenty-five times in the rest of the New Testament.) Instead, the Bible's use of the word for heart is the closest equivalent to the concept of conscience. According to Scripture we can possess a clean heart or speak from an insincere heart. We can ponder God's word in our hearts and take it to heart, or we can be stubborn and harden our hearts. We pray for an upright heart and an understanding heart. The times we go astray we need a change of heart.

Of course, the "heart" that Scripture talks about does not mean the physical organ that pumps blood throughout our body. Rather, it means our entire being. To be conscientious persons we need to develop the "habits of the heart," the virtues mentioned in chapter 2, so that acting with sensitivity and concern for others flows naturally from our awareness of the goodness of God, of our own dignity, and of our oneness with others. When the prophets of old tell us to "change our hearts," they are reminding us that we need to view everyone and everything with this freshness of vision. When John the Baptist and Jesus call for a change of heart—sometimes translated as "repentance" or "conversion"—they are calling us to see the kingdom of God within us and around us and to act accordingly. **J**

Activity J

Use a concordance to research where and how the words *conscience* and *heart* are used in the Bible.

The Bible reflects the perspective of a people who were sensual, body-centered, experiential. Its frequent use of the word *heart* to denote a concept akin to conscience reminds us that conscience cannot be an intellectual activity that is isolated from our feelings, our experiences, our "gut reactions." *Conscience must be an activity of our whole person—a knowing of the heart as well as of the mind.*

Psalm 119 provides us with a fine description of Scripture's "knowing of the heart." We find in this psalm many of those traits of conscience that we value so dearly as essential to human dignity. In the psalm we pray for honesty and authenticity and not "the way of deceit" in our decision making. We pray to be molded to God's judgment so that we can see ourselves and others through God's eyes. We acknowledge our freedom of heart and ask for guidance and understanding as we strive to make decisions in accord with God's will. We would do well to ponder the psalm's message in our own hearts, for it serves as a fine "prayer of conscience." **K**

A Prayer of Conscience

Put false ways far from me;
and graciously teach me your law.
I have chosen the way of faithfulness;
I set your ordinances before me.
I cling to your decrees, O LORD;
let me not be put to shame.
I run the way of your commandments,
for you enlarge my understanding.
Teach me, O LORD, the way of your statutes,
and I will observe it to the end.
Give me understanding, that I may keep your law
and observe it with my whole heart.
Lead me in the path of your commandments,
for I delight in it.
Turn my heart to your decrees,
and not to selfish gain.
Turn my eyes from looking at vanities;
give me life in your ways.

—PSALM 119:29–37

Activity K

Using your own words, write a prayer of conscience that you could use when trying to decide what is the right thing to do when faced with moral dilemmas.

Conscience in Church Teaching: Does the Church Say "Follow Your Conscience"?

Discussion about Catholic teaching related to conscience usually centers around the question: Have the leaders of the Church taught that we should follow our conscience? While this is an important question, unfortunately it is not easily answered. Where conscience is mentioned in Scripture, most notably in the epistles of Saint Paul, it is presented in a favorable light. Certainly, Jesus calls us to act according to the change of heart that is central to his teaching. However, "conscience" has been a changing, developing concept within Christianity. As we have already pointed out, even today conscience means one thing on a popular level and another on a more technical level.

Nevertheless, thanks to some definitive statements by recent Church leaders, we can answer some questions about Catholic teaching on conscience. *Question number one:* Are Christians called upon to act and live conscientiously, that is, in accord with their consciousness of goodness and truth? The *Catechism of the Catholic Church* states, "In all he says and does, man is obliged to follow faithfully what he knows to be just and right" (1778). Clearly, the answer to question number one is "yes." *Question number two:* Should Christians think through their decisions and not act solely out of blind obedience or on whim and feelings? The Vatican II document "The Church in the Modern World" asserts, "Hence, the more a correct conscience prevails, the more do persons and groups turn aside from blind choice and try to be guided by the objective standards of moral conduct" [DH #3 § 2] (number 16). Thus, the answer to question number two also is "yes." *Question number three:* Should Christians act according to the dictates of an informed and developed conscience in their moral decision making? Turning to the Catechism once again, we read, "Man has the right to act in conscience and in freedom so as personally to make moral decisions. 'He must not be forced to act contrary to his conscience. Nor must he be prevented from acting according to his conscience, especially in religious matters'" [DH 3 § 2] (1782). Again, we find "yes" to be the answer given by Church leaders to this pivotal question. **L**

The Second Vatican Council on Conscience

When all the world's Catholic bishops convened in Rome from 1962 to 1965 for the Second Vatican Council, one issue about which they were very much concerned was that of human dignity in the face of modern trends leading toward dehumanization. Many of them knew firsthand the dehumanizing nature of fascism, nazism, and communism.

They were also concerned about more subtle attacks on human dignity accompanying some expressions of the capitalism, individualism, and consumerism of the West. They approved several documents that dealt with these topics. Later, portions of these Vatican II statements on conscience were included in the official *Catechism of the Catholic Church*.

Activity L

Are the answers to the questions about Church teaching on conscience what you expected them to be? Why or why not?

Conscience represents our dignity as human persons.

Deep within his conscience man discovers a law which he has not laid upon himself but which he must obey. Its voice, ever calling him to love and to do what is good and to avoid evil, tells him inwardly at the right moment: do this, shun that. For man has in his heart a law inscribed by God. His dignity lies in observing this law, and by it he will be judged. His conscience is man's most secret core, and his sanctuary. There he is alone with God whose voice echoes in his depths. By conscience, in a wonderful way, that law is made known which is fulfilled in the love of God and of one's neighbor (number 16). (See also Catechism, #1796.)

Conscience is a universal, human characteristic, operating when people seek truth and solutions to problems.

Through loyalty to conscience Christians are joined to other men in the search for truth and for the right solution to so many moral problems which arise both in the life of individuals and from social relationships. . . . Yet it often happens that conscience goes astray through ignorance which it is unable to avoid, without thereby losing its dignity (number 16). (See also Catechism, #1791.)

Freedom is required for people to choose good.

It is, however, only in freedom that man can turn himself towards what is good. . . . Man's dignity therefore requires him to act out of conscious and free choice, as moved and drawn in a personal way from within, and not by blind impulses in himself or by mere external constraint (number 17).

The bishops approved one document specifically titled, "Of Human Dignity." It is also known as the "Declaration on Religious Liberty." In this document the bishops speak strongly about the need for freedom and free choice if human dignity is to be served:

God calls men to serve him in spirit and in truth. Consequently they are bound to him in conscience but not coerced. God has regard for the dignity of the human person who he himself created; the human person is to be guided by his own judgment and to enjoy freedom (number 11).

The bishops also published a document known as the "Pastoral Constitution on the Church in the Modern World." It, too, teaches that conscience represents an essential element of human dignity that should be cultivated and followed in moral decision making. The above passages from the "Pastoral Constitution on the Church in the Modern World " illustrate the lofty view of conscience held by the bishops.

The bishop's words summarize the Catholic Church's understanding of moral conscience as an exercise of free will. It is a human action grounded in our human dignity that is itself the action of a judicious and loving God.

Pope John Paul II on Conscience

The Splendor of Truth—Pope John Paul II's encyclical on morality

In 1993 Pope John Paul II wrote an encyclical, an official letter from the pope, called *The Splendor of Truth*. In it he offers his thoughts on morality and moral decision making. He reaffirmed what the bishops of Vatican II said: Follow your conscience. However, he expressed great misgivings about the way many modern people interpret that pronouncement. In our strongly individualistic climate, many people view "follow your conscience" as an invitation to do "whatever I want to do." The pope points out that for Christians, following conscience means doing what Jesus would want them to do.

According to the pope, conscience involves intense, honest searching for the truth and then living in line with the dictates of that truth. (Recall the title of his encyclical.) Strangely enough, some people hear "follow your conscience," and they believe it lets them off the hook. To them it resembles a parent taking a child to a candy store and saying, "You can get whatever you want." In fact, conscience more often requires self-denial than self-indulgence and looking out for the good of others more than for oneself. In short, conscientious living requires great *heroism*—a word used frequently in the pope's encyclical.

Thus the pope offers us a more accurate, and more challenging, understanding of conscience. First, for Christians, conscience can never be divorced from the inspiration of Jesus. Secondly, there is a community dimension to conscience. An individual's seeking to be true to his or her conscience is not the same as an individualistic conscience—one that disregards the collective wisdom or the collective concerns of a community. Thirdly, for Catholics, Church teaching holds a privileged place as the source of moral guidance. Finally, being true to conscience requires heroism. Thus, the pope ends his discussion of conscience where this chapter began—with the call to be heroic. **M**

When we follow our conscience we . . .

- always strive for the truth
- look to Jesus Christ, the source of truth
- recognize that what is right and good may not be what we seem to want
- pursue information and guidance as best we can
- take seriously Church teaching
- listen to past wisdom
- look toward possible future consequences
- learn from others, especially from family, friends, and fellow Christians
- are sensitive to others
- investigate personal motives, pressures, and past patterns of behavior
- take positive steps rather than settling for indifference and inaction
- look critically at the messages that surround us in our culture
- make judgments to the best of our ability
- remain open to the possibility that we may be mistaken in our judgments
- evaluate the quality of our decisions during and after making judgments

For review . . .

12. What biblical term is the closest equivalent of the concept conscience?
13. What attacks on human dignity was the world facing that influenced Church leaders to convene Vatican Council II?
14. Name two documents of Vatican Council II that address the question of conscience.
15. In *The Splendor of Truth*, what are the four points about conscience that Pope John Paul II offers?

Activity M

Recall an incident when you tried to follow your conscience. Look over the checklist of steps in the box on the left involved in following conscience. Note which of the steps you took, deliberately or unconsciously, when making your decision. If possible, add to the list any other steps that helped you make a conscientious decision.

Conscience and Moral Maturity

As you can imagine, the message "follow your conscience" can be dangerous unless it is accompanied by a degree of moral maturity. But what is moral maturity? A little less than a half century ago, social scientist Lawrence Kohlberg began trying to determine whether or not there were basic patterns to moral growth similar to the patterns of physical, intellectual, and emotional growth that other researchers had been trying to identify. (For instance, at a certain point children typically realize that a dime is worth more than a nickel, even though it is smaller. Is there a stage of moral development when taking money from a parent or a friend can be grasped as having moral implications?) Through his research Kohlberg arrived at a theory of development that identified three levels of moral maturity. Essentially, he was not interested in *what* his subjects concluded about right and wrong but in *why* they chose what they did. Therefore Kohlberg's theory describes motivation rather than content. In capsule form here are his three levels of moral maturity. **N**

Lawrence Kohlberg's Levels of Moral Maturity

The Pre-Conventional Level: Fear of punishment, promise of reward

A person who reasons, "I'm being good only so that I don't get punished and so that I will get ice cream," is demonstrating this lowest level of morality. The presumption is that a person at this level makes choices based solely on the external tangible punishments or rewards that others provide based on his or her actions. He or she will make a good moral choice to avoid pain and to bring pleasure. Selfish behavior, to whatever degree, is acceptable so long as he or she does not get caught.

pre-conventional level of morality— when a person's motive for behavior is fear of punishment or promise of reward

The Conventional Level: Adhering to the conventions of society

Kohlberg suggested that most people function on the second level of moral maturity—following the norms of their culture, wanting to fit in, and trying to be nice. "Conventions" are the taken-for-granted norms of a society. Conventional morality represents the standard morality of a person's group—family, peer group, community, or country. When young people act a certain way around adults but slip into a different code of behavior when they're with their peer group, they are exhibiting this kind of morality. A conventional person adheres almost uncritically to a society's norms. To stand up against the status quo would require a higher degree of maturity—Kohlberg's post-conventional level.

conventional level of morality— when a person's motive for behavior is fitting in and adhering to conventions of society

The Post-Conventional Level: Self-chosen ethical principles

On a post-conventional level of moral reasoning, universal good is placed over self-good or the good of one's group. Persons operating at this level of maturity respect laws, rules, and social norms. Moreover, they take seriously the principles underlying these laws, rules, and social norms. They seek a just and unbiased application of morality, regardless of whether the beneficiaries belong to their own group or another's. People at this level operate beyond cultural norms. They act counter to accepted wisdom when they perceive that there is a higher good, and they will even risk personal suffering to adhere to their principles. Kohlberg considers such people to be the moral heavyweights, the exceptional ones for whom "conscience" means dedication to selfless and self-chosen ethical principles.

post-conventional level of morality— when a person's motive for behavior places universal good over self-good or the good of the group

A. Divide into small groups. Have each group choose one of the following moral dilemmas. Describe a response that would reflect each of Kohlberg's three levels of moral development.

1. During a test you turn to the person sitting next to you to ask a question. The person looks over and says, "I don't know." Your teacher sees your classmate talking but not you. He walks over to your classmate's desk and removes her test. You realize that this means she will fail the test. What do you do?

   Pre-Conventional response:

   Conventional response:

   Post-Conventional response:

2. A friend of yours decides to run for student-council president. He tells you that he is interested in the office only because it will help him get into a good college. You and he have gone to school together since kindergarten, so he asks you to be his campaign manager. You believe that the student running against him, someone in a group with whom you have little contact, is actually the better candidate. What do you do?

   Pre-Conventional response:

   Conventional response:

   Post-Conventional response:

3. On the phone with a classmate, you are reminded that you have a history paper due tomorrow. You totally forgot about the paper. When you get off the phone, you tell your older brother about your problem. He says, "I had that course two years ago. We had the same assignment. You can hand in my old paper if you want it." What do you do?

   Pre-Conventional response:

   Conventional response:

   Post-Conventional response:

4. An earthquake causes damage to a nearby commercial area. Many store windows are shattered and electrical power is cut off. As you walk behind a large appliance store, someone you know runs by with a few boxes of portable CD players that he took from a storage area in a damaged store. Attention of store employees is directed toward the front of the building where a fire has broken out. What do you do?

   Pre-Conventional response:

   Conventional response:

   Post-Conventional response:

B. Give other examples to describe what each of the following might look like:

   a "pre-conventional conscience":

   a "conventional conscience":

   a "post-conventional conscience":

Are There Different Ways to Be Morally Mature?

Kohlberg's theory has been attacked on a number of fronts. For one thing he describes levels of moral reasoning—why people do what they do—rather than the conclusions they reach about right or wrong. Should morality be reduced to a person's motives? Secondly, a colleague of his named Carol Gilligan notes that his theory describes moral reasoning as it more typically operates in boys. Gilligan suggests that girls tend to reason differently from boys—a position that has interesting implications for a course on morality such as the one you are now taking!

Gilligan observes that girls are more likely than boys to focus on how everyone is getting along than on being true to abstract moral principles. Although Kohlberg's theory would place such concern more at his second level, it can be argued that a concern for relationships actually represents a higher level of moral behavior. Gilligan's main contribution to an understanding of moral maturity is that, while people can be more or less developed in their moral reasoning, we must be careful about assigning too rigidly what constitutes degrees of moral maturity. **O**

Activity O

State your position on the following questions. Explain your answers.

1. Do you agree with Lawrence Kohlberg's theory of moral development?

2. Do you believe that, on the average, boys and men do moral reasoning differently than girls and women do?

3. Do you find that Kohlberg's levels of moral maturity can help us have a more accurate understanding of conscience?

Saint Thomas More

Model of Conscience

Saint Thomas More (1478–1535) is a famous example in history of someone known for following his conscience. More was a lawyer who rose to the rank of Chancellor of England during the reign of King Henry VIII. He was married and had three daughters and one son. While More served as chancellor, the pope was petitioned by King Henry to nullify Henry's marriage to his wife Catherine so that he could marry someone else. (Henry wanted a son as heir to the throne, and none was forthcoming with Catherine.) The pope refused Henry's request. The king then declared himself head of the Church in England and quickly declared his marriage invalid.

Naturally, such an action caused disruption within England. The king wished to rally whatever support he could. Thomas More was a pivotal person who was highly regarded for his uprightness and learning; if he would approve of the king's action, surely most other English subjects would do the same. However, in conscience More could not approve of the king's declaring himself head of the Church in England. When he refused to sign an oath to that effect, More was found guilty of treason and beheaded.

Thomas More was a family man who enjoyed life and in no way desired martyrdom. However, he placed being true to his conscience above all other considerations. He felt that he could not face God if he acted contrary to what he perceived to be the truth in this important matter.

Was More wrong? Many of his contemporaries in England—even important Church people—did sign the oath that More refused to sign. No doubt many acted out of cowardice. But, on the other hand, many signers probably acted in good conscience. Certainly a case can be made for signing the oath as being a good act. (By refusing to sign, More knew that he was in danger of death. What difference would signing the oath make? By his death, he caused great sorrow to those who loved him. Wouldn't he have been justified in signing the oath in order to spare his family and friends this hardship?)

Thomas More was certain of his judgment—even though he disliked tremendously the consequences of remaining true to that judgment. Because of his faithfulness to conscience unto death, More has become a model of integrity and a saint and hero of the Church.

Little as I meddle in the conscience of others, I am certain that my conscience belongs to me alone. It is the last thing that a man can do for his salvation: to be at one with himself.

THOMAS MORE IN ROBERT ELLSBERG, *ALL SAINTS.* [NEW YORK: CROSSROAD, 1997].

For review . . .

16. Name and describe Lawrence Kohlberg's three levels of moral maturity.

17. What did Carol Gilligan add to the discussion about moral development?

18. Why is Thomas More portrayed as a model of conscience?

Conclusion
You and Your Conscience

God has given us many gifts—of speech, of sight, of thinking, of our own unique personality. Yet God's gift of conscience supersedes them all, for it directs us to use all of our gifts for the good of the community, the common good. At times such faithfulness to conscience calls for real heroism on our part.

Christian teaching on conscience affirms that we possess a basic capacity to search for and to choose goodness. Through prayer and reflection leading to a change of heart, we can befriend and become more familiar with this "most secret core" of our being. Through this process of conversion, conscience becomes vital and active in our day-to-day decisions.

We also possess the ability to cultivate and develop conscience. We can do this through the study of Scriptures, through seeking advice, through faithful investigation of Church teaching, and through engaging in discussions on important issues with other Christians and non-Christians. (Chapter 8 outlines a process of moral decision making that suggests an entire program of conscience development.)

Finally, conscience is a God-given gift. We show our gratitude to God by its constant and deliberate use.

Let us pray . . .

God of goodness, we pray that your love takes root within us so that in all cases, in all places, we seek to do your will. We recognize that our hearts are restless until they rest in you. Free us from being timid and fearful; fill us with your spirit of courage and compassion. Amen.

God of truth, we pray that we may grow in wisdom and knowledge. Grant us an understanding heart to know right from wrong, the good from the misdirected, truth from ignorance. May we pursue your truth with endless passion. Amen.

God of love, when we grapple with difficult questions, may we always ask, "What is God's will for me right here, right now? What would Jesus want me to do?" The road that we travel is filled with detours and dead ends. When we stray from the straight path, may your Spirit renew in us the fire of love, the courage of our convictions, and the freedom to choose wisely. Amen.

CHAPTER 4

Jesus
Model of Morality

Jesus is the foundation stone of Christianity and the foundation of Christian teaching on morality as well. If we wish to know Christian moral teaching better, then we need to learn what Jesus himself took most seriously. In this chapter we will examine key Gospel passages related to morality. In particular we will explore the dual messages of consolation and challenge found in Jesus' teachings: God loves us, and we find true happiness only by loving others.

Chapter Overview

- Jesus models moral character in word and action.
- Love is the guiding principle of Christian morality.
- Jesus identifies with outcasts and those who are suffering.
- The Beatitudes describe followers of Christ.
- Jesus models service and calls upon his followers to serve.
- The difficult teachings of Jesus offer a foretaste of God's reign.

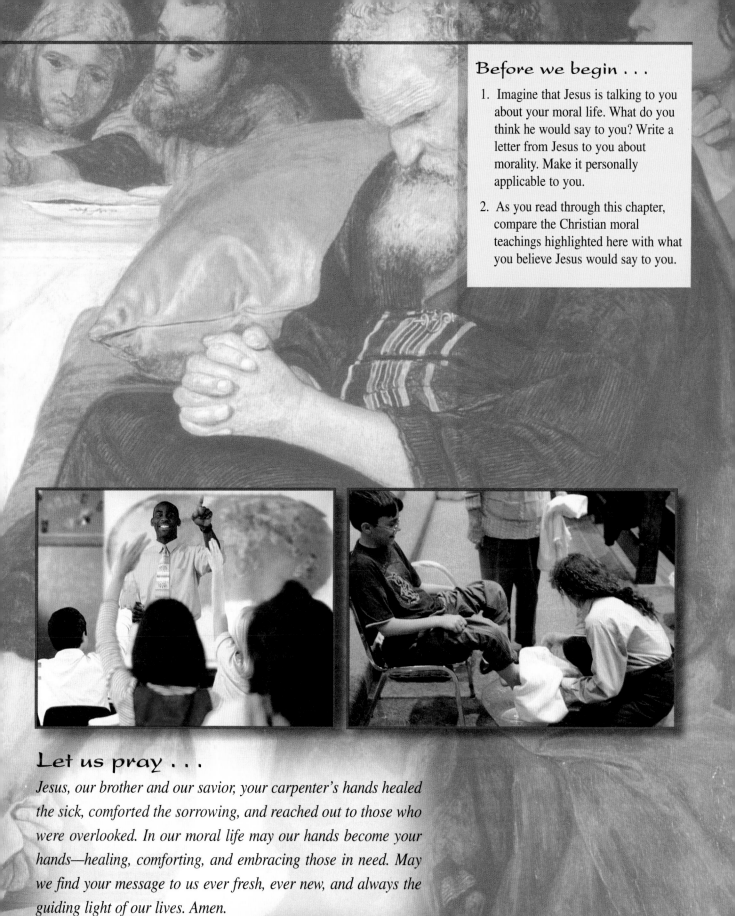

Before we begin . . .

1. Imagine that Jesus is talking to you about your moral life. What do you think he would say to you? Write a letter from Jesus to you about morality. Make it personally applicable to you.

2. As you read through this chapter, compare the Christian moral teachings highlighted here with what you believe Jesus would say to you.

Let us pray . . .

Jesus, our brother and our savior, your carpenter's hands healed the sick, comforted the sorrowing, and reached out to those who were overlooked. In our moral life may our hands become your hands—healing, comforting, and embracing those in need. May we find your message to us ever fresh, ever new, and always the guiding light of our lives. Amen.

Come, Lord Jesus

If Christ were to appear today in our own country, where might we search for him? Upon his birth, the wise men from the East looked for him in a palace. He wasn't there. According to the two accounts we have of his birth, it was a lowly affair. In our modern nativity scenes, shepherds and cattle seem cozy and comforting, even glamorous in their own way. The Gospel writers had another intention in mind with this portrayal. They wanted to shout out how much this child was mistakenly overlooked, an unlikely source by which the glory of God could shine through.

Thus the Gospels hint at an answer to the question: Where might we find Christ today? Perhaps in an inner-city slum, where people of little means live among boarded-up houses and empty factories, while lights from center-city skyscrapers bespeak a world of affluence so close and yet so far away. Perhaps we would find him along a desolate country road, a member of a large family living off an assortment of odd jobs to make ends meet, hoping that the vegetable garden by the house will keep food expenses down. Perhaps he would live with the nurse and the teacher, newly graduated and newly married, trying to make a life for themselves while being true to their professions. Perhaps he would be out in a field bent over a long row of fruits or vegetables, putting in long hours before moving on hoping to find work elsewhere.

When they heard the wisdom that the grown-up Jesus spoke, his townspeople were amazed. "Isn't he the carpenter?" they marveled (Mark 6:3). This is not where we expect to hear the voice of God! His person was surprising, his message baffling. Unless we, too, can look in unexpected places, we are equally in danger of not seeing Christ among us.

The Person of Jesus
The Starting Point of Christian Morality

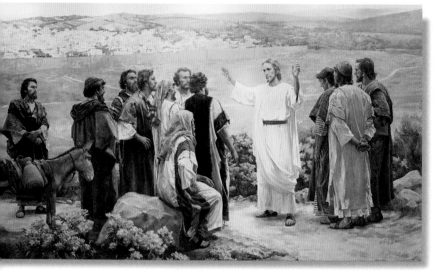

The story of Jesus' life is anything but dull. He is endearing but confusing, confronting but compassionate. Always he gets involved. Jesus' point of view on moral questions is not that of a philosopher, one who stands back and makes pronouncements on right and wrong from an ivory tower. He is not a teacher or rabbi who is associated with any particular school. Instead, Jesus is a preacher and a prophet without credentials. He spends the last three years of his life traveling about Israel, preaching his message and healing people in need.

Jesus' morality is more a *morality displayed on the run* than a systematic presentation of moral principles. That is, the Gospels are peppered with moral pronouncements that Jesus makes as he encounters people who are hurting and people who are hurting others. A morality on the run means that we discover Jesus' view of the moral life through stories about him and by him more than through any specific moral pronouncements that he makes. Nonetheless, we can identify certain Gospel passages, such as the **Sermon on the Mount**, that contain key moral teachings of Jesus. **A** **B**

We can reduce morality to the question, "What ought I to do?" From Jesus' perspective, that question by itself appears to be much too abstract, much too impersonal. Instead, the moral questions Jesus asks are more basic, more person oriented. He asks of us, "How are people hurting?" and "What can we do about it?" He also asks us to consider, "How is God at work in the world today?" and "How can we participate in God's work?" In a sense, in these two sets of questions we have the twin commandments, love God and love your neighbor.

Sermon on the Mount—the account in Matthew chapters 5–7, of Jesus' preaching important moral teachings, beginning with the Beatitudes

Activity A

Describe an experience when you had to do "morality on the run"—making a decision in the midst of an immediate problem. What would you recommend as guidelines for people who find themselves in such situations?

Activity B

The Sermon on the Mount (Matthew 5–7) contains many pronouncements about morality beginning with the Beatitudes. However, a parable such as the Good Samaritan story in Luke, chapter 10, also contains moral implications. Choose several of the Gospel verses below. After reading through them, state the moral messages that they contain. Apply the messages to situations that exist today.

Matthew 13:24–30	Luke 6:32–36	Luke 19:19–25
Matthew 13:33–37	Luke 10:38–42	John 8:1–11
Mark 10:2–12	Luke 12:1–3	John 14–17

The Moral Character of Jesus

Clearly, the Gospels leave us wanting to know so much more about the person of Jesus. The only story we have of him before age thirty can be read as one of youthful rebellion, as a foreshadowing of wondrous things to come, or as both. (Read Luke 2:41–51 about the incident of twelve-year-old Jesus discussing spiritual matters with the priests in the temple while his parents anxiously search for him.)

The first miracle recounted in John's Gospel takes place at a wedding, when, at his mother's request, Jesus changes water into wine. The scene is hardly profound. A couple find themselves running short of wine on their wedding day—a troublesome experience but not exactly earth shattering. So that their celebration goes well, Jesus helps them out. On another occasion Jesus goes to the house of the leader of a local synagogue whose daughter is dead (Mark 5:21–43). Jesus pushes through the weeping crowd and, upon entering the house, takes the young girl by the hand and tells her to get up. Again he saves the day in simple, direct fashion.

Even though we have too few accounts of them, the moral character of Jesus comes through in incidents such as these. He regularly demonstrates courage and compassion. He shares meals with anybody and everybody. He gets upset when anyone is left out. Jesus serves as our model for morality because of who he is. In other words, we find the answer to our moral quest not simply in what Jesus says but even more so in the moral character that he keeps demonstrating in his many encounters with others. As we read these accounts we discover, in the words of Pope John Paul II, that: "The light of God's face shines in all its beauty on the countenance of Jesus Christ, 'the image of the invisible God'" (*The Splendor of Truth*, number 2).

I once took a count of what sort of things Jesus thought important enough to confront people about in the gospel of Luke. Nine times Jesus confronted people for not showing love in their actions. Nine times he confronted folks for their greed and hoarding, which get in the way of single-minded service toward God and loving action toward the needy. Nine times Jesus confronted people for having divided loyalties, rather than serving God alone. Eight times he confronted people for showing by their actions that they did not recognize his authority. Eight times he confronted people who were seeking places of honor and reputation, and urged instead the way of servant-like humility.

Seven times he emphasized that the crucial question is whether we actually do what he teaches, versus the hypocrisy of claiming to be on the side of righteousness while not doing God's will. Seven times he called people explicitly to repent, to take the log out of our own eye, to stop being self-righteously critical of others and insisting on our own way, and instead to be more humble and loving toward him and toward others.

GLEN STASSEN, "INCARNATING ETHICS," SOJOURNERS. MARCH/APRIL, 1999. **C**

For review . . .

1. What moral questions does Jesus view as more basic than "What ought I to do?"

2. What does it mean to say that Jesus does "morality on the run"?

3. What does it mean to say that the moral character of Jesus serves as the basis for Christian morality?

Activity C

Read one of the Gospels. Based on your reading, write your own one-page portrait of Jesus.

The Moral Teachings of Jesus
Love of God, Love of Neighbor

Even non-Christians associate Jesus with love. Jesus embodied love—through his presence, his healing touch, his words of comfort to the sorrowing, and his words of challenge to the comfortable. Indeed, we can imagine no greater expression of love than Jesus on the cross.

Throughout his public life Jesus went to great pains to show us how much God loves us. Once again, Jesus places morality in the context of love and response. That is, the starting point of Christian morality is not, "What ought I to do?" but "What has God done for me?" Here is how the first epistle of John puts it:

> *In this is love,*
> *not that we loved God*
> *but that he loved us*
> *and sent his Son to be the atoning*
> *sacrifice for our sins.*
> *Beloved,*
> *since God loved us so much,*
> *we also ought to love one another.*
>
> 1 JOHN 4:10–11

Guiding Principles for a Christian Moral Life

- All love comes from God.

- Love on our part is a response to and a participation in God's love.

- Love others as we love ourselves, that is, with our whole being.

- Love of others and love of God are not separable.

Clearly, *love is the guiding principle of Christian morality.* Jesus revealed the centrality of love when he was tested by a group of the religious leaders of his day. He responded to their questioning about commandments by proposing his own commandment—love. **D**

> *When the Pharisees heard that he had silenced the Sadducees, they gathered together, and one of them, a lawyer, asked him a question to test him. "Teacher, which commandment in the law is the greatest?" He said to him, "'You shall love the Lord your God with all your heart, and with all your soul, and with all your mind.' This is the greatest and first commandment. And a second is like it: 'You shall love your neighbor as yourself.' On these two commandments hang all the law and the prophets."*
>
> MATTHEW 22:34–40

Activity D

Saint Paul provides in 1 Corinthians 13 a hymn to love. Read the passage in your Bible. Choose one of the characteristics and illustrate it with a collage, a photograph, a drawing, or a poem.

The Last Judgment—Finding Christ in People

After this he [Jesus] went out and saw a tax collector named Levi, sitting at the tax booth; and he said to him, "Follow me." And he got up, left everything, and followed him.

Then Levi gave a great banquet for him in his house; and there was a large crowd of tax collectors and others sitting at the table with them. The Pharisees and their scribes were complaining to his disciples, saying, "Why do you eat and drink with tax collectors and sinners?" Jesus answered, "Those who are well have no need of a physician, but those who are sick; I have come to call not the righteous but sinners to repentance."

LUKE 5:27–32

the Last Judgment—the story told in Matthew, chapter 25, where Jesus identifies himself with the needy of the world

This is my **commandment,** *that you* **love** *one another* *as I* *have loved* **you**.

JOHN 15:12

Imagine if we were brought in by police to identify someone who claimed to be Christ. Before us stood a hardened prisoner, a strange-looking older woman, a young boy in tattered clothes, and a mother carrying a baby crying from lack of nourishment. Where is Christ in this motley line-up? The words of Jesus found in Matthew, chapter 25 (known as **the Last Judgment**), startle us into concluding that Christ is represented in each of them!

When the Son of man comes in his glory, and all the angels with him, then he will sit on his throne of glory. All the nations will be gathered before him, and he will separate people one from another as a shepherd separates the sheep from the goats, and he will put the sheep at his right hand and the goats at the left. Then the king will say to those at his right hand, "Come, you that are blessed by my Father, inherit the kingdom prepared for you from the foundation of the world; for I was hungry and you gave me food, I was thirsty and you gave me something to drink, I was a stranger and you welcomed me, I was naked and you gave me clothing, I was sick and you took care of me, I was in prison and you visited me." Then the righteous will answer him, "Lord, when was it that we saw you hungry and gave you food, or thirsty and gave you something to drink? And when was it that we saw you a stranger and welcomed you, or naked and gave you clothing? And when was it that we saw you sick or in prison and visited you?" And the king will answer them, "Truly I tell you, just as you did it to one of the least of these who are members of my family, you did it to me."

MATTHEW 25:31–40

When we apply the message of this vivid scene to our own lives, we discover that Jesus is calling us to seek him in the people who are part of our lives. For example, the story reminds us that we are to welcome strangers.

Our attitude toward the "strange" student in our school whom nobody likes actually reflects our attitude toward Christ. Likewise, how we respond to people around us who are hungry—for food or for attention or for friendship—indicates how we are responding to Christ. Similarly, actions to alleviate suffering are actions in behalf of Christ.

But Jesus also calls us to reach out to those who are not necessarily in the mainstream of our lives. We also need to find Christ in our prisons, in our hospitals, and in our shelters for homeless people. Just like Jesus, we must treat each person as our brother or sister no matter what circumstances are a part of his or her life.

The passage from Matthew provokes us toward soul searching and great upheaval in the way that we normally view things. (For instance, in contrast to the Gospel story, we probably imagine Christ as being "like us" and not as being some stranger. Similarly, we are probably accustomed to looking for Christ in a church—not in a prison!) The Last Judgment scene offers a forceful presentation of what in chapter 1 was called "costly grace." It calls upon us to care not only for those whom we normally care for but, more importantly, for those whom we frequently overlook and avoid. **E**

For review . . .

4. What word describes the guiding principle of Christian morality?

5. According to the Last Judgment story in Matthew's Gospel, where is Christ to be found?

Activity E

Write a short story with a modern setting about finding Christ in another person.

The Beatitudes
The Christian Measure of True Happiness

The Beatitudes are at the heart of Jesus' preaching. . . . they shed light on the actions and attitudes characteristic of the Christian life. . . . The Beatitudes respond to the natural desire for happiness. This desire is of divine origin: God has placed it in the human heart in order to draw man to the One who alone can fill it.

CATECHISM, #S 1716–1718

Sometimes the eight Beatitudes are viewed as the Christian equivalent of the Ten Commandments. The **Beatitudes** are similar to the commandments in the sense that both lists describe what it means to be a member of God's people. However, while the Commandments represent a specific set of laws, the Beatitudes describe "attitudes" that the early Christians had as they experienced their life in Christ. They remain for us the attitudes that today's Christians should have. They offer hope in time of trouble as they describe the type of blessings and rewards waiting for those who choose to live them. The Beatitudes challenge us to conscientiously think about our attitude toward others so that our attitude reflects love of God above everything else.

As you can clearly tell, the Beatitudes are not a simple list of rules. Neither do they provide us with a series of things to do. Rather, they describe a way of life that results from trying to live the values of Jesus. **Beatitude saints** are people who attempt to live the Beatitudes and who take their message to heart. On the surface, Beatitude saints endure difficult times. Below the surface, they experience joy that comes only from an attitude of trust in God and from acting on that trust. **F**

Beatitudes–eight descriptions of early Christians as they struggled to live their life in Christ

Beatitude saints– people who take the Beatitudes' message to heart and attempt to live it

---

The Eight Beatitudes

When Jesus saw the crowds, he went up the mountain; and after he sat down, his disciples came to him. Then he began to speak, and taught them, saying:

Blessed are the poor in spirit, for theirs is the kingdom of heaven.
Blessed are those who mourn, for they will be comforted.
Blessed are the meek, for they will inherit the earth.
Blessed are those who hunger and thirst for righteousness, for they will be filled.
Blessed are the merciful, for they will receive mercy.
Blessed are the pure in heart, for they will see God.
Blessed are the peacemakers, for they will be called children of God.
Blessed are those who are persecuted for righteousness' sake, for theirs is the kingdom of heaven.

MATTHEW 5:1–10

Activity F

Divide into small groups and choose one or more of the Beatitudes. For each Beatitude make a list of "Beatitude saints"—that is, people living or dead, whose lives and actions exemplify that Beatitude's values.

A Beatitude Examination of Conscience

Each of the Beatitudes suggests attitudes, as well as actions that flow from those attitudes. Use the following questions to determine how close you are to being a Beatitude saint. After reading the entire list, choose one set of questions, and reflect on how you might make these characteristics your own. How might you better follow in the footsteps of the early "Beatitude saints" of the Christian community?

- **The Poor in Spirit.** Do I trust in God? Does my life become so cluttered that I have little time for God? Do I recognize that the world is not a weight upon my shoulders alone? Can I accept help rather than always trying to go it alone? Do I identify with poor people and, together with them, seek reasons for hope? Do I work to change attitudes and structures that oppress poor people?

- **The Gentle.** Do I view other people with profound respect? Do I treat the people whom I meet with care, sensitivity, and even tenderness?

- **Those Who Mourn.** Life always involves suffering. Do I appreciate that the suffering that comes from giving myself for others can also bring joy? Can I feel the pain of others, and do I contribute to relieving their anguish?

- **Those Who Hunger and Thirst for Righteousness.** Do I relate to others with a sense of fair play? Do I push myself to speak out against injustice and to work for just causes?

- **The Merciful.** Do I wish for others what I would want for myself? When others are down, do I try to help them up rather than take advantage of their misfortune? Would people who know me say that I am truly a kind person?

- **The Pure in Heart.** Am I a person of integrity, someone who cultivates wholesome values and stands up for those values? Am I sincerely honest when making decisions about right and wrong? Are my motives pure, that is, not dominated by self-interest to the exclusion of the interest of others?

- **Peacemakers.** Do I search for peaceful means to resolve conflicts? Am I known as a peacemaker in my family, among my friends, and with the strangers whom I meet? Do I try to understand the points of view of those with whom I have disagreements?

- **Those Who Are Persecuted in the Cause of Righteousness.** Are there beliefs and principles that I hold dear? Am I willing to stand up for my beliefs, even when they are unpopular or lead to personal hardships?

The Beatitudes as Descriptions of True Joy

The Beatitudes promise joy. Do you know many people who are truly joyful? That is, do you know people who possess an intense, abiding joy that outlasts and runs deeper than fleeting moments of happiness? Can you name even three people who are joyfilled?

Would you number yourself among this select group? Do you rank "being joyful" as one of your most important goals in life? Do qualities such as those enumerated in the Beatitudes figure into your understanding of true joy?

Clearly, the Beatitudes present a different portrait of joy. The joy of the Beatitudes is not that promised in television commercials or magazine ads. The Beatitudes are not the road usually traveled by people searching for happiness in our contemporary culture. The Beatitudes describe people who recognize the hand of God at work around them and who seek to work hand-in-hand with God. One Christian writer has observed that the secret of true happiness is to find joy in another's joy. Living in such a way does open oneself up to suffering; the Beatitudes are definite about that. However, in the dream of God's reign that Jesus offered his followers, sharing one another's joys and burdens lightens the load for everyone.

Although the Beatitudes as a prescription for joy confound human understanding, it is a joy that even outsiders among the early Christian communities recognized as unique and desirable—even when being Christian subjected one to possible persecution and death at the hands of Roman authorities! **G**

When we think about joyful people, certain images may immediately come to mind. We may think about people who possess every possible comfort, as well as many extra comforts that make life more enjoyable. ("Joy is a big-screen TV and a room entertainment center all to myself!") Or we might name someone who has achieved a high level of success—the most valuable player on the championship basketball team, the number one student in the class who will surely go far in life, or the person chosen as the lead in the school play. We might also bring to mind someone with great looks and a winning personality, someone who always comes across as self-assured and who always seems to be looked up to as a leader.

For review . . .

6. How are the Beatitudes similar to and different from the Ten Commandments?

7. What do the Beatitudes challenge us to do?

8. Define a "Beatitude saint."

9. Contrast a typical view of joy with the Beatitude's understanding of joy.

Activity G

The ancient Greeks and Romans had epic poems that rival any current Hollywood blockbuster films in action and adventure. An interesting event is described in book four of the Latin classic, Virgil's "Aeneid." A severe storm occurs at sea. After a harrowing time fighting the storm, the sailors who survive experience a shipwreck and then struggle to make their way to shore. Wise old Mentor stands up, gazes along the beach strewn with debris and bodies, and says: "Perhaps someday we will be glad to remember even these things."

Have you ever had a painful, challenging, or difficult experience that later you were able to say you were glad you went through? What was the experience? What did you learn from it? Was there any sense of "joy" that actually accompanied or resulted from the experience? Write about your experience.

"Come and Follow Me"

Jesus' request to follow his example offers us his support and presence always. In return we are asked to serve humbly, love completely, and live unselfishly.

Footwashing—Model of Service

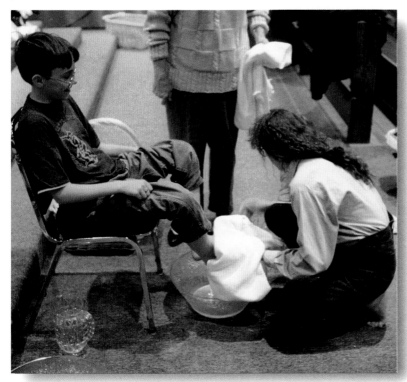

footwashing— the activity Jesus performed prior to the Last Supper that becomes the model for all Christian service

the face and hands of dinner guests; but even servants did not have to wash other people's feet. (Remember that in first-century Israel there were no paved streets, modern sewage and garbage disposal systems did not exist, and people wore open sandals while walking over dusty and dirty roads.)

Jesus' washing of the apostles' feet was both shocking and purposeful. Just as he told his followers to "do this in memory of me" every time they shared bread together in his name, through his washing of their feet he wanted to send a message about the type of behavior he expected of his disciples. As he completed washing the apostles' feet, Jesus said, "For I have set you an example, that you also should do as I have done for you" (John 13:15).

At one point Jesus gathers together his apostles and tells them, "Whoever wants to be first must be last of all and servant of all" (Mark 9:35). Interestingly, when Jesus cures a sick woman and a leper, their immediate response—the sign of their new life—is that they begin to serve. (See Luke 8:43–48 and Mark 1:40–45.) The message of the Gospels is clear: Christians should be tripping over themselves trying to serve one another and those who are hurting in their midst. **H**

Interestingly, some Protestant groups always include a footwashing ceremony whenever they have a communion service. Catholics combine **footwashing** with the Eucharist only on Holy Thursday. According to John's Gospel, on that day, before he shared his last supper with his closest friends, Jesus washed their feet. Although we can't be certain about first-century customs, one belief is that at the time it was common practice for servants to wash

Activity H

1. What message did Jesus wish to convey by washing feet and asking his disciples to wash each other's feet?
2. Name three types of activities that today would mirror the spirit of footwashing.

Placing God First in Our Lives

Granted, most of us can barely stay on top of our own business. Nonetheless, Jesus asks us to "strive first for the kingdom of God and his righteousness" (Matthew 6:33). This request seems overwhelming, an added burden placed upon our already overburdened lives. But read through this section of Matthew's Gospel.

Jesus makes this appeal in the context of the message: Stop worrying! He doesn't want to increase our burden; he wants to unburden us! According to Jesus, placing God first in our lives frees us, relieves us of self-consuming anxiety, and supports all of our endeavors to lead a good life. ◼

The "Hard Sayings" of Jesus

"hard sayings" of Jesus—teachings such as the Beatitudes and the Last Judgment that overturn commonly held values and priorities

Face it. The Gospels contain many hard sayings—teachings such as the Beatitudes and the Last Judgment that overturn commonly held values and priorities. Even his closest friends found many of Jesus' teachings to be **"hard sayings,"** sayings that are hard to understand and even harder to follow.

If we paged through the Gospels, we could find many examples of difficult and disturbing teachings. Here are two Gospel passages that exemplify values and priorities that run counter to those typically found in most cultures.

> *You know that among the Gentiles those whom they recognize as their rulers lord it over them, and their great ones are tyrants over them. But it is not so among you; but whoever wishes to become great among you must be your servant, and whoever wishes to be first among you must be slave of all.*
>
> MARK 10:42–44

> *But I say to you that listen, love your enemies, do good to those who hate you, bless those who curse you, pray for those who abuse you. If anyone strikes you on the cheek, offer the other also; and from anyone who takes away your coat do not withhold even your shirt. Give to everyone who begs from you; and if anyone takes away your goods, do not ask for them again. Do to others as you would have them do to you.*
>
> LUKE 6:27–31

Many of us today are accustomed to hearing the words of Jesus about turning the other cheek, serving others, valuing people over property, and becoming like little children. Because of our familiarity with these sayings, we might overlook the challenge found in them. But imagine if we preached these same sentiments in different words and apart from a church setting. No doubt, we would find ourselves ridiculed, labeled troublemakers, or denounced as some sort of crazy religious fanatics. The hard sayings of Jesus create a tension in anyone who attempts to take them seriously. And yet to be Christian means to take seriously that which Jesus took seriously.

For review . . .

10. What action by Jesus modeled his command to serve others? When did Jesus perform this action?

11. In what context does Jesus put his message to place God first in our lives?

12. What does the text mean by the "hard sayings" of Jesus? Give an example.

Activity I

1. Name three ways that you personally could place God first in your life.

2. If you actually did these things, would your life be more or less burdensome? Explain.

Jesus' Vision of God's Reign

kingdom of God—
Jesus' vision of a world where God reigns–where people serve one another, share their goods with one another, and refuse to retaliate with violence against others

The challenging words of Jesus make sense only in light of his vision about God's reign—the **kingdom of God**. Jesus imagined a world where God reigns. He provided wondrous images to help us appreciate his dream—a heavenly banquet to which everyone is invited; a precious gem found discarded in a field; yeast that appears insignificant but, when added to bread, makes the entire loaf rise. Jesus also pointed out that, even though we may not readily see it, the kingdom of God is already among us and within us.

Jesus wants us to share his dream. As the above Gospel passages remind us, the dream of God's reign on earth can come true only when people serve one another, share their goods with one another, and refuse to retaliate with violence against others. Throughout history, trying to live these lofty ideals has created a great challenge for Christians. This course represents our own attempt at making some sense of Jesus' difficult teachings. The hard sayings of Jesus continue to challenge Christians with the dream of furthering God's reign "on earth, as it is in heaven."

Taking the teachings of Jesus seriously certainly will cause us unrest; we see around us a human community that constantly falls short of his ideals and we know how frequently we ourselves do not measure up. Consequently, we might dismiss the hard sayings of Jesus as unrealistic and unworkable. But in fact, are there any better directives for creating and cultivating God's reign? As lofty and as challenging as his teachings are, the words of Jesus provide our best guide book for transforming the world and for seeking eternal life.

The kingdom belongs to the poor and lowly, which means those who have accepted it with humble hearts. Jesus is sent to "preach good news to the poor" [Lk 4:18; cf. 7:22]; he declares them blessed, for "theirs is the kingdom of heaven" [Mt 5:3]. To them—the "little ones"—the Father is pleased to reveal what remains hidden from the wise and the learned [Cf. Mt. 11:25]. Jesus shares the life of the poor, from the cradle to the cross; he experiences hunger, thirst, and privation [Cf. Mt 21:18; Mk 2:23–26; Jn 4:6–7; 19:28; Lk 9:58]. Jesus identifies himself with the poor of every kind and makes active love toward them the condition for entering his kingdom [Cf. Mt 25:31–46] (Catechism #544).

Making the Jesus Story Our Story

In the midst of his famous Sermon on the Mount, Jesus sums up his challenge to us in these words: "Be perfect, therefore, as your heavenly Father is perfect" (Matthew 5:48). That's quite a proposition he hands us mere mortals! Of course, none of us is perfect. "Perfection" here means *being the person we were intended to be*. So Jesus was perfect because he fulfilled completely the purpose for which he was created. It took Jesus his whole human life to complete this task; just as it will each of us. To help us on our journey, Jesus assures us that *his* story is *our* story. We celebrate our identification with Christ in our Baptism and Confirmation, in our participation in the Eucharist and other sacraments, and through all of our efforts to live a Christ-like life.

> Here is a **test,** to find whether your **mission** on earth is **finished**: If you are **alive,** it isn't.
>
> RICHARD BACH, QUOTED IN ROBERT J. FUREY, *CALLED BY NAME* [NEW YORK: CROSSROAD, 1960].

Celebrations of the Christian life should not be divorced from our attempts to lead a Christian moral life. The sacraments offer us a glimpse into our true Christian identity—that is, how to be those persons and that community we are meant to be. If we truly enter into our reception of the sacraments, they can help us remember, reassemble, and recreate ourselves at our best and in the way God intended us to be. The task of following Jesus is neverending, and we need all the help we can get. As the next chapter points out, the Christian community—its history of truth-tellers and models of sainthood, along with its resources such as prayer and the sacraments—connects us in our imperfection to the perfect one, Jesus. **J**

For review . . .

13. Only in light of what concept do Jesus' hard sayings make sense?

14. Name two images Jesus uses to help us appreciate the kingdom of God.

15. What is the relationship between the sacraments and Christian identity?

Activity J

1. Have you ever had a moment when you felt particularly close to God? Did the experience suggest anything to you in terms of moral behavior? Explain.

2. If the moral message of Jesus can be summed up in the phrase, "Love one another as I have loved you," what would you say are some characteristics of Jesus' understanding of love as this chapter presents them?

Conclusion
Jesus—Moral Teacher, Moral Model

For Christians, Jesus is the great moral teacher. In all of his teachings, Jesus begins with the message of God's love for us. Because of that starting point, Jesus' moral teachings—such as his summary of the Commandments, the Last Judgment, and the Beatitudes—are expressions of a response to God's love. This entire course is meant to be an exploration of Jesus' invitation to respond to God's love—and to love as God loves.

Let us pray . . .

God our Father, we pray that the work we associate with your Son may also become our work: love, service, forgiveness, sharing of goods, relieving burdens, giving ourselves over to you. Sustain us in our attempts to do your will. Carry us by the power of the Holy Spirit when necessary. Forgive us always. Bring us home to you as you promised, through Christ our Lord. Amen.

CHAPTER 5

The Church

Communion of Saints, Communities of Support

The Church provides inspiration, support, fellowship, and guidance as we struggle to be creative and loving with our lives. In this chapter we examine the numerous ways that the Church community can assist us in our moral decision making. A key to appreciating the Church and its relationship to the moral life is to remind ourselves that the Church is "we," not "they" or "it."

Chapter Overview

• The communion of saints refers to all people—past, present, and future—people who were, people who are, and people who will be inspired by the Holy Spirit to use their talents for helping others.

• As the body of Christ, the Church is a community whose members serve different functions.

• In imitation of Christ, the Church stands for reconciliation and forgiveness.

• The Sacrament of Reconciliation celebrates forgiveness and offers Christians an opportunity to take an inventory of their lives in light of the healing message of Jesus.

• The Eucharist is a sacrament that contains many implications for morality.

• Church leaders serve as teachers and guides for living a moral life.

• Church teachings are both continuous with the past and ever renewed.

Before we begin . . .

1. Draw a symbolic image of the Church and its relationship to the moral life.

2. Discuss the following questions:

   • Why did you select the image that you did?

   • Where are you in this image of Church—inside or outside, active or passive, in communion or in conflict?

   • Based on your drawing, what role are you assigning to the Church in your moral life?

3. Draw an image that would depict your understanding of the ideal relationship between the Church and the moral life. Explain this image.

Let us pray . . .

Christ our Lord, you are the head of your body, the Church. You are a living presence, across the globe and in the seat next to us. You are within us and among us. As members of your body, we join with all the saints, living and dead, who proclaim your good news: "Dying, you destroyed our death. Rising, you restore our life. Lord Jesus, come in glory." Amen.

A Teenage Princess
Who Cared for the Poor

Saint Elizabeth of Hungary (1207-1231)

Imagine that you were born a medieval princess. At the age of four, you were sent off to live in the home of your future husband. At age fourteen you married the man chosen for you, and you took on the dual responsibilities of raising children and assisting your husband in making decisions about affairs of state. (The age is not a misprint. The heroine of our story did indeed begin her life as wife and mother at age fourteen!)

We envision a princess as living a fairy-tale life, surrounded by riches and waited on by countless servants. However, this was not the case for the princess who became known as Saint Elizabeth of Hungary.

Born the daughter of a Hungarian king, Elizabeth was betrothed while still an infant to a German prince. She was sent off to live at her future husband's castle, where she married him at age fourteen.

While still a teenager, Princess Elizabeth became a wife and mother. She loved her husband and he loved her. She also felt deep compassion for lepers, famine victims, and suffering peasants— the people most in need during her lifetime. The prince, Elizabeth's husband, admired and respected Elizabeth's untiring efforts on behalf of these people and supported her in her endeavors. Elizabeth saw to it that much of the wealth of the realm went to building hospitals and facilities for poor people. Because of her generosity she gained many enemies, who felt that royal money should be spent on more "important" matters such as grander castles and stronger armies.

One such enemy was her mother-in-law. According to legend, one time Elizabeth even gave up her own bed to a homeless leper.

Elizabeth's mother-in-law felt that this instance of extreme generosity could easily be exposed as misguided. To discredit Elizabeth the mother-in-law dragged her son the prince to the bedroom. However, when the two of them entered the room, instead of a leper they found a vision of Jesus Christ.

After bearing four children and selflessly dedicating her life to caring for the poor and the sick, Elizabeth died at the age of twenty-three. Four years later she was proclaimed a saint of the Church. The speed with which she was named a saint indicates that, even though she was young, many people of her time viewed her as a saint.

As a princess, Elizabeth could have enjoyed all the comforts of courtly life. Instead, she gave herself to the needy people in her realm. For her efforts she suffered rejection, harassment, and physical torment from her enemies. Nonetheless, true to her youthful enthusiasm and deep compassion, she remained undaunted. We can look to Saint Elizabeth of Hungary for inspiration as we search for ways to channel our own enthusiasm and compassion. **A**

Activity A

Do research on someone who has recently made a positive contribution to our world. Write the person's story—if possible include a picture. As a class, collect the stories and make a booklet or bulletin-board display of these models of saintliness. (Some people to consider are Mother Teresa of Calcutta, Jean Donovan, Maximilian Kolbe, Oscar Romero, Mev Puleo, Alfred Delp, Katherine Drexel, Fannie Lou Hamer, Thea Bowman, Peter Maurin, Albert Luthuli, and Edith Stein.)

A Hero Both On and Off the Baseball Field

Roberto Clemente (1934–1972)

To most of us a professional baseball player may seem to lead a life as wonderful and storied as that of a princess. Few ball players played the game with as much delight and enthusiasm as the legendary right fielder of the Pittsburgh Pirates, Roberto Clemente.

While starring in a league in his native Puerto Rico, Clemente drew the attention of the baseball world because of his exceptional defensive skills, his speed, and his lightning-quick bat. Clemente played outfield for the Pittsburgh Pirates from 1955 to 1972. During that time he twice led the Pirates to World Series titles; four times he won batting titles as the best hitter in the National League; and once he was named the league's most valuable player.

When a severe earthquake struck the country of Nicaragua in 1972, Clemente was not comfortable simply reading about the devastation that occurred there. Inspired by his Christian faith and drawn by concern for those suffering, he quickly became involved in raising funds and in collecting needed supplies for the earthquake victims. While accompanying a shipment of supplies to Nicaragua, Clemente died when the plane in which he was traveling crashed into the sea.

Roberto Clemente was elected to Baseball's Hall of Fame in 1973, the year following his death. Because of the way he gave himself both on and off the field, Clemente is an inspiration to us— to give ourselves in all that we do. **B**

Activity B

If you were to die at a young age, what tribute would friends, family, and acquaintances make about you? (Don't hold back. Think positively.)

The Communion of Saints

When we look at the world around us, we are led to ponder difficult questions: Why is there so much suffering in the world? Why do people treat one another so harshly? What kind of God has allowed our world to become what it is? We are overwhelmed by such questions. But here are equally baffling ones: In the midst of such darkness, why are we blessed with the light of so many saintly people? Why are so many people good in situations where selfishness or complacency seems more rewarding?

Christian faith affirms that in our struggles to do good, we can look for inspiration from Jesus and from his Spirit within people.

I believe in the Holy Spirit, the holy Catholic Church, the communion of saints

THE APOSTLES' CREED

Elizabeth of Hungary and Roberto Clemente of Puerto Rico and Pittsburgh are merely two members of "the communion of saints" that is the Church. History provides us with many examples of saintly people, people so Spirit-filled that they lived heroic lives of goodness.

For instance, even in the inhuman circumstances of Nazi concentration camps during World War II, where every morsel of food was life, we find that saintly people shared their bread with others who were in greater need. The recently canonized saint, Maximilian Kolbe, offered and gave his own life at the hands of the Nazi executioners so that another might live. Many equally remarkable stories of saintly, courageous Jews and others from this period can be told. Deserving of recognition are heroes and heroines such as Anne Frank and the Dutch family that hid Anne and her family from the Nazis who were rounding up Jews for execution.

communion of saints—people of the past, present, and future who were, are, and are to be inspired by the Holy Spirit to contribute to the world in some positive way

People will always follow a good example; be the one to set a good example, then it won't be long before the others follow. How lovely to think that no one need wait a moment, we can start now, start slowly changing the world! How lovely that everyone, great and small, can make their contribution toward introducing justice straightaway . . . And you can always, always give something, even if it is only kindness!

ANNE FRANK, "GIVE," MARCH 26, 1944.

The communion of saints is the glory of the Church. The **communion of saints** refers to all those people—past, present, and future—who were, are, and are to be inspired by the Holy Spirit to make God's presence a more visible reality in our world. The Church, then, is the assembly of all the saints. (See Catechism, #s 957–959.) Certainly, the people who make up the Church are sinners as well as saints. Some more than others stand out as beautiful expressions of saintliness—proving that our world continues to produce saints today. Where we find a crisis we also find members of our human family who are trying to deal with the crisis. For instance, after tragedies such as the killing of school children, people typically gather together to pray. At such times they especially feel the need to be reminded of God's presence in their lives and to seek the strength of God to continue living in the presence of such evil.

Where we find people in need we also find saints who are trying to meet those needs. For example, we read about rock musicians who contribute their time, money, and influence to help fight the problems of hunger, homelessness, and racism. We also know that great numbers of young people volunteer their time to help in hospitals, homes for children who have special needs, and hospices for poor people. Many school and parish groups dedicate their time and effort to addressing problems in their local communities. While not everyone working to make the world a better place links their involvement directly to their Christian faith, nonetheless all such people share the

Christian spirit spoken of by the bishops of Vatican Council II:

Today there is an inescapable duty to make ourselves the neighbor of every man, no matter who he is, and if we meet him, to come to his aid in a positive way, whether he is an aged person abandoned by all, a foreign worker despised without reason, a refugee, an illegitimate child wrongly suffering for a sin he did not commit, or a starving human who awakens our conscience by calling to mind the words of Christ: "As you did it to one of the least of these my brethren, you did it to me" [Mt. 25:40].

"Pastoral Constitution on the Church in the Modern World," number 27.

Stories that dominate the news—of politicians engaged in misconduct, parents who mistreat their children, and young people who engage in violence against other young people—should not blind us to the vast majority of people, including politicians, parents, and youth, who work selflessly for others.

The Little Way of Saint Thérèse

As you know, dear Mother, I've always wished that I could be a saint. But whenever I compared myself to the Saints there was always this unfortunate difference—they were like great mountains, hiding their heads in the clouds, and I was only an insignificant grain of sand, trodden down by all who passed by. However, I wasn't going to be discouraged; I said to myself: "God wouldn't inspire us with ambitions that can't be realized. Obviously there's nothing great to be made of me, so it must be possible for me to aspire to sanctity in spite of my insignificance. I've got to take myself just as I am, with all my imperfections; but somehow I shall have to find out a little way, all of my own, which will be a direct shortcut to heaven."

"AUTOBIOGRAPHY OF ST. THÉRÈSE OF LISIEUX," AS QUOTED IN JOSEPH F. SCHMIDT'S *PRAYING WITH THÉRÈSE OF LISIEUX*, [WINONA, MN: SAINT MARY'S PRESS, 1992.]

The communion of saints is not an abstract concept, nor does it refer only to heroes and heroines of old, or exclusively to the good people who make newspaper headlines or who win Nobel prizes. One of the most popular saints of the past century was Saint Thérèse of Lisieux, France (1873–1897). (Notice that she, like Saint Elizabeth, died at a very young age.) Thérèse aspired to do great things but came to realize that she was destined to do little things. She proposed a spirituality called "**the little way**," by which she meant doing the little things of life with great love and awareness of God. Many common folks throughout the world adopted Thérèse's spirituality of the everyday as the best way to give expression to their faith. Today, the communion of saints continues to manifest itself in ways as simple, as unheralded, and as unpretentious as the following:

After an exciting and successful year, football season was now over. To celebrate the winning season, the school's chaplain held a team Mass. Following the ceremony, the captains addressed their teammates with this request: We had a good time representing the school on the football field. Now we'd like all team members to take the lead in this year's Thanksgiving food drive. We'd like to see all of the football players actively involved in collecting and distributing the food baskets and in participating in the Thanksgiving liturgy. We want this year's football team to be remembered as a well-rounded group who gave their best both playing football and helping others.

That year, the Thanksgiving food drive was the most successful ever held at the school.

How do we contribute to the communion of saints? Every time we intervene when someone is being picked on, every time we help out at home when someone is sick, every time we volunteer our time at a nursing home or hospital, every time we stand up for the rights of others, we are making the communion of saints a flesh-and-blood reality. **C**

"The little way"—a "spirituality of the everyday," doing little things to reflect God's love in the world, as advocated by Saint Thérèse of Lisieux

Activity C

1. Describe an incident when you experienced the communion of saints in a real but unheralded way.

2. If you were to publish a newspaper that printed only stories of people doing good works, what would some of the headlines be? Name three or four such headlines.

3. Name three things you already do or could do to practice the "little way" of Saint Thérèse.

The Church Community as the Body of Christ

Sometimes we hear the Church referred to as "it." Some people have experienced the Church as an impersonal institution, one that seems removed from the real concerns of real people. This is certainly not what Jesus intended his community of followers to be. In fact, no matter how diligently we search we will find no such impersonal entity. Instead, we will find some people who believe in Jesus Christ and who seek to carry on his work, such as the various saintly people described earlier. We will also discover some people who are hurting and some who at times hurt others. We will find them all living together in a community called "Church."

We might think of the Church as only the select group of people who hold leadership positions within the Church. For instance, we might say: "Why doesn't the Church do more for homeless people in this country? Why doesn't the Church do more for young people? Why doesn't the Church do more to intervene in the many trouble spots of the world? Why doesn't the Church share its wealth?" Quite likely, we actually mean: Why don't bishops, priests, nuns and other religious, and perhaps the people who are most visible in our parishes do more? However, we need to remind ourselves constantly that the Church is not "they" or "it" but "we."

The Analogy of the Body

In a famous analogy found in his letter to the Corinthians, Saint Paul describes the Church in terms of a body made up of different parts:

> *For just as the body is one and has many members . . . so it is with Christ. For in the one Spirit we were all baptized into one body—Jews or Greeks, slaves or free—and we were all made to drink of one Spirit.*

Indeed, the body does not consist of one member but of many. If the foot would say, "Because I am not a hand, I do not belong to the body," that would not make it any less a part of the body. And if the ear would say, "Because I am not an eye, I do not belong to the body," that would not make it any less a part of the body. If the whole body were an eye, where would the hearing be? If the whole body were hearing, where would the sense of smell be? But as it is, God arranged the members in the body, each one of them, as he chose. If all were a single member, where would the body be? As it is, there are many members, yet one body. The eye cannot say to the hand, "I have no need of you," nor again the head to the feet, "I have no need of you." . . . If one member suffers, all suffer together with it; if one member is honored, all rejoice together with it.

1 Corinthians 12:12–21, 26

In Saint Paul's analogy Christ is the head, and all other community members serve different functions that together make one body. The Church is one body in which all of the members play vital roles.

Let's carry this analogy a step further by including the earth as a part of the image of the body of Christ. When we ourselves are suffering from a stomachache or headache, then our entire body feels discomfort—not just the isolated parts. Similarly, if suffering occurs in one part of the world, the effects will eventually touch every part of our increasingly smaller global community. For instance, if suffering occurs in Africa, China, or Central America, then all parts of the globe eventually will experience the pain. We would be out of touch with our bodies if we commented, "My liver is deteriorating, but that's okay because the rest of my body is fine." Similarly, we would have a poor sense of our interdependent earth if we said, "Rainforests are being destroyed in Brazil, but we have many trees in my neighborhood," or "People are starving in Africa, but that's okay because North Americans have lots to eat."

In addition, if we would imagine our school community, our family, and our city or town as a human body made up of different parts, then we would better understand what Saint Paul meant by the body of Christ. In our family and our communities, the health and well-being of each part are vital for the well-being of every other part. For instance, if one family member disrupts the dinner table, everyone's meal is disturbed. If one family member has a drug problem, then the entire family suffers. While on the opposite end of this same comparison, one small group of students working hard to plan dances and other activities benefits the entire school community.

Saint Paul's analogy of a body remains a forceful and engaging symbol because that is what we collectively are—a body composed of many parts, each in need of the others. **D**

Activity D

Write about one of the following as if it were a body made up of interrelated parts:

- Your school community
- Your country
- Your family
- The world community

"Body of Christ" Means Communities of Support

In one high school, a group of students designs a program of skits to demonstrate to other young people some of the dangers related to teenage sex and drinking. In another school students initiate a suicide prevention program. Elsewhere, a group of young people receives training in peer counseling. Some juniors and seniors prepare to serve as big brothers and big sisters to incoming freshmen in order to ease their transition into high school. Members of the National Honor Society volunteer their time as tutors for other students. Another group of students gathers weekly in the school chapel to pray for the needs of the school community. Youth group members from surrounding parishes organize and participate in sports programs for local youth.

We could easily expand the list of ways that the Church functions as a community of support. One of our words for Church is *ecclesia*, which is also the Greek word for a "duly summoned assembly." This reminds us that Christians are not meant to travel solo on their life journeys. Within the Church, everyone is both giver and receiver. Saint Paul makes it clear that, for the Body of Christ, the weakest members are just as important as the strongest: "On the contrary, the members of the body that seem to be weaker are indispensable" (1 Corinthians 12:22). Weak and strong, good and bad, in the Body of Christ everyone needs one another. **E**

ecclesia—a Greek word for a "duly summoned assembly"; also means "Church"

For review . . .

1. Briefly describe how Elizabeth of Hungary, Roberto Clemente, and Maximilian Kolbe modeled saintliness.
2. What is the communion of saints?
3. Describe "the little way" of Saint Thérèse.
4. How can Saint Paul's analogy of the body be applied to the Church?
5. What does the Greek word for "Church" imply?

Activity E

1. Saint Paul says that the weakest members of a body are just as important as the strongest. Does this principle hold true in any of the community bodies to which you belong? Explain.
2. Name groups or organizations with which you are familiar that function as "communities of support."

The Church Provides Sacraments of Reconciliation

alienation—
an experience of isolation and separateness resulting in uneasiness around others

reconciliation—
an experience of reuniting and reconnecting with others

Then Peter came and said to him, "Lord, if another member of the church sins against me, how often should I forgive? As many as seven times?" Jesus said to him, "Not seven times, but, I tell you, seventy-seven times."

MATTHEW 18:21–22

In biblical symbolism, the number seven means completeness. Jesus' response to Peter about how often we should forgive one another suggests that Jesus knows how often we humans need forgiveness! We are constantly in need of forgiveness, and Jesus tells us here that we should forgive one another completely and endlessly, as God forgives us.

If we were to play a word association game centered on Jesus and the Church, we should arrive fairly quickly at the word "forgiveness." Forgiveness is an important step in eliminating the roadblocks that exist in our relationships, including our relationship with God. If we have truly experienced forgiveness, then we know how refreshing and revitalizing an experience it is. **F**

Without forgiveness we are out of touch with God and with one another. **Alienation**, a sense of distance and separateness from others and of uneasiness around others, is unsettling and saps our energy. To be renewed and revitalized, we need to experience forgiveness. With forgiveness we find **reconciliation**—a word that means reuniting and getting back in touch with others. Therefore, reconciliation is the means of overcoming alienation and of achieving a return to a sense of belonging. It's easy to see how alienation fosters immorality while a spirit of reconciliation supports moral behavior.

A primary function of the Church is to be a community in which forgiveness and reconciliation take place. Within the Church there are ceremonies to celebrate reconciliation. In a sense, all sacraments celebrate reconciliation since all sacraments celebrate different ways of keeping in touch with God and with other people. Two principal sacraments that can serve as avenues of reconciliation are Eucharist and Penance. **G**

Activity F

• Recall a moment in your childhood when your mother or father reprimanded you for doing something wrong. Imagine yourself crying, then your parent hugging you and saying, "It's okay now."

• Imagine that you and your best friend are fighting. You exchange angry words, cutting deeply since each of you knows the other's weaknesses so well. A few lonely and anxious hours later your friend arrives at your door and says, "You know I can't stay angry with you! I'm sorry for those nasty things I said. Please forgive me."

• Imagine that you are baby-sitting a young child. While you are chatting to a friend on the phone, the child scribbles with crayon on new living room furniture. Imagine how troubled and burdened you feel unless you experience forgiveness, both as giver (to the child) and receiver (from the parents).

Write about a time when you experienced forgiveness.

Activity G

1. Write a poem, a story, or an imaginative essay, the theme of which is either "alienation" or "reconciliation."

2. Using specific examples, describe the relationship between alienation, reconciliation, and the moral life.

Reconciliation—Celebrating Our Homecoming

The sacrament most closely associated with forgiveness and the moral life is Reconciliation or Penance. The gospel story of the prodigal son serves as the model for the sacrament. The story tells of a wayward youth's return to his father, who has been waiting for him with open arms and an anxious heart. Through the Sacrament of Reconciliation we celebrate our homecoming.

The Sacrament of Reconciliation offers Christians an opportunity to celebrate God's offer to return to him (no matter how little or how far we have strayed). In this sacrament, we face squarely our faults, our sins, and our shortcomings. We risk taking such difficult measures in order to show how determined we are to experience a homecoming with God and with others. We attempt to name all that stands in the way of our being at home with God and other people so that we can experience health and well-being both individually and as a community.

Clearly, the focus of the sacrament is forgiveness. However, it also offers us an opportunity to make an inventory of our lives. We might say, "I'll talk to God about my life in my own time and in my own way." Nonetheless, the Church's Sacrament of Reconciliation provides us a time, a setting, and a structure for self-examination and for hearing words of forgiveness from an official representative of the Church. Here is one person's experience of reconciliation that for him became a precious gift from Christ's Church. **H**

Starting Over

To begin the Lenten season, John's religion class went to chapel for a Lenten reconciliation service. There were readings inviting students to think about their relationship with God, with family and friends, and with themselves.

During the quiet time of the service, John took seriously the questions about how he could make his relationships better. In this setting he had a chance to think about himself and his family and friends. John knew that for some time now, he had been hanging around with a group of people who didn't really care about others' property. With their encouragement, he had stolen money from another's billfold and shoplifted a CD from a store. He had lied to his parents about where the money and the CD had come from. He had tried not to think about what he had done, but here alone with his thoughts, and calling on the Spirit's guidance, John knew it was time to change his actions and, if necessary, even his friends. After confessing his sins to the priest, he truly felt God's forgiveness. He decided to take this opportunity to change the direction his life was going.

He prayed that, with the help of the grace of the sacrament, he could make a fresh start in his life. He decided he would begin as soon as he arrived home by telling his parents the truth. He knew they would be upset, but he felt that they, too, would forgive him and help him make whatever changes he needed.

Activity H

Private confession began as a means to help people in their spiritual journey. Describe how the Sacrament of Reconciliation could help you in your own spiritual development.

Eucharist—A Reconciliation Meal

One important aspect of the Eucharist is participation in a meal—a highly ritualized meal, but clearly a meal. When we explore the significance of the Eucharist as a meal, then we discover how it is a sacrament of reconciliation.

A meal is meant to be a time for conversation and sharing friendship; if it is not, then the meal is a lie. If we attend a school banquet and end up sitting between two people with whom we recently quarreled, we can look forward to an unpleasant evening. However, if we settle our differences with these people before the banquet begins, then the food will be tastier and the entire event much more enjoyable. Similarly, at the beginning of each Mass, the priest asks those present to "call to mind our sins." When we take time at Mass to think about our lives, we are looking within ourselves to uncover anything that might separate us from God, from our family and friends, and even from strangers. As a means of reconciliation, then, the Eucharist can be used as a time when we set aside our differences and celebrate our oneness with others in Christ.

Furthermore, when we share a meal with others, we would certainly violate all that a meal stands for if we were to follow it up by saying or doing anything harmful against those with whom we shared the meal. At every meal, we are sharing life-giving food and drink. If we act in ways that are life-destroying, then we have entirely missed the meaning of the meal. The Eucharist is a meal like other meals, but it is much more than the most special meal that we can imagine. To participate in the Eucharist is to share Christ with others, life itself!

Finally, according to the Catechism we "dishonor the table" of the Eucharist if we do not move from participating in this meal to sharing with people who are poor and in need (Catechism, #1397). During the Eucharist we share Communion and communion with the small group gathered together. However, the true significance of the Eucharist knows no such boundaries. During the celebration of the Eucharist, we should imagine a table of vast proportions. Around the table sit old and young, rich and poor, citizens of diverse nations, members of different races, persons who exhibit a vast array of personality traits, and people whom we like and whom we dislike. Christ, the Bread of Life, is feeding all in like manner. The symbolism embedded in the Eucharist makes it clear that the sacramental life of the Church, such as celebration of the Eucharist, is intricately tied to our moral life. One way to look at the Eucharist is to view it as further encouragement to reach out to all the people Jesus mentioned in Matthew 25, the Last Judgment. **I**

For review . . .

6. What does the number seven mean in biblical symbolism? What does it say about Jesus' message of forgiveness?

7. Define the terms alienation and reconciliation.

8. What does the Sacrament of Reconciliation celebrate?

9. How does the Sacrament of Reconciliation help our self-examination?

10. What attitude toward others is implied by referring to the Eucharist as a reconciliation meal?

11. What is the relationship between the sacramental and the moral life of the Church?

Activity I

1. Think back on a time when you experienced a meal as real sharing. Write about the experience.

2. Think about a Mass that you have attended. Name words, symbols, or ritual actions of the Mass that have implications for morality. Explain.

Church Leaders and Church Teachings as Moral Guides

rabbi—Hebrew for "teacher," a term frequently applied to Jesus

In the Gospels, Jesus is more often called "teacher" (in Hebrew, *rabbi*) than anything else. Naturally, then, the Church dedicated to following Jesus takes the vocation of teacher very seriously. In the Church the primary teachers of children are parents. However, learning is a lifelong process. Thus, we need guidance throughout our lives.

From the beginning of Christianity, there have been leaders of the community dedicated to preserving and carrying on the teachings of Jesus. Today, the pope and bishops continue that role for Catholic Christians. Together and in various ways, they provide teachings, norms, and guidance. Certainly, "teaching" entails much more than the written word. (We know of only one incident when Jesus himself wrote—a few words written on the ground that caused quite a stir. [See John, chapter 8.]) However, we do use the written word. The following types of writings describe some of the means by which these leaders of the Church teach and guide the Catholic community.

Documents of Vatican II

As a result of all the world's bishops meeting together from 1962 to 1965 at Vatican Council II, numerous documents were published. This council marked only the second such council in over four hundred years, so obviously it was a significant event for the Church. The documents do address some specific moral issues, especially in the document called "The Pastoral Constitution on the Church in the Modern World." In addition to specific teachings, however, the documents provide a sense of direction for the Catholic community as it journeys through our fast-paced world.

Catechism of the Catholic Church

Catechism of the Catholic Church—a document containing official Catholic teaching

No summary of Catholic teaching was produced by the Second Vatican Council. The council billed itself as a "pastoral council," one concerned about the life and the spirit of the Church today, rather than a council whose primary focus was on defining teaching more exactly. Twenty years later, however, a number of bishops petitioned the pope that he begin a process of compiling a catechism that would serve as the primary teaching document for the universal church. In 1994, the *Catechism of the Catholic Church* appeared in English and quickly became a bestseller. It is meant to guide Church leaders and teachers as they try to instruct the members of their community on official Catholic teaching.

Papal Encyclicals

encyclical—an official letter from the pope, usually addressed to all Church members

An **encyclical** is an official letter from the pope to the Catholic community. In the recent past, popes have written encyclicals on such topics as peace, justice, family life, human dignity, treatment of workers, and morality in general. When we look at specific moral topics later in the course, we will refer to various encyclicals to find relevant teachings.

Statements of Vatican Commissions

The pope oversees a large collection of offices dedicated to various areas of Church life, such as education, justice and peace, and relations with other religions. For the most part, members of these commissions work behind the scenes to help make the Church an instrument of peace, justice, and moral betterment in the world. However, on occasion commission members study a specific area of morality or Church life and issue a pronouncement to provide guidance on that question. For instance, as we will examine later, there have been tremendous advances related to artificial reproduction. Such advances are not just matters of technology but of morality. A Vatican commission gathered together experts to examine the issue and prepared a document about it.

Pastoral Letters

Traditionally, the bishops of the Church are known as *pastors*, a word meaning "shepherd." In their local area, known as a diocese, they serve as successors to the apostles. Bishops, either individually or as a regional group, write official letters to their communities. These letters are called pastoral letters. For instance, in pastoral letters the Canadian bishops have addressed concerns of Indian populations in their country. The U.S. bishops have written about immigrant workers and nuclear weapons.

The Catholic Church is both local and universal. Catholic communities celebrating Christ's presence in their lives and seeking to do his will can be found in Hong Kong, Kiev, Nairobi, Detroit—and all over the world. The pope and bishops are visible reminders of the combined local and universal nature of the Church. **J**

Activity J

Read through an official Church document (such as one of those listed above) that addresses moral concerns. Write about key teachings found in the document.

Young people are met by Pope John Paul II during a youth rally at the Kiel Center in St. Louis January 26, 1999.

The Church—A School for Morality

As God's chosen ones, holy and beloved, clothe yourselves with compassion, kindness, humility, meekness, and patience.

COLOSSIANS 3:12

The Church is a school for morality. That is, the people who make up the Church struggle to know God's will and to do God's will in the complex and challenging situations in which they find themselves. The great vision that was offered by Jesus of how the world can be needs the Church to make it real. It takes Church members—pope and bishops along with the rest of us—to be schooled in the imitation of Christ. The moral skills we learn within the Church we bring to the moral dilemmas we face daily. As a school for morality, the Church is not just a place for study but a place for living the Christian life. **K**

Church Teachings Are Continuous and Ever Renewed

Church leaders follow three guiding principles when they make official pronouncements about issues such as abortion, treatment of the environment, or poverty.

- How can the message of Scripture and especially the teachings of Jesus shed light on this question?

- What time-honored insights from earlier Christian teaching can be applied to this question?

- How can the problems facing people as they live their lives today be addressed through official Church statements?

In other words, Church leaders strive to follow time-honored principles and earlier Church teachings, constantly looking to the life and message of Jesus for guidance. Then, they seek to provide teachings that address the very real problems facing people in current historical situations and in diverse cultures.

Activity K

Envision the Church as a school for morality. Name five of the most important messages you received in this school.

This formula, of continuity with the past and of renewal in light of new insights and problems, gives both a timely and a timeless quality to Church teachings. It can be found, for instance, in some of the documents that address economic problems. In those documents, "development" is considered good. In fact, all people have a right to pursue personal development. Advocating the betterment of people is nothing new. However, some encyclicals and pastoral letters have questioned the impact that a free-wheeling and unrestricted approach to "development" has had. For example, Pope John Paul II wrote in 1987:

> . . . natural resources are limited; some are not, as it is said, renewable. Using them as if they were inexhaustible, with absolute dominion, seriously endangers their availability not only for the present generation but above all for generations to come.

ON SOCIAL CONCERN, NUMBER 34

In other words, the pope reminds us that we need to be careful about how we use things in our quest for betterment. Development—of new roads, houses, factories, technology, material goods—affects humans now and in the future. **L**

For review . . .

12. In the Gospels what title is applied most frequently to Jesus?

13. Distinguish among the five types of written Church documents described in the text.

14. What does it mean to say that the Church is a school for morality?

15. What three principles guide Church leaders when they make official pronouncements about moral issues?

16. Use an example to explain the notion that Church teachings are both continuous and ever renewed.

Activity L

Think back on the understanding of "Church" you had before reading this chapter. How has the information in the chapter supported or changed your understanding of Church? Explain.

Conclusion
In Making Moral Decisions, We Are Not Alone

Moral decision making and living an authentic life are important challenges facing all of us. Christian teaching about the Church community reminds us that we are not alone in making decisions and in shaping our lives. We are better decision makers when we look for support, guidance, and direction in the teachings of Jesus, in the great heroes and heroines of Church history, in the community committed to carrying on the work of Jesus, and from the many official teachings found in the Church today.

In a world filled with suffering, Church members need to proclaim that there is a place where suffering can be shared. In a world of confusion, Church members need to proclaim that Christ offers a focus for the search for wisdom. In a world of war, Church members need to proclaim that peace can be sought together in Christ. In a world of intense loneliness and alienation, Church members proclaim that we can live together and love one another in Christ. Indeed, this course is a study of what will be required of each of us if we are to become such a Church today.

Let us pray . . .

We will lovingly follow the truth at all times—speaking truly, dealing truly, living truly—and so become more and more in every way like Christ who is head of his body, the Church. Under his direction the whole body is fitted together perfectly, and each part in its own special way helps the other parts, so that the whole body is healthy and growing and full of love (Ephesians 4:15–16). *Amen.*

CHAPTER 6

Sin and Morality
Bringing Our Dark Side into the Light

In this chapter we examine Christian teaching regarding sin. Sin names the dark side of our human condition. As Christians we can never treat lightly or dismiss our dark side, but neither can we dwell on it. Rather, we view sin in light of the broader Christian message. In the Christian vision, Jesus conquers the sin of the world and graciously offers us forgiveness for our own sinfulness so that we may be free to live our lives lovingly and creatively.

Chapter Overview

- Two images frequently used in Scripture for sin are *missing the mark* and *hardness of heart*.

- In Christianity the primary message about sin is one of forgiveness.

- Distinguishing among types of sin is intended to help people overcome sin.

- In recent decades Catholicism has experienced changes in its perspective on sin.

- Social sin refers to behavior patterns, values, and social structures that encourage or support sin in a society.

Let us pray . . .

Gracious and forgiving Father, we place before you all the misdeeds, unkind thoughts, and hurtful actions that have marked our lives. We thank you for the gift of your Son, Jesus, who sacrificed his life for the forgiveness of sin. Through him, with him, and in him, we possess the wisdom and the strength to live life passionately and creatively. Through him, with him, and in him, we know your boundless love. Amen.

Before we begin . . .

Use of the word *sin* is not as popular today as it once was. And yet wrongdoing certainly continues, almost in epidemic proportions. To begin your examination of this traditional Christian concept, rate the following behaviors in terms of their degree of sinfulness. (Keep in mind that such labeling is unfair. Church teaching recognizes that both circumstances and the persons involved color the sinfulness of actions.) Explain your rankings.

1. A vacationer takes two large bath towels from the luxury hotel where she is staying.

   not a sin 1 2 3 4 5 serious sin

2. An employee at a computer firm quits his job and begins his own business using technology developed by his former company.

   not a sin 1 2 3 4 5 serious sin

3. A senior high-school boy pretends to be interested in a sophomore girl in order to persuade her to have sex with him.

   not a sin 1 2 3 4 5 serious sin

4. Two unmarried sixteen-year-olds have sex, even though they had decided previously that they would refrain from sexual intimacy.

   not a sin 1 2 3 4 5 serious sin

5. A person throws a plastic container out of a car window.

   not a sin 1 2 3 4 5 serious sin

6. In an attempt to fit in, a boy lies to his friends about seeing a strongly violent movie. Actually he hasn't seen the movie, because his parents have forbidden him to see it.

   not a sin 1 2 3 4 5 serious sin

7. A student regularly copies homework from other students.

   not a sin 1 2 3 4 5 serious sin

8. Because of a long-standing agreement with local government officials, a company legally empties harmful chemical waste into a river.

   not a sin 1 2 3 4 5 serious sin

The Pervasive Mystery of Sin

The young teacher told his class, "Today, I have invited a friend of mine to speak with us about our topic, sin. I know him to be old and wise, so listen to his words."

An old man sat at the teacher's desk. He began slowly and thoughtfully. "I cannot define sin. I can tell you only what sin looks like. To me, sin is present when humans hurt one another. When one nation destroys another nation with deadly weapons—that is sin. When we destroy one another with deadly words—that, too, is sin. Sin can be fiery hot like war and fighting, or it can be icy cold like ignoring someone in need. Sin can become very complicated, like the tangled web of lying. Sin can also be as simple as yelling at a younger brother who wants attention, coming home late when we know our parents will worry, or not keeping our part of an agreement. Sin is an unfounded burst of anger aimed at someone who meant well; sin is also being too lazy to help out at home."

The old man paused, then continued. "Unfortunately, we find sin splashed across the headlines of our newspapers: Public officials accept bribes, children gun down other children without reason, corporations place profits over

people, and drugs destroy young lives. But sin also lies hidden in the dark corners of our country, resulting in homeless persons seeking shelter in the subways beneath our cities or nameless farmworkers receiving inadequate pay for harvesting the fruits and vegetables we eat.

"When I think about sin, I picture water heating on a stove. For a while, sin simmers—like pornography peddled in corner convenience stores and at neighborhood video counters. Then later the same sinfulness bubbles forth onto the streets as child pornography and prostitution."

"Why does sin exist?" inquired one student.

"If we knew that answer," responded the old man, "then we would truly be wise. We know that

sins exists—we see too much of it to deny its existence. But we know little of the reasons why it holds such power over us. Ancient wisdom often pointed to selfishness as the root of sin—a misguided placing of our own will and desires above and against the will of God and the needs of others. However, naming the root of sin does not solve its mystery or destroy its power."

"Is there no escape from sin, then?" another student finally asked.

"That is an important question," the old man replied. "I have told you today that sin surrounds us and that it is lodged in our very hearts. And yet, I want to leave you with words of hope. We have this assurance from someone who faced sin with all of its terrible power, the one we call the Christ: Love conquers sin! Therefore, I trust in Jesus that whenever we plant seeds of love, sin is diminished. And where love flourishes, sin withers. The mystery of sin is awesome and frightening, and yet this mystery of love is infinitely greater. Because of the wonder of God's love, I assure you that we can face sin and sing an Easter song: 'O sin, your reign has ended; O sin, you are destroyed!'" **A**

Activity A

If you were invited to address a group of young people about sin, what would you say? What examples would you give? What would be the primary message that you would want to communicate about sin?

Sin Is the Harming or Breaking of Relationships

sin—when people act contrary to their conscience and purposely choose to do wrong.

*Come, my children, listen
as I teach you
to respect the Lord.
Do you want to live
and enjoy a long life?
Then don't say cruel things
and don't tell lies.
Do good instead of evil
and try to live in peace.*

PSALM 34:11–14 [CEV]

As the old man points out, sin surrounds us. That assessment may sound unpleasant and harsh, but even a quick look at our lives and our neighborhoods, our newspapers and our newscasts, our thoughts and our daily interactions with others, leads us to readily agree with his observations. We find evidence of sin and its consequences at every turn. Sin plagues our world, keeping it from being what it can be. Sin also burdens us, keeping us from being what we are called to be.

Sin is an offense against God. In other words, it is a term Christians use to remind ourselves that, through our own perverse choices, we go against God's will and do evil deeds. From its beginning, sin has been part of the Christian story. The Bible begins with a meditation on sin. The story of Adam and Eve does little to explain human sinfulness. (You can read their story in Genesis, chapters 2—3.) It does indicate that God intends the world to be a place of harmony and solidarity and that the way to maintain human welfare is for people to remain faithful to God's will. The story also insists that people are accountable for their actions and that sin violates God's intention for creation. For Christians the story of Adam and Eve sets the stage for another story that places evil and sin in a broader context—the story of Christ's conquering of sin through his death on the cross. Both human sinfulness and Christian salvation remain mysteries all of us need to reflect upon. Due to personal sin we continue to live imperfect lives filled with problems and unhappiness. Due to social sin we find baffling stories of hate and destruction broadcast almost daily on the evening news. We continue to need ways to live out Christ's victory over sin. **B**

Activity B

Draw a symbol or image that you think would picture sin. After completing your drawing, create a written analysis of what the image suggests about your impression of sin.

Sin in Scripture
Two Images

We can gain a better understanding of what Christianity means by sin if we examine the way the term is used in Scripture. The Bible uses many images to refer to sin. Two images used frequently to describe the mystery of sin are *missing the mark* and *hardness of heart*. By exploring the meaning of these two biblical images of sin, we can come to a greater appreciation of how sin might operate in our own lives.

Missing the Mark: The Failure to Love

An image used for sin in Scripture pictures sinfulness as actions that "miss the mark." This is the image of sin depicted in Proverbs 8:34–36.

> *And now, my children, listen to me:*
> *happy are those who keep my ways.*
> *Hear instruction and be wise,*
> *and do not neglect it.*
> *Happy is the one who listens to me,*
> *watching daily at my gates,*
> *waiting beside my doors.*
> *For whoever finds me finds life*
> *and obtains favor from the LORD;*
> *but those who miss me injure*
> *themselves;*
> *all who hate me love death.*

The people of the Bible believed that there was a mark or goal to aim for, and that sin meant missing that mark. The term for "sin" actually was the same word as that used in archery for missing the mark, for being "off center." Ultimately, the mark that we aim for is God—the joy of life with God and with God's family both now and in the future. Since our God is a God of love, sin is a failure to love. We sin—"miss the mark"—when we settle for behavior that does not reflect our love for God, ourselves, and others. **C**

Activity C

The biblical image of sin as "missing the mark" invites us to consider some important questions. In your journal or notebook, write about the following:

- State goals for living a Christian life.

- How are you trying to live out these goals in specific ways right now?

- What actions, attitudes, or values are moving you along toward the goals of living a Christian life? What actions, attitudes, or values are interfering with your attaining those goals?

In our lives, we encounter many opportunities to take positive steps toward our goal of becoming our true and best selves. When we settle for acting out of motives other than love and goodness, then we miss the mark. Here are some examples of behaviors that might not appear on many people's list of sins. However, when we consider that our true goal is God-like love, then we can recognize these actions as "missing the mark."

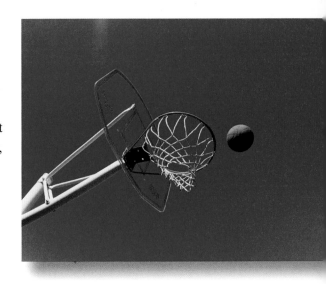

- Sitting at his desk at school, Bill carves obscenities into the desktop. Now the desk looks unsightly, and no one can write smoothly on it. The obscenities will have a negative impact on younger children, other students, or visitors, as well as create added work for school personnel. With little thought, Bill actually has chosen destruction over concern for others.

- Kim's mother asks her to stay home and watch her younger brother on Friday night. Kim says, "You know I always go out with my friends on Friday nights. I'm not giving that up!" In this case, Kim does not see beyond her own wants to another's needs.

- The regular teacher is absent, and a substitute is taking over for the day. When the substitute asks the class where they left off in the lesson, a student purposely directs her to material they covered the previous week. No one else speaks up, and the student who misdirected the substitute snickers with his friends about his successful prank. When presented with an opportunity to rise to a higher level of consideration, the students instead settle for less.

- Hannah's parents have expressly forbidden her to drink. Hannah assures them that she doesn't. Nevertheless, every Saturday Hannah and her friends gather in a section of a local park where they know beer will be readily available. With this weekly routine, Hannah diminishes the level of trust in her family, and she participates in behavior that is illegal and potentially dangerous.

- Steve's homeroom has an intramural basketball team, and one boy who is a terrible player has come to every game. Since everyone who shows up for the games must play, this particular boy enters the championship game, and, largely because of his mistakes, the team loses. Steve joins his classmates in deriding the other boy for losing the game. In so doing, Steve is displaying insensitivity to someone who at this moment needs sensitivity shown to him.

Identifying sin in our lives is not an easy task. To some people the actions described here may seem too trivial to warrant labeling them as sin. However, the biblical image of sin as missing the mark helps us recognize that when we make choices that are uncaring, insensitive, and selfish, we hamper our journeys toward our ultimate goal of being a loving person. **D**

Activity D

If you were to illustrate sin as "missing the mark," what two examples would you use? Explain why these two examples illustrate this understanding of sin.

Hardness of Heart: The Failure to Be Human

Scripture often uses bodily images such as "hard-hearted" and "stiff-necked" to describe sin. These images suggest a tightening up and a closing in upon ourselves—the way we might stiffen when we are being touched by someone whom we don't want to touch us. Such images do not portray humanity at its best. A heart of stone is not a human heart.

It's easy to imagine attitudes that would reflect a stony heart in need of transformation.

- Don't bother me. That's your problem!

- I wish this new student would just leave me alone.

- Can't these homeless people stay off our city streets? They bother me while I'm trying to shop.

- I'm not picking it up. I didn't put it there!

- Why did she get so upset about what I said? I was only joking!

- Mrs. Smith is really having a bad day with the experiments in her biology classes today. Let's give her a hard time.

In the book of Ezekiel, God promises to replace hearts of stone with hearts of flesh:

I will sprinkle clean water upon you, and you shall be clean from all your uncleannesses, and from all your idols I will cleanse you. A new heart I will give you, and a new spirit I will put within you; and I will remove from your body the heart of stone and give you a heart of flesh (36:25–26).

Scripture is reminding us that sin has as much to do with our attitudes as with our actions, with our being as with our behavior. A heart of flesh is one that can be touched and, also wounded. But only with a heart of flesh can we embrace others and allow others to embrace us. **E**

For review . . .

1. What does the story of Adam and Eve indicate about a Christian understanding of sin?
2. How does the story of Jesus respond to and complete the Adam and Eve story?
3. Name two biblical images used for sin.

Activity E

Write a song or a poem about being "hard-hearted" or about having a "heart of stone."

Sin in Christian Tradition
Accepting Our Sinfulness

A number of years ago a noted psychiatrist named Karl Menninger wrote a book titled, *Whatever Became of Sin?* In the book Dr. Menninger decried our modern tendency to avoid speaking about sin. He pointed out two dangers to this tendency. For one, if we lose our sense of sin, then we run the risk of losing authority over our lives. In other words, if we blame our parents or our culture for all of our actions, then we eliminate accountability for our decisions. Rather than subjects, we make ourselves out to be objects. Secondly, without a sense of sin any choices that we make are valueless. If nothing is wrong, then it doesn't matter what we do. Into what kind of murky future would this attitude take us? Menninger and others are reminding us that if we don't recognize our dark side for what it is, then we give it power over us.

Throughout history Christian teachers have preached about sin so that its power over us can be decreased. A basic, common-sense reason why they have done so supports Dr. Menninger's insight: Only when we recognize that a problem exists can we overcome the problem. Imagine if our car became hopelessly stuck in a snowdrift and we told all those who offered to help us, "There's no problem!" Imagine if we forgot that we had an important test one day, and we walked into class totally unprepared and said, "We have a test today? No problem!" Imagine if our drinking became so out of control that even our friends try to tell us to cool it and instead we said, "Don't be silly! I can handle my drinking. It's no problem." By drawing our attention to the reality of sin, Church teachers remind us that we do have problems hampering us from being what we would like to be. **F**

Activity F

In our society there is a tendency for people to blame circumstances rather than to take responsibility for their behavior. What kind of problems are caused by our not taking responsibility for our behavior? Use examples to defend your answer.

Forgiveness of Sins

*The Gospel is the revelation in Jesus Christ
of God's mercy to sinners [Cf. Lk 15].*
CATECHISM, #1846

Once a young boy took down from its shelf a trophy his father had won when he was in high school. The father had received the "most valuable player" award in the state baseball tournament. The trophy was one of his prize possessions. The young boy had been told not to touch it, but he couldn't resist. He was placing it on a table when it fell off, hit the floor, and broke in two.

The boy was stunned. What was he to do? He quickly picked up the broken trophy and hid it in a drawer, hoping no one would notice the empty spot on the shelf.

At dinner, the boy was nervous but no one seemed to have noticed. However, that night while watching television his father asked him if he had seen the trophy. "No, Dad," the boy replied.

Suspicious, the father turned off TV and asked his son again. This time the boy confessed. "I'm sorry, Dad. It was an accident."

After inspecting the broken trophy, the father said, "You were told not to touch this trophy. I hope you've learned a lesson about disobeying and about not lying to your parents. I know you're sorry. I forgive you. Now don't be down on yourself. That's more important than any trophy." **G**

Activity G

1. Is the father's reaction in this story realistic?

2. Do you agree that the son's feelings are more important than the trophy?

3. Do you think it is still important for the son to experience some consequences for his actions? Why or why not?

4. If Jesus were the father, how do you think he would have reacted? Why?

Guilt is a uniquely human experience. It's hard to imagine elephants and lions feeling guilty, but certainly for a person never to feel guilt seems inhuman. However, to experience forgiveness—to feel oneself cleansed of guilt—is a true gift from God.

When we read about sin in the Gospels, we find the word almost always used in connection with forgiveness. When we read about the amount of time that Jesus spends with sinners, we can't help but note his special affection for them. He wants the power that sin has over them to be eliminated. Throughout the Gospels, we find instances of Jesus forgiving sinners. Even when people are seeking a cure for their physical ailments, he forgives their sins as well! As the Catechism says, the Gospel message is one of God's mercy for sinners.

Christ Conquers Sin

The chief reason the Church gives an important place in Christian teaching to sin is neither to emphasize sin nor to accent its power. Rather, the essential message about sin in the Christian story is that Christ conquers sin. Along with death and anything else that can separate us from God, sin is overcome with Christ's death on the cross on Good Friday and his resurrection on Easter. In other words, sin is clearly neither the central theme nor the final chapter in the Christian story. Christ, the sacrificial lamb offering his life for the sins of the world, takes on all evil and leaves it powerless. It is as if the world were two-sided scales. On one side of the scales are placed all the world's sin; on the other side are Christ's death and resurrection. The central Christian belief is that Christ's sacrifice far outweighs sin.

We need to remain ever watchful about sin.

And yet Christian belief is that we can celebrate Christ's victory over sin and that his victory is ours as well. Therefore, we have faith and hope that our participation in transforming evil into good contributes to the grand scheme of the world's design. We should try not to let the fear of sin and its many manifestations prevent us from doing good, from taking a chance on love, or from joining other "sinners" in doing our part in furthering God's reign on earth. **H**

Lamb of God
*who takes away the **sins***
*of the **world**,*
*have **mercy** on us . . .*
*grant us **peace**.*

Activity H

One of the most significant ways that Jesus stands out as unique is in his treatment of sinners. Read the following Gospel passages and for each one describe the attitude that Jesus exhibits toward sin or sinners in the story. Then, use these passages to describe in concrete terms how Jesus' message of forgiveness could be applied today.

Matthew 9:9–13 (the call of Matthew)

Luke 7:36–50 (the penitent woman)

Luke 15:1–10 (the parable of divine mercy)

Luke 15:11–32 (the prodigal son)

Luke 18:9–14 (the Pharisee and the tax collector)

Luke 23:39–43 (the good thief)

John 9:1–14 (the man born blind)

Luke 17:3–4 (the forgiveness of those who sin)

Original Sin: Human Inclination to Evil

The great apostle Saint Paul wrote the following reflection about his own tendency toward sinfulness: "

> . . . *I am of the flesh, sold into slavery under sin. I do not understand my own actions. For I do not do what I want, but I do the very thing I hate"* (Romans 7:14–15).

original sin—the human inclination toward evil

Saint Paul is being brutally honest here. He could be speaking for all of us when he admits to giving in to what he calls "the sin that lives in me." He found the pull of sin to be a powerful force within him. This inclination to evil Christianity calls *original sin*. It refers to our basic human condition which, in the words of the Catechism (405), has been "wounded."

Therefore we find ourselves constantly doing battle with our darker side. Original sin harkens back to the famous story of Adam and Eve mentioned earlier. As you know from the story, humans—created good and filled with bright promise—didn't take long before they gave in to sin and misused their God-given free will.

Through Baptism, Christianity celebrates and makes effectively present in the human community Christ's victory over sin. Nonetheless, too frequently humans seem to be captivated by sin—in fact, held captive by sin. Thus, the human tendency toward sinfulness—also called concupisence—still manifests itself in specific actions, because some of the effects of original sin remain in us even after Baptism. The next question then becomes how do we deal with these failings?

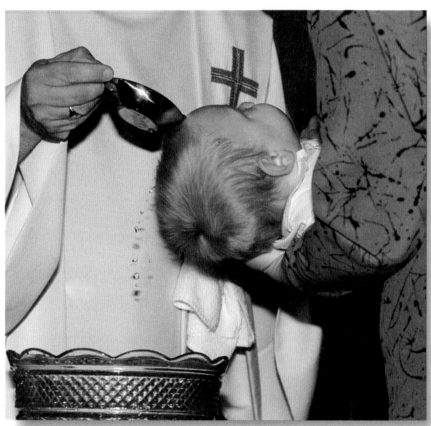

Confessing Sin

During the seventh century, Irish monks introduced a practice to the rest of Europe that today we know as private confession. At the time, part of the regimen for monks was to tell their failings to a confessor who would then suggest ways for each monk to improve his life. In Ireland, people outside of the monasteries sought out monks so that they, too, could have this opportunity. Shouldn't lay people as well as monks have a chance to examine their behavior and to turn their lives around by confessing their sins and doing penance?

Once private confession became standard practice in the Church, then it became necessary to provide priest confessors with guidelines about the degree of seriousness of various sins and about the types of penance that would be appropriate for each sin confessed. Thus, private confession spurred on distinguishing among types of sin.

Distinguishing Among Sins

venial sin—an action that turns us away from God in small degrees

mortal sin—an action so destructive that it mortally wounds our relationship with God; complete rejection of God

sin of omission—not doing an action that is called for

sin of commission—purposely doing an action that is harmful to oneself or another

Church teaching labels acts of sin according to their degree of seriousness—less serious sins traditionally are called **venial sins**; the most serious sins are called mortal. (While venial sins are like wounds to the health and well-being of the soul, **mortal sins**—as the term implies—are "deadly.") In addition, traditional wisdom reminds us that sin can involve our doing something wrong (a **sin of commission**) or not doing something that we should do (a **sin of omission**). Situations in which a person is more likely to sin, Catholic teaching terms as "occasions of sin"—for example, a recovering alcoholic who frequents a bar is in a place where he may be tempted to sin.

Keep in mind that, in the Christian tradition, all this talk of sin is meant to loosen its power over us. We seek to identify and acknowledge sin insofar as it prevents us from cooperating with God's Spirit at work in us. ∎

Mortal Sin—A Complete Rejection of God

As Christians, our lives find meaning through our relationship with God in Christ. When we talk about our Christian life and the place of sin in our life, we are talking about a relationship. Therefore, we can better understand the traditional Catholic concept of mortal sin by comparing it to our relationships with our family members and our friends.

For example, if we claim that someone is our best friend and yet treat that person cruelly whenever we don't want to do what they want to do, then we are not treating that person as a friend whom we love and respect. In addition, rejection of a relationship is also a matter of attitudes that accompany our actions. Sometimes even best friends treat each other cruelly. Usually, it doesn't mean that they wish to completely reject the other person.

Rejecting someone can occur only in an atmosphere of freedom. (At times the pressures of living are great. These pressures, internal and external, affect our freedom to relate to others in healthy and wholesome ways.) Even though friends may live miles apart and not see each other for long periods of time, they may still remain friends. Usually, when a friendship ends, more often than not it is because of a pattern of hurtful behavior on someone's part.

We sin mortally when we reject God completely. Like the death of a friendship, then, mortal sin involves actions, attitudes, freedom, and long-term life patterns. When we explore the possible presence of mortal sin in our life, we need to consider how these four aspects of mortal sin together have affected our relationship with God.

Activity I

Answer agree, disagree, or uncertain to the following statements. Explain your answers.

1. The Church talks too much about sin.
2. Sin is no longer a helpful category for naming the world's problems.
3. The Christian message must include sin.
4. I hear mention of sin regularly in Church circles.
5. More than other Christians, Catholics emphasize sin.
6. When people do wrong, it's important that they understand that they are sinning.
7. Talk of sin leads to feelings of guilt, which are never healthy.
8. Jesus focused quite a bit on sin.
9. My understanding of sin has changed since I was a child.

Venial Sin—Weakens Our Relationship with God

Most of our sinful actions are not so serious as to be considered mortal. We perform small acts, which turn us away from God in small degrees. Venial sins usually result from bad habits or laziness. Each of these actions or attitudes weakens our ability to avoid sinning in the future. Each venial sin turns us a little more away from God. Unless we break these bad habits and try to turn ourselves back to God, we could eventually find ourselves turned completely away from God or in a state of mortal sin. (Again comparing this to a human relationship, think of a marriage relationship—abandonment of one relationship and the beginning of another usually happens in small steps, not all at once.)

A final word about Catholic teaching on sin: Sin is a statement about the way we treat our relationship with God; it does not describe God's relationship with us. We may work very hard at rejecting God, but God never rejects us! We look to Jesus on the cross who died for us and know that God is ever-faithful to us, ever-forgiving, and ever-loving.

For review . . .

4. What modern tendency did Karl Menninger caution against? What two negative consequences can result from this tendency? How does Christian teaching counteract this tendency?

5. In the Gospels what association is frequently made in discussions about sin?

6. What is the essential message about sin in the Christian story?

7. What practice led to private confession of sins?

8. Define original sin.

9. What is the difference between mortal and venial sin?

10. Describe mortal and venial sins in terms of relationship.

11. What does it mean to say that "sin is a statement about the way we treat our relationship with God; it does not describe God's relationship with us"?

Has Sin Changed?
A New Look at an Old Nemesis

IG GIRL HOLDS A ROSE AS SHE IS HELD DURING PRAYER AT A MEMORIAL SERVICE ON SUNDAY, APRIL
)9, FOR THE VICTIMS OF THE COLUMBINE HIGH SCHOOL SHOOTING RAMPAGE IN LITTLETON, COLO.

Vatican II

The United States Catholic bishops have labeled racism a sin. How can they call an abstract notion like racism a "sin"? Doesn't sin refer only to specific actions that we individually do that are wrong? If a young person goes on a rampage and kills a number of fellow students after watching a movie depicting graphic violence, are the producers of the movie in any way responsible for these deaths?

Questions such as these signal changes in the way Christian teachers have been speaking about sin over the past few decades. Developments have occurred in all areas of Church teaching and practice including our understanding of sin. Church leaders have recently made sure that any discussion about sin closely reflects points of emphasis found in the Gospels. Here are five characteristics of a Gospel-based perspective on sin. As you read through the information, think about how it can help you to know yourself better, to take charge of your life more effectively, and to follow Jesus more closely.

A Gospel-based Perspective on Sin

What comes to mind when you think about sin? Here is how the U.S. Catholic bishops spoke about sin in their 1976 reflection on moral life:

> There is vast goodness in our world, yet sin's effects are also visible everywhere: in exploitative relationships,   in loveless families, in unjust social structures and policies, in crimes by and against individuals and against God's creation. Everywhere we encounter the suffering and destruction wrought by egoism and lack of community, by oppression of the weak and manipulation of the vulnerable; we experience explosive tensions among nations, ideological, racial, and religious groups, and social classes; we witness the scandalous gulf between those who waste goods and resources and those who live and die amid deprivation and underdevelopment—and all this in an atmosphere of wars and ceaseless preparations for war. Ours is a sinful world.

TO LIVE IN CHRIST JESUS, NUMBER 10   **J**

Like so many other developments in Catholic teaching, the Second Vatican Council in the mid-1960s served as a major impetus leading to a re-evaluation of how sin is viewed. The Council called for an investigation of all areas of Church life in light of gospel values. Concerning sin and morality, Church leaders and teachers unearthed the following as characteristics of a gospel-based perspective: Views sin primarily in terms of relationships; stresses doing the positive; focuses on overall life patterns as well as specific acts; emphasizes sin as being against God in our neighbors (a horizontal perspective); and considers the social dimension of sin.

Activity J

1. Name five specific examples of sin that would mirror the bishops' description of our "sinful world."

2. Do these examples of sin broaden or deepen your own understanding of sin? Explain why or why not.

Sin and Relationships

For a time in Christian history sin meant breaking a law. More recent discussion typically refers to sin more as a breakdown in our relationships rather than as the breaking of a law. Many Christian theologians note that the Bible contains this emphasis. The foundation of our faith is our relationship with God and with our neighbor. For that reason, the theologians point out that faithfulness to our relationships should be an essential concern in all areas of our life, including our moral life. Therefore, in determining sin we need to ask: What effect do my actions have on my relationship with God? How do my actions harm or enhance the people around me and the quality of my relationship with them? **K**

Sin and Apathy

> ## *No one has a right to sit down and feel hopeless. There's too much work to do.*
>
> DOROTHY DAY, IN *PEACE PRAYERS* [HARPERSANFRANCISCO, 1992].

apathy—an attitude of not getting involved, not caring, not acting when action is called for

Second, an overemphasis on sin as breaking laws could result in morality that concerns itself solely with avoiding the negative rather than with doing the positive. Doing the positive, such as what we earlier referred to as practicing virtue or as being virtuous, was at times not linked directly to morality. In this light, sin essentially meant "I did something wrong." In reality, one great "sin" is **apathy**—not getting involved, not caring, and not doing what needs to be done.

If our personal understanding of morality has been one of avoiding wrongdoing exclusively, then we might consider reckless driving a sin since it involves doing something that is breaking a law. However, we might overlook, as dimensions of the moral life, not visiting a friend in the hospital or not helping someone who urgently needs help. This second set of examples does not involve breaking any law, and the examples describe inaction rather than action. However, if sin includes harming others, then if people continue to suffer because we did not help them, we have sinned against them. We can see how these non-actions rightly belong in the category of sin. To paraphrase the English political writer Edmund Burke, "The only thing necessary for the triumph of evil is for good people to do nothing." **L**

> *When the Nazis came to get the Communists, I was silent because I was not a Communist. When they came to get the Socialists, I was silent. When they came to get the Catholics, I was silent. When they came to get the Jews, I was silent. And when they came to get me, there was no one left to speak.*
>
> MARTIN NIEMOELLER IN ROBERT ELLSWORTH, *ALL SAINTS* [NEW YORK: CROSSROAD, 1997].

Activity K

Complete each of the following sentences.

- Three people with whom I relate on a regular basis are . . .
- I enhance their lives when I . . .
- I would describe the quality of my relationships with them as . . .
- I would harm their lives if I . . .

Activity L

High school yearbooks frequently include a picture of students sleeping in study hall with the caption: "A meeting of the Apathy Club." In your own words, define apathy. Write a story whose theme and plot are "the sin of apathy." If possible, illustrate the story with a drawing or a picture.

Sin and Life Patterns

An overemphasis on delineating specific sins people commit—divorced from any real desire for forgiveness or change—leads to a "grocery list" approach to the Sacrament of Reconciliation. That is, going to confession, and rattling off sins committed and the number of times each was committed, ends up sounding like a grocery list: "I lied three times; I disobeyed four times; and I stole once." The list might be rattled off with the same degree of detachment that someone would express when reading off a grocery list: "Three dozen eggs, two quarts of milk, and a loaf of bread." Though there is an advantage to being specific about the sins we have committed, a more accurate understanding of sin seeks to relate our actions more closely to who we are and who we want to become.

Our earlier discussion of the biblical image of sin as hardness of heart reminds us that our actions flow from who we are. In the words of the Catechism, "sin tends to reproduce itself and reinforce itself . . ." (1865). Because of this focus, Church teachings on the Sacrament of Reconciliation speak about examining our overall life patterns, determining the fundamental direction of our lives, and deciding if we are heading in the direction God wants us to be going. The effect of the sacrament on our lives is that we are offered reconciliation with God, others, and our own conscience. If the Sacrament of Reconciliation is approached with openness to change and forgiveness, we should see a difference in our actions and attitudes. **M**

Sin and Our View of God

The God of the Scriptures is a God of people. A gospel-based perspective on sin links the vertical and the horizontal. That is, sin is not between us and a God who is distant and absent from us; rather, sin is between us and God who is close at hand and present in the people around us. When we choose not to love others, we also hurt God. This notion of sin reflects more closely what "breaking God's law" means in the Gospels. Emphasis on a horizontal understanding of sin is found in other areas of Christian life as well. For instance, modern church buildings are often designed in circles or semi-circles so that as people gather around the altar where we remember Jesus sacrificing his life for our sins, we face one another.

Sin and Our Society

Finally, sin in a gospel vision should not be viewed in isolation from the context in which those actions occur. Since Vatican Council II in particular, the social dimension of sin is being more closely explored. The Catechism speaks of "structures of sin" and of "social sin" (1869). For example, racism and sexism— discrimination against certain races and against women or men—are often called "sinful social structures." Since this emphasis on the social dimension and its relation to the individual dimension of sin is so important for an understanding of sin today, we will examine it more closely under the heading "social sin."

Activity M

In your notebook or journal, write about how the Sacrament of Reconciliation could be a particularly meaningful experience for you.

Social Sin

In recent years, an important development in morality has been the recognition of the social dimension of sin. The Christian life is always a matter of "we" and not "I." Likewise, we must recognize the "we" dimension of our experience of sin. If we wish to identify and overcome sin, then we need to do more than focus on the individual acts that individual persons do. Emphasis on the social dimension of morality has given rise to what can be called **social sin**. Social sin is sin that exists within a society. It refers to the many ways that groups of people suffer in a society even when responsibility for that suffering may not lie solely on the shoulders of specific individuals.

We will look more closely at the social dimension of morality in the chapter on justice. For now, we will examine social sin in terms of the following three categories: sinful social structures, social behavior patterns that encourage or support sin, and societal values that cause harm.

social sin— recognition of the social dimension of sin, both in its causes and in its effects

Sinful Social Structures

Are certain people unjustly hurt because of the way our educational, criminal-justice, business, and health-care systems are arranged? Insofar as the answer to this question is yes, then we can speak of sinful social structures. For instance, if members of one race or gender hold an unfair advantage over others in the workplace or in the court system, then sinful social structures exist in these important social institutions. **Sinful social structures** are ways that a society is organized that can result in certain groups of people being unfairly deprived of the power, benefits, and privileges available to others.

sinful social structures— ways societies are structured resulting in unjust distribution of power, benefits, and privileges

To demonstrate how societal structures can be sinful, ask yourself the question: Would a young, poor, African American person accused of a crime typically receive the same treatment at the hands of our criminal justice system as an older, wealthy, white person? Statistics reveal that if you are young, poor, uneducated, and a member of certain racial groups, you are more likely to go to prison if you commit a crime. Because inequalities and disadvantages exist, when we examine sin in our society we need to consider not only the actions of individuals but also social structures. Sin is at least as much a social affair as it is an isolated, individual one.

Social Behavior Patterns That Encourage or Support Sin

In our society, hardly a family exists untouched by problems associated with alcohol consumption. A disproportionate number of accidental deaths, marital breakups, incidents of domestic violence, and other social problems are directly related to excess alcohol consumption or alcoholism. And yet drinking continues to be an essential element of much of our recreational activity. For many older teenagers and young adults in our country, "partying" means drinking. Is drinking ever a sin? Is a culture of excessive alcohol consumption sinful? Let's consider the following example in order to explore the social dimension of our society's attitude toward drinking.

At the risk of being morbid, but quite realistic, let us imagine that a good friend is struck and killed by a drunk driver. If sin means harming someone, then such a tragedy certainly deserves to be placed in the category of sin. But where does responsibility lie? In our society, we consider an individual who drinks alcohol to excess to be responsible for his or her actions. However, today in most communities someone who serves alcohol to another who is inebriated can also be held responsible for that person's actions. Is serving alcohol to someone who is drunk a sin? If, while her parents are away, a teenage daughter hosts a party where people are drinking and subsequently a fatal accident occurs, can the parents or the daughter be held responsible?

We can step back even farther.

Would it be sinful to portray excessive drinking in a playful light in television ads? Is it wrong for the makers of alcoholic beverages to glorify drinking? Are the producers of films aimed at a teenage audience responsible at all for presenting drinking not just as innocent fun but as an activity whose consequences can be hurtful or even tragic? Might we even include community leaders who provide few alternatives to drinking among those who share responsibility for the problem?

Clearly, deaths related to alcohol point to the social nature of sin. We cannot blame "society" and dismiss individual responsibility. On the other hand, we should not accuse individuals of sin and close our eyes to the society in which the sin occurs. In our society, we find many accepted behavior patterns that actually support or encourage sin. This does not mean that we should lessen our sense of individual responsibility for our actions. Rather, we should broaden responsibility to include indirect influences on behavior.

> We become **victors** **not** by **holding** our adversary **down**, but rather by **not** allowing him to **fall** . . .
>
> St. Gregory of Nyssa

Societal Values That Cause Harm

What are the values that undergird our society? Certainly, many positive values mark our society. However, we also find negative values prevalent and accepted in our society—for example, excessive competitiveness, individualism, and greed.

A value such as individualism can lead to a "me-first" attitude that is destructive; a spirit of competition carried to excess can lead to a "survival of the fittest" attitude that harms weaker members of a society. When combined, these two societal values suggest that there are winners and losers in the game of life. They advocate being a winner— if possible, being "number one"—even if others are disregarded or hurt by an individual's success. Of course, often values such as these have a plus side as well as a negative side. However, when values that are dominant in a society directly or indirectly hurt people, it results in what can be called social sin.

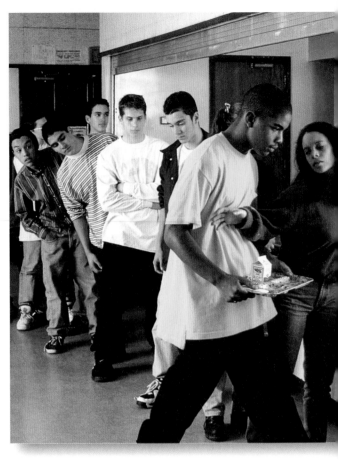

Activity N

Look over the following incidents and identify possible social behavior patterns or societal values that might contribute to such behavior. (Again, social and cultural influences do not eliminate personal responsibility but rather pinpoint factors that help shape people.)

1. At her prom, a girl gives birth and secretly disposes of the baby in a bathroom trash container.

2. Two older teens shake down a twelve-year-old boy who refuses to become involved in their neighborhood drug trade.

3. A month after receiving her license, a girl driving late for work runs through a red light, causing an accident.

4. A boy who has been sexually active for some time contracts a venereal disease.

5. A seventeen-year-old whose friends participate in illegal drug use becomes addicted to cocaine.

6. A group of teens imitate an initiation rite they recently saw in a movie, causing the death of another teen.

Activity O

Think about our culture and the structures that exist in our society. For each set of contrasting values, circle the number that indicates to you how strongly that value currently operates in today's society.

Our society more strongly values . . .

1. nonviolence	1	2	3	4	5	violence
2. concern for the environment	1	2	3	4	5	no concern for the environment
3. respect for people of diverse races	1	2	3	4	5	no respect for people of diverse races
4. people over possessions	1	2	3	4	5	possessions over people
5. church attendance	1	2	3	4	5	not attending church
6. concern for world problems	1	2	3	4	5	lack of concern for world problems
7. family life	1	2	3	4	5	family life as not important
8. trust of those in authority	1	2	3	4	5	distrust of those in authority
9. balance of work and leisure	1	2	3	4	5	imbalance of work and leisure
10. concern for poor and disadvantaged people	1	2	3	4	5	no concern for poor and disadvantaged people
11. God as important	1	2	3	4	5	God as unimportant
12. preference to be different	1	2	3	4	5	preference to conform
13. patriotism	1	2	3	4	5	lack of patriotism
14. pessimism	1	2	3	4	5	optimism
15. youth	1	2	3	4	5	old age
16. importance of physical health	1	2	3	4	5	no importance to physical health
17. equality of women and men	1	2	3	4	5	inequality of women and men

A Final Caution about Sin—Distinguishing Guilt from Shame

Psychologist John Bradshaw makes an important distinction that is helpful in clarifying for us why sin plays a secondary role in the Christian vision. Bradshaw contrasts *shame* and *guilt*. Guilt means I *made* a mistake. Shame means I *am* a mistake. As this chapter has outlined, guilt has a place in the Christian vision. Christian morality recognizes that in our response to life we can make mistakes, we can sin. However, shame as Bradshaw defines it holds no place in the Christian vision. Jesus affirms that we are not a mistake—God's love brought us into being; God's love for us is complete and never-ending. **P**

For review . . .

12. Name the five characteristics of a gospel-based perspective on sin.
13. Define apathy.
14. What is a "grocery list" approach to confession?
15. What is the difference between a vertical and a horizontal view of God?
16. Name three expressions of social sin.
17. Define the concept "sinful social structures."
18. What is the difference between guilt and shame?

Activity P

Write a one-page essay explaining the following distinction: Guilt means I *made* a mistake; shame means I *am* a mistake.

Conclusion
The Mystery of Sin and Forgiveness

We have a dark side, a shadow side that marks us as human. It is important for us to recognize sin, to name it for what it is, and to dread its horror. However, every aspect of Christianity seeks to lead us from a recognition of sin to a celebration of Christ's great victory over sin. Through the power of the Holy Spirit, we are freed from sin so that we can live life and love others in imitation of Christ.

> But the *devil* loves to *distract* one from God's *love* and *mercy* by worry about *sin*. The only *cure* for this worry is to *concentrate*, not on self-perfection, but on the *love* and *tenderness* of God.
>
> CARYLL HOUSELANDER

Let us pray . . .

Lord Jesus,
you opened the eyes of the blind,
healed the sick,
forgave the sinful woman,
and after Peter's denial confirmed him
in your love.
Listen to my prayer:
forgive all my sins,
renew your love in my heart,
help me to live in perfect unity with my
    fellow Christians
that I may proclaim your saving power
    to all the world.
Lord Jesus,
you chose to be called the friend of
    sinners.

By your saving death and resurrection,
free me from my sins.
May your peace take root in my heart
and bring forth a harvest
of love, holiness, and truth.
Lord Jesus Christ,
you are the Lamb of God;
you take away the sins of the world.
Through the grace of the Holy Spirit,
restore me to friendship with your
    Father,
cleanse me from every stain of sin
in the blood you shed for me,
and raise me to new life
for the glory of your name. Amen.

THE RITES OF THE CATHOLIC CHURCH. [NEW YORK: PUEBLO PUBLISHING COMPANY, 1976].

CHAPTER 7

Law and Principles
Guidance for the Journey

As groups fashion an identity, they gain insights about behaviors that either support or subvert their life together. These insights serve as the basis for a community's laws. While laws and general statements about right and wrong (moral principles) are not the only word or the final word when it comes to morality, they do provide guidance for moral decision making. In Christian tradition, two major sources of moral principles emerged—the philosophical investigation of nature ("natural law") and God's word in Scripture.

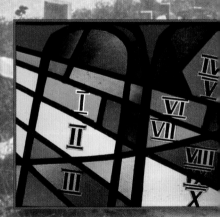

Chapter Overview

• Laws share five characteristics that reveal their role in the moral life of a community.

• The natural-law tradition provides a philosophical foundation for moral principles.

• In Scripture, the law is another word for our relationship with God.

• Jesus encouraged his followers to move beyond simply following the letter of the law.

Before we begin . . .

Imagine that you are the parent of three children, ages seventeen, fifteen, and thirteen. Would you establish the following rules in your household? Why or why not? Are there alternatives to or variations of these rules that you would recommend? What other rules would you consider important?

1. I would set up a block at our local video store so that the children could not rent R-rated movies.

2. I would program child-protection mechanisms into our computer system so that children could not access inappropriate material on the Internet.

3. I would establish and strictly enforce a curfew for each child.

4. I would not allow the children to go to homes or parties where alcohol is available.

5. Each child is responsible for keeping his or her room clean and neat.

6. One hour every Saturday morning is set aside for housecleaning. Each child has a job to do.

7. Each child will assist with doing laundry.

8. Except for serious excuses, everyone is to have dinner together at least twice weekly.

9. Each child takes a turn preparing and cleaning up after meals.

10. Upon graduation, no child will be permitted to go on vacation for a week with friends in Cancun, Mexico.

11. No television is permitted on school nights until 8:00 PM.

12. No phone calls are permitted after 10:00 PM.

13. Phone conversations are not to exceed one-half hour.

14. School grades will determine the degree of freedom that each child receives.

Let us pray . . .

All your works give glory to you, O God. We search for you far and wide, high and low. And yet you carry us always in the palms of your hands. May we live life in tune with the melody of creation, the rhapsody that constantly sings your praise. May we find in nature, in the words of Scripture, and in your Son Jesus guidance for our journey. Amen.

The Nightmare of Lawlessness

In the morning as you leave for school, you rush out of the house to catch your bus. At the intersection, you notice an oncoming car. Since you have a green light, you run across the street; but you wonder if the car will stop or continue on through the red light and run you down.

Fortunately, the driver of the car knows the law, obeys it, and does stop. Once inside the bus, you feel momentarily secure. But are you? Has your school district required that the bus driver receive sufficient training? Does he or she know the driving laws of your state? Does he or she follow them?

At school you open textbooks with lots of information in them, and your teacher tells you many things that he or she expects you to remember. Do the books contain truth? Who regulates what goes into textbooks? Are your teachers certified by the state, and are they really qualified to teach? Does the school meet the requirements of an educational institution?

Distracted from your studies, you look out the classroom window at the passing traffic. You notice a police car driving by. Could these police officers walk into your classroom and arrest you without cause? Are there laws to protect you, or could they haul you off to a dark, secluded prison cell where you would never see family and friends again?

During lunch you have an opportunity to go to a fast-food restaurant. You sit down with your lunch and say to yourself, "It looks like a hamburger, but what's really in it? Am I protected from being given inferior-quality foodstuffs in my sandwich? Are there laws requiring testing meat for the E. coli virus and other potential problems?"

The thought of eating a hamburger that is not really a hamburger starts your head to swoon, and you faint. Not knowing what is wrong, your friends rush you to a nearby hospital. You recover consciousness just in time to see doctors and nurses hovering over you. But are they really licensed doctors and nurses? Can't almost anyone get a white coat and a name tag? Does this hospital measure up to government standards? Are the government's laws regulating hospitals stringent enough? Can these people do anything they want to you, or do you have legal rights as a patient? **A**

Activity A

1. Write a brief science-fiction story describing a nightmare of lawlessness.

2. Review the rules of your school. Are there any that you would change? Are there rules that you would add?

3. Would you forbid smoking and alcohol at school functions attended only by adults?

Characteristics of Law

We could continue "the nightmare of lawlessness" indefinitely, making our everyday life seem perilously similar to one of "The X-Files" episodes. While "anything goes" initially may sound appealing as a slogan for a school or a society, the nightmare of lawlessness quickly reveals itself as a dangerous alternative to law and order. A world without laws is a world without standards of conduct, without rules regulating what is acceptable and unacceptable, and without definite protections for people. When we examine characteristics shared by most legal systems, we can appreciate better the value of laws and the important function that they can serve in any community. One approach to law includes the following five characteristics.

In the first place, *laws provide the basis for good order within a society*. In other words, a law states what is required and what is forbidden for people like:

- citizens in a particular country or community
- representatives of a particular profession
- members of institutions such as schools, clubs, and churches.

As the above nightmare points out, the "good order" that is the aim of laws both restricts us and frees us. (If we attend a party at someone's home and police come and direct us to stop the noise and rowdiness, we may dislike the restrictive quality of laws. However, if we live next door to the house and are trying to sleep, then we might applaud that same quality.) Since laws are concerned with good order among an entire group of people, they seek to bring about what is frequently called "the common good." **B**

The Common Good

By common good is to be understood "the sum total of social conditions which allow people, either as groups or as individuals, to reach their fulfillment more fully and more easily" [GS 26 § 1; cf. GS 74 § 1]. The common good concerns the life of all . . . It consists of three essential elements:

(1) respect for the person,

(2) social well-being and development of the group itself,

(3) and peace (Catechism #s 1906–1909).

Activity B

"The sixties" marked a time of great social upheaval and revolution in many parts of the world. During the late 1960s some groups of people attempted to live in ways that rejected all previous social conventions. Through research or interviews, name some of this movement's expressions as they actually occurred in the 1960s. Comment on the following questions:

1. If such a movement took place among young people today, what might it be like?

2. Would joining a group whose aim is to reject social conventions appeal to you? Why or why not?

3. Is it possible to "reject all previous social conventions"? Is it a noble goal? Explain.

Second, *laws are meant to protect the welfare and the rights of individual members of a particular community.* Without laws the powerless would have no protection against the powerful. Looking back at our opening "nightmare" again, we have some assurance that our rights are looked after by law. For instance, schools have many laws that protect their students' rights—a teacher cannot assign detention or give you a failing grade simply because he or she doesn't like you. Restaurants receive a license to serve food based on their adherence to the laws that protect what a customer eats. And, of course, hospitals have numerous staff regulations aimed at the protection of their patients.

Good laws balance concern for the common good with concern for individual rights and individual welfare. For instance, an individual's right to privacy needs to be balanced with a society's right to have information that would serve the common good. Laws related to the possession and uses of guns often seek to balance the values of individual freedom (for instance, to own firearms) and the dangers that firearms create within a community. Laws prohibiting smoking in public places restrict individual rights but protect the common good—in this case, people's health. **C**

A third characteristic of law is that *laws usually name only the minimum requirements of a community's members.* For instance, laws regarding paying taxes reflect the minimum requirements of good citizenship. Adhering to a dress code and to class-attendance regulations represents only the minimum requirements of being a student at a school. Clearly, laws do not specify all that someone can do to be a good student, a good citizen, or a good church member. **D**

Activity C

Debate the following proposition: Currently, the government infringes too much on individual rights and freedoms. Individual citizens should decide for themselves what they do in matters such as childrearing, smoking, alcohol consumption, wearing helmets while riding motorcycles, and the type of schooling they want for their children.

Activity D

Debate the following proposition: Dress codes are an unnecessary restriction on high school students.

Fourth, *laws typically are stated in negative terms.* "Do not kill" and "Do not steal" exemplify traditional statements of law. "Do not arrive late for classes" and "Do not cheat on tests" are school rules expressed negatively. **E**

Finally, on the positive side, *laws reveal what a society considers important.* For instance, traffic laws indirectly reflect a society's concern for preserving life and health. Laws against shoplifting support the value of private property. A community that requires recycling of aluminum and glass demonstrates concern for the environment. **F**

Laws
• provide the basis for good order
• protect the welfare and rights of individuals
• identify minimum requirements
• are typically stated in negative terms
• reveal what is considered important

Laws and Morality

Law is a rule of conduct enacted by competent authority for the sake of the common good. . . . There are different expressions of the moral law, all of them interrelated: eternal law—the source, in God, of all law; natural law; revealed law, comprising the Old Law and the New Law, or Law of the Gospel; finally civil and ecclesiastical laws.

CATECHISM, #S 1951–1952

What is the relationship between law and morality? For some, the two terms are practically identical—morality means following laws and not acting contrary to the laws of Church and State. According to this view, since laws provide us with standards about right and wrong, then moral decision making simply requires us to decide how to apply the appropriate laws to our lives.

Law is certainly related to morality, but laws, as we commonly understand them, are not the same as morality. Recall from chapter one that morality refers to the actions we do that help or hurt ourselves or others when the actions are done deliberately. As we typically think of them, laws are rules governing members of a nation or an organization. Good morality and good laws share the same goal—to benefit people. However, we can easily view the laws to which we must answer as external to us, as imposed upon us from an outside source.

Unfortunately, in some nations, law ends up being simply the whim of those in power trying to impose their will on the powerless—for example, kings or elected officials, parents or school disciplinarians, declaring, "This is the law because we say it is!"

Activity E

Name three laws that are stated in negative terms. Re-word each law so that it expresses a positive value.

Activity F

If you were one of fifty people stranded on a deserted island with no immediate hope of being rescued, what laws would you establish for the group? Submit ten to fifteen of your most important laws.

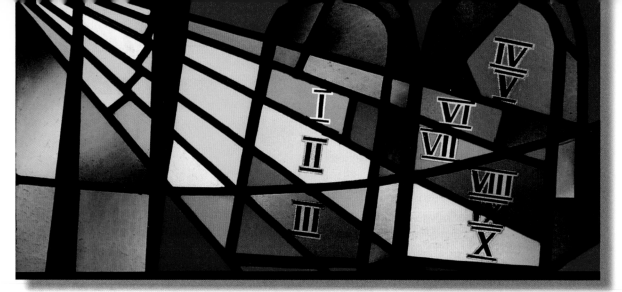

Christianity maintains that we can scrutinize specific laws with the help of general moral principles that are more basic than any laws. In other words, good laws are not simply made up. Rather, they are based on fundamental principles of morality. Laws deserve our obedience or criticism based on these principles.

Moral principles are fundamental statements about right and wrong. The word *fundamental* is related to "foundations." If a building does not rest upon solid foundations, it will soon crumble. Similarly, laws must reflect solid fundamental principles or they, too, are groundless. Traditionally, Christianity has looked to two sources for its general principles of morality: God's law placed in the human heart, called the **natural moral law**, and God's law revealed in Scripture. **G**

moral principles— fundamental statements about right and wrong

natural moral law— moral principles arrived at through rational investigation of human nature

Examples of moral principles expressed in Christian tradition

- Do good; avoid evil.
- Respect all human life.
- Treat all people equally and justly.
- Give all people their rights based on their dignity as persons.
- Provide laws that protect the common good.
- Benefit all people with created goods.
- Do not use evil means to achieve good ends.

For review . . .

1. Name the five characteristics of law.
2. Explain the difference between morality and law.
3. In Christian tradition what two sources have been used to critique specific laws?

Activity G

Put yourself in each of the following situations and defend or condemn the practice by appealing to what you consider fundamental principles of morality.

1. You are a missionary to an island where infants born with a physical defect are killed.
2. You are a member of a society in which women but not men must cover their faces in public.
3. You are banned from smoking in public buildings.
4. You are a parent who decides that your children will not receive vaccinations for common diseases.
5. You are a homeless person who is restricted from panhandling in downtown shopping districts.

Natural Law
A Philosophical Foundation for Moral Principles

The moral law presupposes the rational order, established among creatures for their good and to serve their final end, by the power, wisdom, and goodness of the Creator.

CATECHISM, #1951

For most of its history, Christianity has emphasized an approach to morality built on general moral principles reflecting our shared human nature. If you want to know this basis for Church teaching on morality, you need to journey into the realm of classical philosophy. The approach to arriving at moral principles that is outlined here has been around a long time. As you read through this section, see if what the philosophers have to say can help you in understanding right and wrong and in making more thoughtful moral decisions.

Traditional Christian moral teaching recognizes a "law" that is more fundamental than all the specific laws that we know. This law is not external to the human person. Rather, this fundamental law identifies what it means to be human. For Christians the essence of law is "engraved on our hearts." In other words, God did not create us one way and then impose rules requiring us to act in other ways. God is not a fickle ruler who arbitrarily decrees laws without regard for who we are. Rather, God's ways are the ways of the human heart following its best inclinations. We are faithful to God's law when we are true to who we are; we stray from God's law insofar as we act in an inhuman fashion. The Catechism says:

Man participates in the wisdom and goodness of the Creator who gives him mastery over his acts and the ability to govern himself with a view to the true and the good. The natural law expresses the original moral sense which enables man to discern by reason the good and the evil, the truth and the lie (1954).

Saint Paul expressed this insight in his letter to the Romans. He reminds the young Christian community at Rome that even though the Gentiles (non-Jews) among them did not know the Jewish law, they could "do instinctively what the law requires" (Romans 2:14). They could do this because "They show that what the law requires is written on their hearts, to which their own conscience also bears witness" (Romans 2:15). This basic human law that Saint Paul says is "written on our hearts" reflects the "higher law" that has inspired many persons to challenge laws in society. Appealing to such a higher law, Mohandas Gandhi in India and Martin Luther King, Jr., in the United States disobeyed certain laws of their country that they felt contradicted fundamental human principles.

"Non-violence is the law of our species as violence is the law of the brute. The spirit lies dormant in the brute and he knows no law but that of physical might. The dignity of man requires obedience to a higher law—to the strength of the spirit."

MOHANDAS GANDHI, "THE DOCTRINE OF THE SWORD," IN *BLESSED ARE THE PEACEMAKERS*, EDITED BY ALLEN AND LINDA KIRSCHNER [NEW YORK: POPULAR LIBRARY, 1971].

The natural law approach to morality has been one of the cornerstones of the Western moral tradition. It stresses fundamental human values and the search for universal moral principles. The natural-law approach to morality suggests the following three steps as the way to make moral judgments that are not simply personal opinions.

First, examine nature—especially human nature— to discover the purpose of things built into nature. Secondly, use reasoning to arrive at general principles of morality based on this examination of human nature. Finally, apply these general principles to the particular moral dilemmas in which we find ourselves. **H**

Three Elements of Natural Law

A Morality Based on Nature

- Be yourself.

- Act naturally.

- Be true to human nature.

No doubt such words of advice sound appealing. We want to be true to ourselves and to act naturally. Like a child who really wants to sit on Santa's lap but who doesn't out of fear of being laughed at, we feel inauthentic when we are not true to ourselves. Natural-law morality suggests the same three steps mentioned above. However, when natural law says "Be yourself," it means "Be your best self." When it says "Act naturally," it means "Act the way God intended humans to act." That is, natural law does not

ask, "How *do* we act?" Rather it asks, "How *should* we act?" **I**

By examining human nature, the natural-law approach to morality discovers basic principles that should govern human conduct. Examples of two such moral principles are "Speak truth" and "Respect life." How would advocates of natural law defend such principles? In condensed form, natural-law morality uses the following reasoning process to arrive at these principles.

Humans are endowed with a wonderful, God-given capacity to communicate by using speech. (Granted, other creatures also communicate, but human speech is something special.) Traditional natural-law morality determines that, by its nature human speech is meant to communicate truth. While it can be used for talking gibberish or for deceiving others, the very design of our ability to speak suggests that we use it for telling

Activity H

Natural law refers to principles that are so natural to our human condition that they are "engraved on our hearts." Imagine that you are a member of a United Nations commission established to formulate a declaration of universal moral principles—that is, a list of principles that would apply to everyone everywhere simply because they are human. Create this list of principles as universal pronouncements about how people should or should not act.

Activity I

- Describe human nature in terms of how people do act. (Give examples.)

- Then, describe human nature in terms of how people should act. (Give examples.)

- Which description more closely reflects your understanding of human nature? Explain.

- Which description more closely reflects what natural law means by human nature? Explain.

the truth. The crowning glory of human speech is its capacity to express deep emotions and to convey lofty ideas, to break down barriers between people, and to communicate with others in fashioning a more human community.

After a quick observation of the people around us, we might propose that lying is as "natural" as telling the truth. However, natural law is an investigation into the nature of speech that seeks to determine its purpose as God the Father intended it to be used. Based on such an investigation, natural-law thinkers traditionally have concluded that lying violates the nature and purpose of speech. According to a natural-law approach to moral reasoning, the way to make a case for or against lying is to justify it in terms of the nature, design, and purpose of human speech itself.

Similarly, by nature all people have a right to life. While killing is a too-frequent natural occurrence, we know that the taking of life goes against what people ought to do. We arrive at this principle simply by observing the nature of the human condition. Human life is from God and for God. Creatures must not usurp the power of their Creator. Thus, all creatures have a duty to preserve their own lives and those of others. Destroying life—even our own—contradicts human nature. We abhor those persons who take innocent human life. In our criminal justice system we consider murder a capital offense. We base our condemnation of such action on the universal principle of respect for life inherent in human nature itself.

The United States Declaration of Independence follows natural-law reasoning when it declares that all people have **"inalienable rights"** such as "life, liberty, and the pursuit of happiness." To say that these rights are "inalienable" means that they are ours by our very nature as human persons and are not to be taken away by any other authority. **J**

inalienable rights— rights that all people possess because of their very nature as humans

---

Activity J

The Constitution of the United States contains a Bill of Rights for all of its citizens. For each of the following groups, spell out three rights that you believe that group has. (If you do not believe that a particular group has specific rights, explain why.)

1. Children have a right to . . .
2. Prisoners have a right to . . .
3. Animals have a right to . . .
4. Consumers have a right to . . .

5. Employees have a right to . . .
6. Employers have a right to . . .
7. Hospital patients have a right to . . .
8. Students have a right to . .

A Rational Approach to Morality

Greek philosophers Plato Aristocles (427-347 BC) with the philosopher and scientist Aristotal (384-322 BC)

Christianity emerged in a world dominated by Greek thought. The Greeks placed great emphasis on using reason as the way to truth. To this day, if you take a course in philosophy, you will no doubt begin by studying the ideas of Plato, Aristotle, and other Greek thinkers of old.

Natural-law morality places great weight on the use of reason. Knowing right from wrong is not information available only to people who believe in the Bible or who place their faith in some other special source of wisdom. According to natural-law moralists, all of us can identify what is good by using the capacity within us that is uniquely human—our reason. "Human reason" is the arena in which the search for truth—including moral truth—takes place. All people of good will can examine human nature and discover truths about the purpose of speech, free will, sex, and every other dimension of our humanity.

With its emphasis on human reason as an instrument capable of arriving at truth, natural law presents a very positive image of us humans. It suggests that reasonable people can speak among themselves about right and wrong and that they can attempt to convince one another of truth through the force of reasonable arguments. In other words, natural law believes that, despite cultural and other obvious differences, Americans can seek universal truth about right and wrong in dialogue with Africans, Asians, and others. Similarly, since morality is not a matter simply of religious beliefs but of rationally presented truths, Christians can discuss moral issues with Hindus, Buddhists, Muslims, and Jews. *The United Nations Declaration of Human Rights*, developed by representatives of all the world's nations, is an example of common universal truths.

Activity K

Debate the following statement. Use examples to support your position.
"Human reason should serve as the sole basis for determining right and wrong."

U.N. Declaration of Human Rights

In 1948 the United Nations drafted a declaration listing rights that all people have. Following this historic act the assembly called upon all member countries to publicize and advocate these rights. The following is a summary of some of the rights listed.

Everyone is entitled to:

- Freedom without any distinction based on race, colour, sex, language, religion, national origin or birth.

- The right to leave any country and the right to have and change nationality.

- Protection, by society and the State, for families.

- The right to seek and enjoy asylum from persecution.

- The right to participate in the arts and cultural life.

- Special care and assistance for children and their caregivers.

- The right to life, liberty and security of person.

- Freedom from torture and cruel, inhumane or degrading punishment.

- The right to a fair and public hearing, and the right to be presumed innocent until proven guilty.

- The right to equal pay for equal work and to favourable work conditions.

- No arbitrary arrest, detention or exile.

- The right to take part in the government, directly or through freely chosen representatives.

- The right to fair pay and to a standard of living adequate for the health and well-being of self and family.

- The right to education, which should be free in elementary stages, and should be available at high levels.

- The right to an effective remedy for acts violating fundamental rights.

[For complete text of the Universal Declaration of Human Rights, see the following Internet site: http://www.un.org/Overview/rights.html]

GENERAL ASSEMBLY OF THE UNITED NATIONS. "BASIC HUMAN RIGHTS."
UNIVERSAL DECLARATION OF HUMAN RIGHTS. <HTTP://WWW.REAL
WORLD.ON.NET/EXPOSURE/ISSUES/HUMAN RIGHTS/RIGHTS.HTML>

An Emphasis on General Principles

follows a "top-down" approach to problem solving. It reasons from general to specific, from the abstract to the concrete.

To demonstrate this process in natural-law moral reasoning, let us consider a simple moral decision that we might face. We are walking along a street and notice a bike parked outside of a house. How do we decide whether or not to take the bike? Natural-law morality asks: What principle can be applied to this situation? *Respect for private property* and *Do not steal* are general principles of morality that serve as a guideline for us in this decision. Therefore, we reason that we should not take the bike.

Of course, the art of determining general principles of morality and of applying these principles to concrete situations is seldom so simple. And, certainly, the process is easier to do when we are not immediately faced with making a difficult decision. As teachers of morality, Church leaders provide us with well-thought-out moral principles that we then can apply to our specific moral decisions. **L**

Third, natural law emphasizes general principles of morality. According to this approach, by using reason to examine nature we arrive at principles that we can apply to the concrete moral situations in which we find ourselves. In other words, natural-law morality

Activity L

Imagine that someone comes to you seeking your opinion on one of the following questions. Provide an answer by completing the following sentences:

- A general moral principle (or principles) related to this question is . . .

- A person can apply that general principle to the particular question by the following use of logical reasoning . . .

1. Is it okay to cheat on income tax?

2. Should hand guns be banned to private citizens?

3. Should a customer who receives $20 extra in change from a store cashier return the money?

4. Is it okay to sell illegal drugs to willing customers?

5. Can a couple who has exchanged marriage vows later decide that it is okay to engage in sex with other partners?

Applying Natural Law— Cautions and Clarifications

> *Application of the natural law varies greatly; it can demand reflection that takes account of various conditions of life according to places, times, and circumstances. Nevertheless, in the diversity of cultures, the natural law remains as a rule that binds men among themselves and imposes on them, beyond the inevitable differences, common principles.*
>
> CATECHISM, #1957

Nature Is Concrete

Natural law can be very helpful to us in our struggle to make good moral decisions. We benefit from exploring the designs and purposes of nature and in particular of human nature as they relate to our moral decisions. Natural law reminds us that we should look to the human condition when deciding what we ought to do. Only then will we truly do the "human" thing.

However, we must avoid viewing "human nature" as something divorced from the concrete earthiness of the humans who inhabit our world. In other words, we discover what is "human nature" by observing and examining actual humans. We misuse the concept if we try to fit all humans into an overly narrow understanding of what it means to be human. **M**

Nature Is Dynamic

> *History itself speeds on so rapid a course that an individual person can scarcely keep abreast of it. . . . Thus, the human condition has passed from a rather static concept of reality to a more dynamic, evolutionary one. In consequence, there has arisen a new series of problems, a series as important as can be, calling for new efforts of analysis and synthesis.*
>
> DOCUMENTS OF VATICAN COUNCIL II, "THE PASTORAL CONSTITUTION ON THE CHURCH IN THE MODERN WORLD," NUMBER 5.

Our next step is to remind ourselves that nature is not something static and unchanging. Rather, it is a **dynamic**, growing, ever-changing

dynamic—developing, growing, changing

reality. Certainly, in our moral decision making, we need to seek "timeless truths" and to act in accord with them. We also need to be sensitive to new insights, new implications, and new applications of timeless truths. Since, in the not-too-distant past, slavery was considered "natural" by some people and the question about whether or not women should be allowed to vote was hotly debated by reasonable people, it is helpful for us to develop a sense of history when considering moral questions. Used properly, timeless moral principles can help us to critique laws and practices common in contemporary cultures and to replace those with laws and practices more in line with timeless principles.

Activity M

Write a report on a unique characteristic of a particular culture. (For example, choose its view of marriage and family life, its approach to wrongdoers, its approach to business exchanges, its attitude toward strangers.) Make a case that this unique characteristic does or does not reflect what it means to be human.

We Are Not Just Rational Creatures

Third, we need to add a word of caution about natural law's emphasis on reason. As natural law suggests, we should attempt to be as reasonable as possible when making moral decisions. However, we are not just rational creatures. We are a combination of mind, body, and spirit. While striving to be "rational" decision makers, we should not disregard our feelings, our bodies, and spiritual discernment. Moreover, we need to remind ourselves that, no matter how reasonable we are, our reasoning is imperfect. We should be reasonable when declaring moral principles, but we should also accept that we still might be mistaken about them.

The More Specific Principles Are, the More Likely They Are to Have Exceptions

Lastly, because for many centuries thoughtful people have struggled to shed light on common moral problems, we now have available to us a great deposit of the "wisdom of the ages." We possess general principles that can guide us in our own decision making. However, we need to keep in mind the cautions mentioned above, and we need to recall a word of caution that comes from the natural-law tradition itself. Namely, the more specific principles are, the more we encounter exceptions to them. (For example, we would have difficulty finding exceptions to the principle "Do good; avoid evil." However, the principle "People have a right to private property," because it is more specific, does leave room for exceptions without denying its validity as a valuable general moral principle.)

Activity N

The following are generally perceived to be valid, useful principles that typically should be adhered to. However, a case could be made that occasionally circumstances would make exceptions acceptable. Can you envision circumstances that would call for making exceptions to these principles? If so, describe those circumstances. Is there another principle that makes an exception acceptable? If you believe that no exceptions are acceptable for one or more of these principles, explain why.

1. The principle of confidentiality (lawyer-client, doctor-patient)

2. Making a solemn promise to keep information secret

3. Respecting private property

4. Freedom to practice the religion of one's choice

Use Natural Law Wisely

If we remember these practical concerns about the interpretation and application of natural law, then it can serve as a valuable ally in our decision making. Natural law helps us to appreciate that moral truth is more universal than simply our view of it. By using "reason" and "human nature" as reference points, natural law allows us to enter into discussion with all other seekers of truth in our search for how to live an authentic human life.

For review . . .

4. Name the three elements of natural law.

5. What did classical thought emphasize as the way to truth?

6. What does it mean to say that natural-law morality follows a "top-down" approach?

7. According to the text what four cautions or clarifications must be kept in mind when using natural law?

8. What is the difference between a dynamic versus a static view of nature?

9. Explain the statement "The more specific principles are, the more likely they are to have exceptions."

Activity O

The bishops of Vatican II list the following categories of behaviors that are wrong by their very nature. For each category, name a positive principle that underlies the behaviors being condemned.

- whatever is hostile to life itself, such as any kind of homicide, genocide, abortion, euthanasia and voluntary suicide

- whatever violates the integrity of the human person, such as mutilation, physical and mental torture and attempts to coerce the spirit

- whatever is offensive to human dignity, such as subhuman living conditions, arbitrary imprisonment, deportation, slavery, prostitution and trafficking in women and children

- degrading conditions of work which treat laborers as mere instruments of profit, and not as free responsible persons

Documents of the Vatican II, "The Pastoral Constitution on the Church in the Modern World," number 27.

The Biblical Foundation for Moral Laws and Principles

> *If you **continue** my **word**, you are truly my **disciples**; and you will know the **truth**, and the truth will **make** you free.*
>
> JOHN 8:31b–32

A quick reading of the Bible reveals that it is not primarily a law book. Within its pages we find stories, sermons, sayings, poems, proverbs, and songs. How can we best use such a book as the basis for morality? For one thing, we would diminish the value of the Bible as a source-book for morality if we simply read through it and underline all the statements about morality, as if the rest is insignificant for moral decision making. In fact, the entire Bible is a source of moral guidance. Indeed, when Jesus referred to "the law and the prophets," he meant the entire Old Testament. For Christians, therefore, the Bible—especially the words and actions of Jesus—serves as a foundation for moral laws and principles.

According to Christian tradition, the teachings of Scripture parallel truths arrived at through natural law. Since God is the Creator of nature and since the Bible is God's word, then the "law" and principles discovered by investigating the one source of truth complement and reinforce the other. On the one hand, we look to creation for insights into how to act according to God's plan. On the other hand, the stories of the struggles of the Israelites and of God's unfailing love for them, the teachings of the prophets, and in particular the words and deeds of Jesus and his followers, tell us what it means to be human. In other words, natural law and Scripture go hand in hand as sources of moral wisdom.

In this section, rather than discuss specific laws found in Scripture, we will explore the way that law is viewed in the Old Testament and then by Jesus.

Law in the Old Testament— Guideposts for Friendship

The days are surely coming, says the LORD, when I will make a new covenant with the house of Israel and the house of Judah . . . this is the covenant that I will make with the house of Israel after those days, says the LORD: I will put my law within them, and I will write it on their hearts; and I will be their God, and they shall be my people.

JEREMIAH 31:31, 33

Does your family have rules? Do your family members take turns setting up and cleaning up for meals? Are you required to do weekly household chores? Is there a weekend curfew and a limit on television watching? When we establish family rules, we are making a statement about who we are and about what our relationship is to others in our family. In the first place, we are recognizing that we are not alone—we are members of a family. Second, we are affirming that our identity is intimately tied to this community called our family. Finally, by being faithful to these rules we are showing our care and concern for the other members of our family.

For the Jews of old, the Law spelled out what they were meant to be as individuals and as a people. The spirit underlying the Law in the Hebrew Scriptures resembles that of a family's rules and regulations. Because God chose to impart the Law to them, the Jews knew that they were God's family. Their Law reflected their intimate, family-like relationship with God and with one another. They viewed their Law as a gift from God. They still do. Observing the Law would keep them close to God; breaking the Law would be an offense against God. The Law spelled out how they could best show care and concern for one another. It even provided for returning land to its original owners if some community members gained an advantage over them. **P**

Activity P

Describe a specific incident when having and keeping rules can add to a relationship.
Describe a specific way that having and keeping rules can provide an identity to a group of people.

Ten Commandments

1. I am the Lord your God. You shall not have strange gods before me.
2. You shall not take the name of the Lord your God in vain.
3. Remember to keep holy the Lord's day.
4. Honor your father and your mother.
5. You shall not kill.
6. You shall not commit adultery.
7. You shall not steal.
8. You shall not bear false witness against your neighbor.
9. You shall not covet your neighbor's wife.
10. You shall not covet your neighbor's goods.

covenant—in the ancient Middle East, an agreement between two parties. Israelites applied the concept to their relationship as a people with their God.

Covenant is the term used to designate this special relationship between God and the Jewish people. It means "agreement," like the agreement that a wife and a husband make when they marry and become family. As the quote from the book of Jeremiah can be read to imply, the covenant between God and the Jewish people was meant to be written not merely on stone tablets like the Ten Commandments, but rather on their very hearts.

According to Jewish tradition, the Hebrew Bible contains 613 commandments. The Ten Commandments serve as the cornerstone of these laws, and Jewish teachers have often attempted a summary of the Law such as, "What is hateful to you, do not do to others. That is the whole Law; all the rest is interpretation." Whether the laws are as broad in scope as the Ten Commandments or as specific as what foods may be eaten, they are always presented as an expression of God's loving concern for the Jewish people. For that reason, the Law is frequently described in the Old Testament as a "delight."

The twentieth-century rabbi Abraham Heschel sums up in these words the spirit underlying Jewish law:

The law . . . is not designed to be a yoke, a curb, a strait jacket for human action. Above all, the Torah asks for love: thou shalt love thy God; thou shalt love thy neighbor. All observance [of the law] is training in the art of love.

BETWEEN GOD AND MAN [NEW YORK: THE FREE PRESS, 1965]. **Q**

For review . . .

10. How does the text suggest that Christians should use the Bible as a source of moral guidance?

11. According to Christian tradition what is the relationship between Scripture and natural law?

12. How did the Jews of biblical times view their laws?

13. Define covenant.

Activity Q

1. Read over the Ten Commandments in Exodus, chapter 20. If you were asked your opinion, would you vote to repeal the Commandments as being out-dated and no longer of value? If you would vote to do away with them, explain why. If you would vote to keep the Commandments as valuable norms for behavior, explain practical applications that they could have in our world today.

2. Read Leviticus, chapter 19. Identify four laws listed there that still contain valuable messages for today. What important message underlies each law?

Jesus and Law

If we look at the incidents when law is mentioned in the Gospels, we discover that, more often than not, Jesus is presented as being in conflict with the Law. He is confronted for violating Sabbath laws—for healing on the Sabbath and for allowing his disciples to pick grain on the Sabbath. He is challenged by advocates of the Law to name the greatest commandments and to pronounce judgment on difficult legal matters. He is baffling to many because he frequently spends time with people who do not keep the Law and who are officially the "outlaws" of his society, such as tax collectors and prostitutes. By examining the references to law in the Gospels, we can name certain perspectives on law held by Jesus.

Jesus Is Not Primarily a Teacher of Law

Sometimes we imagine that Jesus replaces Jewish law with Christian law. Actually, Jesus is primarily concerned about communicating God's love for us. On our part, he calls for a change of heart, a conversion in response to our experience of God's love. *Jesus' teachings center much more on what God does for us than on what we are supposed to do.*

Of course, Jesus is concerned about the behavior of his followers, but his teachings primarily describe what happens when we change our hearts. For example, we have already studied the famous list of Christian characteristics known as the Beatitudes. In them, Jesus describes the loved ones of his Father as the poor in spirit, the gentle, those who mourn, justice seekers, the merciful, the pure in heart, and peacemakers. Elsewhere he reminds us to "change and become like children" (Matthew 18:2–3) and to "sell your possessions, and give the money to the poor" (Matthew 19:21). Statements such as these are not "laws" but rather are descriptions of people completely changed by the experience of love.

Jesus Does Not Renounce the Law, but Emphasizes the Spirit of the Law

Do not think that I have come to abolish the law or the prophets; I have come not to abolish but to fulfill. For truly I tell you, until heaven and earth pass away, not one letter, not one stroke of a letter, will pass from the law until all is accomplished.

MATTHEW 5:17–18

As this passage from Matthew's Gospel makes clear, for Christians Jesus brings the Law to fulfillment. Jewish law names the terms of friendship between God and us; Jesus embodies and makes complete that friendship. Jesus knew and approved of the Law. However, he strongly disapproved of certain attitudes toward and uses of the Law.

For one, Jesus criticized those who used elaborate reasoning to get around the letter of the Law. Secondly, Jesus emphasized the spirit of the Law. Merely following the letter of the Law means doing what the Law commands only because it says so. Following the spirit of the Law means acting in response to the Spirit of God who dwells within us. The difference is one of attitude. We can approach a school project with the attitude that it is required for a certain grade or with an attitude that of itself it can be a great learning experience. We can give a gift because we are expected to or because we truly want to show the person our love. We can recycle our paper, aluminum, and glass products because of local laws or because we feel strongly about the benefits of recycling. As these examples point out, actions based solely on the letter of the Law or based on the underlying spirit of the Law can look the same from the outside and can achieve the same external results. However, whether we follow the letter or the spirit of the Law makes a great difference regarding who we are and regarding our relationship with others. **R**

Activity R

Give two examples of someone following the letter of a law but not its spirit. Give two examples of someone following the spirit of a law. In light of your examples, explain the difference in terms of possible intentions and results.

Jesus Proclaims Love as the Summation of the Law

As you no doubt already noticed, love is a recurring theme in any course on Christian morality. Law and love need not be contradictory. More often than not, following the law is the loving thing to do. However, it is possible that when we emphasize strict observance of the law we can lose sight of the true purpose of law, namely, love of God and others. When Jesus' disciples are accused of violating the Sabbath laws by plucking grain, Jesus reminds his accusers that "The Sabbath was made for humankind, and not humankind for the Sabbath" (Mark 2:27–28).

Legalism is a term that refers to emphasizing strict observance of the law. For that reason, legalism misses the heart of the matter when it comes to the intention of laws. We are legalistic when we begin counting words after writing one sentence of a 500-word essay assignment. We are legalistic when we drive the speed limit even when conditions indicate that lower speeds are called for. We are legalistic when we stick to the rules of a game even when doing so is unnecessarily hurting certain players. We are legalistic when we scheme to figure out how laws and rules can best serve our personal interests. We are legalistic when we decide that people are "good guys" or "bad guys" simply on the basis of whether or not they keep the law.

Clearly, Jesus places concern for people and love of God over observance of law. There must have been many people who held a legalistic attitude toward law during his time, because reminding his listeners of the importance of love over law is a central theme of Jesus' teaching.

legalism—an attitude of strict observance of laws, regardless of circumstances and possible harm to people involved

Do More Than the Law Requires: Exercise "Moral Muscle"

You have heard that it was said to those of ancient times, "You shall not murder"; and "whoever murders shall be liable to judgment." But I say to you that if you are angry with a brother or sister, you will be liable to judgment; and if you insult a brother or sister, you will be liable to the council; and if you say "You fool," you will be liable to the hell of fire . . .

You have heard that it was said, "You shall love your neighbor and hate your enemy." But I say to you, Love your enemies and pray for those who persecute you, so that you may be children of your Father in heaven . . . For if you love those who love you, what reward do you have? Do not even the tax collectors do the

same? And if you greet only your brothers and sisters, what more are you doing than others? Do not even the Gentiles do the same? Be perfect, therefore, as your heavenly Father is perfect.

MATTHEW 5:21–22, 43–45a, 46–48

Typically, laws state the least that a person ought to do. Jesus responds to such an attitude toward law with a resounding: Do more! "Do not steal" tells us the minimum of how we should treat property. It does not tell us when we should share our property with others. "Obey traffic laws" does not require us to be exceptionally courteous drivers or to stop and help others who are in trouble by the side of the road. "Do not cheat" specifies what we cannot do during a test. It does not stipulate that we use a test as an educational experience. Performing the two or three weekly chores that we have been assigned says nothing about the many ways that we can also help our households run smoothly. Voting and paying taxes are merely the minimum requirements of good citizenship.

Minimalism refers to an attitude of doing the bare minimum required of us by law. Minimalism and legalism are deceptive partners in our attempts to lead moral lives. Instead of concentrating on the minimal requirements of the law, Jesus invites us to exercise what one moral theologian calls **"moral muscle"**—

pushing ourselves to take extra steps in making our world a better place. Faithfulness to laws holds a valuable place in Christian morality. However, of itself such faithfulness is merely a limited part of the Christian moral vision. Divorced from personal initiative and thoughtfulness, law keeping is merely moral laziness. Jesus wants more from us. **S**

For review . . .

14. What is most striking about Gospel stories related to Jesus and the Law?

15. Name four perspectives that Jesus held about law.

16. Rather than focusing on what we are supposed to do, what does Jesus focus on in his teachings?

17. According to the text does Jesus renounce the Law?

18. Define legalism and minimalism.

19. What does the text mean by the phrase "exercise moral muscle"?

minimalism— an attitude of doing only the least that is required by law in our moral life

moral muscle— pushing ourselves to do more than the minimum in our moral life

Activity S

Write an essay describing either legalism or minimalism as an attitude toward law. Include in your essay the message of Jesus: Do more!

Conclusion
Law, Principles, and Christian Morality

At their best, moral laws and principles specify what it means to be human and what actions promote or diminish our human community. Isn't it true that we want to be known as persons of principle, living our lives true to the grand vision of humanity spelled out in noble principles such as "respect life" and "do unto others as you would have them do unto you"? Laws deserve respect and obedience insofar as they flow from the values and principles that we discover in God's creation and in God's word. For Jesus and his followers, love represents the summation of all law.

Let us pray . . .

Our Lord, you bless everyone
who lives right
and obeys your Law.
You bless all of those
who follow your commands
from deep in their hearts
and who never do wrong
or turn from you . . .
Teach me your laws.
With my own mouth,

I tell others the laws
that you have spoken.
Obeying your instructions
brings as much happiness
as being rich.
I will study your teachings
and follow your footsteps.
I will take pleasure
in your laws
and remember your words. Amen.

PSALM 119:1–3, 12–16 (CEV)

CHAPTER 8

Moral Decision Making

A Process

A text on moral decision making cannot be reduced to a "how to" book. Moral decision making is more than a skill. Nonetheless, we can identify action steps that can make our moral decision making better. As with all important projects in our lives, moral decision making deserves careful planning and thoughtful execution. Some steps listed in this chapter will appear obvious; others are frequently overlooked. Attention to the process results in moral decisions that are closer to being the best judgments that we can make—that is, judgments in line with the values and teachings of Jesus.

Chapter Overview

- A first step in responsible moral decision making is identifying the facts.

- Discernment, the second step in making moral decisions, means calling upon as many resources as possible to evaluate whether an action is right or wrong.

- Finally, Christian moral decision making involves seeking God's help in Jesus' name to arrive at a judgment on the matter.

Let us pray . . .

O Lord our God, you have fashioned us in your own image—creators and decision makers with thought and feelings. May we use your gifts wisely and lovingly. May your Spirit enlighten us with clear thinking and enliven us with care for others as we seek to do your will. Amen.

Before we begin . . .

1. A friend of yours is away from home at a sports camp. Your friend mentions that all team members are going into town that night to get matching tattoos. Your friend asks you for advice, as to whether you think it would be wrong for him to get one, too. How would you recommend that your friend make this decision? What questions should be asked? Who should be consulted? What steps do you recommend that he or she take in order to arrive at the best course of action? Make your list of suggestions as complete as possible.

2. Another friend of yours has been a lifeguard at a neighborhood pool for the summer. Part of her responsibility is to check the chlorine level of the pool on a regular basis. Now that it is getting near the end of the season, she has stopped checking the chlorine level. Instead, she merely writes down on the chart the same information as the previous lifeguard reported. If you wanted to convince your friend that her actions are wrong, what arguments would you use? What questions should she be asking herself? What steps should she consider in determining whether or not this is acceptable or unacceptable behavior?

3. Ask two or three other people how they typically go about making an important moral decision. Compare the steps you suggest for the above cases with the steps that they follow. Would you add any of their steps to your process?

Preparing for the Big Game

The school band marched along the driveway in preparation for Friday's big football game. In the parking lot, cheerleaders practiced their cheers until the entire squad could clap and kick and shout in unison. Students and staff in charge of sound equipment and video-taping checked microphones, loud-speakers, and camera equipment. Ticket-takers were assigned. Programs informing others of the player numbers and positions were printed and folded. Concession-stand workers double-checked their supplies and made sure that extra help would be available on Sunday.

On the playing field itself, the football team ran through its drills. Quarterbacks and receivers worked on pass patterns. Place kickers and punters practiced by the goalposts. Running backs coordinated their timing with the offensive line. The defensive team captain yelled out different numbers, and the defense scrambled to set up its predesigned defensive patterns.

On this day filled with preparation, each facet involved in making the championship game a success stood apart as a separate unit. Yet everyone involved knew that attention to these seperate details was important for creating a winning combination and a day the entire school would be proud of.

The Skill of Moral Decision Making

discernment—
investigating and
analyzing the moral
implications of choices
we are faced with;
taking whatever steps
necessary to help
make the best possi-
ble decision

Moral decision making is like a football game. Attention to the many factors involved in a football game results in a better overall game. Similarly, if we are seriously ill we would seek as much information, advice, and guidance as possible to help us make the best decision about how to treat the illness. If we are faced with other decisions such as what kind of car to buy or whether or not to go to college, we would take steps to insure that our decisions are thoughtful and responsible. Likewise, the decisions that affect our moral life should not be made quickly or without forethought. Being alert to the many factors involved will improve our moral decision making. Therefore, in this chapter we will examine the many "parts" that can make a better "whole" out of the many moral choices each of us has to make in our life-time. Paying special attention to each of the following steps will result in better moral choices.

In moral decision making, we need to be as objective as possible, determining the facts of the matter as best we can. The Catechism says the following about moral decision making. The morality of human acts depends on:

• the object chosen;

• the end in view or the intention;

• the circumstances of the action (1750).

In other words, there are objective and subjective components involved in determining right from wrong. Determining facts should be a straightforward, non-controversial matter, shouldn't it? For instance, abortion is abortion, right? However, as you know, some people refer to abortion as "terminating a pregnancy" while others label the same action "murder." In other words, on this important moral issue disagreement exists even on the fact level. Therefore, identifying the facts involved is an important first step in deciding the morality of actions. In this chapter we will refer to a series of questions that can help us identify the morality of our decisions.

Secondly, moral decision making is not just a fact-finding mission. It also involves discernment. **Discernment** moves analysis from the level of facts to one of responsibility. This concept refers to a process of sifting through things, like a prospector panning for gold amid the sand and stones in a stream. That is, discernment means thinking through the moral implications of our possible actions. What wellsprings of wisdom and insight can we tap into as we try to discern right from wrong? Discernment brings to bear on our decision making all the resources that can help us make more thoughtful moral choices. In debates about morality, people can agree on the facts of a matter and still disagree on what ought to be done. For instance, people can agree on the facts about what a nuclear explosion will do. That doesn't mean all people will agree about whether or not to use nuclear weapons during a conflict. The difference depends partially on how they determine right from wrong on the question— the process of moral discernment. Of course, according to Catholic moral teaching certain actions are just plain wrong. Nonetheless, discernment is an important step in helping us understand why certain acts are right or wrong in themselves while intentions and circumstances color the morality of other acts.

Finally, moral decision making is a matter of judgment. Certain skills, such as prayer, can assist this move from discernment to judgment. We might not think of it as a skill, but during decision making, prayer adds an important dimension to the process. In prayer we seek to diminish our self-absorption in order to be more open to God and God's will. Indeed, every aspect of our moral decision making has as its goal making the best judgments we can—that is, judgments in line with the values and teachings of Jesus.

Moral Decision Making:
Another Name for Conscience

It's important that you do not seperate the process for moral decision making outlined in this chapter from the rest of the course. For instance, the process actually describes what "follow your conscience" should involve. Also, the process helps us answer the question posed early in the course, "What would Jesus do"? Aspects of the process can serve as building blocks upon which to foster virtuous living ("Yes, Jesus would do this") and to avoid sin ("No, Jesus would not do this"). Moral principles and laws, the subjects of the last chapter, play a central role in the discernment process discussed in this chapter. Finally, the process can be applied to the specific areas of morality addressed in the second part of the book. **A**

Activity A

Think back to the situations mentioned earlier—the case of the friend contemplating getting a tattoo and the lifeguard who discontinues testing the pool water. Look over the steps involved in moral decision making that you arrived at for those cases. Then read over the following case study. Based on the information you have just read, what additional steps, if any, would you now take to arrive at a decision? What would your decision be on the following case? Explain why you would take this position.

Friday night and all day Saturday the radio station of the local university featured the music of a group known for its graphic lyrics suggesting violence against women. On Saturday night at a club near the university, three women are attacked by a group of men chanting lyrics from one of these songs.

After the incident some campus student groups argue that such songs should be banned from being played on the radio station. They want a committee to oversee the type of music played. Other students argue that free speech would be compromised if these songs were kept off the air.

Since your high school is near the campus and the radio station is popular with your fellow students, you are invited to present your views on the subject at a special on-the-air forum. You gather together some of your classmates to decide what position you will advocate at the forum and what arguments you will use to support your position.

Fact-Finding
Morality Is Concrete

If we actually took time to investigate situations calling for moral decision making, what questions could we ask ourselves to help us understand moral dilemmas that come our way?

Questions That Help Identify the Facts
What is the problem that needs to be talked about?
Who performs an action or who is affected by an action?
Why do I act as I do? (motivation)
How will my goals be achieved? (means)
When and **Where** will the problem happen? (time and place)

What?—Opinion or Fact

As in all areas of life, in morality it is important to know what we are talking about. Before we jump to conclusions about moral questions, we need to make a "reality check." For instance, imagine that we confronted a friend about her drinking. "Marci, we think that you have a drinking problem. We believe you need help." Upon what basis would we make such a statement? If we expect Marci to take seriously our observation, we would need to present her with a number of facts to back up our claim.

To arrive at good moral judgments, we need to know what we are talking about. To illustrate the importance of the "what" question to moral decision making, let us examine two different statements. A necessary first step in evaluating each statement's moral content is to determine whether it is an unfounded opinion or an observation based on facts.

Statement one: "Don't buy that product. It destroys the earth's ozone layer."

This opinion suggests that the purchasing of certain products is immoral because of their effect on the ozone layer. Before we can say that this opinion has merit, we need to know:

- What is ozone? What purpose does the earth's ozone layer serve?

- Is there, in fact, something in this particular product that harms the ozone layer?

- If yes, how serious is the damage to the ozone layer caused by the product?

- How essential is this product? Do alternative products exist?

Based on the information gleaned from asking these questions, we now should be clearer as to whether the statement is an opinion or a fact.

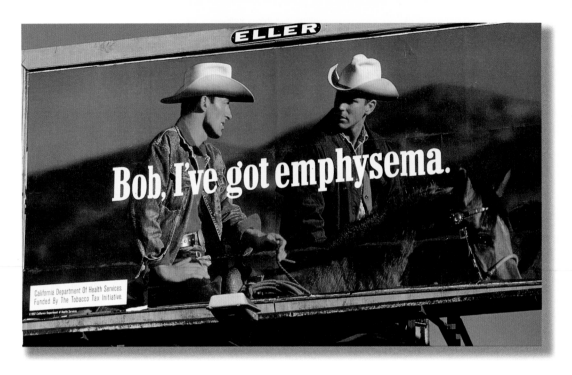

Another such example would be: "No cigarette ads should be allowed. They purposely mislead people, especially children."

Concerning this second statement, many cigarette ads portray athletic-looking people engaged in strenuous exercise. Some tobacco companies have sponsored sports events, such as tennis tournaments. Also, some companies have been accused of purposely aiming their ads at a youth market. In other words, cigarette advertising associates smoking with youth and vitality. To seek the truth, we need to ask:

- Do medical facts about the effects of smoking support or deny the accuracy of this portrayal?

- Is making this association false advertising?

- Is it immoral to advertise in this way?

Before taking a stand on laws regulating smoking and cigarette ads, it is important to gain an accurate picture of the groups targeted and of smoking and its effects.

The "what" question reminds us that moral decision making always occurs in concrete circumstances. Generalizing serves a purpose, but moral decision making does not occur "in general." It occurs only when real people make choices in concrete situations. In other words, we need first to ask, "What are the facts about the topic?" before we jump to the second question, "Who will be affected by my decision regarding this topic?" **B**

Activity B

For each of the following topics, write down questions about basic information that a person should have before coming to a moral position on the matter. As a follow-up, research one of the topics and seek answers to the questions you posed.

- Buying a fur coat
- Nuclear energy plants
- Gun control legislation
- Laws on the driving age
- Violence in sports
- Violence on television

Who?—What's Right for One Person May Be Wrong for Another

The person or people involved in an action can make a difference in moral decisions. "Who" figures into morality in two ways: Who does an action and who is affected by an action. The following examples demonstrate ways in which the people who are involved in the decision can be significant.

- Marie is sitting at a cafeteria table at lunchtime with her friends and jokes about two students' eating habits. To one person, Marie's comment is taken all in fun; to the other it is devastating.

- Even though they come from fairly wealthy families, a group of young people regularly steal just for the fun of it and are finally caught. In a similar situation Anthony, too, is caught stealing. His family has been having a rough time financially and needed food.

- As he enters the restroom at school, John overhears a group of students joking about him. Their comments are cutting and not playful. When he realizes that his good friend Steve is among those cutting him up, John is particularly upset.

Just as morality always refers to specific actions—the *what* of our moral decisions—so, too, morality always involves individual persons. Therefore, *who* is involved can make a difference in deciding how to act. In the above examples, the emotional state of the person acting or being affected, economic differences, and our relationship to another person all need to be taken into consideration in deciding on how to act.

Age differences and cultural backgrounds are other factors that need to be raised when studying the "who" question. For instance, in traditional Vietnamese culture it is considered impolite to say no to someone. This uniqueness suggests a need for sensitivity to cultural differences in our interactions with others. If a history of racial tension exists in our community, greater sensitivity is required when we make general comments about a person of another race. Actions that are acceptable for children may not be acceptable for adolescents or adults, and vice versa. The various age ratings for television and movies are an example of this. **C**

Activity C

Give three examples in which "who" is involved can make a difference regarding the morality of actions.

Why?—Examining Our Intentions

motives— why people do what they do

For some moralists, the "why" question is the only yardstick that we should use to measure morality. (If you recall from the chapter on conscience, those who study moral development make much of the "why" question when determining levels of moral maturity.) Certainly, whether we act out of selfish motives or out of concern for others colors the morality of our behavior.

Here are examples of actions that, on the surface, may appear acceptable or even good. However, the motive underlying each action paints a much different picture of the persons involved.

- Mr. and Mrs. Smith invite some of their friends to their house for a party. When the guests arrive, the Smiths use the occasion to attempt to get financial support from everyone for a business scheme they have recently begun.

- Now that the school year is coming to a close and warm weather is coming, Ted and Angelo have begun to include P.J. in their activities. P.J. has a pool in his backyard; Ted and Angelo do not.

- Amelia knows that she and her brother are supposed to clean the house right after school. In an attempt to avoid cleaning, she stops at the library on the way home to work on a report that's not due for two weeks.

In these examples, even though the acts themselves seem positive, negative or self-serving intentions are obviously at work. The question of **motives** adds a very personal touch to our moral decision making. Our motives tell us a great deal about who we are. Regardless of whether our decisions are right or wrong, we can have good or bad intentions for those decisions. For that reason, the "why" question moves us from morality as *doing* to morality as *being*. While our intentions are seldom if ever pure, they do make a statement about our integrity as persons and are important for us in evaluating our moral decision making. **D**

Activity D

1. Describe how motives could affect the morality of the following decisions:

   - A student volunteers to help the school chaplain because it will get him out of after-school detention.

   - A politician running for office promises more jobs for the community if she is elected.

   - A male student realizes that a female student is having difficulty with course work and offers to help her study.

2. Describe three other situations when motives can affect the morality of actions.

How?—The Question of Methods

• Katie wants to break up with Ron, a boy she has been going out with for a few months, in order to go out with Joe. At this point, Ron feels madly in love with Katie and presumes that Katie's feelings for him are mutually intense. Katie sees Ron and casually says to him, "I really like you, Ron, but can we just be friends from now on?"

• Dan is concerned that his weightlifting program is not sufficient to help him rehabilitate his knee and get him back into shape for his final year of college football. He feels that if he has a good senior year he has a chance to make a pro team. He

considers taking illegal drugs that he thinks will speed up his rehabilitation.

• The big game between O'Hare High School and Wilson is two days away. Late that night, some O'Hare students go to their rival school and spray-paint "Beat Wilson" in big letters on the sign by the school's entrance.

"How" we do things influences the morality of our actions. In the three examples described above, each person has a goal to achieve. Katie wishes to break up with her current boyfriend, Dan wants to play football at his best, and some students decide to exhibit school spirit. While their goals are honorable, they can choose any number of different means to achieve them. Those means would be more, or less, caring for the people involved.

An overemphasis on goals can lead to losing sight of the importance of the means used to achieve those goals. For instance, a goal of "Win at any cost" can result in harmful behavior by a student, an athlete, or a friend. Likewise, a business philosophy that advocates "Do whatever it takes to close the deal" opens the door to possible immoral business practices. Even during warfare, some means of attaining goals have traditionally been deemed unacceptable. According to the Catechism, "the end does not justify the means" (1752). Both the goals and the means to our goals need to be examined in determining a course of action. "How" we do things is one more important factor in determining the morality of our decisions. **E**

Activity E

Choose one of the following conflict situations and describe possible positive and negative approaches to resolving the conflict:

• Breaking up with a boyfriend or girlfriend

• A disagreement with a parent

• Hearing that someone is telling harmful stories about you

When and Where?—Circumstances That Can Color Our Actions

- Karen's mother and father are having a heated discussion about important family matters. Nevertheless, Karen walks in and says, "Mom, can you drive me to Denise's house right now?"

- Barbara's religion teacher invites a missionary to speak to her class. During the speaker's very personal and emotional presentation, Barbara sits in front of her and completes her math homework.

- It's 11:00 PM. Mike decides to play his favorite CD at full volume while the rest of his family tries to sleep.

We could continue this list, naming cases in which *when* or *where* significantly alters the impact of our actions. Of course, questions about when and where do not always tip the scales from right action to wrong or vice versa. However, since our moral decisions always occur in a time and a place, "when" and "where" are two more questions that can help us ground our moral decisions in concrete reality. **F** **G**

Activity F

Describe three situations in which "where" or "when" are important factors affecting the morality of a person's action.

Activity G

Here are twelve situations in which questions about the facts affect the morality involved. Explain how using one or more of the questions What? Who? Why? How? When? and Where? help determine the morality of the actions described.

1. A teenage boy irritates his younger brother while on a long trip in the family car.

2. In class a tenth-grader hoping to delay a scheduled test asks a lot of questions to which she already knows the answers.

3. A girl tells her father, "In driver's education class today we saw a film about using seat belts and air bags. From now on I know the first thing I'm going to do when I get in a car."

4. A boy comments to some friends who are trying out for the school play, "All theater people are gay."

5. In order to get money to attend an upcoming rock concert, three boys canvass their neighborhood pretending to be collecting money for a charity.

6. Because he doesn't want them to feel left out, a boy invites to a party some classmates whom his friends dislike.

7. As he boards a plane a passenger jokes about carrying a bomb in his suitcase.

8. A sports figure known for using illegal drugs is invited to speak at an awards banquet for young athletes.

9. A teenage girl seeking to lose weight takes diet pills that are potentially harmful.

10. A farmer uses chemical fertilizers and insecticides on his crops.

11. A coach who wants to embarrass the opposing team's coach tells his players to run up the score even though victory is already assured.

Stretching Our Point of View

Issues of morality are frequently heavily laden with emotion. Unless we're completely out of touch, the opinions we hold are supported by strong feelings. And the more personal and pressing the issues are, the more strongly we feel about them. In the midst of heated controversy, we may reduce a moral question to having only two answers—one right answer (the one we hold) and one wrong answer. While our feelings about an issue deserve to be taken seriously, we also need to step back at times and look at the subtleties that surround an issue. If we stretch our point of view, we might open the door to possibilities that we never knew existed. One way to do that is to seek alternatives.

For instance, on the issue of the use of nuclear weapons as moral or immoral we might want to jump quickly to a "yes" or "no" stance. However, if we force ourselves to arrive at a number of alternatives to simple yes or no answers, then we are engaging in a critical reasoning process.

For example, before concluding that nuclear weapons are or are not immoral, consider a few alternative positions on that issue:

- Nuclear weapons are moral. In the right hands they help prevent large-scale war.

- Offensive nuclear weapons are immoral, but strictly defensive weapons are acceptable.

- The spread of nuclear weapons to more and more countries is wrong and should be prevented.

- Building more nuclear weapons is wrong, but maintaining minimal levels of nuclear arms is acceptable.

- Nuclear weapons are not going to go away. Therefore, all countries possessing nuclear weapons should follow strict regulations concerning number, placement, and testing of such weapons.

Using such a process widens our perspective and makes our choices more thoughtful. **H**

Activity H

Choose one of the following issues and name six to ten different positions that a person might have about it:

- marijuana and other illegal drugs
- pollution
- treatment of people convicted of crimes
- terrorism
- world population

Considering Possible Effects

Another way to stretch our point of view and to identify facts is to imagine possible effects of different choices that we might make. Our present actions are the seeds out of which future consequences grow. As mentioned earlier, moral decision making is not an exact science. We cannot know beforehand all that will result from our actions. However, we can envision possible effects. For instance: The excuse, "I didn't mean it!" rings hollow from someone who plays baseball dangerously close to backyard windows. We are equally unsatisfied with, "I didn't mean it!" from the boy whose friend hurts herself after he pulls a chair out from under her. Similarly, someone who consistently drives recklessly should not be surprised when an accident happens. In each case, the people involved would benefit from considering possible effects of their actions.

The fast pace of much modern development makes attention to foreseeable effects difficult. A philosophy that states, "If it can be done, then do it," has led to scientific and technological developments whose effects have not always benefited humanity.

For example, in the case of cloning, test-tube babies, and chemical warfare, the jury is still out as to the possible long-term benefits or harm these experiments may have on society.

Issues such as these, as well as many of our everyday decisions, remind us: *Our actions have consequences.* We are shortsighted when we fail to consider probable effects of our actions.

For review . . .

1. Name and explain the questions that we can ask ourselves in trying to understand the acts involved in moral decision making.

2. Name two ways that *who* is involved can make a difference in moral decision making.

3. Explain how people could distort the means used in achieving their goals.

4. Name two ways that we can stretch our point of view during moral decision making.

Activity I

Name some possible effects that should be considered before doing any of the following:

- Attending an unsupervised party where young people will be drinking

- Going for a drive with a friend who does not have a license

- Signing a petition stating that one of your teachers is unfair

- Teasing someone whom you don't know very well about his family

- A community granting a permit to a developer to build a shopping mall on the site of a wheat field

- Staying out an hour past your curfew

Moral Discernment
Deciding for Yourself, Not by Yourself

What assistance is available to us in our attempts to evaluate our choices? If morality is a prescription for leading a good life, what would a "moral prescription" typically include? Here is a list of helps that we can call upon when we are honestly and thoughtfully trying to make the best moral decisions possible.

Talking to Others

In making our moral decisions, we need all the help we can get. Contrary to what we might feel at the moment of a crisis, we are probably not the first or only person to face this problem. Many people are available to us for assistance. If we have a friend or friends with whom we can share our deep concerns, then we may be able to talk our problem through to a solution. They need not be experts, and they may not always provide us with the answer to our problems. Usually, the most important function served by a friend is to be an active listener while we sort out the jumbled thoughts and feelings that we are carrying around inside us.

However, we need not confine our resources to the shared wisdom of friends from our own age group. Often young people rule out seeking help from parents, teachers, priests, or school counselors by declaring, "They wouldn't understand." Yet when they finally do talk over their problems with responsible adults, they exclaim, "Their understanding really helped!"

Consider the following questions about how you typically respond to difficult decisions that you face:

• Do I talk over my decisions with anyone?

• Who are the people from whom I normally seek counsel?

• Are there other people whom it would be beneficial for me to consult when faced with a difficult decision?

When faced with moral decisions, remember: Deciding *for* yourself does not mean deciding *by* yourself. **J**

Activity J

• Has there ever been a time when talking things over with a friend proved helpful? If so, describe the situation.

• Has there ever been a time when talking things over with a responsible adult proved helpful? If so, describe the situation.

Consulting the Church

The Church's teachings are a great depository of resources that can assist us in making moral decisions. The Church community of which we are a part is committed to carrying on the message of the great teacher, Jesus. As such, this community should be called into play when we consider the ways that we, too, can best mirror the message of Jesus in our lives.

Consulting the Church's teachings necessarily includes reading the Gospels, those crucial first statements of Christian teaching. That is, Jesus and his Church can never be separated. In chapter 5 we looked beyond Scripture and Jesus' teachings to the "many instruments and agents" of the Church that also assist us in moral decision making. When we examine specific areas of morality later in the course, we will refer to insights from official Church teaching on the issues involved. Sometimes Catholics of high-school age or older believe that they received the final word on Church teaching during their grade-school years. More often than not, actual Church pronouncements on moral matters are much more subtle and insightful than Church members expect. (Imagine how silly it would be to believe that we heard the full story about science or history in grade school. The same is true for Catholic moral teaching.) This entire course considers consulting the Church's teachings as an essential component of moral discernment.

Learning and Applying Principles

The last chapter discussed general statements about morality known as principles. Moral principles may be stated positively: "Do good; avoid evil." "Do unto others as you would have them do unto you." They might be stated negatively: "Do not kill." "Do not steal." Time-honored moral principles are part of our human legacy. They provide insights accumulated throughout history. We should not view moral principles as a straitjacket that confines us but rather as part of "the wisdom of the ages." When we treat principles with respect and analyze their possible meaning for today, we are participating in the great, ongoing search for truth that has been the glory of human history. Bringing general principles into our determinations is a valuable addition to moral discernment.

Knowing and Respecting the Law

The last chapter also discussed how important various expressions of law are in moral decision making. People who seriously protest laws that they consider unjust or immoral want laws changed not eliminated. They know that laws are an important part of public discussion about right and wrong. We live dangerously if we do not respect the laws of our various communities when we engage in moral discernment. **K**

Activity K

For many people—devout Jews, Christians, and Muslims—The Ten Commandments are perceived as valuable universal principles of morality. Choose one commandment and describe five implications it can have for your own decision making.

Check with Your Feelings

"If I could talk face to face with the pilot who dropped the bombs I would tell him we cannot change history, but we should try to do good things for the present and for the future to promote peace."

JOHN PLUMMER, "THE MEETING AT THE WALL," *GUIDEPOSTS*. OCTOBER, 1997.

Phan Thi Phuc placing a wreath at the Vietnam Veterans Memorial in Washington, Monday November 11, 1996

During the Vietnam War, which occurred during the late 1960s and early 1970s, one particular photograph received much media attention. It showed a young Vietnamese girl, Kim Phuc, running away from a village in flames, screaming in pain because she was burning from a plastic explosive known as napalm. Over twenty years later, this young girl—now a woman—again made the newspapers when she paid a visit to the Vietnam War Memorial in Washington, DC.

The picture of the burning girl touched many people in a way that news reports about the war did not. We might wonder why this particular picture should have had the impact that it did. Young children were being burned with napalm bombs for years during this particular war. The difference was that this picture moved people; it touched their feelings as no news reports of war casualties had previously done.

We know that our feelings can lead us astray. They can be manipulated and misguided and should not be the only word and certainly not the final word in our moral decision making. As the Catechism says, "Strong feelings are not decisive for the morality or the holiness of persons; they are simply the inexhaustible reservoir of images and affections in which the moral life is expressed" (#1768). However, feelings can also lead us to an awareness of truth that we might otherwise miss if we left feelings out of our decisions. Since morality involves actions in response to others, our feelings can serve as the driving force that leads to action on behalf of others. To be moral does not mean to be cold, passionless, and inhumanely detached from our feelings. Rather, it means to live life impassioned, afire with love. **L**

Activity L

1. Write an essay about an incident when your feelings influenced your behavior in a positive way.

2. How important a role do feelings play in your moral decision making? What role would you like feelings to play in your moral decision making?

Learn from Personal Experience

Everything that you have lived through, or will ever live through, has a message for you, a message you are to keep—a message that may appear meaningless or too painful to hold but that, after a time, reveals itself as essential to your missions in life.

ROBERT J. FUREY, *CALLED BY NAME*. [NEW YORK: CROSSROAD, 1996].

We are narrow minded if we never branch out beyond our limited experience of things. However, we are wise to learn from past experiences and to consider their lessons in our current moral decision making. Here are examples of viewing current dilemmas in a fruitful way through the lens of past experience.

- I'm not going to go to a party with those guys. I know from experience what will happen.

- Maybe you're better at writing a paper the night before it's due, but I need to work on it for days before I come up with something.

- One drink may not affect you, but I know what one drink does to me.

- Whenever I come home from visiting my father, I know my mother will be upset. I need to be very careful about what I say.

As we go about living, we experience many things about life, about people, and about who we are. When we reflect on our personal experience, we might notice how we instinctively respond to different people, such as authority figures, members of the other sex, family members, and people who belong to a group other than our own. We might discover that certain circumstances bring out the best in us, while in other situations we tend to fall short of what we would like ourselves to be. We might recall that certain past decisions were good ones and others were not.

Such reflection on personal experience is a valuable asset in moral decision making. Each of us is unique. Each of us carries around some information that no one else has; each of us has an exclusive viewpoint that no one else has in exactly the same way. In moral decision making, we should tap into our unique resource known as personal experience. **M**

Activity M

Reflect on your past experiences with the following. Give an example of how an experience with each—positive or negative—can help you in future decision making.

- an experience with an authority figure
- an experience with someone of the opposite sex
- an experience with someone very different from my usual acquaintances
- an experience that brought forth positive qualities in me
- an experience in which I responded with concern for another

Recognize and Scrutinize Your Values

- To me, being popular is very important. I want people at school to know me and to like me. I take care that I say the right things and wear the right clothes. I pay attention to the people who hang out with me. I want to belong to the group that people look up to.

- I value having a good time. Sure, I want to go to college and do well in life. But for now my philosophy is, "You're only young once."

- When I get older, I want to make lots of money so that I can lead a comfortable life and buy the things that make life enjoyable. I know that many people are deprived of basics, but I think that if you work hard you deserve the fruits of your labor. I intend to be one of those who are a success in life.

scrutinize—to examine various dimensions of a dilemma, especially so that overlooked aspects come to light

What we do over a long span of time depends very much on what we value. Our values are shaped by our culture, by our Church, by our family and friends, by all the persons and things that influence us. Sometimes the mix of influences on our values blends together smoothly—for example, family and friends agree on what's important, or our religion and our culture advocate similar values. Sometimes we experience values in conflict. Values, such as those expressed in the three statements above, influence the choices that people make.

Values are often subtle. Sometimes the values that are the most influential are so much a part of us that we don't even recognize them. (For example, if you are a North American and truly want to know what American values are, you would do well to spend time abroad. You may find that you value the availability of certain resources when you cannot obtain clean water, a heated or air-conditioned bedroom, or gas for your car. You may become more aware of the wastefulness of a typical North American lifestyle when you encounter people who share a bowl of rice for a family meal.) Since our values will come into play in our decision making, it is important to recognize them as much as possible and to **scrutinize** where they tend to lead us. **N**

For review . . .

5. According to the text what is typically the most important function that talking to others serves?

6. What does it mean to say that principles are "the wisdom of the ages"?

7. What contribution to decision making do feelings make?

8. Name three influences on our values.

Activity N

How could the elements of moral discernment —talking to others, consulting the Church, principles, feelings, experiences, and values—be applied to the following cases?

1. At a friend's party, seventeen-year-old Mitchell became intoxicated and while driving home struck a twelve-year-old boy crossing a street on his bike. Mitchell is found guilty of drunk driving and death by homicide. Since you have known Mitchell for many years, you are brought to court as a character witness before sentencing. While you are on the stand, a lawyer asks you, "What do you think should happen to Mitchell?"

2. You have just completed a lifesaving course and would like to work as a lifeguard at your local pool. A friend of yours who worked at the pool last year informs you that a sure way to get the job is to help in the re-election campaign of a local politician with whose views on major issues you disagree.

Judgment Guided by Prayer

The people of God believes that it is led by the Spirit of the Lord who fills the whole world. Moved by that faith it tries to discern in the events, the needs, and the longings which it shares with other men of our time, what may be genuine signs of the presence or of the purpose of God.

DOCUMENTS OF VATICAN COUNCIL II, "THE PASTORAL CONSTITUTION ON THE CHURCH IN THE MODERN WORLD," NUMBER 11.

Making a judgment about what is right or wrong can feel like a solitary, isolated experience. In Christianity, it is not meant to be. The moral discernment process already described indicates how we are to decide for ourselves but not by ourselves. When we turn our gaze inward, we imagine that we are alone there. However, Christian teaching proclaims that God resides in the very depth of our being. Prayer refers to the ways that we speak to and attempt to listen to our God. For Christians, turning inward to discover God's will is an important part of moral decision making. As the Catechism points out, "How can the Holy Spirit be our life if our heart is far from him?" (2744) In regards to morality, prayer means calling upon God, within us and among us, to help us in our decision making.

Many years ago a priest gave the following advice to a group of ninth-grade boys about to depart on summer vacation: "Never do anything you wouldn't do in front of your mother!" After the priest's talk, the boys joked about all the possible "summer fun" activities that this would rule out. However, the priest's folksy advice contained a kernel of wisdom. While we are not always under our mother's gaze,

communal prayer— praying together with a group of people

Christians believe that God looks upon us always as a loving, compassionate parent. Prayer serves to remind us of God's enduring presence with us.

Before Jesus made the decision about beginning his active life of ministry and preaching (after thirty years of unassuming work as a carpenter), he went aside to a desert place to be alone with God. Before facing the trials of his upcoming torture and death, he went to a garden to pray. In similar fashion, as part of our own judgment process, we would do well to go to a desert place—our room, a walk around the neighborhood, a church—to be alone with God. When faced with a difficult decision, praying about it echoes Jesus' prayer in the garden: "not what I want but what you want. . . . your will be done" (Matthew 26:39, 42). In praying we step back to listen to God. We pray to participate with God in creating the world through our actions. Indeed, "Prayer is an indispensable condition for being able to obey God's commandments" (Catechism, #2098).

Moreover, just as talking to others can reveal new possibilities to us in our moral decision making, so also praying with others can awaken us to new dimensions of God's will for us. Praying with others at Mass, before a class or a meal, or during a penance service—is an important way that Catholics demonstrate their prayer life. Again, in prayer the Spirit is at work within us and among us. Sharing prayer means sharing our deepest selves. **Communal prayer**, or prayer with others, adds a valuable dimension to moral judgment. **O**

Activity O

Write a prayer that you would find helpful to say prior to making an important decision.

Cultivate Humility and Humor

Having a process to follow when making moral decisions is helpful but not foolproof. No matter how much time and thought we put into making moral decisions, there will be times when we will make errors in judgment. We can cultivate attitudes and activities that can strengthen our capacity to pick ourselves up, ask for forgiveness, and move on with our lives.

You may not initially connect the words **humility** and *humor*, but actually they share the same derivation. Both humor and humility are rooted in the Latin word *humus*, meaning "earth," "ground," or "soil." Certainly, moral decision making is very serious business. However, when making judgments we shouldn't take ourselves so seriously that we are afraid to act. We are earthly creatures, prone to mistakes and filled with human faults. To remind ourselves of our human condition, we should laugh at ourselves, even while we do our best to make loving and correct judgments. A spirit of humor enables us to laugh at the mistakes we make because we are imperfect creatures. A spirit of humility nudges us to seek God's truth and not to think we are God. Applied to moral judgment humility keeps us grounded in who we are—creatures of God who should seek always to do God's will. **P**

humility—admitting the truth about who you are, especially about limitations that you possess

Dianne had a 4.0 grade point average. While in driver's education, she had no trouble acing the tests. The actual driving experience was another matter however. On her first day out with the instructor, she carefully backed out of a diagonal parking space but didn't back up quite far enough. As she began pulling forward her bumper hit the bumper of the instructor's car, which had been parked next to the driver's education car. Dianne was embarrassed as the story spread throughout the school, but soon she was laughing along with the other students about the irony of having hit the instructor's car.

Activity P

Describe in writing—or draw a cartoon depicting—a humorous look at moral decision making. Seek to demonstrate how humor can serve as a helpful addition to moral decision making.

Journey with Jesus

Thomas said to him, "Lord, we do not know where you are going. How can we know the way?" Jesus said to him, "I am the way, and the truth, and the life. No one comes to the Father except through me. If you know me, you will know my Father also."

JOHN 14:5–7a

In chapter four we looked specifically at the unique approach to morality that Jesus offers us. If we are moral decision makers worthy of the name, then we are seekers of truth and life. In Jesus we have someone whom we acknowledge as the Way, the Truth, and the Life. Our life's journey is filled with constant challenges and decisions. If we center constantly on Jesus, our journey may not go more smoothly, but it will certainly go more faithfully to what we hold dearest. After all, we want to make judgments that we are not only comfortable with but that we feel Jesus is calling us to make.

In our moral decision making, we journey with Jesus when we pray that his love so overwhelms us that we act lovingly toward others. We journey with Jesus when we pray the Gospels, hear the words of Jesus, and apply them to our lives. We journey with Jesus when we seek to listen to his direction each day.

Where does journeying with Jesus fit in a moral decision-making process? For Christians, it must color and shape every step of any process that seeks to make right judgments.

For review . . .

9. Why is moral decision making not meant to be a solitary experience for Christians?

10. What is the role of prayer in moral decision making?

11. What prayer did Jesus say in the garden the night before his death?

12. What Latin root meaning do the words *humor* and *humility* share? What does this Latin derivation remind us about our human condition?

13. What is the goal of our journey with Jesus in our moral decision making? **Q**

Activity Q

Read through recent newspapers or news magazines. Find a situation that called for moral decision making. Look back over the many elements of moral decision making described in this chapter. Apply each one to the problem you selected. Explain whether—and if so, how—each step could help a person in making a responsible decision about the problem.

Conclusion
Moral Decision Making—A Multifaceted Process

Looking back at all that conscientious decision making involves, we realize the enormity of the task. If we sincerely want to do it right, then we will make all of our moral decisions on the basis of what it means to act as Jesus would want us to act. We begin by trying to uncover the facts. From there we engage in discernment, seeking to determine the morality of all the possible choices we could make. Finally, we arrive at a judgment—as best we can, seeking to do God's will. Remember: Through the many decisions we make, we are creating who we are and we are contributing to our world. Decision making, especially in the big decisions we face, deserves such careful attention. Keep in mind these many steps involved in moral decision making as we examine specific areas of morality in part two of our course.

Let us pray . . .

Lord, grant me the serenity to accept the things I cannot change, the courage to change the things I can, and the wisdom to know the difference. Amen.

A Review of Part I

1. Write down key themes that you find expressed in each of the first eight chapters of this book.

2. For each theme, write a question that would apply that theme to topics covered in Part II of the book.

3. Keep these themes and these questions in mind as you examine specific moral issues during the second part of the course.

CHAPTER 9

Sex and Morality

Caring for Our Bodies, Ourselves, and Others

According to the Christian vision, we were created out of love, through love, and for love. Literally, sex has been associated with love and creativity from the moment of conception. Like all good things, misuse and manipulation of sex can cloud its beauty and goodness. The decisions that we make regarding our sexual capacities can enrich us or dehumanize us. In this chapter we will look at how our culture and Catholic tradition have perceived sex. We will name fundamental principles about sexual morality that reflect the Catholic vision. Finally, we will look at some specific cases to help us explore our own beliefs and attitudes related to sexual morality.

Chapter Overview

- Sexuality is more than physical; it is a drive toward fruitful union and reaching out to others.

- Some Christian groups have viewed bodily existence negatively.

- With its sacramental vision, Catholicism holds physical-sexual intimacy in high esteem.

- As with all dimensions of the human person, sexuality is open to abuse.

- Christian moral principles provide guidance for decision making in areas of sexual behavior.

Let us pray . . .

We praise you, Jesus, as Word-made-flesh. The holy finds a home in your earthy, bodily existence. You are one with us, a constant reminder that we, too, are holy—spirit and flesh. May the physical urges we experience lead us to appreciate the awesome wonder of the human body. May we always treat ourselves and others with respect, especially in our sexual behavior, ever conscious that we carry your Spirit within us and share that Spirit through word and touch, smiles and laughter, hugs and handshakes. Amen.

Before we begin . . .

Answer agree, disagree, or uncertain to the following statements.

1. Most sixteen-year-olds cannot have a deep love relationship.

2. If I were going out with someone, I would expect that person to be my best friend.

3. A double standard about sex exists in our society—one for boys and one for girls.

4. The majority of boys will go as far as girls will let them.

5. Boys are more interested in sex; girls are more interested in romance.

6. Most guys think that girls owe them something physical after they've gone out for a while.

7. I would be very upset if I were treated as a sex object.

8. Sexually explicit movies, magazines, and books are harmful and should be illegal or at least highly restricted and regulated.

9. Making available sexually explicit materials on the Internet should be a crime.

10. My religious upbringing has helped me understand and appreciate sex.

11. Values cannot be taught. Schools should concentrate on conveying factual information about sex rather than on shaping values about sex.

12. Sex is one of the most important aspects of a marriage relationship.

13. Generally speaking, young people today have healthier attitudes toward sex than their parents' generation.

14. Sexual morality has deteriorated over the past thirty years.

Sexual Expression

- Tracy and Rick, both juniors in high school, were in the school play together when they started dating. Their involvement became more and more intense. They began to spend most of their time alone with each other or talking on the phone. Gradually, Tracy began feeling a need for other people in her life. She wanted to tell Rick, but she didn't want to hurt him. Though their relationship continued, it became uncomfortable and unpleasant for her. She wondered how she could resolve this dilemma without hurting Rick.

- Marci and Frank have been married for fifteen years. They have never gone on a vacation alone since the first year of their marriage. Now they are about to be together without the children for an entire week! They feel like newlyweds—nervous, playful, excited, and yet anxious about how they'll get along without focusing on the children.

- Tom had found the magazine discarded on a bench weeks before. Since that time he has hidden the magazine amid the sports books in his room. Most nights when he is alone in his room doing homework, he takes out the magazine for a few minutes and pages through it, stopping briefly to look at each photo of a nude or a scantily dressed woman. At this point Tom has seen the pictures of each woman so many times that he feels as though he knows them. To Tom they are like family—a family that inhabits his world of secret fantasies. Lately, however, Tom has been thinking that he should throw out the magazine. He finds that something just doesn't feel right about looking at these pictures. He feels that he is violating himself and, perhaps surprisingly, violating the women in the pictures as well.

- Since Joe has become friends with Michele, he spends little time with his old crowd. Joe is happy to spend time joking and talking about life with Michele. From his new-found distance, Joe finds his friends' routine terribly immature. They drink and then act "macho." They get girls to drink with them and, if they're "lucky," to have sex with them. Joe thinks about telling his old friends that they should change their ways before any more damage is done.

Sex
Definitions and Attitudes

Sex! Few words are as exciting and frightening, as stimulating and alluring as the word *sex*. If we find that we are talking but that nobody is listening to us, we can change the topic to sex and immediately we have an attentive audience. Popular novels, television shows, and movies know that sex in the media will keep their audiences awake and attentive. (Honestly, isn't this the first chapter that you turned to when you picked up this book?)

Sex is part of the allurement that draws us out of ourselves and urges us to seek union with others. When we speak about sex, we can mean a great variety of behaviors, feelings, and experiences. Sexual activity includes kissing, flirting glances, holding hands, words of comfort and support, passionate embraces, as well as more intimate forms of sexual expression. Concerns about sex range from what we think about and talk about to how physically intimate we are with others.

All the incidents on the previous page relate to sex. Both the young couple struggling to hold in check the intensity of their sexual expression and the married couple seeking to rekindle the intensity of theirs describe real-life dramas in which sex plays a central role. The joys, the excitement, the attractions, and the problems related to sex are not limited by age, culture, social class, or lifestyle.

As with everything human, sex has a darker side. Sex can seem to control us, or it can be used to exploit us where we are most vulnerable. For instance, Tom's fascination with his sex magazine can become an obsession, while Joe's friends exploit others sexually.

Before discussing the morality of various sexual behaviors, we need to define terms and explore cultural attitudes that have influenced how we view the important dimension of our identity known as our sexuality. **A**

Activity A

Our attitude toward sex is greatly shaped by our culture. List at least five messages that various segments of our popular culture communicate to you about sex. Analyze those messages. (That is, are they positive or negative, do they help us appreciate ourselves and our sexuality better, do they provide helpful guidance for decision making regarding sex?)

Defining Sex: Sexuality Is More Than Our Bodies

> *. . . sexuality . . . is by no means something purely biological, but concerns the innermost being of the human person as such.*
>
> POPE JOHN PAUL II, *ON THE FAMILY*, NUMBER 11.

When it comes to describing what it means to be human, our language fails us. We may say, "I have a body" and "I have a soul." Such use of language is just a manner of speaking, an attempt to capture in words the richness and the subtlety of the human condition. In fact, as we live our lives, we cannot divide ourselves into such clear-cut dimensions as "body" and "soul." Similarly, our sexuality is not something that we have—as if our sexuality were merely something non-essential added onto who we are.

We are sexual creatures to our innermost being. That is, we do not simply have a body— male or female. Rather, sexuality names the way that we express ourselves as physical-spiritual creatures. Sexuality is a psychological, spiritual, and physical reality. These interlocking dimensions of our identity cannot be isolated one from another. As sexual beings, we are drawn out of ourselves to seek connections and fulfillment with others. (Even the boy who spends his nights gazing at sex magazines or searching the Internet for provocative web sites is seeking relationships of sorts.)

We can show love in different ways—with a touch or with a kiss, with words or with flowers. Likewise, we need to recognize that a great many of our actions are "sexual." In other words, when we talk to another person, we do so as sexual persons. When someone smiles at us or touches us, sexuality comes into play. Whether we are physically intimate with our friends or not, we communicate with them through our bodies; and our bodies are manifestations of our sexuality.

We lose the richness of who we are as sexual beings if we reduce sexuality to the "sex act" alone. In fact, sexuality does not always mean using our sex organs. Since our sexuality is not simply a biological function, we can actually achieve "sexual fulfillment" without ever experiencing physical sexual union. Similarly, we could be very involved physically with one or even with a number of people and still be sexually unfulfilled. By extension, "sexual harassment" means mistreating someone not only physically but also emotionally or psychologically because of their gender— including, of course, rape, the extreme form of physical abuse. Similarly, we are "sexy" insofar as we are alluring, exciting, intriguing, and interested in others. In short, *we are more than our bodies; and sex is more than a bodily function.* If we reduce sexuality to its physical component alone, we dehumanize sex. **B**

Activity B

Our sexuality draws us out of ourselves to seek union with another. Besides physical union, what are some ways that we can develop closeness with others? Besides physical-sexual abuse, what are some ways that people can mistreat others because of their gender?

Traditional Perspectives on Sex

When we attempt to identify the Christian vision of sexuality, we discover that throughout the ages two conflicting views about sex have existed. We can name one a *dualistic* view of sex and the other a *sacramental* view of sex. While the sacramental view has become more emphasized recently, both views have had a home in Christian thought. Before we identify the Christian vision of sexuality found in Scripture and in Church teaching, we need to appreciate these different ways that sex has been portrayed in our culture and tradition.

A Dualistic View—Good and Evil

dualistic view of the human condition— dividing the human into higher and lower components and labeling one evil

The *Catechism of the Catholic Church* notes that from the very beginning of the Christian story, some thinkers "have affirmed the existence of two eternal principles, Good and Evil, Light and Darkness, locked in permanent conflict . . . According to some of these conceptions, the world (at least the physical world) is evil, the product of a fall, and is thus to be rejected or left behind . . ." (285). Often accompanying such a **dualistic view** is a negative perspective on sex. In this type of dualism, sex is associated with the body, with the lower or inferior dimension of our humanity; and it is perceived as evil. In this view physical-sexual activity is simply animalistic behavior, giving ourselves over to uncontrolled drives that originate in our base instincts. Therefore, sex is a bodily drive that distracts us from developing our higher powers, our spirituality, and that keeps us from grace. At best, sex is a necessary evil, a duty performed by married couples only to create new "souls." Self-control is the primary virtue needed to overcome this evil. To lose oneself in sexual pleasures smacks of sinfulness akin to drunkenness and gluttony.

While this negative attitude toward sex is described here in an oversimplified manner, nonetheless it does represent one strain that has been present within our Catholic tradition. When we too readily associate sex with sin, and when we perceive moral teaching about sex to be only a "thou shalt not," then we are reflecting the dualistic view of sex that authentic Christian teaching has been trying to correct from the Church's beginning. **C**

Activity C

The Catechism identifies six movements that it indicates have historically promoted an inadequate view of the relationship between the physical and the spiritual sides of human nature. Look up each of the following and briefly describe that movement's point of view:

- Pantheism
- Manichaeism
- Deism
- Dualism
- Gnosticism
- Materialism

A Sacramental View—A Holistic View of Being Human

Another view of nature and of our human condition has also been present in our religious and cultural tradition. This view is a more holistic perspective—that is, it focuses on the *whole* person as an integrated unit. It seeks to avoid rejecting any facets of who we are as physical-spiritual creatures. It affirms the fullness of our human reality as holy. This view cautions against too readily separating natural from supernatural, body from soul, or the physical from the spiritual. It especially cautions against labeling physical reality as evil. Rather, it portrays our bodies as sacred vessels to be distinguished but not separated from our total being.

We can name this viewpoint "sacramental" because it views the physical as a doorway into the sacred, just as the sacraments do. In other words, sacraments rely on physical objects and bodily actions to help us keep in touch with God. Immersion in water, anointing with oil, sharing bread and wine, the touch of hands, and a kiss as a sign of peace are integral to Christian sacraments. In a sacramental vision these physical objects and actions convey the holy to us. Therefore, the holy is not separate from nature. On the contrary, nature is revealer of the holy.

In this view sex is seen in relationship to the whole person. Our spirituality cannot be divorced from our sexuality. Our sexuality is a significant expression of our spirituality and is meant to be an instrument of grace. God's goodness can be found in our sexuality just as it can be found in everything that is "natural." God's gift of sex is part of the beauty and goodness of creation urging us toward union with others. Marriage is a sacrament, and the life-giving sexual expression shared by married couples is sacred.

For various reasons the inherent goodness of sex has not always been a strongly conveyed message in our Christian tradition. ("Be sexy!"

is a phrase that we hear in popular magazines, at our local video stores, and from radio stations but not from our parish pulpits.) However, the sacramental view of sexual reality, which is so central to Christian and especially Catholic tradition, reminds us of the goodness of our bodies and of the sacredness of our bodily activity. Our physical-spiritual "wholeness" is a "holiness"— a good gift given to us by God, who is good and holy. **D**

For review . . .

1. Explain the statement, "As with all aspects of our humanity, sex has a darker side."
2. What does it mean to say that "Sexuality is more than our bodies"?
3. Name and describe the two views toward sex present in our tradition.

Activity D

How has your religion helped you appreciate sexuality and your body to a greater degree?

Fundamental Christian Teaching about Sex

God created humans out of love for us. God created us to love each other. The basic Christian teaching about sex is that it is good because it was created for love.

Sexuality Is Part of the Good News of the Christian Message

If it truly mirrors the vision of its founder, then Christian teaching about sex is meant to be good news. If God's message in Christ is Word of God made flesh, then we, too, should trust that our own bodily existence—our flesh—is also part of God's good news. However, "good news" about sex does not mean that the Christian message is easy or simple to follow. **E**

Activity E

Each of the following statements has been made in reference to sex. However, some of the statements reflect the Christian message about sex; others do not.

For each statement decide:

- Which statements do you agree with or disagree with?
- Do certain statements more than others reflect the attitude toward sex that members of your peer group exhibit?
- Which of these statements can you imagine Jesus saying?
- Which statements do you think truly convey good news about sex?

1. If it feels good, do it.
2. Our sexuality is a treasure to be cherished.
3. How do you know what it's like until you've tried it?
4. Our bodies are sacred and sacramental signs of the holy.
5. It's okay to have sex as long as you don't hurt anybody.
6. Any level of sexual activity is a sacred trust—to be shared honestly, caringly, and responsibly.
7. Enjoy it now; worry about the consequences later.
8. Sexual intimacy is sharing on a very deep level. Physically, it symbolizes psychological and spiritual intimacy of equal depth.
9. When we did it, we agreed there would be no strings attached.
10. Sexual involvement with another represents a serious commitment.
11. If two people truly love each other, then it's okay to have sex.
12. Sometimes love means saying "no."
13. Everybody does it. If I don't, then there must be something wrong with me.
14. I feel a lot of pressure to experience sex, but such intimacy is too important for me to give in to such pressure.
15. Nowadays it's expected that teens have sex. If I have a chance, why should I be any different?

Sex in Scripture—Sex Is Good but Corruptible

Song of Solomon— a book of the Hebrew Scriptures; a love song between a man and a woman that also serves as an analogy for the love God has for people

adultery—sex between two people at least one of whom is married to someone else

idolatry—being all consumed with one thing and treating it as if it were more important than God

To discover Christian teaching about sex, we turn initially to the Scriptures. In the Hebrew Scriptures, discussion about sexual morality is often intermingled with other matters, such as concern for property rights. Jesus himself says little on the matter. (In Matthew's Gospel Jesus addresses sexual morality-related questions in only three passages; in Mark's Gospel only once. John's Gospel contains a story in which, as we will see, Jesus saves the life of a woman who was accused of **adultery** and about to be stoned to death.) However, two general principles regarding sex that we can deduce from Scripture are: Sexuality is part of God's good creation; like all dimensions of our humanness, sexuality can be corrupted and become sinful.

In light of the first principle, we need constantly to remind ourselves that God created us as sexual beings and said, "It is good." From a Christian viewpoint, our bodies—including our sexuality—are temples of the Holy Spirit. When we were created, sex was not an after-thought. Our lovemaking and life-giving sexual expression are essential to our existence. That is, God did not say, "I've made perfect humans, but now I have to mess things up and add sex." Rather, the refrain echoed throughout the biblical creation story is that "God saw everything that he had made and indeed, it was very good" (Genesis 1:31).

The God of the Bible is passionate about creation, especially about the wonderfully intricate creature known as the human person. The Bible also constantly warns about the danger of **idolatry**—that is, of being all consumed with one thing and treating it as if it were more important than God.

The two biblical principles regarding sex are manifest in the following two quotes.

The first quote, from the **Song of Solomon**, beautifully portrays the first principle's positive outlook on sex. (Also known as the "Song of Songs," this book of the Bible does not hesitate to use sexual imagery to speak about our passionate God.)

> *Let him kiss me with the kisses of his mouth!*
> *For your love is better than wine,*
> *your anointing oils are fragrant,*
> *your name is perfume poured out;*
> *therefore the maidens love you.*
> *Ah, you are beautiful, my love;*
> *ah, you are beautiful;*
> *your eyes are doves.*
> *Ah, you are beautiful, my beloved,*
> *truly lovely.*
>
> SONG OF SOLOMON 1:1–3, 15–16

The second quote, from Saint Paul's letter to the Romans, is a reminder of the second principle, that we need to take care that sex not become distorted, an instrument of harming ourselves or others.

> *Therefore, do not let sin exercise dominion in your mortal bodies, to make you obey their passions. . . . but present yourselves to God as those who have been brought from death to life.*
>
> ROMANS 6:12, 13b

The first Christian principle about sexuality affirms that sex is a gift that is meant to be used creatively and lovingly, to be linked to concern for others and community life, and to be enjoyed and refined. In that sense sexual passion mirrors the passion that God feels for creation. The second principle about sexuality reminds us that regarding sexual activity we need to be critical of our actions, our motives, and our society's values. We can misuse our sexuality; we can subvert what is meant to be creative and turn it into a destructive force. (For instance, sex can be used to show love or to sell cars, to give of ourselves or to take from another, to show someone we care or to demonstrate carelessness.)

It is important to remember: *The fact that sex can be corrupted in no way diminishes its beauty, its blessedness, and its awesome power to be an expression of creativity and love.* Actually, the two principles about sex found in Scripture apply similarly to all other dimensions of human life—each gift that we are endowed with is meant to serve the good, yet each can be corrupted. Our capacity for speech can be used

creatively or destructively. Also our capacity for eating and drinking can be used creatively or destructively. Indeed, our use of dancing and writing, of sunshine and water, of automobiles and electricity, and of all other natural resources and manufactured products can be used for good or evil purposes. However, sex is such an intimate dimension of who we are that to misuse it in ourselves or to abuse it in another violates our deepest self. **F**

Activity F

- Describe ways that two natural, human capacities can be used either destructively or creatively.

- Describe ways that two manufactured products can be used either destructively or creatively.

Sex in Christian Tradition
The Marriage Ideal

The spouses' union achieves the twofold end of marriage; the good of the spouses themselves and the transmission of life.
CATECHISM, #2363

Christian teaching about sex holds physical-sexual expression in high esteem. By viewing sex in the context of marriage, it links sex with the creation of new life, and with love, community, and sacramentality. Church teaching proclaims that physical union between two people should not be divorced from these four important elements. Because of this exalted view of physical intimacy, traditional Church teaching considers marriage to be the only state ideally suited for sexual union. Sexual union is meant to be so precious and such a deep level of sharing that it finds its natural home amid the love, the commitment, the permanence, and the public affirmation that marriage provides.

Church Teaching on Sex in Marriage

Church teaching views sex in marriage as serving the following four goals:

First, physical-sexual activity is intimately linked to bearing and raising children.

Second, but of equal importance, physical union represents full and complete sharing of life in love between two people. That is, sex in marriage is both life giving and love giving, an expression of mutual commitment to each other and to family life.

Third, sexuality finds meaning in relation to community. In other words, our sexuality is not for ourselves alone. In marriage, the "community" involved is at least two people and potentially a third—namely, a child who could be born as the result of sexual union. In addition, sexual activity has an impact on a larger community. A goal for Christians is to become more caring individuals, people more sensitive to others' needs. Sex and marriage cannot be divorced from these community goals. A happy and wholesome sex life can help married couples love life and share themselves more lovingly with others.

Finally, marriage is a sacrament. In marriage a couple may experience their God and may serve as a sign of God's presence to each other and others. God, who is creator and lover, is present in every aspect of the life of a married couple—including their "sex life." **G**

Activity G

Answer agree, disagree, or uncertain to the following statements. Write a sentence or two explaining each of your answers.

1. The commitment of marriage is outdated in today's society.

2. I view marriage more as a restriction than an opportunity.

3. Married couples today experience more pressure on their relationship than married couples in the past did.

4. Practically everyone I know who is my age would like to marry when they are older.

5. Most people today still consider marriage to be a serious and sacred commitment.

Sex as Language

The *Catechism of the Catholic Church* speaks about sex in many ways. For instance, it describes sex as "language." If sex is a language, a means of communication, what possible messages does it communicate? According to the Catechism it should speak of a love so strong that a man and a woman would want to commit themselves totally to each other until death. It should speak of self-giving and the joy and the pleasure that come from giving yourself exclusively to another for the rest of your life. In other words, sex speaks most profoundly in the intimate sexual expression of marriage.

However, in today's society there are voices calling for an acceptance of intimate sexual expression apart from marriage. What does sex communicate when it is detached from marriage? Here are three alternative views of what sex may communicate as advocated today.

Recreational Sex

recreational sex— a view of sexual activity as the pursuit of pleasure with no constraints other than mutual consent

Only the most insensitive person would consider sex to be a form of communication equal simply to a handshake or a phone call. On the other hand, there are those who recommend that engaging in sex for the fun of it is reason enough. *Recreational sex* says, "If it feels good, do it." The only prerequisite is mutual consent—both parties agree that "whatever happens, happens. I am not responsible for you; you are not responsible for me." (Of course, even if the sex is consensual, if a child is born of the union both people will be legally responsible for the child. The father is responsible for paying child support until the child is eighteen, and both parents are legally responsible for seeing that the child is taken care of and raised in a loving environment.) We will explore this position further in the upcoming discussion of the "playboy philosophy."

Emotional-Relationship Sex

emotional-relationship sex— a view of sexual activity as being acceptable when the two people involved feel love for each other

The second perspective on sex as language is "If two people feel as though they truly love each other, then intimate sex is a natural and accept- able way to express those feelings." In contrast to recreational sex, **emotional-relationship sex** takes the quality of a relationship into account. Two people who have established a relation-ship add sexual intercourse to the ways they relate to each other. Supposedly, they engage in sex with a sense of mutual responsibility and respect. However, the responsibility ends as soon as circumstances change, such as when one of the two no longer feels love for

the other or a relationship with someone else starts growing. Surprisingly, what the couple plans to do if the woman becomes pregnant is an issue often not addressed. Rules underlying sex in such a relationship are unwritten and subject to change. For instance, sex that begins as a desire to express love can continue even after love dies. In this case, it becomes sex for convenience rather than sex as an expression of love. To the pleasure principle, emotional sex adds the feelings one has for the other as the basis for sexual intimacy. Thus the term *emotional-relationship sex.*

Almost-Committed Sex

almost-committed sex— the view that intimate sexual activity is acceptable when the two people have expressed a degree of commit- ment to each other, such as during engagement

Today, long engagements are more the rule than the exception. There are those who suggest that an "almost total commitment" makes intimate sex acceptable and even beneficial. "**Almost total commitment**" situations might include a couple who are living together, who are planning on getting engaged sometime in the future, or who are already engaged. However, if you talk to any married couple, invariably you will hear from them that "living together" or being engaged is not the same as being married. There is something total and transforming about the union of two people in marriage.

Church teaching sees full physical sexual expression as communicating more than just pleasure, more than just a serious relationship, and even more than an almost total commitment between two people. Rather, Church teaching affirms that the fullness of sex is meant for the fullness of marriage. Only married sex combines

the recreative (pleasure-sharing) with the unitive (love-expressing) and the procreative (life-giving) characteristics of sex. These three qualities together manifest what the fullness of sexual expression is meant to communicate. **H**

For review . . .

4. Name two general principles regarding sex that can be deduced from Scripture.

5. How could sex become a form of idolatry?

6. What imagery does the Song of Solomon use to describe the relationship between God and God's people?

7. List the four goals of marriage as put forth in recent Church teaching.

8. Name and describe the three types of sex-as-language described in the text.

Activity H

For each of the types of sexual expression listed above, write a paragraph describing what message it communicates. Begin the paragraphs:

Recreational sex says . . .   Emotional-relationship sex says . . .

Almost-committed sex says . . .   Married sex says . . .

Examining Specific Situations Related to Sexual Morality

Forty years ago in a Catholic high school religion class, typically a time would be assigned for a priest to take aside the boys and a nun to gather the girls together. A series of classes would be given over to "sex talks." During that time the sexual thoughts, words, and actions that were declared sinful would be clearly spelled out. Often the teacher would painstakingly delineate those thoughts, words, and actions that were lesser sexual sins from those that were more serious sexual sins. There was something comforting and reassuring about this approach to sex instruction. Everyone knew what was allowed and what was forbidden in regard to sex. No one needed to worry about differences in who was involved, about their ages, about their relationship, about their motives, or about any other variables. Church teaching on sexual matters was clear and precise. In addition, all of society—including television, popular songs, books, and movies—generally upheld the same standards of conduct.

The approach to sex instruction employed forty years ago has generally been discarded today as being too legalistic, too focused on the negative, and not adequately effective. Nowadays, sex education in religion or health classes is more likely to start in kindergarten.

A discussion about sexual behavior is not just about sin but is also likely to refer to physical and psychological dangers. The change in approach, however, does not mean that the Church has changed its stance on what is sexually right and wrong. This stance may appear old-fashioned to young Christians because the messages they are receiving from other dimensions of their culture have changed dramatically. In the current culture young people are being hit with a great barrage of conflicting opinions and viewpoints about sex. At times, it may feel as if Church leaders and teachers are pushing them in one direction while much of popular culture is pulling them in another. Meanwhile, young people must contend with intense and newly awakened sex drives but with prospects of marriage postponed to an increasingly distant future.

In the midst of such turmoil and confusion, naturally our sexuality seeks expression in fact and in fantasy. Boys might dream the "playboy fantasy": "There are sexy girls out there who want to go to bed with me, with no strings attached!" Girls might dream a romance-novel dream: "There's a boy out there who is strong but sweet and who will love me deeply enough for me to give myself to him completely!"

Certainly, with something as important and personal as our sexuality, we need more to go on than our fantasies and dreams. We also want more to base our decisions on than the plots presented to us by movies and television. A film-maker's primary concern is to make a movie that will show a profit rather than a movie presenting sexual values. And we live dangerously and not very responsibly if we wait to decide where we stand on the pre-martial sex issue until we find ourselves in the heat of passion, in the frenzy of a party, or in an alcohol-aided lethargy.

Sexually transmitted diseases, the epidemic of unwanted teenage pregnancies, the availability of abortion, and the lack of guidance from many elements within society create the need for us to develop a thoughtful, careful, and responsible sexual morality. Self-control, restraint, saying "no," and concern for more than immediate gratification continue to play a much-needed role in our decisions about sex. Moreover, we need guidance from more than television talk shows and magazines sold at supermarket checkout counters. In other words, decisions about our sexuality are so important that they deserve our fullest effort and attention. ▮

Jim and Joann

How Should We Respond to Our Sexual Urges?

Jim and Joann's relationship began slowly. They met at a party and started to seek each other out at social gatherings. Eventually, they started dating and spending most of their time together.

For the entire next year, Jim and Joann dated each other exclusively. Although they didn't talk about sex directly and although sex has not been the major focus of their relationship, Jim and Joann have become increasingly intimate physically. During the times when they are alone together, they have held to an unspoken rule about "how far to go." Neither Jim nor Joann take their physical involvement lightly.

Whenever they step beyond the boundaries that they unconsciously set for themselves, they feel uncomfortable and find themselves pulling back.

With the junior prom just a few weeks away, Jim and Joann want the night to be special. It seems to be an appropriate time to show how much they love each other; and, with a little planning, the opportunity for privacy will be available. Without discussing the matter with each other, both Joann and Jim wonder if prom night would be the perfect occasion to overstep the boundaries that they have established for themselves.

Activity I

1. Interview someone over fifty. Ask them to name two television shows and two movies from their youth that dealt in some way with sex or boy-girl relationships. What messages do they remember being communicated in those shows? How were the messages communicated?

2. Name two television shows and two movies of today that deal in some way with sex or boy-girl relationships. What messages do they communicate? How do they communicate these messages?

3. Compare and contrast the shows of forty years ago with those of today. What trends do you see?

This scenario is too brief to capture all of the subtleties that are present in a relationship. However, let us consider some questions that this young couple might ask themselves.

Imagine that the prom night arrives, and, after the planned festivities, Jim and Joann steal away and have sexual intercourse for the first time. What effect would this experience have on them individually and on their relationship? What are possible far-reaching effects the experience might have? Or imagine that before prom night arrives, Jim and Joann talk to each other about their desires and decide that they will refrain from becoming more intimate physically—especially on prom night. What effect would this decision have on themselves and on their relationship? Which decision would more likely lead to personal growth and more clearly reflect concern for each other?

A decision to engage in full physical-sexual intimacy outside of marriage usually leads to a less than satisfying, maturing, and loving experience of sex. Studies indicate that intimate physical-sexual activity among teenagers never solves problems and more frequently worsens them. The following is a list of problems that can develop for sexually active adolescents:

- Experiencing a type of commitment to another without the structures and supports of a marriage commitment

- Changing the focus of a relationship from enjoying each other and growing together to experiencing physical sex with each other

- Experiencing a change in other significant relationships, such as with parents and with other close friends of both sexes

- Feeling pressure to continue a relationship which statistically has little chance of ending in marriage

- Feeling more invested in and committed to the relationship than either person originally intended

- Feeling as though the relationship is a grown-up relationship rather than one of youthful fun

- Feeling pressures resulting from deep *physical* intimacy and self-giving, unmatched by *total* intimacy and self-giving

- Fearing pregnancy

Activity J

Look over the reasons listed here why unmarried teens should refrain from engaging in full physical-sexual intimacy. Do you think any of the reasons mentioned should not be included? Are any of the reasons not ones that you had thought about? Can you think of other reasons that you would add to the list? Write your response to the list.

Activity K

Straightening up desks at the end of the day, the morality teacher picks up a piece of paper that had been dropped on the floor. She reads the note scribbled in a student's handwriting:

Chrissie,

Is this class boring or what? I can't wait until tonight. I'm definitely going to hook up with Mike 'cause he's so hot! Anyway, do you think I should hook up with Russ, too? I don't know. I'll wait and see. This weekend will be great!

B.J.

If you were the teacher who found this note in her classroom, and you wanted to design a lesson to address sexual attitudes and behaviors among your students, what would the lesson plan look like? What messages would you want to communicate most strongly? What activities would you recommend to get across your messages? Are there approaches to dealing with this topic that you would caution the teacher NOT to use? What would some of these be? Why would the methods you recommend be more effective than others?

Playboy/Playgirl Philosophy

When we consider decisions about physical-sexual involvement, we need to recognize the values and pressures placed upon us by our culture. For the past few decades, a persistent message given to us by the dominant culture has been the **playboy/playgirl philosophy**. We can paraphrase that philosophy in these words:

playboy/playgirl philosophy— the belief that sex should be engaged in strictly for pleasure, with few if any restrictions

All of us—men and women, young and old—have a right to sexual pleasure with no strings attached. We should seek it and get it as often and with whomever we want. Anyone who suggests otherwise is "hung up," "out of it," and definitely not "cool."

Essentially, the playboy/playgirl philosophy advocates "anything goes" in sexual matters. This type of person thinks restricting sex to relationships involving love and commitment may make sense for older people but not for youth who are supposed to be experimenting and having fun. The fear of AIDS has added some caution and hesitancy to this mentality, but it has not eliminated it. Certain restrictions apply.

Until we scrutinize the unrealistic sexual values advocated by much of the Hollywood dream machine and recognize the pressures that they place on us, we will not be free to make wholesome, mature, and loving choices regarding our own physical-sexual behavior.

For example, a healthy diet involves planning, restraint, and thoughtful selection of the foods that we eat. Similarly, healthy sex involves restraint as well as planned, thoughtful, and conscientious decision making. Our diet affects ourselves directly and others indirectly. Sexual involvement directly affects at least two

people and, to varying degrees, a wide circle of family, friends, and acquaintances.

Finally, as married couples can attest, there are many ways to show love in a relationship. When questioned about what keeps them together, married couples typically rank physical sexual activity closer to number ten than number one on their list of important factors. Open communication and even cooperation with household chores and family responsibilities rank as more important for most married couples. As one writer puts it, "Real love is very ordinary: putting-out-the-garbage love, visiting the hospital love, cutting down on the drinking love" (William J. O'Malley SJ in *America*, 15 April 1989). **L**

Activity L

Our sexuality can add to the intensity, the excitement, the joy, and the meaning of our lives. Thoughtfulness, consideration of others, responsibility, and even restraint in sexual expression do not negate these positive aspects of our sexuality. Write about a novel, a television show, or a movie that you feel depicts sexuality in a positive light. Explain why.

Playboy/Playgirl Restrictions

- Don't rape. (Nevertheless, 90,000 rapes are reported annually; and it is estimated that almost forty percent of rapes and attempted rapes are not reported to the police. More than forty percent of all rapists know or are "friends" of their victims.)

- Don't get pregnant if you don't want to. (And yet abortions outnumber live births in some communities, and the number of "children having children" places a burden on families and social-service agencies alike.)

- Don't spread or contract sexually transmitted diseases, especially AIDS. (However, it is important to remember that most people infected with AIDS show no symptoms of illness and may not know that they are carriers of the disease. Moreover, popularly advocated methods of protection are far from fail-safe.)

- Don't become committed. Some voices in our society have been calling for more responsible attitudes toward physical-sexual activity. However, we still find a persistent playboy/playgirl message in much of our media—television, movies, and popular magazines. The television show that glorifies the leading man who sleeps with a different beautiful woman each episode—or at least tries to— suggests to us that we fall short of the playboy/playgirl ideal if we desire to love someone rather than to sleep with someone unattached. Many movies espouse the pleasure of sex and downplay the joys of committed relationships. The excitement of "casual sex" sells movies. In the real world, sex cannot be casual. Too much is at stake.

CROWDS LOOK AT **AIDS** QUILTS ON DISPLAY OUTSIDE THE **WHITE HOUSE**, **WASHINGTON DC.**

Nikki and Bonnie

Developing Our Sensitivity toward Others

Already by eighth grade, Nikki and Bonnie had developed a reputation. They were two girls who were physically mature for their age and often hung out with boys a few years older than they were. Their classmates began to look upon them as "easy." Many of the other girls avoided them so that they, too, wouldn't get a "reputation." Boys called the two girls names and joked about them, even though quite a few boys thought, "I wouldn't mind doing it with Nikki or

Bonnie. They're experienced and they want it anyway, so nobody would get hurt."

For whatever reasons, at times both Nikki and Bonnie lived up to their reputation, and many times they were hurt. Throughout their high school careers, the love that both girls desperately wanted eluded them. Hopefully, Nikki and Bonnie will grow to love themselves more. Hopefully, someday each of them will find someone who will love her for herself—body, mind, and soul.

The story of Nikki and Bonnie reminds us that in sexual morality, as in all other areas of morality, a central question is, "Are people getting hurt?" That is, by my attitudes, my words, or my actions is anyone being used or abused, treated as less than a precious, unique, invaluable expression of God's goodness?

In pondering these questions, we can gain insight by reading the Gospel story of Jesus and the adulteress. The story contains two important teachings: Our moral condition is a matter that involves our God and us, and God loves us in spite of our faults.

Early in the morning he came again to the temple. All the people came to him and he sat down and began to teach them. The scribes and the Pharisees brought a woman who had been caught in adultery; and making her stand before all of them, they said to him, "Teacher, this woman was caught in the very act of committing adultery. Now in the law Moses commanded us to stone such women. Now what do you say?" They said this to test him, so that they might have some charge to bring against him. Jesus bent down and wrote with his finger on the ground. When they kept on questioning him, he straightened up and said to them, "Let anyone among you who is without sin be the first to throw a stone at her." And once again he bent down and wrote on the ground. When they heard it, they went away, one by one, beginning with the elders; and Jesus was left alone with the woman standing before him. Jesus straightened up and said to her, "Woman, where are they? Has no one condemned you?" She said, "No one, sir." And Jesus said, "Neither do I condemn you. Go your way, and from now on do not sin again."

JOHN 8:2–11

In this incident—one of the few passages in which Jesus addresses matters related to sexual morality—we encounter a compassionate, not a condemning Jesus. We meet someone who perfectly models the difficult balance expected of Christians between condemning the sin but loving the sinner. In fact, Jesus seems much more upset with those who would cast stones at her than with the sinner herself.

Jesus sees the adulteress as a sinner but even more as a child of God, something forgotten by her accusers. Nikki and Bonnie also experienced this forgetfulness in attitudes and actions of "good" people. From the story about Jesus and the adulteress, we can readily identify what Jesus' attitude toward Nikki and Bonnie might be. **M**

Denise's Yearbook—What Makes Something Obscene?

While looking through Denise's yearbook, her mother finds notes from boys written to Denise that contain sexually suggestive drawings and that are filled with harsh words about sex. When her mother confronts her about these notes, Denise simply tells her that some boys at her school just like to joke around that way.

Obscene literally means "offstage." During classical Greek and Roman drama, certain actions—namely, physical-sexual activity and dying—were not performed on stage, in public view, but took place only offstage. Sex and dying have a sacredness about them that makes them deserving of special treatment. When we cheapen either experience, we risk cheapening our deepest, most intimate human experiences. Language, movies, and magazines are obscene when they insensitively portray material that deserves more careful treatment.

The boys who scribble sexually suggestive sayings and drawings in Denise's copybook

risk belittling the wonderful human capacity for life and love. While sexuality can be discussed and displayed humorously and playfully, we need to be sensitive to how we might slip into or condone an obscene treatment of sex. As one theologian puts it, "Physical sex, therefore, is the language or expression of love. . . . The language we use should mirror properly the love we actually have" (Matthew F. Kohmescher, *Good Morality Is Like Good Cooking*. [New York: Paulist Press, 1987]).

obscene—
literally means "offstage." An insensitive, public portrayal of what should be kept private and intimate, such as sex and dying

Activity M

Place yourself in the scene of Jesus and the adulteress. Answer the following questions.

1. What is the difference between Jesus' attitude and treatment of the woman and that of the scribes and Pharisees in the story?

2. What do you think Jesus was writing on the ground? Why would this cause the elders to walk away? Or was it what he said?

3. Can you think of how the attitude of the elders and that of Jesus could be exhibited in a situation today?

4. In what specific ways might you practice the attitude of Jesus toward others?

Rape: When Sex Becomes Violence

"Can you believe it?" he asked his friend. "We had more than a few drinks. We were having a good time. She was definitely into it. We had already gone pretty far when at the last minute she yells, 'Stop! Don't!' and pushes me away. Well, it was too late then. I wasn't about to stop! Now she's calling it rape!"

rape—forcing sex on an unwilling partner

acquaintance rape—forcing sex on someone known by the assailant

date rape—rape that occurs in the context of a date or a dating relationship

Rape *is the forcible violation of the sexual intimacy of another person. It does injury to justice and charity. Rape deeply wounds the respect, freedom, and physical and moral integrity to which every person has a right. It causes grave damage that can mark the victim for life.*

CATECHISM, #2356

Based on the information provided in this story, do you think that the young man is correct in his assessment? Does this incident describe a young woman who led him on and then refused to take responsibility for the consequences; or is this a case of inflicting unwanted, forced sex upon an unwilling partner? If the latter is true, as it appears to be, then the young man is morally and legally wrong in his actions. By definition, rape is forcing sex upon an unwilling partner, regardless of the circumstances. Rape occurs if forced sex occurs when a couple have been dating, when a couple are married, when both parties are drunk, and when—as in the above story—one party initially appears willing. **N**

Both women and men can be raped. Recent studies indicate that a surprisingly large number of men were raped when they were growing up. This revelation is surprising because men, like women, often hide this information even from their closest friends and family members. When a victim knows the person who rapes him or her, it is known as **acquaintance rape**. (One form of acquaintance rape is **date rape**—rape that occurs while two people are on a date.) As the following quote points out, acquaintance rape accounts for the greatest percentage of rapes that occur.

Statistics on rape are notoriously unreliable, but most observers now agree that a conservative estimate suggests that at least one out of three women will be raped or will be the victim of attempted rape in her lifetime. . . . What is particularly troubling is the context in which rape occurs. . . . Rape is not committed only by strangers. In a study of nearly one thousand women, Diana Russell found that only 11 percent had been raped (or had been the victims of attempted rape) by strangers, while 12 percent had been raped by "dates," 14 percent by "acquaintances," and 14 percent by their husbands.

KAREN LEBACQZ, "LOVE YOUR ENEMY: SEX, POWER, AND CHRISTIAN ETHICS," IN LOIS K. DALY, EDITOR, *FEMINIST THEOLOGICAL ETHICS* [LOUISVILLE, KY: JOHN KNOX PRESS, 1994]. **O**

Activity N

Do you think that most teenagers and young adults would label the above scenario as rape? Do you think men and women would typically view the situation similarly or differently? Explain.

Activity O

Search the Internet, an almanac, or other reference source to find the most recent statistics on rape, including incidents of acquaintance rape. Read about organizations concerned about rape and report on any guidelines they provide concerning precautions to prevent rape and what a person can do if she or he has been a victim of rape.

To understand the phenomenon of the frequency of rape in American society, it is important to examine our society itself. At the beginning of this chapter, the point was made that the meaning of sex is strongly shaped by our culture. Although it has been challenged recently—perhaps even eliminated—one theme that is deeply imbedded in our culture is that men should play a dominant role in society. Flowing from such a theme, men should be the aggressors and women either the passive receivers or the resistors when it comes to determining the extent of sexual involvement. In a sense, a case could be made that a culture that emphasizes male dominance fosters rape more than mutuality in sexual activity. On the other hand, emphasizing mutual respect and love above self-seeking and control over another supports an atmosphere that clearly rejects rape.

Homosexuality and the Christian Life

Even in high school, Jackie sensed that she was different. She always had friends, both boy and girl friends. She was a leader in many school activities. But dating never appealed to her much. She preferred group activities and working on projects with classmates.

When Jackie entered her state university, she looked forward to continuing her involvement in clubs and activities. One organization that caught her eye during orientation week was the "gay and lesbian students' association." At first she laughed: No such organization existed at the Catholic high school she attended! However, she felt drawn to exploring what the organization and its members stood for. Perhaps she could find out more about why she always felt different from her friends who were into dating so much. Jackie decided to seek out the campus minister who worked at the Catholic Newman center at the college. Maybe she could help her with her dilemma.

homosexuality— sexual attraction toward persons of the same sex. Homosexual activity is sexual activity engaged in by persons of the same sex.

heterosexuality— sexual attraction toward persons of the other sex. Heterosexual activity is sexual activity engaged in by persons of different sexes.

As if sexual morality isn't complicated enough when it involves two adults of different sexes, same-sex activity requires an even more sound moral analysis. Frequently today even young children who watch TV know about homosexuality—at least popular stereotypes of homosexuality. In the past few years a number of television shows featured groundbreaking episodes that revealed the homosexual orientation of cast members or the characters in the shows. (**Homosexual activity** is sex engaged in by two people of the same sex; **heterosexual activity** is female-male sex.) On this matter, official Church teaching is clear.

Sexuality and Church Teaching

- Marriage is the norm for full sexual expression.

- Intimate sexual activity finds its true and complete meaning in a marriage between an adult woman and man who love each other, who are committed to each other and to the possibility of having and raising children.

- Homosexual sex does not measure up to this norm any more than non-marital heterosexual sex does.

Beyond that, both Church and society have been grappling with two other questions related to homosexuality:

- How can the Church and society help persons with homosexual inclinations to fulfill their Christian vocation to be loving and life-giving people?

- How can the Church and society direct non-homosexual persons to treat persons with homosexual inclinations in loving and just ways?

In other words, the existence of persons who have strong homosexual inclinations rather than heterosexual ones creates a variety of moral dilemmas for homosexuals and heterosexuals alike. For instance, should a homosexual couple be allowed to legally marry? (Church leaders say that this would distort and undermine the nature of marriage and therefore is unacceptable.) Should a couple who have lived in a long-standing relationship be entitled to benefits similar to those received by married couples? (Some municipal governments and corporations have granted benefits to such couples.) Can an organization deny employment or promotions to someone who publicly states that he or she is homosexual? How can the Church and other institutions provide guidance and set rules about how heterosexual and homosexual persons should live their lives and how non-homosexuals should view and treat homosexuals? For instance, how can the Church help prevent violence in word or deed against people who are gay or lesbian? (A term for violence against persons suspected of being gay or lesbian is gay bashing.) **P**

Jesus asks his followers to love their neighbors—most especially those neighbors whom others would prefer not to love. The presence of homosexual persons in a predominantly heterosexual society represents another way that Jesus' fundamental commandment is put to the test. For instance, recall once again the story of the Good Samaritan in Luke's Gospel, chapter ten. When a person is found hurting by the side of the road, Jesus wants us to treat that person as neighbor regardless of whatever prejudice we might hold against that person. The one who helps another in need is being a neighbor. If within the Christian community people with homosexual tendencies and people with heterosexual tendencies do not treat each other in neighborly fashion, then the Christian community is a sham.

Activity P

Church leaders insist that their teaching about the immorality of homosexual activity must not be viewed as a rejection of homosexual persons. For instance, in the late 1990s the U.S. Catholic bishops wrote a letter titled "Always Our Children" in which they cautioned parents to treat homosexual children with the love and care that all God's children deserve. Why do you think that the bishops felt a need to remind Catholics to love young people who discover that they possess homosexual tendencies? Does gay bashing continue to be a problem in our society? In your community? Explain.

For review . . .

9. What was emphasized forty years ago in the approach to teaching sexual morality?

10. What is the playboy/playgirl philosophy about sex?

11. Where do married couples typically rank physical-sexual activity in their list of important factors affecting their relationship?

12. What image of Jesus is portrayed in the Gospel story about the adulteress?

13. What is the original meaning of the word *obscene*? What attitude toward sex is implied in this original meaning?

14. According to the text approximately what percentage of women are victims of rape or attempted rape? What does the text say is most striking about the context of most rapes?

15. How is official Church teaching regarding homosexual activity similar to its teaching on other forms of non-marital sexual activity?

16. What two problems do the Church and society seek to address regarding persons with homosexual inclinations?

Conclusion
Sex and Morality

Our sexuality is integral to who we are. Our attitudes, values, and behaviors related to sexuality tell us a great deal about ourselves. Through the creative and responsible ways that we express our sexuality, we celebrate ourselves—body and soul, female and male— as made in God's image and as reflections of God's love.

Let us pray . . .

Jesus, we pray that you caress us with your gentle touch. Like us, you experienced bodily pain and pleasure. Like us, you were drawn to other people; and people were drawn to you. You touched people, and they were healed. We pray that our bodies and our emotions, our physical urges, our capacities for thinking and deciding, and our need for one another will unite to help us to know and love you, and to love others throughout our lives. Amen.

CHAPTER 10

Medical Ethics I
Moral Issues and the Beginning of Life

During the course of Hollywood history, the theme of intelligent life on other planets has captivated moviegoers. In films, such life may be portrayed as either fearful or friendly, but always fascinating. We might forget that outside movie theaters, we are also surrounded by magnificent creatures worthy of profound respect—the awesome and miraculous mystery that is the human person. Christian morality calls upon us to treat human life in all its manifestations and in all stages of its development with the special care that it deserves. Due to recent advances in science and technology, possibilities that never existed before are currently available for intervening with human life. It is now possible in a laboratory to start a person on his or her life journey. Ending human life in its most vulnerable period can be accomplished with pills or with relatively uncomplicated surgery. As with all matters where human life lies in the balance, Christian morality asks us to step back and evaluate technological intervention in light of its impact on the dignity of the human person.

Chapter Overview

- Respect for life underlies all Church teaching about medical technology and practice.

- Procedures that are now scientifically feasible are not necessarily moral.

- Church teaching on the beginning of life rejects abortion.

Let us pray . . .

God our Father, creator of the universe, support us in our continuing attempts to know your will and to follow the right path. Even in the midst of constant change and new challenges, may we compassionately join together with others in a search for truth. Guide those who work in science and with technology so they may become instruments of life not death. In our explorations into new ways of healing and making life better, may we never forget the preciousness of each person. Amen.

Before we begin . . .

Answer agree, disagree, or uncertain to the following statements. Where possible, refer to specific examples to explain why you agree or disagree.

1. Modern science and technology have increased our appreciation for the dignity of human life.

2. By its very nature, science seeks truth. Therefore, scientists should pursue every possibility when it comes to developing new techniques for intervening into human life.

3. Human lives, especially when most vulnerable, are being viewed more and more like commodities—kept, used, or disposed of according to the desires of whoever has power over them.

4. Medical technology is progressing so rapidly that moral evaluation of it is increasingly difficult.

5. We need clear guidelines about moral issues related to medical technology.

6. Morality related to the beginning and early stages of life affects only a few people. I don't envision that I will ever be personally involved in deciding about such matters.

7. If I were married, before planning a family I would use all medical technology available in order to ascertain personality traits and health risks my children might face.

8. My religion has helped me appreciate the preciousness of all human life.

Medical Possibilities

- Pam and Ned want children desperately. After four years of trying, Pam still is not pregnant. They decide to look into whether or not a fertility clinic can help them. Their physician at the clinic puts each of them through a series of tests and then reviews available medical options. Sometimes exercise or a change in diet helps. One or both partners might need corrective surgery. Fertility drugs could be used to stimulate Pam's ovulation. Pam and Ned could consider artificial insemination with Ned's sperm or sperm from an anonymous donor.

  The fertility doctor recommends the latter—combining in the lab some of Ned's sperm with several of Pam's ova and then inserting one (or more) "embryo" into Pam's uterus. The financial cost is fairly high and not always covered by health insurance. The possibility of success cannot be guaranteed—a twenty-percent success rate is typical, although some clinics have recently increased their successes to about forty percent. The clinic representative explains that a number of embryos, or fertilized eggs, would be obtained and frozen so that they would be available if needed. Pam and Ned leave the office to ponder the choices available to them. On the way home, Pam says, "Both of us definitely want children. Do you think this is the way to go? I'd hate to lose out on an opportunity,

but I don't want to overlook doing the right thing to get what we want either. What do you think, Ned?"

- Part of what drew Carl and Caitlin together is that they are both short in physical stature. Both can joke about the comments they heard growing up, but they also both know the disadvantages they faced because of their height. However, their short stature has not interfered with their success in life or in their marriage.

  Not surprisingly, routine medical exams indicate that their young son Chris is destined to reach only about 5'2" or 5'4" at most. When Carl reads about the availability of an artificial growth hormone that, administered regularly over a period of years, can increase a child's height, he runs the information by his wife. "What do you think, Caitlin? Wouldn't it be great to spare Chris the jokes and the problems we faced by being short? How about if we look into it?"

- "Human cloning is no longer the stuff of science fiction. Its possibility can no longer be ignored," the noted biologist began his lecture. "We should not dismiss the opportunities cloning provides, especially for infertile couples who wish to have children without resorting to a third party. If a child can be created that contains the genetic makeup of at least one of them, surely this is an option that many such couples would choose. Isn't it premature to condemn this practice before we have explored its many potential benefits? Don't we have an obligation as rational beings to use our intelligence to foster and utilize new avenues of human development?"

- Senior year began smoothly enough for Dennis and Trina. Since they started going together over the summer, they have spent much time together. They've had sex a number of times. They know about the risks of pregnancy. Usually they're cautious, but not always. So far they've been lucky.

  In the last couple of weeks, Trina has become irritable and rebuffs Dennis' attempts to become physically intimate. Finally, Dennis asks, "What's the matter with you? You're not much fun to be with lately. If it's over between us, let me know." Trina breaks down sobbing, "I think I'm pregnant." Dennis turns pale and feels a huge knot tightening in his stomach. After a moment of silence he asks, "What are you going to do about it?" **A**

Activity A

Apply the steps of the process described in chapter 8 to each of the above stories. Which steps are particularly important for evaluating each dilemma? Based on your evaluation, what recommendations would you make to the persons asking questions at the end of the stories?

Respect for Life
The Foundation of Medical Ethics

medical ethics—
moral decision
making related to
medical research and
practice

When I look at your heavens,
the work of your fingers,
the moon and the stars that you
*   have established;*
what are humans beings that you are
*   mindful of them,*
mortals that you care for them?
Yet you have made them a little
*   lower than God*
and crowned them with glory and
*   honor.*

PSALM 8:3–5

Medical ethics refers to moral decisions related to medical research and practice. Included under medical ethics are the following questions: How can the limited funds available for health care be distributed most fairly? How should candidates for organ transplants be selected? What should be included in professional codes of behavior for health-care providers such as nurses and doctors? What rights do medical patients have? Obviously, medical ethics takes in so many pressing issues today that it deserves close examination.

Recall from chapter five that the Catholic Church has dedicated many of its resources to health care. The Church of Jesus the Healer is intimately concerned about all aspects of the healing profession. Thus, Church leaders and health-care providers are very familiar with this area of morality and have offered both underlying principles as well as practical guidelines for addressing medical ethics issues. A recurring theme in Church teaching is that the fundamental principle for evaluating all areas of medical ethics is respect for the dignity of human life. Thus, the Church has condemned any practice that shows irreverence for a person at any stage or age of life. In the next two chapters we will look specifically at two important areas of concern that fit under the category medical ethics: moral concerns related to the beginning of life and moral concerns related to the end of life. **B**

Activity B

Interview someone who works in a hospital or in a medical profession, or someone who has had personal experience related to a medical ethics decision. Find out about a moral concern or concerns that the person has encountered. As part of the interview, try to determine whether, and if so how, "respect for life" was considered or ignored in the decision. Write a report on your interview.

Reproductive Technologies and Responsible Parenting

reproductive technology— scientific procedures related to procreation and the early stages of life

DNA—the intricate interlocking chain of genetic material that makes up all living cells

We live in an age of technology. Routinely, monitors tracking progress or signaling problems now accompany both birth and death. In addition to providing information, technology can also interrupt, hasten, or alter the birth or death process. Technologies applied to reproduction are called **reproductive technologies**. For instance, with the help of increasingly sophisticated machines, scientists have identified **DNA**—the intricate interlocking chain of genetic material that makes up all living cells. Due to advances in technology, doctors can provide a great deal of information to parents about their baby—months before the actual birth of their child. Today, technicians can manipulate, as never before possible, and at their earliest stages, sperm, egg, and embryo.

"What does all this technology have to do with me?" you might ask. "I'm not interested in becoming a parent right now—either through natural means or artificial, technological means!" Nonetheless, if surveys are accurate, well over 90 percent of young people expect to have children sometime during their life. Parenting is an awesome responsibility, a

responsibility that has been at the center of the success of the human enterprise since the beginning of the human race. The introduction of modern technologies complicates but does not diminish the need for responsible parenting. There are time-honored moral principles related to reproductive technology worth your consideration now before parenthood becomes a reality for you.

Although the wonders of reproductive technology, and moral dilemmas associated with it, are not addressed in Scripture, Scripture and the Christian tradition do provide us with perspectives and values regarding respect for life. These perspectives and values can guide us as we search for moral ways to use the technology of today. As we examine moral issues related to the beginning of life, we will encounter many strange sounding terms. "Ovum" and "insemination" sound like words that we should be studying in biology class, not in religion. It is important not to lose sight of the human reality underlying the procedures described here and to apply the Christian value of respect for life to each of them.

IN VITRO: LIQUID NITROGEN STORAGE OF DONOR AND PATIENT SPERM TO BE USED IN IN VITRO FERTILIZATION

From Artificial Insemination to In Vitro Fertilization

artificial insemination by husband (AIH)— mechanically introducing a husband's sperm into his wife's uterus to bring about fertilization

artificial insemination by donor (AID)— mechanically introducing sperm from a man other than the woman's husband into the woman's uterus to bring about fertilization

ovum— egg cell

embryo— a fertilized egg possessing a unique genetic makeup

surrogate mother— a woman who agrees to be artificially impregnated by a man married to another woman and to relinquish at birth legal custody of the child to the man and his wife

For many millennia, human reproduction occurred using the same means. During the past century, however, the possibility of reproduction through other than the natural, traditional means has become available. Artificial insemination began as a way to improve breeding of cattle and other animals—the sperm of one bull could be used to produce many offspring. For humans it involves a technique whereby the semen of a husband or another donor is placed in the vagina, cervical canal, or uterus by means other than sexual intercourse. In this procedure both fertilization of the egg and subsequent development take place entirely within the womb. **AIH** (artificial insemination by husband) and **AID** (artificial insemination by donor) are the earliest and simplest of the reproductive technologies currently available.

The year 1978 marked a further dramatic development in reproductive technologies—the first "in vitro" baby was born. The life of this baby began when the wife's **ovum** had been injected with her husband's sperm in a petri dish, or "in vitro" (literally, "in a glass"), and the **embryo** was then implanted in the wife's uterus where it continued development until birth.

Once an egg could be inseminated artificially and outside the womb—that is, egg and sperm could be joined in a laboratory—then various possibilities opened for sperm and ovum to come from persons other than the husband and wife. Someone's sperm, other than the husband's, could be combined with the wife's or another woman's egg. Similarly a woman, other than the wife, could donate her egg. A still further combination possible with this technology is called **surrogate motherhood**. A woman can carry another couple's child until birth—serving as a "host womb." Instead of using the wife's or another woman's egg, a surrogate mother may also donate her own egg for artificial insemination with the husband's sperm. In this case she is the biological mother but intends to relinquish the child to the biological father and his wife at birth.

Chance of Live Birth from Various Artificial Reproduction Methods

Intra Cervical Insemination
10–15%

Intra Uterine Insemination
8–26%

Intra Tubal Insemination
8–26%

In Vitro Fertilization
30%

CENTER OF DISEASE CONTROL AND PREVENTION, 1996

How might we possibly evaluate the incredible series of technological breakthroughs that combined are called reproductive technologies? Two factors that make using the technology attractive are the following. For one thing, reproductive technologies in general, and in vitro fertilization (IVF) in particular, have improved and expanded since the 1978 event described above. Couples interested in considering what reproductive technologies have to offer can find qualified doctors and clinics in many communities. Secondly, due to a number of known and unknown factors, infertility rates have gone up in recent years. **Infertility** in married couples refers to an inability to conceive or bear a child through natural methods. An expert in medical ethics describes this phenomenon in these words:

> It is estimated at the present time that 15–16% of U.S. couples are infertile, i.e. have been unable to bear a child after one year of normal efforts. About 40% of the time this has been due to male deficiencies, 40% due to female deficiencies and 20% due to deficiencies originating in both parties. Among women 20–24, infertility has almost trebled since 1965. In 1990 one million new patients sought treatment for infertility. It is estimated that 50% of these will not profit from any therapy available at this time. **C**

RICHARD J. DEVINE CM, *GOOD CARE, PAINFUL CHOICES* [NEW YORK: PAULIST PRESS, 1996].

infertility—an inability to bring about conception (for a man) or to conceive or bear a child (for a woman) through natural methods

For review . . .

1. Define medical ethics.
2. What principle serves as the foundation for Christian moral discussion about medical ethics issues?
3. Define artificial insemination by a husband; by a donor.
4. What is in vitro fertilization? For how long has in vitro fertilization been practiced?
5. Define surrogate motherhood. What are the three forms surrogate motherhood can take?
6. How common is infertility in the U.S.?
7. How successful are reproductive techniques in helping infertile couples have children?

Activity C

Apply the moral decision making process outlined in chapter 8 to the following dilemma. Indicate which steps in the process are particularly important for determining the morality of this situation.

George and Trina, who have been married for five years, discover that Trina is incapable of conceiving a child. Through a local fertility clinic, they receive the name of a woman who, for a fee, will serve as a surrogate mother for George and Trina's child. Although the woman is poor and can use the money, she declares that her intention is simply to help out a childless couple. Through the process of artificial insemination, she would be the biological mother and George the father. However, she is willing to sign a statement renouncing any legal claims to her offspring when the child is born.

The Church Responds: Four Principles for Reproductive Technology

Various procedures now make it possible to intervene not only in order to assist but also to dominate the processes of procreation. These techniques can enable man to "take in hand his own destiny," but they also expose him "to the temptation to go beyond the limits of a reasonable dominion over nature."

CONGREGATION FOR THE DOCTRINE OF THE FAITH. QUOTE FROM POPE JOHN PAUL II IN THE INTRODUCTION OF *INSTRUCTION ON RESPECT FOR HUMAN LIFE IN ITS ORIGIN AND THE DIGNITY OF PROCREATION: REPLIES TO CERTAIN QUESTIONS OF THE DAY.*

ASHI DE SILVA IS ONE OF THE FIRST TWO PEOPLE IN THE WORLD TO BENEFIT FROM GENE THERAPY, THE EXPERIMENTAL TECHNIQUE OF TREATING DISEASE BY TRANSPLANTING GENES.

Are the two factors previously mentioned in regards to reproductive technologies sufficient to outweigh moral constraints against IVF or other reproductive technologies? As the number of reproductive technologies increased during the last part of the century, Church leaders began looking at the serious moral questions that were also evolving with these technologies. Consequently, in 1987 a Vatican commission issued a document, that Church leaders have used ever since, for setting forth key principles for evaluating new technologies related to the medical field. Before it addresses specifics, *Instruction on Respect for Human Life in Its Origin and the Dignity of Human Reproduction* offers four principles to be kept in mind when considering the morality of medical technologies in general.

According to the document, the first principle underlying all medical ethics decisions is: *Life is a gift of inestimable value*. In other words, all moral decision making related to the laboratory or the hospital should begin and end with the fundamental principle mentioned at the beginning of this chapter, respect for life.

Second, the document affirms that science and technology are indeed very valuable resources that can serve people well. In other words, it looks upon modern science with its technological developments in a positive light; a technology is not immoral just because it is a technology. Rather, the question the document wants us to keep in mind is: Does this technology assist the natural process or replace it? In all cases, *science and technology must be used to benefit people*. The document calls scientific research and development aimed at helping people "science with a conscience."

Third, the document affirms that *humans are a unity of body and spirit*. This familiar Christian teaching about the nature of the human person has implications for all medical practice. For instance, the document points out a simple fact that can actually be forgotten during the course of the high-tech medical practices of today: "An intervention on the human body affects not only the tissues, the organs and their functions, but also involves the person himself" (number 3). An illustration of this principle is the reminder that a doctor does not operate on a kidney or on lungs but on a human person. Of course, the principle affirming unity of body and spirit can be violated even more unthinkingly when the subject of technological intervention exists in a laboratory and is not even visible to the naked eye—for example, embryos kept frozen waiting upon technicians, couples, or judges to decide their fate.

Finally, the document includes a principle that provides a word of caution about how we view technology and its marvelous advances. It states that "*what is technically possible is not for that very reason morally admissible*" (number 4). Just as not every weapon that might be developed *should* be developed or used in warfare, so also not every proposal made by medical researchers should be pursued. Indeed, not every potential medical "breakthrough" necessarily serves humanity. Once again, technological advancements in the medical laboratory must be measured in terms of respect for life. **D**

Activity D

Use the Internet or other research instrument to identify a number of issues related to recent medical ethics and reproductive technology. Apply the four principles listed above to each issue. How can these principles help determine the morality involved? What would practicing "science with a conscience" mean for these issues? Explain.

In Vitro Fertilization and the Nature of Marriage

unitive function of marriage—the love-making and love-giving dimension of a married relationship

procreative function of marriage—the life-giving dimension of a married relationship, including—but not exclusively—openness to children

The 1987 document addressed the issue of in vitro fertilization in the context of the nature and purpose of marriage. Traditional Catholic language refers to marriage as both unitive and procreative, that is, as having both love-making (**unitive**) and life-giving (**procreative**) characteristics. IVF can be procreative, although it is important to keep in mind that it typically involves great expense, financial and otherwise; and, as mentioned earlier, more often than not it results in failure. The more significant concern voiced in the document is that both artificial insemination and IVF are physically divorced from the unitive aspect of marriage. Instead of resulting from an act of love between a wife and husband, a child's life is initiated through the manipulations of various technicians and laboratory personnel.

> *Consequently fertilization of a married woman with the sperm of a donor different from her husband and fertilization with the husband's sperm of an ovum not coming from his wife are morally illicit. Furthermore, the artificial fertilization of a woman who is unmarried or a widow, whoever the donor may be, cannot be morally justified.*
>
> CONGREGATION FOR THE DOCTRINE OF THE FAITH. *INSTRUCTION ON RESPECT FOR HUMAN LIFE IN ITS ORIGIN AND ON THE DIGNITY OF PROCREATION*, SECTION II, PART A, PARAGRAPH 2.

The document also expresses concern over the embryos produced in this fashion. Keep in mind that more embryos are produced than are used. After eggs are extracted from the mother and sperm donated by the father, the production and handling of embryos are given over to technicians. What is to be made of these embryos—that is, what is their moral and legal status? What is to be done with unused embryos? Might the sacred beginnings of life be reduced to lab material?

> *In the usual practice of in vitro fertilization, not all of the embryos are transferred to the woman's body; some are destroyed. Just as the Church condemns induced abortion, so she also forbids acts against the life of these human beings.*
>
> CONGREGATION FOR THE DOCTRINE OF THE FAITH. *INSTRUCTION ON RESPECT FOR HUMAN LIFE IN ITS ORIGIN AND ON THE DIGNITY OF PROCREATION*, SECTION 1, PARAGRAPH 5.

The document continues to advocate the principle that children are to be viewed as gifts from God. They have a right to be created and nurtured in the environment of a loving and life-giving marriage. The document makes this final observation:

> *By defending man against the excesses of his own power, the Church of God reminds him of the reasons for his true nobility; only in this way can the possibility of living and loving with that dignity and liberty which derive from respect for the truth be ensured for the men and women of tomorrow* (conclusion).

For review . . .

8. Name the four principles for examining medical technologies spelled out by the Church in 1987.

9. What does "science with a conscience" mean?

10. What are the two characteristics of marriage traditionally identified in Catholic teaching? How do these characteristics call into question in vitro fertilization?

11. Why does the 1987 document consider the treatment of embryos as it occurs in IVF to be morally unacceptable?

12. How does the 1987 document help the men and women of tomorrow?

Genetic Engineering

genetics—
the study of
characteristics
inherited from one
generation to another

The beginning of this chapter talked about Chris, a child predisposed to be short. The fact that he is almost certain to be short because his parents are short is an example of genetics. **Genetics** is the branch of science that examines characteristics inherited from one generation to another. **Genetic engineering** refers to attempts to change a person's inherited characteristics by changing her or his genetic makeup. Genetic engineering can potentially be used to try to eliminate inherited diseases or to change hair color. It can also be used to search out and possibly alter genes associated with certain types of behavior or personality traits.

genetic engineering—
changing inherited
characteristics by
changing genetic
makeup of a plant,
animal, or person

Immediately, it is obvious that genetic engineering is fraught with potential risks and rewards, positive and negative aspects. Advances in genetic engineering could lead to a utopia, but would this "brave new world" be a paradise or a prison?

therapeutic—
directed toward
healing a disorder,
disease, or illness

As with IVF, the morality of genetic engineering is not based on whether it is "artificial" as opposed to "natural." The key is how it affects the dignity of the human person, a mystery of body and soul. The Vatican's 1987 document makes a distinction that it considers crucial in evaluating genetic engineering. A procedure is **therapeutic** when its aim is "the healing of various maladies such as those stemming from chromosomal defects" (section I, number 3). The document says that: "Such an intervention would indeed fall within the logic of the Christian moral tradition" (section I, number 3). On the other hand, procedures that are not strictly therapeutic, for instance "those aimed at the improvement of the human biological condition," are unacceptable (Introduction, number 3). **E**

Cloning—Life After Dolly

cloning—creating
a plant, animal, or
person asexually
that is genetically
identical with a donor
plant, animal, or
person

Early in 1997 a **cloned** sheep named Dolly was born. Dolly was an identical genetic match to another sheep. After that event, speculation intensified about whether or not we could or should clone humans. Within the scientific community the general answer to the first question was "yes." While cloning a human would be more complicated than cloning other animals, it could conceivably be possible to do so sometime in the not too distant future.

However, the answer to the "should" question, both within the scientific community and beyond, has generally been a resounding "no" to human cloning.

Activity E

Classify the following as either therapeutic or nontherapeutic uses of genetic intervention. Explain why you label them as such

1. seeking to increase a child's height
2. eliminating a gene that causes obesity
3. preventing sickle cell anemia
4. altering a gene linked to homosexuality
5. eliminating the gene causing cystic fibrosis
6. eliminating a disposition for smoking cigarettes

..LY, RIGHT, THE FIRST CLONED
..EEP REPRODUCED THROUGH
..UCLEAR TRANSFER FROM
..FERENTIATED ADULT SHEEP
..S, AND DOLLY, THE WORLD'S
..IRST TRANSGENIC LAMB.

Thus, over the past few decades reproductive technologies have made available a gradual substitution for the natural process of human procreation and birth. Artificial insemination separated reproduction from the sex act, eliminating the link between sexual intimacy and procreation. IVF replaced both sexual intercourse and the beginning of life within the womb. Cloning would replace a whole partner in the process of procreation. Each technological advance moves the procreative act farther and farther away from the physically intimate and unitive dimension of marriage.

In 1968 Pope Paul VI wrote a famous encyclical called *Of Human Life* in which he condemned the use of artificial contraception (artificial birth control) by married couples because it separates the unitive and the procreative aspects of marriage. For the same essential reasons, the 1987 document condemns the various forms of artificial conception described above. **F**

In light of our discussion about Catholic views on IVF and genetic engineering, it's easy to imagine what Church leaders have to say about the matter. Principles of Catholic medical ethics in general apply as well to cloning. For instance, producing a person through cloning clearly lacks the intimate connection to marriage, especially the unitive dimension of marriage that Church teaching calls for. Secondly, the nature of cloning is an affront to the dignity and rights of a child. A representative of the U.S. Catholic bishops spoke to the issue soon after the Dolly story made the news.

> *Catholic teaching rejects the cloning of humans, because this is not a worthy way to bring a human into the world. Children have a right to have real parents, and to be conceived as the fruit of marital love between husband and wife. They are not products we can manufacture to our specifications. Least of all should they be produced as deliberate "copies" of other people to ensure that they have certain desired features.*
>
> RICHARD M. DOERFLINGER, "REMARKS IN RESPONSE TO NEWS REPORTS ON THE CLONING OF MAMMALS," IN RONALD COLE-TURNER, ED., *HUMAN CLONING: RELIGIOUS RESPONSES* [LOUISVILLE, KY: JOHN KNOX PRESS, 1997].

For review . . .

13. Define the terms *genetics* and *genetic engineering*.

14. What is the difference between therapeutic and nontherapeutic medical procedures? What is the Church's moral position on each of these?

15. What year marked the first successful cloning of a mammal?

16. Name two ways that human cloning would violate Catholic principles of medical ethics.

Activity F

Find out what you can about the current state of cloning. What is the legal status of experiments seeking to determine the possibility of human cloning in various countries? What arguments do advocates of human cloning make? How do others counter these arguments? Write a report on your findings.

Abortion and Respect for the Unborn

For the past thirty years or so, no moral issue has been more divisive and controversial than abortion, the deliberate cessation of prenatal human life. If we polled a group of North Americans and asked them to name the first moral issue that came to their minds, the vast majority would probably answer "abortion." The emotional intensity surrounding abortion often clouds any attempt at an open exchange of viewpoints on the issue. Discussions about the rightness or wrongness of abortion often focus on peripheral rather than central questions. For instance, abortion debates often center on a woman's right to privacy or on the acceptability of abortion in certain circumstances but not in others. People answer such questions differently depending in large part on how they view prenatal life, that is, human life before birth.

A Single Mother's Story

When Elisha became pregnant in her junior year of high school, she initially felt as though her life was over. She was certain about one thing: No matter what anybody else thought or said, she would never have an abortion. She managed to have her child, a healthy baby boy, and to make it through high school. Now she works and also takes college courses part time. Life has been a struggle for Elisha these past few years. She would caution other young people not to have premarital sex. Raising a child as a single mother has been an unending struggle. Sometimes she doesn't think she will make it. She had to grow up fast and learn to be responsible as she provides for herself and her son. However, every night when she hears about her son's day at kindergarten, she is thankful for the beautiful gift that her child continues to be in her life. **G**

Activity G

Abortion is a much-debated issue in religious, political, and social circles. No doubt you have heard many viewpoints on it. List all the different arguments and opinions that you can think of regarding abortion. As you read through this section, keep this list in mind. Then write a response to each argument and opinion in light of Church teaching on the subject.

When Does Human Life Begin?

One of the central questions in the abortion debate is: When does human life begin? More precisely, when in the course of the continuing development from fertilized egg to newborn infant does a human person exist? Because disagreement exists on this pivotal question, there is disagreement about what abortion actually involves.

On the one hand, someone who believes that a human person does not exist until later stages of prenatal development sees concern for respect for life primarily in terms of concern for the life and health of the pregnant woman. In other words, if no human person exists until sometime late in pregnancy or only at birth, then denying a pregnant woman an opportunity to terminate her pregnancy is denying her access to a medical procedure that can benefit her and harms no one.

On the other hand, if a person believes that a human exists at the earliest stage of development, that person will view abortion as unjustified killing—taking the life of an innocent human who deserves care and protection as every person does. In other words, someone holding this view thinks that from the moment of conception when sperm and egg are united, a distinct and unique human person exists. From this perspective, abortion clearly violates respect for life—the life of an unborn child.

Church Teachings on the Beginning of Life

What guidance does Church teaching provide on this important topic? A comprehensive statement addressing the abortion issue came out from the Vatican in 1974. Concerning the beginning of life, the document titled

Declaration on Procured Abortion states that: *From the time that the ovum is fertilized, a life is begun which is neither that of the father nor of the mother; it is rather the life of a new human with his own growth. It would never be made human if it were not human already. . . . Modern genetic science offers clear confirmation. It has demonstrated that from the first instant there is established the program of what this living being will be: a man, this individual man with his characteristic aspects already well determined. Right from fertilization the adventure of a human life begins, and each of its capacities requires time—a rather lengthy time—to find its place and to be in a position to act. The least that can be said is that present science, in its most evolved state, does not give any substantial support to those who defend abortion* (numbers 12–13).

This part of the statement makes two essential points that modern Church teaching has consistently voiced about the beginning of life.

1. A new and distinct human life begins at the moment of conception.

2. Information from modern science affirms the statement "Right from fertilization the adventure of a human life begins."

The document continues:

Moreover, it is not up to biological sciences to make a definitive judgment on questions which are properly philosophical and moral, such as the moment when a human person is constituted or the legitimacy of abortion. From a moral point of view this is certain: even if a doubt existed concerning whether the fruit of conception is already a human person, it is objectively a grave sin to dare to risk murder. "The one who will be a man is already one" (number 3).

In this passage, the document makes two other key points about what our stance should be regarding the beginning of life.

More than a fifth of all pregnancies around the world end in abortion and unplanned pregnancy remains common.

Each year, about 35 of every 1,000 women of childbearing age have abortions. The rates are similar in developed and developing countries, although abortion laws are generally more restrictive in poorer nations.

BETH GARDINER, "FIFTH OF THE WORLD'S PREGNANCIES END IN ABORTION, REPORT SAYS," *PHILADELPHIA INQUIRER*, 22 JANUARY 1999, PAGE A28.

3. Questions about the beginning of life and abortion are not just scientific; they are more properly philosophical and moral.

That is, science provides us with intricate information about the physical development of a fetus. However, it is not the role of science to   make a judgment about the moral status of a fetus. In other words, we cannot simply step back and expect science to determine when a human person begins to exist. "What constitutes a human person" is a philosophical and religious question. The long tradition of philosophical and religious understanding about what is a human and how a human is to be treated plays a deciding role in answering this pivotal question.

4. If we are not sure when, in the course of development, a human person exists, then we should presume that a human person is present at the earliest stage.

This statement is addressed to people who say, "How can we be certain when a human person first exists? If we can't be sure, shouldn't the decision be a matter of choice?" The document answers that, considering that human life hangs in the balance, we sin because we take a life if we are mistaken. **H**

Abortion and Values in Conflict

People who argue that abortion is morally acceptable raise many questions. The best arguments demonstrate sensitivity to the difficulties that can accompany pregnancy and having children.

• What about in the case of rape—isn't abortion okay then?

• How about if we know that a child will be seriously deformed—shouldn't that be considered?

• Shouldn't the physical and psychological health of the pregnant woman be considered?

The Declaration on Procured Abortion recognizes that circumstances leading a person to contemplate abortion are often difficult, at times even tragic. It recognizes that women seek abortions to prevent physical, psychological, financial, or other hardships to themselves or to their unborn child. However, the declaration calls people to consider the fundamental value of life which underlies an abortion decision. In its view, the right to life itself, once conceived, outweighs all the other values and concerns involved.

Activity H

One commentator draws the following analogy to dramatize the position that, in the face of doubt about the status of a fetus, abortion is wrong: If a hunter hears a rustling noise behind some bushes and he or she is uncertain whether it's a deer or a human, the hunter is not justified in firing a gun in that direction.

• What point is the analogy trying to make?

• Is it a valid analogy for helping us understand the abortion debate?

• Write your comments on this analogy.

The gravity of the problem comes from the fact that in certain cases, perhaps in quite a considerable number of cases, by denying abortion one endangers important values which men normally hold in great esteem and which may sometimes even seem to have priority. We do not deny these very great difficulties. It may be a serious question of health, sometimes of life or death, for the mother; it may be the burden represented by an additional child, especially if there are good reasons to fear that the child will be abnormal or retarded; it may be the importance attributed in different classes of society to considerations of honor or dishonor, of loss of social standing, and so forth. We proclaim only that none of these reasons can ever objectively confer the right to dispose of another's life, even when that life is only beginning. . . . Life is too fundamental a value to be weighed against even very serious disadvantages (number 14). ▯

For review . . .

17. According to the text what is the central question in the abortion debate? What are the two dominant positions people have on this question?

18. List the four key points made about the beginning of life in the *Declaration on Procured Abortion*.

19. What stand does this document take regarding the many difficulties that pregnancy can cause for some people?

Activity I

Read over the following passage from Psalm 139. Then write your own "respect for life prayer," focusing on some concerns raised in this chapter.

> *For it was you who formed my inward parts;*
> *you knit me together in my mother's womb.*
> *I praise you, for I am fearfully and wonderfully made.*
> *Wonderful are your works; that I know very well.*
> *My frame was not hidden from you*
> *when I was being made in secret,*
> *intricately woven in the depths of the earth.*
> *Your eyes beheld my unformed substance.*
> *In your book were written*
> *all the days that were formed for me,*
> *when none of them as yet existed.*

PSALM 139:13–16

Conclusion
At All Stages, in All Cases—Human Life Deserves Respect

Christian moral teaching calls for respect for human life. Today, due to earthshaking developments in science and technology, the very concept "human life" has been called into question. Legalized abortion has been with us for a number of decades. The reproductive technologies may sound futuristic, like the stuff of science fiction, but now they are realities that all of us must deal with. The moral dimension accompanying each of these developments must never be lost amid the high-tech atmosphere that surrounds them. In the midst of complexity, confusion, and constant change, it is important for us always to heed the words of Scripture (Deuteronomy 30:19): "Choose life."

Let us pray . . .

God said to Isaiah:

"Can a woman forget her nursing child,

or show no compassion for the child of her womb?

Even these may forget,

yet I will not forget you.

See, I have inscribed you on the palms of my hands . . ."

ISAIAH 49:15–16

Gracious and loving God, you have told us through your prophet Isaiah that you will never forget us. May we show to all persons, born and unborn, the care that you have for us. Amen.

CHAPTER 11

Medical Ethics II

Moral Issues Near the End of Life

If they are to have any validity, all religions must grapple with the question of death. Essential to Christianity is the story of the suffering, death, and resurrection of Jesus. In a sense, this story lays the foundation for all other Christian beliefs. The Church founded upon the life and teachings of Jesus not only holds out hope for all of us faced with death, it also seeks to bring its vision of reverence for life to the many moral issues surrounding death and dying. As we will discover in this chapter, death and dying have become more complicated than people would ever have envisioned even a half-century ago. For the end of life as for its beginning, each new medical or technological advancement brings with it new moral dilemmas. As with all areas of medical ethics, the dignity of the human person and respect for life are the principles underlying evaluation of proper care and treatment of those who are sick, near death, or dying.

Chapter Overview

• A Christian view of death balances realism and hope.

• Euthanasia must be viewed in light of respect for human life.

• A living will and hospice care offer assistance in facing dying in our complex modern world.

Before reading this chapter discuss and write up a response to the following questions.

1. Over the past few decades, what developments have shaped moral discussion about death and dying?

2. In Catholic tradition there is a patron saint of a "happy death"—Saint Joseph, who was blessed to die in the presence of his wife Mary and Jesus. Describe the role, if any, that each of the following would play in fostering a good death. What are some policies and practices that could help people experience such a death? If you were to arrange this list so that it reflects your own concerns, what would the list look like?

- a minimum of pain and suffering

- the presence of caring family and friends

- a deep faith and hope in God's love

- a sense of being "right" with God and other people

- a firm belief in an afterlife

- a sense of personal accomplishment

- a sense of the meaning of life

- knowledgeable and compassionate healthcare providers

- the ability to make choices

Let us pray . . .

Gracious God of life, may we savor all the moments of our own lives and provide comfort for those dear to us whose lives are ending. Through your son, Jesus Christ, may we find meaning in life, consolation in suffering, and faith in the world to come. Grant us peace, now and at the hour of our death. Amen.

The Quality of Life

- Everything changed for Laurie the day she received the diagnosis. In fact, everything changed for her family, her friends, and her classmates as well. The tumor was cancerous. Surgery to remove it provided some relief, but the cancer itself had already spread. She began aggressive treatments immediately. Side effects were not pleasant. Laurie continued attending school, but she no longer looked seventeen. Her friends couldn't help but notice that she began to take on an ageless look.

  Her classmates didn't know what to do. Usually it was Laurie who set them at ease and calmed their fears. Even though it was "business as usual" at school, everyone had it in the back of their minds: Laurie, our friend, is sick; she may be dying. Not surprisingly, Christian teaching about life and death took on special meaning during liturgies and religion classes at Laurie's school. Although some students questioned and got angry at God, Laurie's faith grew stronger. She sustained her classmates and inspired everyone with her courage and trust in God.

  Laurie fought the spreading cancer as best she could, but her body grew progressively weaker even while her spirit remained strong. Appropriately enough, Laurie's death came shortly after Valentine's Day, a day when Laurie was showered with love. The funeral was tear-filled and sad but also uplifting. Death claimed victory; but those gathered in the church celebrated that a greater victory had been won for Laurie—the victory of eternal life in Christ.

- It happened suddenly. While vacationing in Florida Tanya collapsed in front of her husband Bill. Without warning she lost consciousness and stopped breathing. Bill called immediately for medical assistance, and paramedics arrived in just over fifteen minutes. They were able to revive Tanya's breathing and rushed her to a nearby hospital.

  After stabilizing her condition and completing a series of tests, doctors notified Bill that Tanya, his youthful sixty-seven-year-old wife, was now over 90 percent brain dead. Artificial nutrition and hydration along with the oxygen she was receiving could keep her functioning at this level indefinitely, but barring a miracle she would never regain consciousness.

  Bill gathered with other family members to ponder the best course of action. Both Bill and Tanya had written up a statement about what they wanted done if such an event occurred—a living will. The medical staff treating Tanya explained to the family available options and potential consequences of each one. Through their sadness the family talked and prayed over what to do. They didn't want to let go of their wife and mother. They also wanted rest and peace for her.

- Now forty-one, Mack has been a paraplegic since the crushing block he received while playing football in his senior year of high school. For the past twenty-some years, he has maintained a steady level of activity, even though his condition makes even simple tasks burdensome. Fortunately, Mack has received help from some family members who assist him on a regular basis and from home-care workers paid for by insurance. Lately, his pain has increased, and he has been wondering if it's all worth it. Wouldn't everyone be better off without him? What does he really have to live for? Does he contribute anything to those around him other than added hardship? Can he take living like this much longer? He has decided that he wants to consider all the options available to him. **A**

Activity A

Today, in addition to priests, laypeople also make up hospital ministry teams. Imagine that you are a member of such a team. For the three persons mentioned above—Laurie, Tanya, and Mack—write a prayer that would be appropriate to say if they ended up in your hospital.

Death and Dying

Leo Tolstoy, the great nineteenth-century Russian novelist, is best known for his long epics such as *War and Peace*. Besides being a great writer, Tolstoy also constantly struggled with spiritual questions. Only near the end of his life did he realize that Christianity held the answers for which he had spent his life searching. One of his shorter stories raised questions about how death is looked at—or, more accurately, how people tend to avoid looking at death.

In *The Death of Ivan Ilych,* the title character is dying. From this starting point the story centers on how various people respond to the main character's illness and gradual slide toward death. His wife and family encourage him to go on as if he weren't in peril of death. More than anything they are annoyed that he isn't getting better and is thus disrupting their lives. Rather than exhibiting sympathy for his patient, even the doctor expresses disappointment in Ilych for not getting better despite his treatment.

Whenever friends stop by to see him, the family always says, "There, you feel better now, don't you," denying the reality so clearly evident in his chalky complexion and his frail body. Ilych feels as though his tormenting pain and his increasing neediness are a burden to everyone, and no one close to him tells him otherwise. Thus, on top of his anxiety about dying, he feels embarrassed that he is putting everyone through the unpleasantness of it all. His dying, with its accompanying anguish and fears, has isolated him in a prison that he shares with no one.

At least not until Gerasim, a peasant servant boy, is assigned to clean up after Ilych. Only Gerasim acknowledges that Ilych is dying. "You are sick. You are dying. Of course I will help you in whatever way I can," Gerasim says innocently and forthrightly. He spends time holding the dying man's legs to give him comfort. Only Gerasim admits the tragedy that Ilych is experiencing and responds sympathetically. Consequently, Ilych feels at ease only with his young servant. Gerasim becomes Ilych's constant companion as he sinks further into his sickness and closer to death. **B**

> The *dying* are often *out* of the *loop*, particularly if they have *suffered* a lengthy *disease* or are among the *elderly*. No one says their *name*, no one cherishes their *presence*.
>
> KENNETH L. AND VAUX AND SARA A. VAUX, *DYING WELL* [NASHVILLE, TN: ABINGDON PRESS, 1996].

Activity B

1. Fold a piece of paper in half. On one side of the paper, draw a symbolic representation of life. On the other side, draw a symbolic representation of death. Open up your paper so that both drawings are visible. What do they suggest about your view of death?

2. What are the prevailing views toward death and dying present in our contemporary society? How are they similar to or different from what you believe to be a Christian view toward death and dying?

3. Read Tolstoy's *The Death of Ivan Ilych*. Take note of how Tolstoy describes stages in Ilych's response to dying, and how Ilych experiences his moment of death. Write a report on the view of death and dying presented in the story.

A Christian View of Death Balances Acceptance and Hope

What is a Christian view of death and dying? For instance, in Christian teaching is death friend or foe? Because of hope in an afterlife, should Christians actually approach death serenely or even welcome it? Is a Christian view of death and dying realistic or is it a lie told in order to ease suffering in the face of tragic human mortality? Does a Christian view of death and dying help us in responding to specific moral challenges brought on by modern medical advances? Of course, the person we should look to for answers to these questions is Jesus himself. However, before looking at what Jesus had to say on the matter of death, it is interesting to contrast his death with that of another famous figure of old—the Greek philosopher **Socrates** (BC 470–399).

Like Jesus, Socrates underwent a trial by the state to determine whether or not his ideas were subversive. He was found guilty and sentenced to death. He had recourse to alter-

Socrates—
fifth-century BC Greek philosopher

natives to the death penalty but for various reasons he refused them. Instead, Socrates gathered his students together and defiantly drank the poison hemlock, thus ending his life.

The picture we have of Jesus during the week before his death is quite different from that of Socrates. Far from welcoming death, Jesus prays the night before his death, "My Father, if it is possible, let this cup pass from me" (Matthew 26:39). The next day, while on the cross, Jesus cries out, "My God, my God, why have you forsaken me?" (Matthew 27:46) These are not the words of someone who welcomes death or who views it as a friend. For Jesus, dying is not a serene experience, free of fear and anxiety. Rather, dying is a "bitter cup" to be avoided if at all possible; and death itself usually is a great tragedy. Jesus does not seek out a poison to end his life; earthly life is too precious for that. He dies not because he wants to but because he remains faithful to his message and his mission.

Is the question of how Christians are to view death thus settled? Obviously, there is more to the story. For Christians, this life pales in comparison to "eternal life." The Catechism puts it in these simple terms: "In death, the separation of the soul from the body, the human body decays and the soul goes to meet God" (997). Thus, the pain and suffering of dying, worse for some than for others, should not blind us to the promises Jesus gave us through his own death and resurrection. Christians call the day he died *Good* Friday not because Jesus suffered and died then, but because his death led to resurrection—for himself and for us. In other words, from a Christian perspective death *is* an enemy, but an enemy overcome.

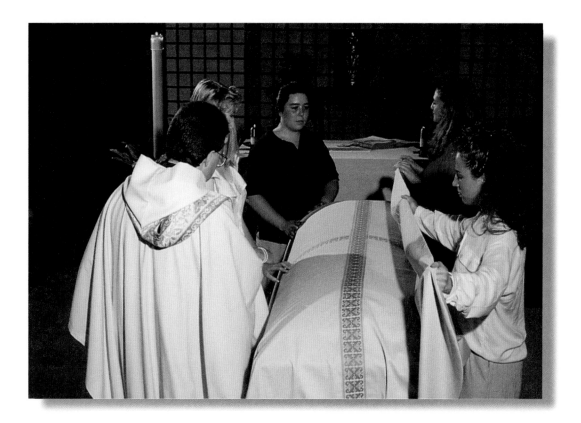

A Christian view of death and dying, therefore, balances two perspectives. On the one hand, death and dying are affronts to human dignity. Dying eats away at our ability to care for ourselves or to give anything to others. It attacks our thought processes and calls into question the value and meaning of our lives. The cold, lifeless body of a dead person is a sacred but pitiable sight. On the other hand, a Catholic funeral liturgy is celebrated with joyous alleluias because it affirms that ultimately the sting of death has been overcome forever in Christ Jesus. For Christians, then, death is in fact going home: "In death, God calls man to himself" (Catechism, #1011). Saint Paul offers this message of joyful expectation to one of the early Christian communities he visited:

> *For we know that if the earthly tent we live in is destroyed, we have a building from God, a house not made with hands, eternal in the heavens. . . . He who has prepared us for this very thing is God, who has given us the Spirit as a guarantee.*
>
> 2 CORINTHIANS 5:1, 5

As we look at specific moral issues related to death and dying, it is important to keep in mind this balance that Christian teaching gives us. For instance, as Christians we are concerned about pain relief and compassionate care and comfort for the dying: "'Heal the sick!' [Cf. Mt. 10:8] The Church has received this charge from the Lord and strives to carry it out by taking care of the sick as well as by accompanying them with her prayer of intercession" (Catechism, #1509). On the other hand, Christians are also very much concerned about how we can best enable one another to die a good Christian death. On this point it is important to recall that the root of the word *health* is the same as that for *salvation*. In the end, therefore, being healed means not avoiding death but being saved—life with Christ after death. If we don't distinguish between our concern for healing and a Christian vision of death and resurrection, we can end up with simplistic but misguided positions on some important moral dilemmas.

Lazarus

The story of Jesus' response to the death of his friend Lazarus illustrates why all Christians can greet death with both sadness and hope. Hearing of the death of Lazarus, brother of his friends Mary and Martha, Jesus comes to their hometown. The Gospel of John describes the scene in these words:

The Jews who were with her in the house, consoling her, saw Mary get up quickly and go out. They followed her because they thought that she was going to the tomb to weep there. When Mary came where Jesus was and saw him, she knelt at his feet and said to him, "Lord, if you had been here, my brother would not have died." When Jesus saw her weeping, and the Jews who came with her also weeping, he was greatly disturbed in spirit and deeply moved. He said, "Where have you laid him?" They said to him, "Lord, come and see." Jesus began to weep. So the Jews said, "See how he loved him!" But some of them said, "Could not he who opened the eyes of the blind man have kept this man from dying?"

Then Jesus, again greatly disturbed, came to the tomb. It was a cave, and a stone was lying against it. Jesus said, "Take away the stone." Martha, the sister of the dead man, said to him, "Lord, already there is a stench because he has been dead four days." Jesus said to her, "Did I not tell you that if you believed, you would see the glory of God?" So they took away the stone. And Jesus looked upward and said, "Father, I thank you for having heard me. I knew that you always hear me, but I said this for the sake of the crowd standing here, so that they may believe that you have sent me." When he had said this, he cried with a loud voice, "Lazarus, come out!" The dead man came out, his hands and feet bound with strips of cloth, and his face wrapped in a cloth. Jesus said to them, "Unbind him, and let him go."

JOHN 11:31–44 **C**

Activity C

Do you agree that it is important not to reduce "dying well" merely to dying a painless death? What else might be involved in dying well?

A Christian View of Suffering Finds Comfort in Christ's Suffering

The Church assigns feast days for various saints to most days during the week. Many Christian saints, especially those from the early centuries, were very familiar with suffering and even with painful deaths. Actually, all of us at some time will be put to the test by suffering. When it comes, Christians can find hope in the fact that Jesus himself suffered and, in so doing, gained eternal life for all of us.

When talking about a Christian view of suffering and physical pain, we need to be careful. There is a psychological disorder known as **masochism**. A masochist seeks out and welcomes pain and suffering. In our day, some young people starve themselves or purposely bring on pain by slashing their bodies with razors. Such behavior is not a ticket to sainthood but a cry for help. However, Christianity recognizes that suffering can put our human condition into clearer perspective. In our suffering—physical or psychological, personal or social—we come to realize our frailty and our neediness. In those times when we are most needy, we are likely to call upon the only one who ultimately fulfills our needs and provides healing ointment for our pain—

masochism—a psychological disorder marked by deliberately seeking out pain

God. A telling example of this is the man about to undergo life-threatening surgery who, although he hasn't prayed since he was a child, now welcomes the prayers of family and friends. Granted, suffering can shake our faith: why does God allow suffering, we wonder. However, suffering can also awaken faith in us. From a Christian perspective, nothing—not even suffering and death—can separate us from God's love. In fact, suffering can even introduce us to a love that we never knew before. **D**

For review . . .

1. In Tolstoy's story, why does Ivan Ilych prefer the company of the servant boy Gerasim?

2. Contrast the responses of Jesus and Socrates to the prospect of dying.

3. What two views about death are balanced in Christian teaching?

4. Describe the Christian view of suffering. How is it different from masochism?

Activity D

Interview an older person to discern answers to the following questions:

1. What are your most pressing needs, concerns and interests right now? How have these changed as you have grown?

2. What should be essential characteristics of a caregiver working with frail older people?

3. Do you think it makes a difference to have a Christian caregiver? If so, what difference might it make?

4. What dimensions of Christian faith could help a person prepare for becoming older? Sickly? Prepared for dying?

Living While Dying

Here is a story from a nursing journal about an older woman's experience of being seriously ill.

I am a prisoner. The bars to my cell are the cold metal handrails of my wheelchair. The walls of my prison are the gloomy, painted block of the nursing home that houses me.

I live; yet I am not really living. I breathe and my heart beats, but my chance to affect the world is over. My ability to work, to clean my room, to write to a friend, to converse with my husband, to hold my granddaughter—all are gone now. I am living in a shell, able to see all that is around me, yet able to connect with nothing.

I overhear the doctor say to my husband, "Organic brain syndrome, Mr. Coffey, is a slowly progressing disease of the elderly. It is a destruction of brain cells. The person loses the ability to function. Eventually she will lose any communication skills she possesses."

Is that why I open my mouth to speak, yet words don't come out? Is that why I can't lift my hand to my mouth to feed myself?

I watch people come and go from the lobby where I spend my time. They bustle around me; everyone is busy, as if on a mission. Mostly when they glance down at me, they quickly look away before I even have a chance to smile at them. I see their color-ful blouses, their bright ties. Color is a pleasure to me, as my world is so empty. . . .

I am awakened from my reverie by a quick kiss on my forehead, and my husband leaves. Now I really feel alone. I dread the long evening ahead. An orderly wheels me to my familiar spot in the lobby. Two nurses walk by, engrossed in animated conversation. "Shirley, how did your meeting go last night?" Their chatter gets faint as they saunter down the hall.

Talk to me! Tell me what the weather is like outside. Bring me the roses on the nurses' desk and let me sniff them. Share with me the funny thing your little boy said to you the other day. Show me the newspaper's front page and discuss it for a while. Pat my arm. Rub my back. I need you to give me some feeling of self-worth . . .

I have plenty of time to contemplate things. I can judge, for example, what distinguishes a good nurse from a bad one. A person becomes an expert at such matters when allowed to view them intimately. A bad nurse sees a curled up, ratchety old lady in me: a *body* to get pills down, a *child* to put to bed at night, an *item* to write on the chart about. A good nurse sees a human soul, a person with a family in her past and a future yet unwritten. A good nurse understands that, while I can't communicate with her, I still need her to communicate with me. I still need love. I hurt. I dream.

BETTY KAUPP, "IMPRISONED: WHY CAN'T YOU SEE ME?" *JOURNAL OF CHRISTIAN NURSING*, 16:1 [WINTER, 1999].

Euthanasia
The Difference between Dying and Killing

euthanasia— deliberately taking steps to bring about a person's death for the purposes of eliminating suffering

When we move from a general discussion about Christian views on death and dying to specific moral issues related to the topic, we come quickly to the topic of euthanasia. Just as moral discussion about abortion centers around the question of when human life begins, so the morality of **euthanasia** is complicated by questions about *when human life ends*. In life, our lungs automatically inhale life-giving oxygen, our heart pumps blood throughout the body, and our brain serves as a control center for all the conscious and unconscious activities which keep the body functioning. When a person is dead, these essential life systems no longer function. Thus, the threshold between life and death would seem to be clearly defined. Yet, more and more we are hearing of instances in which this threshold is not so clear. Because of increased complexity in the dying process resulting from improved medical technology, important new moral decisions face us.

Church teaching condemns euthanasia. However, we need to be clear about what the word *euthanasia* specifically means. A 1980 Church statement on issues related to dying recalls that "in ancient times *euthanasia* meant easy death without severe suffering" (*Declaration on Euthanasia*, number 3). In modern times euthanasia has come to mean mercy killing—mercifully putting to death someone who is dying or who is experiencing extreme suffering, as we might put to death a dying beloved pet. However, to understand the moral issues surrounding euthanasia today we need to distinguish among a number of actions and inactions that sometimes are identified with the term.

Pope John Paul II gives the following definition of euthanasia: "Euthanasia *in the strict sense* is understood to be an action or omission which of itself and by intention causes death, with the purpose of eliminating all suffering" (*The Gospel of Life*, number 65).

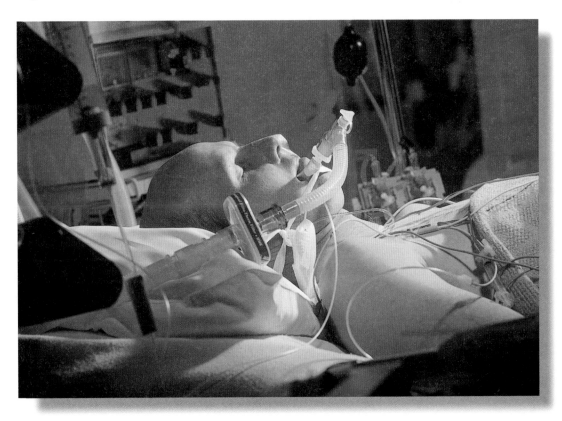

Notice that the pope refers to "euthanasia in the strict sense." In other words, he recognizes that sometimes people use the term to refer to actions that are not, strictly speaking, euthanasia. He also is pointing out that the same action may or may not fall under this strict definition of "euthanasia" depending on the kind of act involved and the intention behind the action. Here are the varying types of euthanasia as performed today.

Active or *direct* euthanasia means taking deliberate steps to end the life of a suffering and incurably ill person. This is what the pope means by "euthanasia in the strict sense." This action may happen with (voluntary) or without (involuntary) the consent of the patient. (*Involuntary euthanasia* occurs when the person [being unconscious or suffering from an irreversible brain disorder] cannot decide for herself or himself.) Regardless of whether the euthanasia was performed at the request of the suffering and dying person himself or herself or decided upon by another, active euthanasia involves the direct and intentional taking of life.

Passive or *indirect* euthanasia means deliberately not taking steps to prevent a sick person's death, precisely with the desire and intention that this "withholding" will lead to or cause his or her death. An example would be refusing a relatively minor, almost always successful, stomach surgery for a Down's syndrome newborn because he or she is mentally handicapped and the parents would prefer the child not to survive. In this instance, while the method is passive or indirect, the intention—just like active euthanasia—is to take a life, however well- or ill-meaning the intention.

Like active euthanasia, this action may happen with or without a patient's consent. Passive or indirect euthanasia, like active euthanasia, is considered wrong by the Church because the intention is the taking of a life. **E**

Activity E

In 1968 Harvard Medical School first listed criteria to indicate when a person is "brain dead." In 1981 a presidential commission updated these criteria. Find a recent statement that specifies what factors are used to determine if a person could be declared dead. (Such a determination carries many ramifications. For instance, defining what constitutes the moment of death is important because of the quick decisions that must be made in cases of organ donors.) Write a report on the factors that in recent decades have made the criteria for determining death more and more complicated.

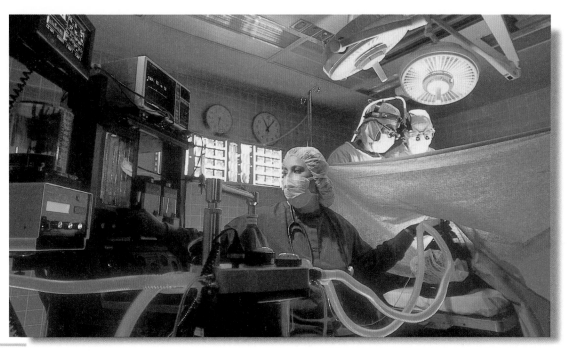

Allowing Death to Occur Is Not the Same as Killing

Visit a hospital that features the latest medical equipment. Immediately, you will notice the array of machines, monitors, and other apparatus available for seriously ill or injured patients. In such an atmosphere euthanasia distinctions appear to become blurred. As a result many people today fear that if their health becomes seriously impaired, the decision about whether to live or die will end up out of their hands. They imagine with dread being kept alive with machines without any hope of serious recovery. With all the medical treatments and equipment available today, the dying person can be forgotten as keeping the body alive becomes the driving force behind treatment. For instance, the body functions of a comatose person with no medical hope of recovery can remain functioning indefinitely with the help of machines and artificial nutrients.

The *Declaration on Euthanasia* addresses this problem by stating that: "When inevitable death is imminent in spite of the means used, it is permitted in conscience to take the decision to refuse forms of treatment that would only secure a precarious and burdensome

prolongation of life" (number 4). This statement acknowledges that at times modern medical technology and medical practices will not *cure* a person but will only *delay death* indefinitely. In such cases, medical treatments that do no more than prolong life at great expense or with excessive burden may be discontinued. Such a decision is not "mercy killing" or euthanasia in the strict sense, since it allows the natural dying process to occur. Thus, the focus is on foregoing excessively burdensome treatment, not on killing the patient.

Medical personnel who work with dying patients often find themselves faced with decisions that rely on these subtle but important distinctions. For instance, what is acceptable when a frail and incurably ill person is experiencing pain and has been prescribed medicine to relieve the pain? At some point, increasing the dosage of certain pain medications might inadvertently hasten or contribute to death. In this situation it is important to recall Pope John Paul II's definition of euthanasia in which he reminds us that the *intention* behind an act must be considered.

Ordinary Versus Extraordinary Means

ordinary means of life support—medical procedures that offer sufficient or reasonable benefits without excessive or undue burdens to the patient or his or her family

extraordinary means of life support—medical procedures that offer little hope of benefits or which cause undue or excessive burdens to the patient or his or her family

Around fifty years ago when modern medical technology was making great advances, Pope Pius XII made a distinction between taking ordinary means of preserving life versus taking extraordinary means. He indicated that extraordinary means of life support need not be taken. Since then Church leaders have further clarified the difference between **ordinary** (necessary) **means** and **extraordinary** (unnecessary) **means**. The important distinction here is not so much a matter of what is done, as it is a matter of the burdens and benefits of available procedures. In other words, the questions to ask are: First, what are the costs and the risks—the burdens—of a particular procedure on a patient, the family, and the community? Secondly, what are the likely results—the benefits—of performing the procedure? Thus, life-support measures that can reasonably be expected to improve a seriously ill person's condition are ordinary means. On the other hand, procedures that merely delay death temporarily but that offer no real hope of reversing the dying process tend to fall into the category of extraordinary means.

Defined in these terms, the same medical interventions can be labeled ordinary in one situation and extraordinary in another. For example, if an otherwise healthy person suddenly stops breathing, putting that person on a ventilator would be expected and necessary if at all possible. Timely use of a ventilator could lead to recovery and avoid death. However, if a person were already near death due to complications from cancer and then stops breathing, a ventilator might be an extraordinary life support, optional rather than necessary. **F**

Activity F

Determine whether or not the following decisions fall under Pope John Paul II's definition of "euthanasia in the strict sense." Explain your decisions.

1. A seventy-year-old woman suffers her third stroke in five years, leaving her paralyzed on her left side and unable to raise herself from her bed without assistance. She notifies the nursing home staff that if she stops breathing she would like not to be revived.

2. A sixty-five-year-old man discovers that he has colon cancer. His father died of this disease many years ago, and the man fears undergoing the same suffering. He plans to take a lethal dosage of painkillers before the condition gets much worse.

3. A couple's daughter is born with severe mental retardation and also with a blockage in her intestines preventing her from taking in regular nourishment. Since they do not want their child to live with the degree of retardation that doctors indicate she suffers from, the couple refuses to sign papers allowing doctors to remove the blockage. Without this operation the child will soon die.

4. An eighty-five-year-old woman is hospitalized with numerous ailments. She suffers from pneumonia, and persistent coughing has weakened her considerably. She complains of chest pain and is prescribed morphine which is administered intravenously to help ease her pain. During the night she calls for a nurse and requests additional pain medicine. According to the patient's medical chart, her doctor permits an increase in morphine as requested. The nurse knows that with the woman's already terminal condition, the amount of morphine being prescribed might indirectly hasten her death. Nonetheless, the nurse does increase the dosage.

Physician-Assisted Suicide

A fairly recent addition to the euthanasia debate is the question of **physician-assisted suicide**. This practice is really a form of active-voluntary euthanasia, since it involves a seriously ill person seeking out a physician to assist him or her in ending his or her own life. Until recently, the question of medical professionals either killing or helping in the killing of their patients wouldn't even have been considered. Such actions go against long-standing professional principles of health care. The role of the physician is to heal, as well as to provide comfort and care, not to kill. Now physician-assisted suicide has become a matter of national debate. As might be expected, the impetus for legalization of this practice originates within the same concerns that lead some people to advocate euthanasia in general. That is, they hope that the availability of a doctor's assistance in ending their lives will free them from needless pain, physical and mental debilitation, and undue prolongation of the death process. Part of their hope is that by killing themselves they will not become a burden to their loved ones or deplete their family's financial resources.

In the chart below, notice the nature of the concerns expressed by someone who may be dying and leaning toward physician-assisted suicide.

physician-assisted suicide—a person who is incurably ill killing himself or herself with the help of a physician

Concerns of the Dying

- I fear pain and suffering.

- I don't want to lose control, especially of my mental faculties.

- I don't want to relinquish my decision-making to health care professionals who may not follow my wishes or have my best interests at heart.

- I don't want to become a physical and financial burden to loved ones.

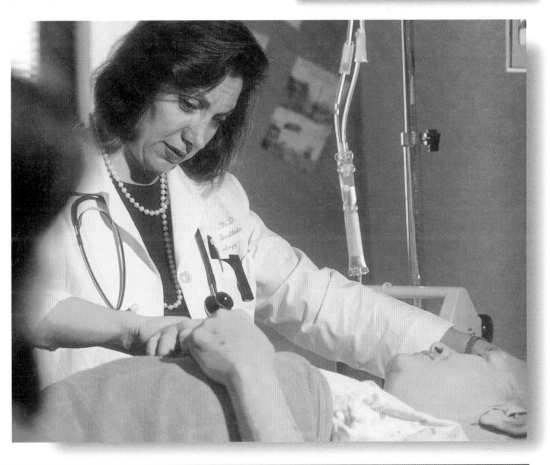

Each of these fears and concerns is understandable, but each one requires questioning and analysis. Physician-assisted suicide seems to reflect the "quick-fix" mentality that permeates our society. Relying on physician-assisted suicide rules out seeking alternative approaches to meeting the fears and concerns of seriously ill persons. It also fails to see possible benefits that can be achieved from time spent undergoing the natural dying process and preparing for death, both for the patient as well as for his or her family and friends. In his encyclical *The Gospel of Life*, Pope John Paul II calls this practice an instance of "false mercy." He asks, what does a person who seeks assistance in ending his or her life really want? He suggests the following:

The request which arises from the human heart in the supreme confrontation with suffering and death, especially when faced with the temptation to give up in utter desperation, is above all a request for companionship, sympathy and support in the time of trial. It is a plea for help to keep on hoping when all human hopes fail (number 67).

The pope recognizes that advocating physician-assisted suicide can arise from positive motivations, from a caring and compassionate human heart. However, he asks people to look behind such a request. Every suicide is a plea for help. The pope sees physician-assisted suicide as a plea for companionship, sympathy, and support. It is a cry for help in attaining the hope beyond human hope that the Christian message provides. He points out that taking a life, even one's own and even during difficult times, attacks the fundamental respect for the dignity of human life that should underlie all decisions about how to view people and how to treat them. That is, human life is precious, even to the very end. Suffering does not diminish the preciousness of life, nor does imminent death or apparent uselessness. The pope implies that, instead of the false mercy of suicide or euthanasia, we serve human life better when we address the deep concerns that sick and dying persons have. **G**

For review . . .

5. What is the difference between active and passive euthanasia?

6. What is the difference between voluntary and involuntary euthanasia?

7. What two questions determine whether a life-support measure is an ordinary or an extraordinary means?

8. What is the Catholic teaching regarding extraordinary means to preserve life?

9. Define physician-assisted suicide.

10. Why does Pope John Paul II call physician-assisted suicide "false mercy"?

Activity G

Use the Internet or other research instrument to find out the current state of physician-assisted suicide. Is it legal in any countries or states? Is it under consideration in any other countries or states?

Make a case for or against the following statement:

Physician-assisted suicide is the beginning of a "slippery slope." Once active-voluntary euthanasia is accepted, then active-involuntary euthanasia will follow that. In other words, we could be headed toward a society in which people who are deemed noncontributing or burdensome may be gotten rid of.

Care for the Dying
Two Movements

Two ways that society has developed to address the deep concerns that sick and dying persons have are living wills and hospice care. The Church not only approves these movements but also encourages proper use of them.

Living Will

living will—a declaration that a competent adult makes identifying the medical care desired if she or he becomes incapacitated

One instrument designed to address concerns that people have about modern technology and dying is the living will. Other names for a living will are advance directive or power of attorney for healthcare purposes. **Living wills** are declarations made by competent adults about the health care they would like for themselves if in the future they are seriously ill or injured and incapable of making their wishes known. Thus, living wills address two concerns that many people have about the medical treatment they will receive if they are helpless: First, individuals retain some control over the administration or the withdrawal of medical treatment. Secondly, family members are relieved from making life or death decisions.

The first state to recognize living wills was California in 1976. Initially, Catholic leaders feared that those who supported living wills were by that very fact advocating euthanasia. Now, Catholic leaders recognize that it can be beneficial for people to make decisions about

designated decision maker—someone appointed to make medical decisions for a person who is incapacitated

their medical treatment or to designate someone else to make decisions for them. A **designated decision maker** is someone appointed by a person to make decisions about his or her health care should he or she beome incapacitated. Most doctors and hospitals appreciate when their patients have living wills. Some hospitals even ask patients, when appropriate, to fill out advance directive forms. **H**

Activity H

One author summarizes a living will in these words: "If there is no reasonable expectation of my recovery from mental or physical disability, I request that I be allowed to die and not be kept alive by artificial or heroic measures. . . . I ask that medication be mercifully administered to me for terminal sufferings even if it hastens the moment of death—I am not asking that my life be directly taken, but that my dying not be unreasonably prolonged" (Alfred McBride, *Death Shall Have No Dominion* [Dubuque, IA: Brown Publishing–ROA Media, 1984]). Would you sign such a document? Why or why not?

The stories of Karen Ann Quinlan and Nancy Cruzan helped shape the evolution of living wills. Find out what you can about the two women. Write a report on their stories and how they influenced living wills.

Hospice Movement

hospice—an intense, multi-faceted, spiritually based approach to assisting people through the dying process

The hospice movement, begun in the 1960s by Dame Cicely Saunders of England, also addresses important concerns of people who are dying. The word *hospice* is taken from the word *hospitality*. Those who travel far from home know how important hospitality is. Travelers need people to welcome them and to assist them on their journey. Hospice recognizes dying as the last and perhaps the most important journey that people will take. Hospice offers an intense, multi-faceted treatment for people with a fatal illness. Hospice refers not to a place but to an approach to being with and caring for dying persons. Hospice care incorporates a wide variety of services, all designed for people who have weeks or at most months to live.

What has the hospice movement added to health care for dying persons? For one thing, keep in mind that medical professionals traditionally see their job as being healers. What are health care providers to do when they can no longer heal their patients but recognize instead that their patients will die shortly? The hospice movement proposes that it is precisely at this time that all the resources of a society should come into play to help make the journey to death as painless, as comfortable, as meaningful, and as communal an experience as possible. When people are nearing death, then health care workers should join with family members, social workers, representatives of religious organizations, and concerned volunteers to offer hospice—support and companionship for the final journey in life. The hospice movement has a strong Christian component to it. Hospice care for dying persons takes place within a network of family and friends and as part of a spiritual community.

Hospice does not try to hasten or postpone death. Instead it seeks to help people live as fully and as comfortably as possible during the last days of their lives. Before the hospice movement, family members often did not talk openly about death or dying when one of their number was nearing death. Everyone tried to spare everyone else the painful reality that someone close to him or her was dying. Hospice rejects a "let's not talk about it" approach to dying. Unlike earlier perspectives, hospice realizes that pain and suffering associated with dying have social and spiritual dimensions that must be talked about and brought to closure before the family member dies. **I**

Hospice's approach to the human reality of dying

1. Hospice considers death and dying as normal aspects of life.

2. Hospice advocates family involvement in caring for the dying person, including care within the person's home for as long as it is beneficial.

3. Hospice seeks to help those who are dying to be givers as well as receivers of care in a community of mutual support.

4. Hospice, as much as possible, actively involves dying persons in decisions.

5. Hospice sees the spiritual dimension as very important for dying persons and fosters spiritual preparation for death.

Activity I

1. If you were in charge of designing a program for persons entering the last stages of their life, what would you include in that program? Name the people and professions you would want to see represented in the program. What attitude toward death and dying would you promote? What activities would you include in order to foster this attitude?

2. Use the Internet or other resource to find out more about the hospice movement. Does a program such as hospice address concerns of dying persons in ways that are wholesome and respectful of the dignity of human life? Report on your findings.

For review . . .

11. Define living will.

12. What two concerns that many people have does a living will address?

13. What concern did Catholic leaders initially have about the living will movement?

14. What is a designated decision maker?

15. Who began the hospice movement and when did it begin?

16. What is the original meaning of hospice? How does the hospice movement apply this meaning to care for the dying?

17. Before the hospice movement, in families and communities what was often the approach to dealing with death and dying?

18. What approach does hospice take to pain and pain management for dying persons?

19. What role does spirituality play in hospice care?

Conclusion
The Healing Message of Jesus Today

We cannot know Jesus apart from his ministry of healing. Is there any activity that he spent more time on than healing the sick? Clearly, Christians seeking to live the message of Jesus today are called upon to heal, and when death is inevitable, healing means for Christians the salvation promised by Jesus. Modern technology has opened up for us many new avenues of healing, some of which come into play precisely during the dying process. The primary moral challenge of today is determining when true healing means allowing a person to die a natural death, while finding hope in the words Jesus offered the thief who was dying with him: "Truly, I tell you, today you will be with me in Paradise" (Luke 23:43).

Let us pray . . .

Father,
God of all consolation,
in your unending love and mercy for us
you turn the darkness of death
into the dawn of new life.
Show compassion to your people in their sorrow. . . .
Your Son, our Lord Jesus Christ,
by dying for us, conquered death
and by rising again, restored life.
May we then go forward eagerly to meet him,
and after our life on earth
be reunited with our brothers and sisters
where every tear will be wiped away.
(We ask this) through Christ our Lord. Amen.

FROM THE CATHOLIC FUNERAL SERVICE, IN *THE RITES OF THE CATHOLIC CHURCH*. [NEW YORK: PUEBLO PUBLISHING CO., 1976].

CHAPTER 12

Morality and Money

Integrity in the Marketplace

As we go about living our lives, all of us will buy—and many of us will sell—products made worldwide. We will earn wages and decide how to spend money. We will work for, invest in, and buy from numerous businesses. Perhaps we will even be responsible for hiring or firing employees. In fact, throughout our lives, whether or not our profession is business itself, we will be involved in many business decisions. If we want to live our lives morally, we will seek to apply our Christian moral vision to all areas of our lives, including our business activity. In this chapter we will aim to become better informed about values and virtues that relate to the marketplace and about moral dilemmas related to business.

Chapter Overview

- Business decisions always have moral implications.
- The world of business presents moral challenges to all of us.
- Christian values can help us make our business decisions more moral.

Let us pray . . .

Jesus, Light of the World, guide us in the holy use of all things. May we value money and material possessions for the good that they can do. Throughout our lives may we engage in right livelihood—providing for ourselves and our families while also contributing to building up the human community. Show us how people are burdened through the workings of our economic system; help us create an economy that is a blessing to all. Keep us ever watchful of the ways material possessions and money can be misused and wrongly viewed. Make us ever mindful of where our true treasure lies. Amen.

Before we begin . . .

Answer agree, disagree, or uncertain to the following questions. Explain your answers.

1. Even though they are private citizens and not public servants, business leaders wield an excessive amount of power in the world today.

2. I trust business leaders more than government officials when it comes to just and sensible use of money.

3. Business leaders must always place the highest priority on the "bottom line," that is, on whether or not their company is making money.

4. The wealthiest people in a country should be more socially responsible than those who are poorer.

5. Wealthier people should be taxed more than poorer people.

6. If I knew that a piece of electronic equipment was stolen from a store but that it was in good working condition, I would buy it if the price were right.

7. If I knew that a product—such as sneakers that I particularly liked— was being manufactured using child workers in deplorable conditions in a poor country, I would refuse to buy that product.

8. If the employees of a store went on strike and I felt that their cause was just, I would not cross their picket line.

9. Advertising is meant to sell products. Therefore, statements in ads need not be true.

10. It is sinful how much people in the U.S. consume.

11. It would be good if all parts of the world could enjoy the level of prosperity that the U.S. enjoys.

12. I consider work to be a blessing, an opportunity for self-expression and service.

Moral Dilemmas in the World of Business

- For a tenth-grade student, Logan displays unusual skill and an avid interest in electronics. He possesses an elaborate, high-tech entertainment system. To help pay for his constant upgrading of equipment, Logan copies CDs, cassette tapes, and videotapes. He sells them at reduced prices to friends and classmates who know that Logan can always be counted on for high-quality products. Logan and his customers know that his "business" is officially illegal, but they don't see that anybody is getting hurt. Besides, Logan claims that "everybody does it." If he didn't make a little money in this way, someone else would.

- A distributor knows that apple juice diluted with sugar is practically indistinguishable from undiluted apple juice. He approaches Ryan, an executive from a leading baby food company, with the following proposal: "Would you like to make a lot of money for your company? I can supply you with diluted apple juice at a reduced rate. Labeling it '100% natural' is not really lying, and no one will know the difference."

- As the quality-control representative during the evening shift at her factory, Marta is responsible for overseeing the quality of the finished product coming off the assembly line—toys designed for young children. She notices that one particular toy is consistently coming through with one crooked bolt, creating a ragged edge and thus a hazard for the small children who might play with it. By the time she notifies her supervisor, thousands of defective toys have been packaged and ready for shipment. Discarding these toys at this time, just before the Christmas season, would create a serious financial crunch just when the company needs all the revenue it can get. "Perhaps the defect isn't so bad," the supervisor tells Marta. "Let's just say we were unaware of the problem and hope it's never discovered."

- Despite occasional disastrous accidents, out-dated oil tankers continue to transport oil across the seas. Disruption of oil supplies would present an economic downturn for countries now heavily dependent on it for industry and transportation. When an oil-spill occurs and transforms miles of coastline into a burial ground for fish, birds, and other wildlife, conservation groups complain. Meanwhile, businesses and agencies debate about who should be financially responsible for the clean-up. The debate could go on for a long time, and prompt action is necessary. As the head of the petroleum company that was importing the oil, Mitchell is trying to determine what his company should do.

- Dianne is the major buyer for the clothing division of her department store chain. While traveling in Asia, she comes upon a company that assures her that they can produce the type of clothing her corporation wants and that they can do so at a reasonable price. Looking into the matter, she finds that workers in the factories run by this company are beaten and made to live under guard in cramped, rat-infested quarters. When she asks the company's representatives about these conditions, she is told that this is standard practice for workers in their country. If she doesn't subcontract with this company, some other buyer will. A deal with this subcontractor could prove to be very lucrative for her corporation and for her personally. **A**

Activity A

1. Imagine that you have been called in to advise the people in the above scenarios: Logan, Ryan, Marta, Mitchell, and Dianne. What course of action would you recommend for each person? Explain the moral basis for your suggestions.

2. Describe three other moral dilemmas related in some way to business. For each one, describe what you believe is the appropriate course of action. Explain why.

3. Finally, based on these examples, consider the following question: Does business activity create unique problems regarding moral decision making? Explain.

The World of Business
Conflicting Images

In our society, we tend to admire those who are successful in business. Heads of businesses hold leadership positions in civic organizations on local, national, and international levels. Business success can even make a person appear qualified to be president of the United States. When cabinet posts are to be filled, heads of government often look to business leaders for potential candidates. Business-related professions rank among the top career choices of today's high school graduates, and a sizable number of incoming college freshmen make business their area of study. A great number of young people view the world of business as the best ticket to financial success and security.

Although business leaders are admired in our communities and even though business-related fields are appealing, our culture often paints a negative picture of the business world. In television and movies, business people are frequently stereotyped as involved in illegal or immoral activity, as being coldhearted and greedy, or as being cunning and deceptive. In a popular media stereotype, business people worship before the altar of the "almighty dollar" and show little concern for who gets hurt from their business decisions. Invariably, that is, they are portrayed as placing profits over people and money over morality.

Which image offers the more accurate portrayal of the world of business today? Does concern for "the bottom line"—that is, making a profit—tend to lead to immorality in business? Do pressures to make ever-increasing amounts of money cause business people more than people in other professions to bend or stretch morality? Or, do the vast majority of people who are successes in business serve an important and honorable function in our society and deserve whatever respect we can give them? **B**

Activity B

Debate the following statement: By the very nature of their work, people involved in business tend to be less moral than people involved in other professions.

Examining Morality in Business

To begin with, it is important to recognize that people involved in business at the highest levels do wield a great amount of power in our world today. The largest businesses are worth more than the gross national product of some nations. Top businesses are international in scope. Clothing featuring Disney characters, manufactured in any number of countries, is worn by African, American, European, and Asian children alike. People in Taiwan drive Fords and eat at McDonald's; Americans drive foreign-made Mazdas and Volvos while drinking a favorite beverage that originated in some tropical country. The closing of a factory can turn a thriving community into a ghost town. Business decisions can help preserve the environment or send it toward destruction.

The powerful impact of business on our lives and in our world is not going to go away. Businesses play an important role on the world scene, and decisions by business leaders affect us in innumerable ways. In fact, a case could be made that *no segment of society has a greater impact on our world today than business does*. Since so many people can be harmed or helped by them, business decisions need to be examined in light of morality. **C**

Recognizing the Problem—Business Decisions Are Moral Decisions

The first step toward examining morality in business is to recognize that *every business decision is at the same time a moral decision*. Morality concerns itself with how people are helped or hurt, how people are benefited or burdened, and how people are nurtured or negated. Like morality itself, all business decisions affect people positively or negatively. Often business decisions affect many more people than simply those directly involved in a business transaction. Morality applied to business, therefore, seeks the welfare of people who are either directly or indirectly affected by business decisions.

The beginning of this chapter presented five incidents describing business decisions that clearly held moral implications. At all levels, the business world offers temptations to choose a self-serving but immoral path to economic success. If we read newspapers regularly, we discover that some business persons do make choices that seem immoral, such as in the examples given at the beginning of the chapter. The point of this chapter is to help you be a consumer who is aware of unethical business practices and to give you a basis on which to become a moral business person in the future.

Activity C

Use examples to make a case for or against the following statement: No segment of society has a greater impact on our world today than business does.

1. Imagine that you are the president of a large international corporation. Write a "code of morality" for your company.

2. Using the Internet or other reference source, find the mission statement or the stated policies and goals of a company. Look for indications that the company advocates moral business practices. What specific moral concerns, if any, do they address?

There is a growing awareness among many business leaders of the importance of morality in business; and more and more business leaders are exploring the relationship between the two. They realize that the business world is a world in which temptations to act immorally are great and in which "realizing a profit" can quickly turn to greed. Certain practices that are officially legal may not necessarily be moral. To complicate matters, common business practices in one country would be viewed as immoral in another. People involved in business may come to the recognition that seemingly acceptable business tactics would in other contexts be labeled lying, cheating, and stealing.

Many business leaders want businesses to take the lead in upholding morality. In this way they wish to set a tone within the entire business world and beyond that says harmful practices will not be tolerated. Recognizing the important global impact that businesses have, they want that impact to be a positive one.

Most successful businesses now have clear policy statements about their business ethics—proper conduct in business. Large companies typically have outside, independent directors who oversee complaints based on a company's conduct policies. Many companies hold courses and seminars to educate their employees about acceptable moral behavior related to their work. Such seminars tend to address practical issues that arise in the course of business dealings. When they examine specific dilemmas that they might face, business workers at all levels discover a wide assortment of moral and legal challenges. In the end, over-arching principles of morality that apply elsewhere also apply to business. **D**

Activity D

• Refer to specific cases to defend or refute the following statement:

Morality in business is different from morality in other areas of life. Certain practices are acceptable in business that would be unacceptable and immoral in other contexts, such as in personal relationships, family life, education, and religion.

• If you were in charge of designing a workshop for business employees on business ethics, what specific issues would you address? What activities would you include to help people appreciate morality in business?

Beyond the Bottom Line—Balancing Concern for Many People

If you broke into another student's locker and stole the contents, you would have a pretty clear notion of who benefits and who is hurt by that action. In business activity, such clarity seldom exists. Many people can be affected by business decisions, such as corporation owners and stockholders, managers and employees, consumers, local communities in which companies are located, and suppliers of the resources used by a company.

Obviously, business decisions affect far more than a company's owners. Moral decision making in business requires weighing the concerns of many different constituents.

Because business involves so many different people, moral decision making in business belies easy solutions. Keeping a plant operating might be good for a community but not good for the company's stockholders. Exploitative advertising might be financially beneficial for stockholders but damaging to the public. Firing an ineffective employee could be detrimental to the employee but good for the company. Keeping the cost of natural resources low benefits consumers but can harm workers who harvest those resources. **E**

For review . . .

1. Describe the two conflicting viewpoints on business that people typically have in our society.

2. What does it mean to say that "every business decision is at the same time a moral decision"?

3. Name two steps that many businesses have taken to address the issue of morality in business.

Activity E

What would you do in each of the following situations:

1. A woman secretary has been arriving late and missing quite a bit of work lately. She tells you that she is a single mother who sometimes has trouble finding day-care for her child.

2. You are in an administrative position for your company. The head of the company informs you that the office where you are working will be shutting down in a few months and that you are not to tell anyone. She assures you that you will continue to have a job elsewhere with the company. However, many of your friends who work at this office will be losing their jobs.

3. You have inside information that your company will soon be merging with another company, which will send your company's stocks soaring. At a social gathering, a friend asks, "Do you have any suggestions for how I might invest my money?" Do you tell him about the future merger?

4. You work for a car dealership. The person in charge of sales tells you that unless many of the used cars on the lot are sold by the end of the month, some people will have to lose their job. An older couple comes in looking for a car. They are attracted to one that you know will be trouble down the line. Do you alert them to potential problems?

5. You are the one woman among the six executives at your company. At meetings, the men often make remarks about women that you feel are inappropriate. When you point this out to the head of the company, he tells you that you are being much too sensitive. What do you do?

Stockholders and Stakeholders

stockholders—
people who invest
money in a company

bottom line—
in business, realizing
a profit

stakeholders—
people who are
affected by a
particular business

A large corporation has **stockholders** to whom corporate executives are responsible. Stockholders entrust their money to a company with the intention that company managers will manage their money wisely—so that they, the stockholders, will realize a profit. The larger the profits, the more successful a corporation's managers are considered. This scenario represents a **bottom-line** perspective on business.

However, beyond the bottom line, many others besides stockholders are **stakeholders** in a corporation's activities. That is, many people have a stake in what businesses do. In a global economy, people on the other side of the earth are affected by a company's decisions.

Especially because of the immense power possessed by large corporations, factors besides the financial gains of stockholders must be included in measuring a company's success.

A corporation's decision to operate a plant in a particular community or country can mean life or death for that region. Research by corporations on such things as pollutants and alternatives to pollutants, safer medicines, safety features in automobiles, health foods, and better farm equipment can benefit vast numbers of people. Beyond the bottom line, business and business leaders play a major role in the welfare of people worldwide. **F**

Activity F

1. List at least two ways that a corporation's decisions could have an impact on each of the following:
   - employees
   - stockholders
   - the local community
   - the environment
   - consumers

2. Think of the world's business activity as one giant enterprise. Make a case that business has or has not made great positive contributions to the people of the world.

Establishing a Rationale for Morality in Business—Why Be Good?

Clearly, business involves moral decision making. However, are good business and good morality compatible? That is, do moral practices enhance or interfere with the economic success of a business and do immoral practices show a positive or negative effect on a business? These questions can be addressed in different ways.

First, some studies indicate that many of the most financially successful companies are also among the most moral in their principles, policies, and practices. Such studies might lay to rest the question: Are good business and good morality compatible? However, other studies find no conclusive evidence that good morality supports good business. Those who advocate high moral standards as the best way to achieve financial success point out that poor quality and poor service will definitely affect profits negatively soon enough. Also, in today's climate businesses that do not adhere to high standards can find themselves drained financially just by paying out substantial lawsuits.

In response to the studies that link good morality and successful business, some skeptical analysts reply that more successful companies can afford to be more moral. Consider this analogy: A student who has studied hard and is prepared for a test is under less compulsion to cheat than a student who is unprepared and anxious about failing. Similarly, a company teetering on the brink of bankruptcy may feel a greater temptation to settle for a quick fix, even if immoral, than a company that is highly successful. In other words, high moral standards often go hand-in-hand with business success. However, when a business faces failure or stiff competition, then lowering moral standards is a temptation. **G**

Activity G

Over the years, your company has built up a reputation for quality products. However, due to changes in the marketplace and some poor business decisions, the company now finds itself in financial difficulty. The CEO recommends to the board of directors the following measures:

- save money by cutting back on the quality of materials used
- close all U.S. plants and move all operations to countries where labor is cheaper
- fire all middle-management personnel who are over forty-five and earning large salaries
- initiate an ad campaign that belittles major competitors of your products

If you were a member of the board, how would you vote on each of these measures? Why would you vote this way? Do any of the proposals strike you as immoral? Explain.

Secondly, in moral decision making related to business, we can distinguish long-term effects from short-term ones. For instance, if we cheat on a quiz we may find that it results in a short-term good—namely, a higher grade for that quiz. However, it can have any number of negative long-term consequences, such as not understanding the material or being unprepared for future college tests. In business, immoral practices can also have short-term positive results but long-term negative ones. For instance, a company that produces inferior merchandise and opts to pass it off as high quality can make money short-term. However, long-term it might establish a reputation for shoddy production and, therefore, lose sales. On the other hand, a company that insists on high-quality merchandise, even when it means incurring the expense of discarding or recalling some of its products, may prove to be more successful in the long run because it may gain sales based on its reputation for quality products.

Finally, in business, why be moral? If a teacher lectures your class about cheating and states the following reasons for not cheating, how will you respond? Would any of these reasons persuade you to not cheat?

- You might get caught and the consequences would be grave.

- Cheating is only a short-term solution to a long-term problem. Cheating does not eliminate the problem. It only postpones it or might actually aggravate it.

- By cheating, your personal integrity and honesty will be damaged.

Notice the difference between the first two reasons and the third one. The first two suggest that cheating may not "work" and therefore we shouldn't do it. The last reason suggests that, whether or not cheating is effective, when we cheat—just as when we choose any immoral behavior—we are damaging and belittling ourselves. The same principle holds true for business. Beyond the question of whether or not good morality equals greater economic success, the moral questions that business persons must face have an impact on their integrity as persons. Just like cheating on a test, moral compromise in business means compromise of personal integrity. In the words of the Book of Proverbs, "Bread gained by deceit is sweet, but afterward the mouth will be full of gravel" (Proverbs 20:17). **H**

whistle blower— an employee of a company who discovers illegal or immoral practices and makes that information public

Activity H

- A good friend of yours works for a company seeking a contract with your company. Over lunch, she tells you that she desperately needs to close a deal with your company or else her job is in jeopardy. If you recommend that your company purchase supplies from your friend's company, your supervisors would take your advice seriously. However, you know that your friend's company's offer is not the best one for your company. What do you do?

- A **whistle blower** is an employee of a company who discovers illegal or immoral practices occurring in the company and goes public with that information.

Is whistle blowing always, sometimes, or never the right thing to do? Use examples to explain your position.

The Challenge of Sustaining Morality in Business

Business transactions involve money or some other exchange between people. Business is a game of winning and losing in which winning can involve making a great deal of money. If we take a game seriously, then we want to be a winner at that game.

However, for every winner at the game there is also at least one loser. The game of business often brings into question basic moral values, without providing opportunities to consult wise counsel or to think things through. When you find yourself in the hustle and bustle of the business world, you will find that decisions often must be made quickly and that the rules of the game are not always so clearly spelled out or easy to follow. Certainly, your values will be called into question.

Evaluating Morality in Business

Guidelines business persons can use to help them evaluate the morality of their decisions.

1. **The Golden-Rule Test**—Act the way you hope others will act toward you.

2. **The "Sixty Minutes" Test**—Act as if your decision and the reasons for it were the subject of a nationally broadcast TV program.

3. **The Pride Test**—Act so that you feel genuine pride in your decision. You would be proud to tell your family all about the decision over Thanksgiving dinner.

4. **The Universal Principle Test**—Act in such a way that you would like the action to be part of a universal code of behavior.

5. **The Fellow-Professional Test**—Act as if your action is subject to review by a panel of the best members of your profession.

The business executive who bribes a government official in order to gain a lucrative contract may applaud herself for knowing how to play the game, but she is diminishing her moral fiber and that of the country. The sales person who lies that "the dress fits fine" is losing touch with the important virtue of truthfulness. The investor who buys stock in corporations that he knows are engaged in immoral practices is limiting his understanding of personal responsibility. Advertising agencies that dupe consumers into believing that certain products are necessities rather than luxuries need to question themselves about the acceptable limits of their profession.

Naturally, people who run and work in businesses exhibit a range of moral development—just like people in all professions. The challenge facing business persons is to stand up for morality and to remain true to principles even during trying times and in the heat of battle. In this regard, the challenges facing business persons are the same challenges facing the rest of us. If we develop virtues and values early in our lives, we will be better equipped to act morally when larger amounts of money are at stake. ∎

For review . . .

4. What is a "stakeholder" in relation to business? Name four groups who would fit this designation.

5. According to the text are the most moral businesses always also the most successful? Explain.

6. Illustrate how moral or immoral business practices can have different long-term versus short-term effects.

7. What three reasons does the text list for not cheating? In what sense is the third reason listed different from the other two?

Activity I

For each question listed, rank yourself from 1 to 10 (10 means "I exhibit the highest moral values"). Write a brief response as to how you think your values will affect business decisions that you might face in the future.

• What value, personal or otherwise, do you place on wealth?

• How frequently does personal benefit alone determine your relationships with others? That is, do you usually ask, "What's in it for me?"

• At how great an expense to others do you seek your own gain?

• Do you act fairly even when you could get away with cheating?

• If you found yourself wealthy, what would you do with your wealth?

• Do you think you could maintain your highest values and virtues if you were regularly involved in business?

Biblical Values and Business

Thirty-eight of Jesus' parables are recorded in the Gospels. Of them, sixteen deal directly with finances.

RON BENTZ, *GOD, MONEY AND YOU* [KANSAS CITY, MO: SHEED & WARD, 1989].

When we read the Bible we discover that the Israelites of old knew quite a bit about shady business practices as opposed to just ones. In particular the prophets warned people that God would not tolerate the rich getting richer at the expense of the poor or needy people being overlooked in society. Unjust practices cause disruption; eventually, everyone will pay the price. According to the prophet Amos, setting the price of grain so that poor people are deprived of what they require will cause the earth to tremble and cause darkness at noon. (See Amos, chapter 8.) According to Jeremiah the prophet, one sure sign that people have strayed from God is that "from the least to the greatest everyone is greedy for unjust gain" (Jeremiah 8:10). When we practice deceit we are like "a horse plunging headlong into battle" (Jeremiah 8:6). For the prophets of old, treating others justly is the only way we can truly know God and live according to his will.

Business morality also figures strongly into the concerns of the earliest Christians. One of the marks of this new-style community was its system of distribution of wealth and goods: "All who believed were together and had all things in common; they would sell their possessions and goods and distribute the proceeds to all, as any had need" (Acts 2:44). The letter of James offers the following words of caution for those who continue to show favoritism to the rich over the poor:

> *My brothers and sisters, do you with your acts of favoritism really believe in our glorious Lord Jesus Christ? For if a person with gold rings and in fine clothes comes into your assembly, and if a poor person in dirty clothes also comes in, and if you take notice of the one wearing the fine clothes and say, "Have a seat here, please," while to the one who is poor you say, "Stand there," or, "Sit at my feet," have you not made distinctions among yourselves and become judges with evil thoughts? Listen, my beloved brothers and sisters. Has not God chosen the poor in the world to be rich in faith and to be heirs of the kingdom that he has promised to those who love him? But you have dishonored the poor. Is it not the rich who oppress you? Is it not they who drag you into court? Is it not they who blaspheme the excellent name that was invoked over you?* **J**

JAMES 2:1–7

Activity J

Read the following passages from Scripture. Write down a possible implication that each passage has for business morality.

Leviticus 19:9–15	Luke 18:18–30
Deuteronomy 10:16–19	Acts 4:32–35
Jeremiah 7:1–11	1 John 3:16–18
Amos 2:6–7	1 Timothy 6:6–10
Matthew 6:24	Hebrews 10:32–34
Luke 6:20–26	Revelation 18:1–3

The U.S. Catholic Bishops Address Economic Concerns

Economic Justice for All—The U.S. Catholic bishops' 1986 pastoral letter on the economy

Business matters continue to occupy the attention of Church leaders. The U. S. bishops addressed the issue most forcefully in 1986 with their pastoral letter entitled *Economic Justice for All*. At the time, many people felt that the bishops should not speak out on a subject that is not "religious" and on matters about which they are not experts. The bishops countered that "no dimension of human life lies beyond God's care and concern" (number 31) and that many central biblical concepts and stories "provide a foundation for reflection on issues of economic and social justice" (number 30).

The following quote from that document raises questions about, and suggests principles for, applying Christian values to our business lives.

> We know that, at times, in order to remain truly a community of Jesus' disciples, we will have to say "no" to certain aspects in our culture, to certain trends and ways of acting that are opposed to a life of faith, love, and justice. Changes in our hearts lead naturally to a desire to change how we act. With what care, human kindness, and justice do I conduct myself at work? How will my economic decisions to buy, sell, invest, divest, hire, or fire serve human dignity and the common good? In what career can I best exercise my talents so as to fill the world with the Spirit of Christ? How do my economic choices contribute to the strength of my family and community, to the values of my children, to a sensitivity to those in need? In this consumer society, how can I develop a healthy detachment from things and avoid the temptation to assess who I am by what I have? How do I strike a balance between labor and leisure that enlarges my capacity for friendships, for family life, for community? What government policies should I support to attain the well-being of all, especially the poor and vulnerable?
>
> ECONOMIC JUSTICE FOR ALL,
> INTRODUCTION, NUMBER 23.

The bishops have developed four themes on Catholic thought about business and morality that appear throughout their documents on economics. In the concluding section of this chapter, we will look more closely at each of these themes. By examining them, we can gain a sense of how the Christian vision of morality can interconnect with business decisions. **K**

Contemporary Catholic Themes about Business and Morality

1. Ultimately, all wealth, goods, and property belong to God. We humans are merely caretakers of wealth and material goods.

2. Our work is not just a means of making money but is connected to our call through which we serve God and other people.

3. All dimensions of our lives, including our business affairs, should be evaluated in terms of how poor and vulnerable people are affected.

4. True success is measured by the enrichment of ourselves, our families, and our communities.

We Are God's Caretakers

With what care . . . do I conduct myself at work?

In the early chapters of Genesis, the first book of the Bible, humans are commissioned by God to be stewards of creation, a term that means "caretaker." All of creation, with all of its beauty and goodness, belongs to God. We humans are called upon to take care of creation and indeed to be creative in our use and distribution of the goods of the earth. In the words of the Catechism, "In the beginning God entrusted the earth and its resources to the common stewardship of mankind to take care of them, master them by labor, and enjoy their fruits" [Cf. Gen 1:26–29] (2402).

Stewardship offers a very exalted image of our relationship to the goods and services that we humans provide one another in our businesses and professions. According to the Bible, our work is to be God's work. We represent God when we decide how money is spent, who works and who doesn't, which products are manufactured, how we treat the environment, and so forth. Such an exalted view of our human dignity carries with it an equally awesome view of our human responsibility.

Among other services, business leaders often oversee the manufacture of products, the harvesting of crops, and the disposal of waste. A company that develops environmentally safe products and takes seriously the problem of excessive waste is operating with a spirit of stewardship. A company that ignores environmental concerns is not acting as a caretaker of the earth as all of us are called to be.

stewardship— biblical concept that humans represent God in caring for the earth's resources

Activity K

How might each of these four themes be applied to the following business-related decisions:

- A state legislature debates whether to fund a highway project or a deteriorating public transportation system.

- A college graduate tries to decide whether to take a high-paying job that she knows she would not like or a lower-paying job that she truly would enjoy and find meaningful.

Work as Ministry

In what career can I best exercise my talents?

According to Christian tradition, all of us are called to minister to one another. We gain insight into the true importance of work if we think of all forms of work as a type of ministry—work that serves God and others. We are usually comfortable with the idea of teaching and social work as forms of ministry. However, shouldn't the same view of work apply to other professions? Farmers and stockbrokers, factory workers and plumbers, newspaper carriers and food handlers—besides hopefully earning a living—are also doing service to God and to the human community. Similarly, factory workers, store clerks, and day-care providers serve essential roles in maintaining our society. Every profession is an important dimension of Christian ministry.

When we exercise our talents for the good of others, then our career is part of our response to God's call. The bishops' letter on the economy emphasizes community and **interdependence** as important concepts in evaluating our economic system. They are reminding us that God does not call us to the work we do apart from everyone else. We do business or nursing or factory work within a community, and within our community everyone is interdependent. When we view only certain professions as important, then we destroy their religious, communal, and interdependent reality. In the Christian vision, all of us are called by God and our work is part of our response to God. Our profession is an important dimension of our Christian call.

Of course, if all work is important, and if a career can be a dimension of our ministry, then whatever we do deserves a **just wage** and also deserves to be viewed with respect. Just wages can be based on a number of factors, such as educational background, talent, or amount of experience. As long as some companies gain their profits and pay huge salaries to CEOs while depending on a workforce many of whom are making wages that will not move them out of poverty, then the business world has a long way to go. **L**

just wage—fair and adequate monetary compensation for one's work

interdependence—the proposition that within a community all members depend upon one another

---

Activity L

1. Consult an almanac or other reference source to find out the average wages of various professions and types of workers (for example: teachers, professional athletes, CEOs, lawyers, hospital orderlies, factory workers). Based on your findings, write a response to the following statement: Just wages are not really a problem in our country today.

2. Name a profession that you would have some interest in entering when you are older. Write an essay describing how that profession could be a form of ministry. In particular, write about how the profession could be a means of self-expression and service to people who are poor or otherwise in need.

Business Decisions and Their Impact on the Poor

. . . To attain the well-being of all, especially the poor and the vulnerable.

Regarding special concern for people who are poor, the bishops' statement in *Economic Justice for All* is very clear and very strong:

As a community of believers, we know that our faith is tested by the quality of justice among us, that we can best measure our life together by how the poor and the vulnerable are treated (Introduction, number 8).

As followers of Christ, we are challenged to make a fundamental "option for the poor" (Introduction, number 16).

The bishops recognize that work, businesses, corporations, and the system within which they exist have an impact on all people. However, the bishops are particularly concerned about the effects that business decisions have on people who are poor. They see a situation in which a small minority of the most wealthy people profit greatly while the large number of very poor people are left out of most of the benefits of the economic systems governing our society and our world. Therefore, the bishops call for an evaluation of our society and its institutions in light of their impact on poor people.

True Business Success

To serve human dignity . . . contribute to the strength of my family and community, to the values of my children, to a sensitivity to those in need . . .

The bishops affirm that all work has moral significance. They describe three dimensions of the morality of work:

- It is a principal way that people exercise the distinctive human capacity for self-expression and self-realization.
- It is the ordinary way for humans to fulfill their material needs (earn a living).
- Work enables people to contribute to the well-being of the larger community. (Chapter 2, number 97)

What is true of work in general is equally true of business in particular. Business activities

are a wonderful means for people to exercise self-expression. Business-related work can provide a livelihood and help people attain material goods. However, like work in general, business activities are never for oneself alone. Rather, they are "for one's family, for the nation, and indeed for the benefit of the entire human family" (Chapter 2, number 97).

When we overemphasize the second purpose of business and work—earning a living—and downplay self-expression and service to others, we make work and ourselves less than human. All professions need to be scrutinized in light of basic moral questions about how people are helped or hurt. True business success is measured not only in dollars and cents but also in terms of self-realization and service to others. **M**

Activity M

Respond to the following questions:

1. Do you think that Church leaders should become more or less outspoken regarding morality in business? Why or why not?

2. Is their impact on those who are most poor and vulnerable the key question to ask of business decisions and economic systems?

8. What message did the Hebrew prophets give to their community about distribution of wealth?

9. How does the letter of James suggest that we should treat people?

10. Name the four Christian principles related to business morality presented in the U.S. Catholic bishops' pastoral letter *Economic Justice for All.*

11. What does the Bible mean when it refers to humans as "stewards"?

12. What does it mean to refer to work as ministry?

13. What types of work does the text suggest should be viewed as ministry?

14. Name the three dimensions of the morality of work identified by the U.S. Catholic bishops.

Conclusion

Morality in Business Is Not Just Good for Business, It Is Necessary for Our Survival

As we become more and more aware of immorality in business, we cry out for businesses with a moral sense. If we find ourselves stranded by the side of a road with a broken car, we want an honest auto mechanic. When we purchase food at a supermarket or a restaurant, we need food producers and food handlers who take pride in their work. Indeed, we cannot survive on our planet without heads of businesses who cherish the environment.

Many business leaders today realize how far-reaching the decisions of major companies are. More and more they are placing moral and social concerns near the top of the list of what their companies stand for. As we ourselves become more active participants in the high-pressure world of the marketplace, we need to maintain the Christian vision that looks beyond the bottom line of profits to the bigger picture of personal integrity and concern for others.

Let us pray . . .

Let us praise God for the community of laborers who make our world work. May we respect each worker and look forward to finding our own way of contributing to the intricate web of life. May all people find security, self-fulfillment, and a means of livelihood in their chosen profession. We ask this through Christ our Lord. Amen.

CHAPTER 13

Technology
Morality in the Information Age

Where does most of your education take place—in school or in front of a television? What are some of the lessons—both the obvious ones and the more subtle ones—that you have learned from your television viewing? In addition to opening up unlimited opportunities for communication, does the Internet also hold out moral dangers different from face-to-face encounters? When a young boy shoots a gun at life-like figures on a screen at a video arcade, is his activity merely the moral equivalent of throwing baseballs at milk bottles during a carnival—or is it fundamentally different? Seemingly overnight our world has become high tech. Much good has come from modern technology. However, along with every other area of life, technology deserves moral scrutiny to help us evaluate how it can be used for human betterment.

Chapter Overview

• Television viewing time must be used wisely.

• Computers and the Internet offer potential good but they can also be misused.

• Video games are an important part of youth culture and deserve moral scrutiny.

Let us pray . . .

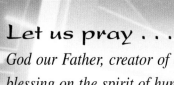

God our Father, creator of all that is good, we ask your blessing on the spirit of human inventiveness that has so enriched our lives and has transformed our world into a global village. May we use the wonders of technology to do your will and, together with you, build up the human community. Amen.

Before we begin . . .

Answer agree, disagree, or uncertain to the following statements.

1. On school nights I would restrict television viewing for school-aged children to one hour or less.

2. I would want a child of mine to have a computer and a phone with a private number in his or her private room.

3. I see no point in discussing computers and other technology in a morality course.

4. If someone comes to our house to visit, the television is turned off.

5. In our house the TV often remains on even if no one is watching.

6. If nothing on TV particularly interests me, I always stop watching and do something else.

7. In general, I believe that family televisions and computers should be in family rooms and not located in bedrooms.

8. I would restrict computer use on school nights to educational uses only.

9. Because computer skills are very important, I would encourage children to spend as much time as possible at a computer.

10. Internet chat lines and instant message services are a good way to make friends and to build communication skills.

11. Playing video games is a harmless and healthy recreational activity.

12. I would not allow a child under twelve to play video games that depict violence.

13. If I had a young child, I would strictly limit the amount of time he or she spends playing video games.

Morality and Technology
Is There a Conflict?

Walk into any large bookstore and you will find stacks of books about computers. They will explain the latest software programs, introduce you to the Internet, and describe the wonderful world of computers in user-friendly language. However, you will have difficulty finding any books raising broad moral questions related to computers.

Schools that want to attract students today typically include in their promotional literature a scene in a computer lab. Students are working away on the latest computer hardware, while a teacher with sleeves rolled up leans in a helpful pose over a student. When politicians talk about improving education, invariably they include a call for more computers in schools and greater computer literacy among students. Are the ever-growing numbers of computers and their increased use an unquestioned positive development? Is there a need for moral discussion about computers and related technologies?

Television has been with us for over fifty years now. Few people remember what life was like "B.T."—Before Television. Today's "screenagers" include older people in nursing homes who depend on television to keep them connected to the larger world and toddlers for whom "Sesame Street" serves as a regular baby-sitter. If you are an average American teenager, you have already spent close to 30,000 hours of your life—that's three and one-half years—in front of a television. How has that investment of time and mental energy affected you? Are there moral dimensions to television viewing?

Do you own a video-game system? Have you recently replaced an older model system with a newer one? If so, how much money has gone into games and equipment? How much time do you spend playing video games? What activities are depicted on your favorite games? Do you or any of your friends have restrictions on video-game use? Would it be possible to put together a report on video games and morality? If so, what might be in such a report?

Unless a worldwide and irreversible power outage occurs and all communications satellites fail, we will continue to become increasingly dependent on technology. New moral questions accompany each technological advancement. Since technology is a "work in progress," it is difficult to identify precisely what the most significant moral implications of various technologies are. However, we need to analyze carefully what the technology that shapes our lives so strongly is doing to us, to our values, and to our moral lives. **A**

Activity A

Interview someone over sixty-five about what life was like before television and before computers. Ask him or her what positive or negative consequences have resulted from the widespread use of TV and computers.

Television
A Journey through the Looking Glass

The means of social communication (especially the mass media) can give rise to a certain passivity among users, making them less than vigilant consumers of what is said or shown. Users should practice moderation and discipline in their approach to the mass media. (Catechism, #2496)

Today's adolescents were born into "the television age." During the time of the advent of TV, Pope Pius XII declared Clare of Assisi to be the patron saint of television. (A friend of Saint Francis of Assisi, Clare adapted his ideals to form a religious order of women.) As a saint of the Middle Ages, Clare knew nothing of NBC's Thursday night line-up of shows,

Saturday morning cartoons, or MTV. One morning she awoke too sick to get out of bed. She was unable to attend Mass that day, as was her custom. Mysteriously, the Mass appeared on the wall of her bedroom, just as if she were actually attending it. Because of this experience, the pope decided that Clare would serve as an appropriate patron saint of this new invention, television.

Why did Pope Pius XII conclude that television should have its own patron saint? Perhaps he wanted to caution its users that this new technology could be used for good or for ill. Certainly it represented a great leap forward in the ongoing march of human progress. However, like any new invention, it opened the door to new challenges and to new possibilities of misuse. Not only did television *deserve* a patron saint, indeed it *needed* a patron saint to remind people to oversee its use so that it would continue to be an instrument for good.

Television Viewing—
A Growing Addiction

In the western world today people are spending between a third and a fifth of their waking lives watching television. . . . In the United States, first graders will spend the equivalent of one entire 24-hour day per week watching television, more time than they spend in the classroom. For most people in the United States, viewing television has become the third most common activity after sleep and work.

JEREMY MURRAY-BROWN, "VIDEO ERGO SUM," IN *VIDEO ICONS & VALUES*, EDITED BY ALAN M. OLSON, CHRISTOPHER PARR, AND DEBRA PARR [ALBANY: STATE UNIVERSITY OF NEW YORK PRESS, 1991].

Some evening when you're not watching television, take a walk through your neighborhood. As you stroll around, notice the number of distinctive glares from wide-screen color televisions lighting up most homes. It's fair to say that many Americans are addicted to television. A question is whether TV addiction is a more benign form of addiction—like drinking coffee—or more hazardous to our health— like smoking cigarettes. To answer that question, it is necessary to discuss possible effects of television viewing. **B** **C**

Seeing the World as a More Hostile Place

Before discussing what is typically shown on television, it is important to think about the effects of TV viewing itself. George Gerbner, a prominent researcher into the effects of television, finds that *the more people watch TV the more they tend to view the world as a hostile, dangerous place.* He calls this unintended side-effect of television viewing the "**mean-world syndrome.**" In other words, our watching television affects our view of other people— especially our view of strangers. Also, while we usually watch TV to relax, increased television

mean-world syndrome— the proposal that increased television viewing leads to a perception of the world as being a more hostile, dangerous place

viewing actually tends to make us feel more anxious, insecure, and angry. More time spent viewing television means less time visiting people and becoming socially involved. Other leisure activities, even solitary ones such as reading and listening to music, tend to push us out into community involvement. Watching television is a cocoon-like activity. Today, the average American home has one more television in it than it has people living in it. As a result, watching television often takes place apart from other family members.

Activity B

If your school decided to sponsor a "no TV week," would you participate? On a scale of one to ten, how challenging would it be for you not to watch television for a week? What was the longest period of time you went without watching television? Did the experience have a positive, negative, or neutral effect on your life?

Activity C

If you were in charge of creating guidelines for "Making TV a Choice, not a Habit," what would you include in the plan? Make suggestions as specific as possible.

Sex and Violence on the Tube

A second moral concern related to TV viewing has to do with the content of most shows. Television shows, even news programs, stay on the air by attracting an audience. Two activities that have been titillating from time immemorial are sex and violence. Films and television make frequent use of both to lure and hold an audience, sometimes even juxta-posing sex and violence.

If you watch TV regularly, you are probably receiving a steady diet of sexually related material. Especially in the U.S., television also regularly serves up programming featuring murder, robbery, rape, and other acts of violence. This characteristic of television has been studied more than any other—especially the effects on children of watching violence on TV. Most studies agree that watching violent programs does have a negative impact on children. The American Psychological Association identifies the following three primary negative consequences resulting from children viewing violence on television:

1. Children become less sensitive to the pain and suffering of others.

2. Children may be more fearful of the world around them.

3. Children may be more likely to behave aggressively.

REPORTED IN JOAN ANDERSON AND ROBIN WILKINS, *GETTING UNPLUGGED* [NEW YORK: JOHN WILEY AND SONS, 1998]. **D**

Activity D

1. You may be familiar with some of the following films available at video stores and frequently shown on TV. Each film features violence. Based on your knowledge of them, would you allow a ten-year-old to watch the following movies? A thirteen-year-old? A seventeen-year-old? Explain why or why not.

   - The "Die Hard" series
   - The "Rambo" series
   - The "Lethal Weapon" series
   - The "Home Alone" series
   - The "Halloween" series
   - The "Jaws" series
   - The "James Bond" series
   - The Jackie Chan movies
   - The animated Disney movies

2. Hong Kong action-film star Jackie Chan points out that he includes "outtakes" (scenes in which mistakes were made so the scenes are not included in the film) following his movies and also intersperses humor throughout so that children realize that the violence is fake and done in fun. Do you believe that his techniques diminish negative effects of viewing on-screen violence? Are there acceptable and unacceptable ways of portraying violence in movies and television shows? What guidelines would you suggest?

"If it bleeds, it leads"

Primary offenders of featuring heavy doses of violence are local news programs. Keep in mind that commercial television is in the business of selling audiences to advertisers. Higher viewer ratings for particular shows result in increased revenue from advertisers. Essentially, "the news" is whatever professionals in the news business decide it is. These professionals are under great pressure to put together a show that draws in the most sizable audience possible.

In response to the fierce competition for viewers among TV stations, a maxim commonly adhered to for local news programs is "If it burns, pleads, or bleeds, it leads." In other words, producers of news programs start out with the most sensational and tantalizing recent events they can find. Consequently, "the news" generally means the coverage of crimes. News broadcasts feature primarily murders, fires, tragic accidents, and serious wrongdoing by public figures.

Are there alternative ways of reporting on crime? One problem with a quick, "just the facts" presentation of crimes is that it leaves viewers feeling helpless. If other information were given that would place crime into a broader community context, then people might feel less helpless. For instance, when reporting a crime committed by a mentally ill family member, news programs could also mention local mental-health centers that provide services for troubled families. Programs could also regularly spotlight successful community crime- prevention programs. Such reporting might not improve the ratings of news programs, but it would provide a service to the communities news programs claim to serve. **E**

Talk Shows—Appealing to Our Base Instincts

Another kind of television program that appeals to viewer fascination with the darker side of human nature is the talk show. Granted, some talk-show hosts have held the line against constantly focusing on deviant and destructive behaviors. Those who feature sensationalistic programming often defend themselves by saying, "Everyone knows it's just entertainment." However, a steady diet of news programs and talk shows would easily lead a viewer to conclude that it's a strange, hostile, threatening world out there. If the world "out there" is so dangerous, we're better off staying inside—watching more TV!

Activity E

Watch a local news broadcast and chart the stories included. What story begins the program? What types of scenes are included to tell the story? What are the second and third stories covered in the broadcast?

Use the following questions to debate the value of local news programs on television:

- Does the way television news packages its stories lead to a trivializing of human tragedy? (For example, what effect does a tragic story have on us when it is packaged into a two- or three-minute docudrama and then a smiling news anchor immediately moves onto another story or breaks for a commercial?)

- Does television news inform us or are television news programs using tragedy and suffering to entertain us?

- What would a news program look like that would set as its goal improving the community to which it is broadcast?

What's on TV Tonight?—The Make-Believe World of Prime Time

Television . . . has taught over the long haul that the elderly and the poor are unimportant (few are ever shown); that there are far fewer female role models than male ones; and that almost everyone you want to emulate is well off, is white, and often lives in a Manhattan apartment too expensive for average people to afford.

STEPHEN SEPLOW AND JONATHAN STORM, "HOW TV REDEFINED OUR LIVES," *THE PHILADELPHIA INQUIRER* 30 NOVEMBER 1997, PAGE A16.

The greatest impact that television has on our moral perspective is subtle and indirect. In large measure, television determines our understanding of what it means to be beautiful and what the beautiful people are doing—in short, what's "in" and what's "out."

With the advent of cable television, many observers were hopeful that there would be an increased variety of programs to choose from. However, most television shows stick to a relatively safe and familiar formula. For instance, studies indicate that white males in the prime of life far outnumber other groups depicted on television. Women are fifty percent more likely to be portrayed as being victims than as being aggressive in social relationships. Portraying social relationships that involve violence and solving problems through violence fit more neatly into an hour program than other, less dramatic conflicts and resolutions.

prime time— the evening hours when television viewing is heaviest

One tell-tale sign that young children are watching an excessive amount of television and shows inappropriate for their age is that their language is overly mature. By the time the average American child reaches adulthood, she or he has viewed thousands of references—either direct or indirect—to sexual activity by other than married persons. Hardly ever are any possible negative consequences of engaging in sex a part of the story line—effects such as unintended and unwanted pregnancies, venereal diseases, a lingering sense of guilt or of being taken advantage of, or uneasiness with physical intimacy unaccompanied by personal bonding. As we discussed in the chapter on sexual morality, sitcom sex is casual sex; real-life sex is seldom casual in its consequences. Many sitcoms with this type of plot are shown during **prime time** when the largest numbers of children are watching. **F**

Activity F

1. List what you consider to be positive contributions and negative effects of television. Make your list as inclusive as possible.

2. Make a list of five of the most popular shows watched by you and your friends. Rate them on a scale of one (very poor) to ten (very good) based solely on their moral message. Explain your ratings. What conclusions can you draw from this exercise?

3. Do you believe that it is harmful for young children to watch television shows that discuss or depict sex or other adult themes? Why or why not?

Commercials—Selling "the Good Life"

For better or for worse, some of the most creative, artistic, and professionally done material on television can be found in commercials. Ad agencies are charged with putting together a captivating thirty-second drama that also brings to the public's attention the item and the brand name being advertised. Unlike regular TV programs, commercials are designed to air over and over again, thus making the investment in them worthwhile. The most successful thirty-second sound bites have created cult figures more familiar to Americans than the president.

Few people admit that they are influenced by commercials. Companies spend millions of dollars a year on commercials because they have found that this is not true. Some stations, featuring infomercials and buying clubs, have even gained a portion of the viewer market by running commercials all the time, uninterrupted by non-commercial programs! Regardless of the success of ads to sell specific products, the constant barrage of commercials that TV viewers receive—on average, over one hundred a day—supports and promotes a particular vision of a consumer culture. In short, *more than any*

specific product, commercials sell values and a version of "the good life." Own this car and you will be happier. Men, use this deodorant and you will become more alluring to beautiful women. Women, this is what it means to be beautiful or sexy. Drink this brand of beer and you're one of the guys. Eating at this fast-food restaurant is as American as apple pie. This brand of soft drink is the choice of a new generation. In other words, people want to be happy, attractive, and one of the crowd. Commercials say "Buy this product!" and you will be all you want to be.

Is it any wonder that, after TV viewing, one of the most popular pastimes of Americans is shopping? The constant stimulation we receive to buy happiness is a hard sell and extremely hard to resist. Should we even try? Is there a problem in buying and owning lots of stuff? We can't help but consume things, and we have it on the authority of the Bible itself that material things are good. However, one problem with a consumer mentality is that we come to view consumption—buying and owning things—as a cure-all. (For instance, are you bored? Then rent a video. Are you depressed? Buying a new outfit or an expensive game is the cure.) More importantly, an overemphasis on being consumers can prevent us from developing other dimensions of our human existence—being friends and lovers, sharing life's goods with those who are truly in need, and recognizing that our dignity cannot be measured by how much we own or by the brand names we wear. In a sense, getting caught up in consumption makes *us* consumer goods!

Commercials are often clever, inventive, captivating, and memorable. Quite possibly you know a number of commercials by heart. The moral concern associated with commercials consists in how much they distract us from, and set us in a direction different from, where we know our true happiness lies. While the Bible assures us of the goodness of creation, it also reminds us that our role is not to be "owners" at all. Rather, we are charged by God to see to it that created things are used for the good of all. **G**

For review . . .

1. Whom did Pope Pius XII declare patron saint of television? What experience led to her receiving this title?

2. On average, how much time do people in the western world spend watching television?

3. What is "the mean-world syndrome"?

4. What two types of activities are frequently used in television shows to attract an audience?

5. The American Psychological Association identified three primary consequences of children viewing violence on television. Name them.

6. What is the business of commercial television?

7. Explain the phrase, "If it bleeds, it leads."

8. What is the problem with a "just the facts" presentation of violence on news programs?

9. Name an alternative approach to this type of presentation of violence on news programs.

10. According to the text what would a steady diet of talk shows lead a viewer to conclude?

11. Name three subtle, indirect messages conveyed by television shows overall.

12. What is a sign that young children are watching television shows inappropriate for their age?

13. What is a primary way that the portrayal of sex on television is usually unrealistic and harmful?

14. What type of television programming tends to be the most creative and professionally done?

15. According to the text what is the underlying product that commercials sell?

Activity G

1. Name three commercials that are currently popular. Besides the product they sponsor, what values and what image of "the good life" are they selling? Are these values in any way supportive of, in conflict with, or a distraction from the Christian understanding of the good life?

2. Do you agree that "you can't buy happiness"? Does our consumer society promote the opposite message? Do you in fact live your life in line with this statement? Is it particularly hard today trying to live out the message that "you can't buy happiness"? If you have taken steps to oppose the notion of buying happiness, how have you done so? What other steps might you take to oppose this notion?

Computers
A Window into Virtual Reality

Luddites—English workers who, early in the industrial revolution, destroyed machines that were taking away their traditional means of livelihood

saboteurs—originally, French factory workers who temporarily dismantled industrial production by throwing their wooden shoes into machines

Man's genius has with God's help produced marvelous technical inventions from creation, especially in our times. The Church, our mother, is particularly interested in those which directly touch man's spirit and which have opened up new avenues of easy communication of all kinds of news, of ideas and orientations . . . .

The Church, our mother, knows that if these media are properly used they can be of considerable benefit to mankind. They contribute greatly to the enlargement and enrichment of men's minds and to the propagation and consolidation of the kingdom of God. But the Church also knows that man can use them in ways that are contrary to the Creator's design and damaging to himself.

DOCUMENTS OF VATICAN COUNCIL II, "DECREE ON THE MEANS OF SOCIAL COMMUNICATION," NUMBERS 1–2.

In the early 1800s, the beginning of the industrial revolution in Europe, a group of English textile workers called "**Luddites**" went about smashing the newly invented cloth-making machines because they saw them as taking away their means of livelihood. In France during the same period, some angry workers would throw their wooden shoes (*sabots*) into the machines that they now had to tend, bringing industrial production at least in their factories to a temporary standstill. Thus, the word "sabotage" entered the English language.

It is highly unlikely that any modern-day Luddites or **saboteurs** will bring to a halt the proliferation of computers and the computer-dependency that have taken over contemporary society. For an understanding of how Church leaders view this development, read again the quote from Vatican Council II that begins this section. Even as early as the 1960s, the bishops of the Council had such things as computers in mind when they said that technological advances were enlarging and enriching humanity's mind. The bishops even saw the possibility that computers and related technology could contribute to the "propagation and consolidation of the kingdom of God"! However, they could also foresee the potential for self-damaging misuse of technology.

Essentially, a computer is a highly sophisticated and complex pencil. A pencil can be used to write great poems or to scribble obscenities on bathroom walls. A pencil can help us keep in touch with loved ones far away or spread lies about people we don't like. Computer technology contains the same promise as well as the same possibilities for debasement as an ordinary pencil, except at mega-speeds and over a global network.

Rash Judgment, Calumny, and Slander on the Internet

slander—revealing information that could harm another person's reputation

*There are six or seven kinds of
   people the Lord doesn't like:
Those who are too proud or tell lies
   or murder,
those who make evil plans or are
   quick to do wrong,
those who tell lies in court or stir
   up trouble in a family.*

PROVERBS 6:16–19 [CEV]

When you sit down at your keyboard and use your mouse to click onto an Internet site, what possible moral implications might that activity hold? For one thing, the Internet has opened up new doors to some very old sins. From its beginning Christianity has alerted its members about the power of public speech. Some traditionally identified offenses against the use of public speech are the following:

rash judgment—assuming as true negative comments made about another person

- **Rash judgment** refers to assuming as true, without sufficient foundation, moral faults in others. When we hear something negative about another person and readily accept it as true, we are judging rashly. As in our law courts, traditional Christian morality declares that people should be presumed innocent, and treated as such, until proven guilty.

- **Calumny** refers to spreading untruths about people that could damage their reputation or harm them in some other way. Calumny means lying with the intention of hurting someone.

calumny—telling lies that could damage a person's reputation

- **Slander** refers to revealing information about another person, without valid reasons, that could harm his or her reputation. In other words, even telling true stories about others is wrong when the intention is to dishonor others, make fun of them, or not help them. A popular term for calumny and slander combined is *gossip*.

Christianity takes seriously the dignity of the human person as a starting point for morality—indeed, our course began with that premise. Clearly, people's dignity can be enhanced or diminished by what we say about them. What role does the Internet play in regards to rash judgment, calumny, and slander?

Activity H

1. Have you or someone you know ever been the victim or perpetrator of rash judgment, calumny, or slander? What were the circumstances? What resulted from the incident?

2. Do you know of any incidents when the Internet served as a vehicle for rash judgment, calumny, or slander? What were the circumstances? What were the results?

3. If you were writing a code for reporting on stories via the Internet or on television, what rules would you establish?

4. Describe one potential moral problem related to e-mails, chat rooms, and web sites.

Some people have decided to use the Internet as a place to post information that does not hold up to the stringent rules of professional news reporting. The Internet provides a forum for hate groups to disseminate material that would subject them to a libel suit if they posted the same information in a newspaper or another public forum. When rumors circulate via electronic media, legitimate news organizations—who always want to be first with a story—experience great pressure to report on stories whose sources cannot be definitively traced. Even individuals sitting alone before their computers can feel less constrained in what they write and read about others in e-mail, chat rooms, or web sites. Gossip over the back fence is one thing. Spreading derogatory stories over the Internet increases the audience, and the potential harm, a thousand-fold.

The Internet opens up to us a vast ocean of information. We can't be sure what information on it is valid and true and what is a fabrication. If we are going to browse through the Internet, as more and more people are, then we need to be careful, responsible, and shrewd in its use.

Internet Etiquette: Morality On-line

A few friends are at your house on a Friday evening. You decide to spend some time on the Internet. One friend says that he knows a web site that has available term papers on various topics. He suggests going there to see if you can get a ready-made report that you can hand in for an upcoming school project. Another friend suggests going to a chat room that he knows about to make fun of the regulars who spend much of their time on-line. He also says that he knows the addresses of web sites that you're not allowed to access at school, ones that detail how to build bombs and ones that make available pornographic portrayals of some Hollywood stars. Instead, you consider sending some kind of e-mail to a classmate whom you can't stand, hoping to get her in trouble with her parents.

The Internet is a means of communication. Our society has established rules of etiquette for various types of exchanges between people. (For example, holding a door open for someone else as you enter a building is proper etiquette; letting a door slam in someone's face is improper etiquette. Introducing yourself when a stranger comes to your house is proper etiquette; ignoring someone who comes into your home is improper etiquette.) The Internet is a relatively new form of communication. Rules of etiquette and, beyond that, moral and immoral uses for the Internet are in the process of being established. However, we need to keep in mind that Internet use does hold out potential for people getting hurt, just as surely as a door slamming in a person's face does. For that reason, **Internet etiquette** and ethics are important concerns for Internet users. **I**

Internet etiquette— using the Internet in ways that do not cause harm to others

Activity I

1. Compose a list of Ten Commandments for proper computer and Internet use.
2. When finished, compare your list to the "Ten Commandments of Computer Ethics" put together by the Computer Ethics Institute (http://www.cpsr.org).

Pornography on the Internet

Before "caller ID" was available for phone services, some men would call up single women and either threaten them or make suggestive comments to them. Often it turned out that the perpetrators were actually wimpy guys who lacked the courage and the social skills to speak to women in mature, appropriate ways. Now the Internet provides a venue for people to pursue interests electronically that they would never even admit to having in face-to-face encounters. On the Internet, a fifty-year-old man can pass himself off as a fifteen-year-old in search of a loving relationship. Some people say things over the course of an exchange in a chat room that they would not say in other contexts.

Hiding behind the anonymity of their computers, people can make illegal materials available over the electronic superhighway. Anonymity cannot hide behind the fact that what was wrong previously is still wrong even when we cannot see the faces of the persons being hurt by our actions.

The Internet holds out great promise for serving humanity. For the price of a local phone call we can keep in touch with friends in China, make new friends in Europe, and access sources of information worldwide. The same technology that helps make our world a global village also provides an outlet for people to manifest their more base instincts in new ways. **J**

Getting Unplugged: What Can We Do When We Turn Off the Screen?

One of the sad things is that the increase in computer technology does not get you out into the world more, into nature, into the community, dancing, singing, and so on. In fact, as the technology expands, there is more expectation that you will spend more of your life at a screen. . . . The more that the use of computers is demanded of us, the more we shall be taken away from truly deep human experiences.

GEORGE LAKOFF, IN JAMES BROOK AND IAIN A. BOAL, *RESISTING THE VIRTUAL LIFE* [SAN FRANCISCO: CITY LIGHTS BOOKS, 1995].

If you had a child, would you spend money on piano lessons or on computer software? Would you prefer your child draw with crayons or with a computer program? Would you consider your child's time at a computer to be educational but his or her time playing outdoors to be just for fun? If a young person enters ninth grade with little computer experience, is she or he educationally deprived compared to other students? Has the time you have spent at a computer generally been more beneficial than time spent on other things?

As the Lakoff quote suggests, the key underlying problem with computers is not so much what we do with them but rather what we don't do because of our time spent on them. Earlier in this chapter, the computer was compared to a pencil. This association is misleading if we mean that computers are "only tools" that do not affect us otherwise. The invention of writing affected humanity mightily, as did the printing press and television. For better or for worse, the computer and all that comes with it have altered how we think and how we view the world.

Activity J

You are a member of Congress. A bill is introduced that would make it a crime to send pornographic material over the Internet. Would you vote for the bill? Why or why not? Are there provisions or restrictions that you would add?

In a 1995 survey Americans ranked "computer skills and media technology" third among the skills students will most need in the future. They considered computer skills to be more important than "values," "good citizenship," and "curiosity and love of learning." Our current fascination with computers is misguided if we lose sight of the importance of basic human qualities and values. Using computers need not run counter to concern for other dimensions of human living. However, all use of technology needs to be examined in terms of how it serves personal well-being and the common good. For one thing, we need to be realistic about the limitations of computers. As one computer programmer puts it, "No matter what anyone tells you about the allure of computers, I can tell you for a fact that love cannot be programmed" (Ellen Ullman, in James Brook and Iain A. Boal, *Resisting the Virtual Life* [San Francisco: City Lights Books, 1995]). **K**

For review . . .

16. What was the response of Luddites and saboteurs to the machines of the early industrial era?

17. What attitude did the bishops of Vatican Council II have toward technological advances such as the computer?

18. In what sense is a computer an artificial appendage?

19. Explain the difference among rash judgment, calumny, and slander.

20. In what sense does the Internet expand the possibilities for rash judgment, calumny, and slander?

21. Define Internet etiquette.

22. What is it about the Internet that makes it a powerful place for distribution of pornography?

23. According to the text what is the key underlying problem with computers?

24. In a 1995 survey how highly did Americans rank computer skills as needed for the future?

Activity K

The 1995 survey found computer skills to be considered very important by Americans. Why do you think such skills ranked so high in the survey? Do you think this assessment of computer skill has changed today? Where would you place computer skills in terms of "skills young people will need for the future"? What other skills would you also consider to be important? Where would you rank these compared to computer skills in terms of importance?

Video Games
A Different Screen, A Similar Story

"You've watched enough TV. Go do something else." Today when a parent gives this command, it can simply mean that a child goes to another room and begins playing a video game. The essential activity remains the same. A young person sits before a screen. Even though he or she now pushes buttons, time flies by and the same glaze settles over the eyes as the gaze stays focused on a screen. At a video arcade, young people face a machine pushed against a wall; each person plays in isolation from those around him or her. The content of the game most likely includes some form of violence or make-believe destruction.

Are video games a problem or a pleasant diversion? As with other technology, it depends on how they are used. An important question to ask is: How does the amount of time I spend on this activity affect the quality of my life in general? For some, moderate use is the answer. Some others might find that "getting unplugged" is the best way to go.

Does "Virtual Violence" Lead to Real Violence?

A popular video-game scenario depicts a man traveling through buildings or over the countryside picking off as many "bad guys" as he can. The main variation on this theme centers around the type of weapons used, the nature of the victims, and the realism of the destruction portrayed. In some games, intended victims are not "bad guys" at all but rather cops or even innocent bystanders. As the technology improves, the display of violence becomes more and more realistic. Studies indicate that games featuring violence are the favorites of fourth through eighth graders. Following an incident in which two youths who were fond of particularly violent video games entered their high school and killed a teacher and a number of their classmates, one commentator made the following observation:

> *Psychologist David Grossman of Arkansas State University, a retired Army officer, thinks "point and shoot" video games have the same effect as military strategies used to break down a soldier's aversion to killing. During World War II, only 15 to 20 percent of all American soldiers fired their weapon in battle. Shooting games in which the target is a man-shaped outline, the Army found, made recruits more willing to "make killing a reflex action."*

JOHN LEO, "WHEN LIFE IMITATES VIDEO," *US NEWS AND WORLD REPORT* 3 MAY 1999, PAGE 14.

This same psychologist refers to violent video games as "murder simulators," functioning in much the same way as computer flight simulators initially train pilots for real flights. If nothing else, he cautions, we as a society need to be attentive to what we are putting into the minds of our young. **L**

Activity L

1. Recreation does not need to serve a particular purpose. It is meant simply to be fun. However, do you find time spent playing video games to be more or less rejuvenating than other recreational activities? Explain.

2. Propose a design for a video game that would not feature violence. Would such a game have any appeal? Why or why not?

Video Games and Youth Culture

youth culture—
the belief that young people have values, interests, and activities distinct from those of other age groups

Video games have become an important part of **youth culture**. For some parents, video games have become the birthday or Christmas gift of choice for that hard-to-buy-for junior high school-aged child. Kids playing video games are at least close to home, occupied, and "staying out of trouble." As with much of the rest of youth-culture types of entertainment, video games are actually passive entertainment created by adults for youthful consumers. Young people playing video games are passively consuming a culture foisted upon them by others rather than actively participating in creating culture themselves.

Keep in mind that the very concept of a youth culture is a relatively recent phenomenon—probably originating in the U.S. in the 1950s. The concept suggests that young people, approximately ages thirteen to eighteen, make up a subgroup that has its own values, its own interests, its own morals, and its own music and other forms of entertainment. If it exists, then this culture is decidedly different from a culture of childhood, adulthood, or old age. In such a scenario, adults can be viewed as at best "out of it" and at worst a necessary evil.

What does Catholicism have to contribute to a discussion about culture and cultural conflicts? Earlier in this course we talked about Vatican Council II. This gathering of the world's Catholic bishops took place during the sixties—the height of modern cultural upheaval and the beginning stages of today's youth culture. At the time the bishops wrote that they recognized that "in each nation and social group there is a growing number of men and women who are conscious that they themselves are the craftsmen and molders of their community's culture" ("The Church in the Modern World," number 55). The bishops believe that people, including young people, should be the authors of culture and not just passive inheritors of it. *Culture* is a living, growing thing. In a sense, it is for humans what agriculture is for food crops. Given this dynamic view of culture, the bishops of Vatican II propose that "one must aim at encouraging the human spirit to develop its faculties of wonder, of understanding, of contemplation, of forming personal judgments and cultivating a religious, moral and social sense" (number 59). Does spending time on a particular video game achieve any of these aims? Video games, along with television and computers, can contribute to human culture or detract from it. In making a moral evaluation of video games and their use, it is important to determine the effect they have on the human spirit and on development of human culture. **M**

For review . . .

25. How are playing video games and TV viewing similar?

26. What type of activity is most popular in video games?

27. According to one psychologist, what effect can "point and shoot" video games have on young people?

28. According to the bishops of Vatican Council II, what role should people play in culture?

Activity M

1. Do you believe that a youth culture exists in our country? If so, what are the dominant characteristics of this culture, both positive and negative?

2. Are video games an important component of youth culture? Explain the positive and negative aspects of video games and their use among young people today.

Conclusion
A Caution for the Plugged-in Generation

Sitting before a screen—the television, the computer, or the video game—has become the great guzzler of one of our most precious commodities—time. What payoff do we receive from this investment? How is our moral world being shaped by such modern technologies? As with all wonders, natural and manufactured, we are called to be both thoughtful and moral in their use. Each has potential for good. Each also requires caution. We are a plugged-in generation. We are also called to be a moral one.

Let us pray . . .

God our Father, how wonderful are the works of your hands! May our work and our play always be a blessing to you. As your son, Jesus the carpenter of Nazareth, was one with you even as he transformed wood into a table and chair, may we always be mindful of you as we create with a computer or enjoy the delights of TV, video, and other technology. All creation, past and present, gives you glory. Amen.

CHAPTER 14

Violence and Peace
Respect for Life at Home and Abroad

Respect for life is a recurring theme in Christian moral teaching. Is the deliberate taking of life ever justified? Does taking a life always diminish the human family? In this chapter we will look at a number of key moral issues related to violence and peace. No country is immune from violence. In the U.S., state-sanctioned violence—capital punishment—continues to be practiced. In our world, nations and groups of nations still rely on acts of war to achieve their ends. As with all moral matters, a Christian looks deeply and lovingly at these issues, seeking always to determine: What would Jesus have me do?

Chapter Overview

- Christians are called to counteract violence in its many forms, both explicit and hidden.

- Gun violence, although decreasing, remains a serious problem in the U.S.

- Church leaders have declared capital punishment an unnecessary affront to the dignity of human life.

- The Church seeks alternatives to war and calls for restriction of warfare as much as possible.

Let us pray . . .

Jesus, we praise you as the Prince of Peace. Your message rings just as true today as it did long ago: How blessed are your peacemakers! Instead of a world divided, may we see one body—your body. Where this body is broken and disconnected, may we be your peacemakers—resetting breaks, reconnecting disjointed parts, and healing the hurts that lead to violence. May we always move beyond anger, hatred, and vengeance. Make us channels of your peace. Amen.

Before we begin . . .

Answer agree, disagree, or uncertain to the following statements. When necessary, write an explanation of your response.

1. Violence is on the rise in our country.

2. Violence is a particularly serious problem among young people today.

3. Incidents of violence occur more frequently in the U.S. than in other western countries.

4. I would feel safe walking alone in my neighborhood late at night.

5. The best way to decrease violence is to address deep-seated social problems such as poverty and drug abuse.

6. All firearms should possess childproof safety devices.

7. Keeping a gun readily available in one's home is a helpful safeguard against being victimized by crime.

8. In order to counteract violent crimes, clerks at convenience stores, gas-station attendants, and classroom teachers should carry guns.

9. The purchase and possession of handguns should be illegal.

10. Automatic weapons not clearly intended for sport use should be illegal.

11. I believe that the death penalty should be used more frequently and more publicly to serve as a more effective deterrent against crime.

12. Executing criminals violates the principle of respect for life.

13. Threat of the death penalty cuts down on violent crimes.

14. Someone who claims to be a follower of Jesus should oppose the death penalty.

Violence and Respect for Life

U.S. incidents of crime have been decreasing steadily over the past decade or so. Yet the United States continues to be the most violent and crime-ridden nation of the Western world. A faculty member at Harvard Medical School reports the following:

> The United States is a violent country. Episodes of violent crime . . . are not exceptions to the rule. Indeed, comparative statistics among nations (Dobrin, Wiersema, Loftin, and McDowarr, 1996) indicate that the United States out-ranks most other nations of the industrial world in violent crimes like assault, rape, and robbery. In the category of murder, we are far and away the most violent industrialized nation on earth.
>
> RAYMOND B. FLANNERY, *VIOLENCE IN AMERICA* [NEW YORK: CONTINUUM, 1997].

In the adolescent age-range, crime has also dropped over the past 10 years, yet the number of victims and perpetrators of violence among adolescents is still at an unacceptably high level.

> In 1997, there were 31 serious violent juvenile crimes committed for every 1,000 children ages 12 to 17. That's down from 52 per 1,000 in 1993 and is the lowest rate since 1986, according to the Justice Department. Still, in 1997 there were 706,000 violent crimes involving one or more of these teens.
>
> "STUDY SHOWS IMPROVING TRENDS AMONG YOUTHS," *PHILADELPHIA INQUIRER* 9 JULY 1999, PAGE A20.

Where Does Violence Begin?

The following scenarios depict situations that could easily turn violent.

• Matt's fascination with guns began at an early age. Matt's father, an avid hunter, did not discourage this interest. Matt's favorite picture of himself is the one of him at age eleven wearing army fatigues and holding the first gun his father bought him. Unfortunately, this "macho" pose did not translate into kind treatment or popularity among his schoolmates. To the contrary, he was often picked on by classmates. This was so common an occurrence that now he often imagined people making fun of him even when they weren't. During target practice, Matt began to imagine that he was shooting at the boys and girls at school who taunted him the most. These moments were the ones that gave him the greatest satisfaction. "If they're not careful, I'll show them who's the tough guy," he often mused.

• Once again Michael was spending the night at his regular street corner with a few friends from the neighborhood. Even though the night air was chilly, he felt more at home here than he did at his house where his father was, as

usual, sprawled out on the sofa half sleeping, half watching TV. Since his father didn't care and his mother was too distracted by other things to pay much attention to him, Michael left the house as much as possible.

Meanwhile, tensions were heating up between Michael's crowd and the group of kids who hung out at the pizza place a few blocks away. This night, two of his friends showed up with baseball bats. They claimed that a carload of kids from the other group had yelled obscenities at the girls on Michael's corner, and they were going over to the pizza place to teach them a lesson.

Michael didn't want to get involved, but he didn't want to go against his crowd either.

"Maybe I'll just go along and watch," he thought.

• Scott first learned about the group from the Internet. They spoke out against the ways American society is being taken over by foreigners, non-Christians, and non-whites. Their views made sense to him. Scott saw non-white superstars making millions in the sports, music, and motion-picture industry. And weren't a lot of non-whites living off the government, not working at all, while he and his family were following the rules, paying taxes, but just scraping by? The government was no help. Actually, it was part of the problem. The group posted guidelines about what people who shared their views could do about affronts to a true, pure American culture. They described how bombs could be made from materials available at hardware and feed stores. When they announced that a convention was to take place in a nearby state, Scott decided he would attend. Finally, he felt as though he had found an outlet for the anger and hatred that had been welling up inside him. **A**

Activity A

Look for an account of violence that occurred sometime over the past year. Make a list of factors that might have contributed to the violence. Describe possible changes that might have prevented the violence or lessened its damage.

The Gospel of Life for a Culture of Death

The Gospel of Life—
1985 Encyclical by Pope John Paul II about the value and sacredness of human life

In 1995 in a lengthy encyclical called *The Gospel of Life,* Pope John Paul II wrote about his concern for what he called a "culture of death"— the violence that disfigures our human community. Here's what the pope had to say about our violent culture of death:

> *And how can we fail to consider the violence against life done to millions of humans, especially children, who are forced into poverty, malnutrition and hunger because of an unjust distribution of resources between peoples and between social classes? And what of the violence inherent not only in wars as such but in the scandalous arms trade, which spawns the many armed conflicts which stain our world with blood? What of the spreading of death caused by reckless tampering with the world's ecological balance, by the criminal spread of drugs, or by the promotion of certain kinds of sexual activity which, besides being morally unacceptable, also involve grave risks to life? It is impossible to catalogue completely the vast array of threats to human life, so many are the forms, whether explicit or hidden, in which they appear today!* (number 10)

explicit violence—
a situation in which someone is physically harmed or killed by direct action

hidden violence—
a situation in which someone is harmed or killed indirectly, because of various social factors

Interestingly, the pope does not mention stories of violence that typically make newspaper headlines—ethnic and racial conflicts, young boys shooting classmates, or home-bound older women who are beaten and robbed of the little money they have managed to save. Instead, he speaks mostly about broader social issues, such as the violence of poverty and the violence of unjust distribution of resources. Obviously, the pope has a more inclusive understanding of what constitutes violence than the one we normally hear about. He distinguishes between **explicit violence**, in which people are physically harmed or killed by the direct actions of another, and **hidden violence**, in which people are harmed or killed indirectly because of various social factors. He wants us to recognize that allowing a child to go hungry is as much an expression of a culture of death as beating the child would be. The final chapter of this book, which discusses the issue of justice, provides many examples of what the pope means by "hidden violence."

Underlying Causes of Violence

skepticism—in general, a doubting and questioning attitude. As defined by Pope John Paul II, a lack of belief that there are fundamental truths, dismissing any sense of right or wrong

In this same encyclical the pope also identifies what he considers to be four factors accounting for the violence that stains our world. The first factor he names is one of attitude—**skepticism**. Skepticism can be a positive characteristic when doubting or questioning is used to examine reports such as the sighting of the Loch Ness monster or the abominable snowman. However, the pope uses a more negative understanding of the word. By skepticism he means disbelief, in this case dismissing the idea that there are clear standards of right and wrong. This kind of dismissal of standards leads to an "anything goes" philosophy of life. Instead of crying out against violent behavior and social conditions, a skeptic in this narrow sense of the word looks the other way since he or she has no basis upon which to condemn violence and no hope that things can change for the better.

fosters other types of violence. The pope also includes here violence against women as a social problem that the world community must address.

Finally, the pope sees a dangerous trend in how people view one another. Namely, many people are denying their solidarity with everyone else. This denial leads to "a war of the powerful against the weak" (number 12). In such an atmosphere, the comfortable and self-sufficient treat those who are weak and have special needs either with indifference or as being the enemy to be ignored, resisted, or eliminated. **B**

Secondly, the pope blames violence on a breakdown of family and community life. He points out that today many individuals and families are left alone with their problems. Making a go of it in our modern world is difficult enough even with a great deal of support. Instead, too many people are forced to face challenges alone, causing pressures to build up that can bring on violence.

Thirdly, the pope lists social and economic problems, the many forms of hidden violence that easily spill over into explicit violence. Here again he places poverty first. Besides being a form of violence in itself, poverty creates anxiety and pressure which, in turn,

For review . . .

1. In what violent crimes does the United States out-rank other industrial nations?
2. What is Pope John Paul II's term for the violence that disfigures the human community?
3. What is the difference between explicit and hidden violence?
4. Define skepticism as Pope John Paul II defines the term. How does the pope see this brand of skepticism contributing to an acceptance of violence?
5. According to the pope, what three other problems lead to violence in our culture?

Activity B

1. Name three examples of "hidden violence" as Pope John Paul II understands the term. Explain how each is a form of violence in itself and also how it might spill over into more explicit violence.

2. Pope John Paul II identifies four underlying causes as central to the problem of violence. Give examples that might support his position. Can you name other key causes of violence?

3. Do you believe that it is an added burden to be poor in a predominantly affluent country compared to being poor in a predominantly poor country? Why or why not?

4. Do you agree or disagree with the following statement: Most wealthy people don't realize the difficulties that people who are poor must face. If they did, they would do more to help them.

The Debate over Guns and Gun Control

The United States has by far the highest rate of gun deaths—murders, suicides and accidents—among more than 30 of the world's richest nations, a government study found. . . .

> *"If you have a country saturated with guns—available to people when they are intoxicated, angry or depressed—it's not unusual guns will be used more often," said Dr. Rebecca Peters, a Johns Hopkins University fellow specializing in gun violence. "This has to be treated as a public-health emergency."*
>
> CHELSEA J. CARTER, "AMERICAN RATE OF GUN DEATHS IS BY FAR THE HIGHEST IN STUDY," *PHILADELPHIA INQUIRER* 17 APRIL 1998, PAGE A3.

> *More than 40 percent of American households with children age 3 to 17 also have guns, according to a poll conducted for a gun-control advocacy group.*
>
> *Among the households with children, 42 percent have a handgun and a rifle or shotgun, 23 percent say they keep a gun loaded at least some of the time, and 28 percent keep a gun hidden and not locked, according to the survey sponsored by the Center to Prevent Handgun Violence.*
>
> "POLL: GUNS IN 40% OF HOMES WITH CHILDREN," *PHILADELPHIA INQUIRER* 14 NOVEMBER 1998, PAGE A2.

A number of years ago, *Time* magazine published a snapshot of and a brief statement about every American killed by a gun during the previous year. This photo yearbook was sobering indeed. Here were old and young—sometimes even very young—men and women, rich and poor, people of all races. Their one common characteristic was that a bullet from a gun had ended their life.

Of course, on *Time's* part this was making an emotional appeal for the nation to take steps to curb gun violence. It did not represent a complete argument. In fact, both gun-control advocates and those opposed to any form of gun control want to see gun violence curbed. Beyond that, each side differs as to how to achieve a safer, less crime-ridden environment.

Advocates of Gun Control

gun control—a variety of measures intended to cut down on gun accidents and gun violence

Gun control does not necessarily mean banning the possession of all firearms by individuals. Gun-control advocates propose a variety of measures that they believe will cut down on gun accidents and gun violence. For instance, the group "Texans Against Gun Violence" reviewed statistics indicating that in

1995 fifteen times as many children were killed by gunshots in the U.S. as in the countries of Japan, Great Britain, Germany, France, and Canada combined. Statistics such as these have led gun-control groups to call for legislation aimed at keeping guns out of the hands of children and at making them inoperable when a child does get hold of one. For instance, guns can now be "personalized" so that they can operate only with a code that only the owner can supply. Also, guns can be produced with child-safety locks on them.

iron pipeline— the practice of buying large quantities of guns where gun-purchasing laws are lenient and re-selling them in high-crime areas

Another concern of gun-control advocates is the "**iron pipeline**." This term refers to the fact that a great number of guns used in crimes in northern cities are originally purchased in southern states where gun regulations are more lenient. One piece of legislation suggested for addressing this problem is a "one-handgun-a-month" law. This law is aimed at restricting the purchase of handguns by an individual to one a month. The presumption is that people who purchase multiple quantities of guns at a time are likely re-selling them, often in cities with high crime rates, to people who have criminal intentions.

domestic violence— violence that occurs in close relationships, such as husband-wife, parent-child, or boyfriend-girlfriend

A third proposal of gun-control advocates is increased regulation of handguns, especially of the least expensive guns currently available. While imported guns must adhere to governmental regulations, guns manufactured in the U.S. do not need to comply to the same degree of safety restrictions.

Finally, proponents and opponents of carrying concealed weapons differ about who benefits. Those who want concealed weapons legal suggest that potential victims of crime would have an edge if they were carrying a gun. Opponents of allowing concealed weapons to be legal suggest that this intended effect would actually backfire. Using an extreme example, they point out that a seventy-year-old woman, even with a gun, is still no match for a twenty-five-year-old man with a gun. A more commonplace scenario is that of **domestic violence**. Statistics regarding domestic violence indicate that men with aggressive tendencies, rather than women threatened by these men, are the ones more likely to use a gun. Thus, the ready availability of guns does not necessarily protect victims but rather may actually increase the stakes involved.

Opponents of Gun Control

appeal to authority— defending one's position by citing a respected source, such as the Constitution

A natural starting point for those opposed to gun control is an **appeal to authority**: The U.S. Constitution itself and documented statements by the country's founding fathers clearly support the right of individual citizens to own firearms. Other arguments used against gun control make more practical appeals. Those opposed to gun control argue that most people use their guns for sport or collecting purposes. Why should all gun owners be penalized when only a small percentage of them use guns to commit crimes? A second point they state is that even if we restrict legal possession of guns, people with criminal intent will disregard the laws and get hold of guns anyway. Only law-abiding citizens will be denied guns.

Gun control opponents also suggest that when average citizens own guns, they have an effective and legitimate means of protecting themselves against becoming victims of crime. Guns in the hands of upright, responsible people are a better deterrent against crime than restricting their access to guns. Yes, guns can be misused; but so can automobiles, over-the-counter drugs, and other products. Those who oppose gun control believe the solution is in proper training in the use of guns, not their restriction. **C**

Whatever steps are taken in the country to reduce gun violence, it is clear that such violence is a public health hazard, an expression of sin on a societal level, and a moral problem that cannot be ignored. To counteract the violence that they see in our culture, the U.S. Catholic bishops call for curbing the easy availability of deadly weapons (*Political Responsibility: Proclaiming the Gospel of Life, Protecting the Least Among Us, and Pursuing the Common Good*, 1995). Along with the pope, they want people of our time to do all that they can to replace a culture of death with a culture that affirms life. The high number of fatalities due to guns in our country is one manifestation of the culture of death. **D**

For review . . .

6. Name four arguments against gun control.

7. What are two changes that could be made to decrease gun accidents by children?

8. Define "iron pipeline." What legislation is proposed to diminish its effectiveness?

9. Why are inexpensive guns made in the U.S. a particular problem?

10. Who are intended to be helped by allowing the carrying of concealed weapons?

11. What is domestic violence? According to gun-control advocates, what type of person is more likely to carry and use a concealed weapon?

12. What "appeal to authority" can American opponents of gun control make?

Activity C

Look for gun-control articles on the Internet or in some other source. Search for information for and against increased regulation of guns. What proposals do gun-control advocates make? What arguments do those who oppose gun control use? Based on the information provided, write your own proposals for curbing gun violence in the U.S.

Activity D

If you were a parent and your son or daughter very much wanted a gun for his or her thirteenth birthday, would you allow your child to own one? Explain your answer. Are there circumstances that would cause you to change your decision?

Capital Punishment

Are We a Better Society with It or without It?

In 1972 the U.S. Supreme Court declared the death penalty as practiced in individual states to be unconstitutional. At the time, the country was in effect moving toward the position of most other Western nations who have determined that **capital punishment** is ineffective, unnecessary, and immoral. In 1976, however, the Supreme Court declined to disallow new state laws and procedures, thus making it possible for 38 states to currently have legalized capital punishment. There are currently 3,565 persons on death row. Five hundred and fifty prisoners have been executed since 1976. The average stay on death row for those who have been executed was 10 to 11 years (Death Penalty Information Center, 1320 18th Street, NW Washington, DC).

The Catholic Church's position on the death penalty is that it is acceptable only in rare situations, if at all. According to Pope John Paul II, capital punishment is acceptable only when society has no other means of defending itself (*The Gospel of Life*, number 56). The pope stresses that the existence of high-security prisons thus make capital punishment unnecessary and immoral in modern societies. In order to appreciate why Church teaching comes to this conclusion, it is necessary to examine the goals and purposes of punishing wrongdoers.

capital punishment— death penalty; state-sanctioned execution of persons convicted of serious crimes

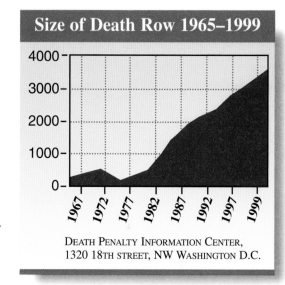

Size of Death Row 1965–1999

DEATH PENALTY INFORMATION CENTER, 1320 18TH STREET, NW WASHINGTON D.C.

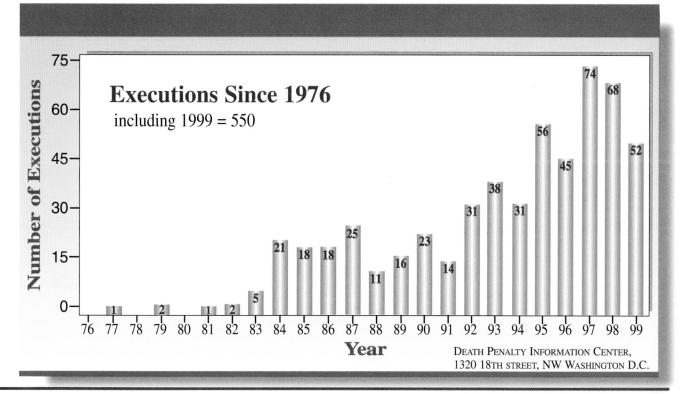

Executions Since 1976
including 1999 = 550

DEATH PENALTY INFORMATION CENTER, 1320 18TH STREET, NW WASHINGTON D.C.

In any event, the principle set forth in the *Catechism of the Catholic Church* remains valid: "If bloodless means are sufficient to defend human lives against an aggressor and to protect public order and the safety of persons, public authority must limit itself to such means, because they better correspond to the concrete conditions of the common good and are more in conformity to the dignity of the human person." (*The Gospel of Life*, number 56)

The United States Catholic bishops addressed the issue of capital punishment most thoroughly in a 1980 document titled *Statement on Capital Punishment*. Before speaking to the issue itself, they let it be known that they are concerned about security within society, about the victims of crime, and in a special way about members of law enforcement whose lives are endangered through crime. However, they don't want these concerns to result in a misguided search for simple and easy solutions to the complex problem of criminal justice. Capital punishment does not automatically make our society safer, nor does it relieve the pain of crime victims and their families. In their statement, the bishops review capital punishment in light of the three justifications traditionally advanced for punishment—deterrence, rehabilitation, and retribution. **E**

Deterrence—Does Capital Punishment Lessen Crime?

deterrence— punishment or fear of punishment can help prevent crime

particular deterrence— preventing by imprisonment or execution someone who has committed a crime from committing crime again

general deterrence— the belief that fear of punishment will prevent people from committing crime

Deterrence means that punishment or fear of punishment can help prevent crime. **Particular deterrence** means that an individual who committed a crime in the past is deterred from committing any future crime. Obviously, capital punishment can serve this purpose. However, alternative forms of punishment such as life imprisonment without the possibility of parole can also serve as a particular deterrent. **General deterrence** means that fear of punishment inhibits people in general from committing certain crimes. On the effectiveness of capital punishment as a general deterrent, the bishops report what many studies have indicated: "Empirical studies in this area have not given conclusive evidence that would justify the imposition of the death penalty on a few individuals as a means of preventing others from committing crimes" (*Statement on Capital Punishment*, page 3). **F**

Activity E

List as many arguments as possible for and against capital punishment. Give possible pros and cons to each argument. Which arguments do you believe are more convincing? Which arguments do you believe reflect a Christian perspective? Explain.

Activity F

On the Internet or other research instrument, look for reports on the effectiveness of capital punishment as a deterrent to crime. Do recent studies affirm or refute the bishops' statement from 1980?

Rehabilitation—Capital Punishment Denies Possibilities for Reform

rehabilitation— programs aimed at training and reforming wrong-doers so that they no longer commit crime

Thanks in particular to the Quakers of Pennsylvania, our society for about three centuries now has relied on imprisonment as its principal means of dealing with wrongdoers. From its beginning, the modern prison system had as a primary goal the **rehabilitation** or reform of a wrongdoer. Prisons were "penitentiaries"—that is, places to do penance, to see the error of one's ways, and to return to society a reformed person. In actual fact, prisons have a very poor track record as places where rehabilitation occurs. More often, time in prison makes people feel victimized, angry, and more anti-social than they were before imprisonment. Also, the associations one makes in prison seldom lend themselves to re-entering society with a spirit of gratitude and goodwill.

The bishops realize the difficulties of helping people to reform. Nonetheless, they urge us to be mindful of Jesus' message of forgiveness and conversion. Capital punishment shuts the door to any possibility of reform and reintegration into society. **G**

Retribution—What Is Just Punishment for Crime?

retribution— restoring the social order by punishing wrongdoers, thus declaring that certain behaviors are not tolerated in society

Retribution is the third justification for punishment of criminals. It means restoration of order by insuring that wrongdoers atone for their deeds. If Hollywood wants to make a blockbuster movie, one can't-miss premise is to portray "bad guys" who, at the climax of the movie, get killed by the "good guys." The bad guys must appear really bad, and then novel ways of destroying them can whet our primitive appetite for revenge. In the end, good wins out and order is restored. Retribution seeks to restore order through punishment of wrongdoers in such a way that everyone in a society knows that criminal behavior is totally unacceptable.

The bishops teach that retribution does justify punishment, but that society's methods of punishment are not meant to satisfy instinctual urges to lash back at people who offend us. "An eye for an eye" must be tempered with "Love your enemy." "Thus we would regard it as barbarous and inhuman for a criminal who had tortured or maimed a victim to be tortured or maimed in return" (page 4). In other words, retribution must be distinguished from revenge.

Retribution Versus Revenge	
Goal is to restore order	Goal is to inflict equal or greater harm
Follows legal process	Accepts legal process if punishment is sufficiently severe
Emotion is filtered through impartial judge and jury	Only emotions at work: rage, hatred
Seeks truth through reason	Follows instinctual urges

Activity G

Look for reports on programs that actually exist whose aim is rehabilitation of prisoners. Based on these reports and on your own creativity, design a program aimed specifically at the rehabilitation of eighteen- to twenty-five-year-old prisoners. Why would you choose this model?

Why Capital Punishment Should Be Abolished

In this document the bishops call for abolition of capital punishment. They do so on the basis of four Christian and human values:

First, abolition sends a message that we can break the cycle of violence, that we need not take life for life, that we can envisage more humane and more hopeful and effective responses to the growth of violent crime.

Second, abolition of capital punishment is also a manifestation of our belief in the unique worth and dignity of each person from the moment of conception, a creature made in the image and likeness of God.

Third, abolition of the death penalty is further testimony to our conviction, a conviction which we share with the Judaic and Islamic traditions, that God is indeed the Lord of life.

Fourth, we believe that abolition of the death penalty is most consonant with the example of Jesus, who both taught and practiced the forgiveness of injustice and who came "to give his life as a ransom for many" [Mark 10:45] (pages 7–8).

The bishops conclude their document with the observation that the death penalty does not make our society either safer or better, as much as we might like it to. Instead, it provides the illusion of a "final solution" when in fact it is not. On this point, one expert on capital punishment reminds us that:

In the final analysis, the issue of the death penalty is linked to the funda-mental matter of the kind of society in which we wish to live. The final solu-tion of death is too pat a solution to the problems presented by violent crime. We ought to be wary of easy solutions to problems, particularly when they are utterly final. It is all too easy to kill—the trees for another concrete roadway; the animal for its teeth or pelt; the enemy, the fetus, the aged, the defective—and the killer himself.  **H** **I**

MICHAEL ENDRES, *THE MORALITY OF CAPITAL PUNISHMENT* [MYSTIC, CT: TWENTY-THIRD PUBLICATIONS, 1985].

For review . . .

13. For what five-year period was capital punishment illegal in the United States?

14. According to official Church teaching, what circumstance would make capital punishment acceptable?

15. Explain the difference between particular and general deterrence.

16. According to the U.S. Catholic bishops, has capital punishment been successful as a general deterrent to crime?

17. What was a primary goal of instituting the modern prison system?

18. Why have prisons not been particularly successful in bringing about rehabilitation?

19. Define retribution. How is it different from revenge?

20. Name the four arguments of the U.S. Catholic bishops about why capital punishment should be abolished.

"You have heard that it was said, 'You shall love your neighbor and hate your enemy.' But I say to you, love your enemies and pray for those who persecute you . . ."

MATTHEW 5:43–44

Activity H

1. Read over the arguments given by the U.S. Catholic bishops against capital punishment. Give reasons and examples why you agree or disagree with each argument.

2. Do you agree that capital punishment represents a "quick fix" mentality that does not consider either long-term consequences or Christian principles? Why or why not?

Activity I

A major reason the Supreme Court in 1972 refused states the right to execute criminals was that the court found that the death penalty was not being administered equally and without bias. In 1999 an advocacy group determined that in the city of Philadelphia, a black defendant is three times as likely to receive a death sentence than a defendant of any other race. Do research to create a profile of who are executed in the U.S. based on race, income, education, state, and gender. According to your findings, is the death penalty currently employed without bias? Explain.

What's Wrong with this Picture

A story is told about two soldiers who fought in the U.S. Civil War. The soldiers, one Union and one Confederate, are dug in within earshot of each other. It is the evening before a battle between the two sides is to occur. As the evening progresses, the two men exchange words and eventually ask each other about where they're from, about their families back home, and about the work they did before the war. If the two men weren't holding guns and wearing different-colored uniforms, the scene would appear to be two neighbors exchanging pleasant conversation over a back fence.

At daybreak, leaders on both sides alert their troops to prepare for battle. Dutifully, these two soldiers join the others in strapping on their equipment and in attaching bayonets to their rifles. The two men, each of whom would normally lend a hand if he saw the other in need and would otherwise be kind and courteous, now enter into the deadly business of war—kill or be killed.

As the battle goes on, perhaps these men actually face each other. Perhaps they even try to kill each other. In the grand picture, that is exactly what all warfare is—neighbor fighting neighbor, brothers and sisters killing one another, members of our one human family taking and sacrificing other members' lives. **J**

Activity J

Answer agree, disagree, or uncertain to the following statements.

1. If my country were at war and a draft were called for, all eligible persons have a responsibility to join the armed forces.

2. If I were eighteen and drafted into the army during wartime, I would serve willingly and unquestioningly.

3. If I were a parent and my nineteen-year-old child wanted to enlist in the military during wartime, I would wholeheartedly support her or his decision.

4. If someone believes that a particular war is wrong but is drafted into the army, he should serve in the military anyway.

5. In the event of a draft, there should be an option for people who don't believe in war to perform non-military service.

6. If my country's leaders believed that extensive bombing of civilian sites was called for, I would support whatever decision they made.

7. When a nation is at war, its citizens should not protest or criticize the decisions of its leaders.

8. War is an evil that should be used only as an extreme last resort.

War and Respect for Life

According to Christian tradition, life is sacred. Christian moral teaching asks of war the same question that it asks of abortion, euthanasia, capital punishment, and other issues in which human lives are at stake: Is purposely taking a life ever justified? If so, when?

The past century was scarred by many wars. Given the high stakes involved in modern warfare, upholding clear principles regulating war on the part of the entire world community is absolutely necessary if the coming century is to be less bloody. A thoughtful and thorough statement of Christian teaching on war is the 1983 pastoral letter of the United States Catholic bishops, ***The Challenge of Peace***: ***God's Promise and Our Response***. The letter discusses the morality of war. It enunciates general principles about war and suggests some specific applications of those principles to our contemporary world.

The Challenge of Peace acknowledges that the use of violence in war is a complex moral issue. Neither the Bible nor Christian tradition offers definitive answers about the morality of war. For example, the pastoral letter says that: "Even a brief examination of war and peace in the Scriptures makes it clear that it does not provide us with detailed answers to the specifics of the questions which we face today" (number 55).

However, although the Bible does not give us definitive answers about war, it does aim us always in the direction of peace. The pastoral letter points us in the same direction when it offers us the following as a first principle regarding war: "Catholic teaching begins in every case with a presumption against war and for peaceful settlement of disputes" (Summary, A1).

According to the bishops, Christians can find in defending and working for peace two legitimate options expressed in the tradition: To resist bearing arms or to bear arms. Nonetheless, it's important to keep in mind that both of these options, while in disagreement on means, do agree on the goal—a just resolution of conflict accompanied by the least possible harm to all parties involved. Given this understanding of means and ends, the bishops accept the idea that war is permissible when entered into for defensive purposes. Even then, however, it is subject to rigorous restrictions that have been spelled out since the early centuries of Christian history. For instance, the bishops remind us that "the possibility of taking even one human life is a prospect we should consider in fear and trembling" (paragraph 80). **K**

The Challenge of Peace—1983 pastoral letter of U.S. bishops addressing issues of war and peace

Activity K

Attitudes toward the morality of war can fluctuate with time and with changing circumstances. On a scale of one to ten (one means being totally against any form of war and ten means being totally accepting of war), rate the attitude toward war that currently exists in our society. Explain your rating.

The Just-War Tradition—Principles to Restrict and Regulate War

just-war principles— a set of principles, first proposed in the fourth century, outlining conditions when use of violence would be acceptable

The bishops describe traditional principles called the **just-war principles** that can guide Christians in deciding when war is justified. The bishops consider modern war such a horror that "a decision [to engage in war], especially today, requires extraordinarily strong reasons for overriding the presumption in favor of peace and against war" (number 83). Therefore, the just-war principles "seek to restrict and reduce its horrors" (number 83). In other words, the bishops are reminding us that there is no "good violence." There is only justified, when-all-else-fails, regrettable violence. Violence is not an instrument to bring about victory rather than defeat. Resorting to violence itself is defeat, a defeat of the sacredness and communal nature of all human life.

A listing of the just-war principles clarifies the teaching that warfare, with its frequent wholesale destruction of life, is morally acceptable only in rare instances. **L**

Just-War Principles

Just Cause: War is permissible only to confront "a real and certain danger. . . ."

Competent Authority: War must be declared by those with responsibility for public order.

Comparative Justice: Every party to a conflict should acknowledge the limits of its "just cause." Do the rights and values being defended justify the loss of others' lives?

Right Intention: During the conflict, right intention means pursuit of peace and reconciliation [not, for instance, increased economic power in a region].

Last Resort: . . . all peaceful alternatives must have been exhausted.

Probability of Success: With a fair degree of certainty, intended results are likely to be achieved.

Proportionality: Proportionality means that the damage to be inflicted and the costs incurred by war must be proportionate to the good expected by taking up arms.

THE UNITED STATES CATHOLIC BISHOPS, *THE CHALLENGE OF PEACE: GOD'S PROMISE AND OUR RESPONSE*, 1983, NUMBERS 86–99.

Activity L

Consider a recent episode when military force was used by a particular nation. Using each of the just-war principles, make a case that war was or was not justified.

Based on your evaluation, do you find just-war principles to be valuable instruments for determining whether or not military force should be used in international conflict situations? Why?

Specific Issues Related to War and Peace

The bishops' document also offers some helpful guidelines regarding specific issues related to war and peace. Their pronouncements mirror the strong criticism of modern warfare that has been voiced by Church leaders especially since Vatican Council II in the 1960s.

On nuclear weapons

nuclear deterrence—the proposition that if two nations possess the ability to inflict serious damage on each other, then neither nation is likely to use its nuclear weapons in the first place

Remember that the U.S. bishops wrote *The Challenge of Peace* during the period known as "the cold war" when tensions were great between the two major world powers of the time, the U.S. and the Soviet Union. The bishops did not condemn the U.S. government for maintaining its arsenal of nuclear weapons. It recognized their potential as a deterrent against all-out warfare between the two superpowers. **Nuclear deterrence** means that if two nations possess the ability to inflict nuclear damage on each other, then neither nation is likely to use its nuclear weapons in the first place.

Concerning nuclear weapons, the bishops condemn:

1. Initiation of the use of nuclear weapons
2. Further buildup of nuclear weapons by any nation. (In part, the bishops see money spent on nuclear weapons as taking away from money available for helping people in need.)
3. **Nuclear proliferation** (the spread of nuclear weapons to other nations) **M**

nuclear proliferation—any increase in the number of nations that possess nuclear weapons or that have the capability to build them

On conscientious objection

conscientious objector—one who for moral or religious reasons is opposed to serving in the military

According to the definition used by the Selective Service Agency, which oversees military registration for the U.S. government, a **conscientious objector** is one who on the grounds of moral or religious principles is opposed to serving in the armed forces and/or bearing arms. [See the Selective Service web site at www.sss.gov.] The government does require eighteen-year-old men to register for military service. The laws in place overseeing this registration do allow men to apply for conscientious objector status, in which case if a draft were instituted these men would perform non-military service rather than military service. Being a conscientious objector is a legal position. Not registering for the draft or simply refusing induction into the military (popularly known as being a "draft dodger") is illegal.

The bishops have called for another category to be instituted: selective conscientious objection. A **selective conscientious objector** is one who believes that the particular war in which he or she would be called to fight is against his moral and/or religious principles. While there is currently no legal status for such a position, the bishops state that: "We continue to insist upon respect for and legislative protection of the rights of both classes of conscientious objectors" (number 233).

selective conscientious objector—one who for moral or religious reasons is opposed to serving in the military during a particular war

Activity M

The bishops took a controversial stand regarding the U.S. government and nuclear weapons—that it is okay to possess such weapons but not to use them. As a United States citizen, then as a citizen from another nation, debate the positives and negatives of the U.S. possessing nuclear weapons.

On nonviolence

nonviolence—
conflict-resolving techniques that do not rely on physical or psychological injury of an opponent

Besides its history of wars, the twentieth century is also notable for progress made in developing **nonviolent** techniques for dealing with conflicts. Mahatma Gandhi of India helped his country achieve independence from England without relying on violence, bloodshed, or even hatred. The United States has also been home to a number of nonviolent movements. The civil rights and anti-war movements, especially during the sixties and seventies, featured leaders dedicated to meeting conflict with nonviolent resistance. The bishops would like to see further exploration into nonviolence as an alternative to violence and war as a means of resolving conflicts:

Nonviolent means of resistance to evil deserve much more study and consideration than they have thus far received. There have been significant instances in which people have successfully resisted oppression without recourse to arms (number 222).

Principles of Nonviolence

1. Nonviolence is a way of life for courageous people. It is active nonviolent resistance to evil.

2. Nonviolence seeks to win friendship and understanding. The end result of nonviolence is redemption and reconciliation.

3. Nonviolence seeks to defeat injustice, not people. Nonviolence recognizes that evildoers are also victims.

4. Nonviolence holds that suffering can educate and transform. Nonviolence willingly accepts the consequences of its acts.

5. Nonviolence chooses love instead of hate. Nonviolence resists violence of the spirit as well as the body. Love restores community and resists injustice.

6. Nonviolence believes that the universe is on the side of justice. The nonviolent resister has deep faith that justice will eventually win.

"PRINCIPLES OF NONVIOLENCE" BASED ON THE WRITINGS AND SPEECHES OF DR. MARTIN LUTHER KING, JR. **N**

Activity N

1. Give examples when nonviolence would require courage.

2. According to principle #2, what is the aim of nonviolence? What is the aim of violence? How are the two different?

3. What does principle #3 mean by saying that "evildoers are also victims"? Give examples.

4. Both violence and nonviolence can result in suffering. Is there a difference in the suffering that each entails? Explain.

5. Give examples of "violence of the spirit."

6. We might think of violence as "natural" and therefore as unavoidable, whereas nonviolence runs against the nature of things. In the "Principles of Nonviolence," principle #6 raises the discussion to a spiritual, cosmic level. In a sense, it calls into question our image of the divine. (Is God violent or nonviolent?) It proclaims that in the "big picture" love, justice, and nonviolence are indeed more fundamental than hatred, injustice, and violence. Do you agree?

7. What strategies would you recommend to foster a "culture of life" in our own society and globally? Explain.

21. What first principle regarding war do the U.S. Catholic bishops state in *The Challenge of Peace*?

22. According to the bishops, in working for peace what two options lay open to Christians?

23. Name the seven principles of the just-war theory.

24. Explain deterrence as it applies to nuclear weapons.

25. Concerning nuclear weapons, what three things do the bishops condemn?

26. What is a conscientious objector?

27. What is the legal status of a conscientious objector in the U.S.?

28. What is selective conscientious objection? What is the U.S. Catholic bishops' position on both types of conscientious objection?

29. What was the major achievement of Mahatma Gandhi?

30. Name two U. S. movements that have employed nonviolent techniques?

31. What position do the U.S. Catholic bishops take on nonviolence?

Conclusion
Violence Violates Respect for Human Life

Let us pray . . .

Jesus, you rejected violence but died a harsh criminal's death. Help us to realize that in the end there is no good violence. Before your death you gave us a simple but awesome task, to be neighbors to everyone. You taught us that every human life is sacred and every unjustified act of violence an affront to the human spirit. May we pause and reconsider your message to us when voices echo a culture of death. Keep us faithful to you as we face conflicts at home, in our communities, and in our world. Amen.

Respect for life is a fundamental Christian moral principle. Violence used against any persons diminishes the dignity that human life deserves. Violence fosters a culture of death. In our attempts to further a culture of life, we need to seek ways of cutting back on violence in all forms. We need to be sensitive both to explicit as well as hidden expressions of violence. Among explicit expressions of violence, we need to seek alternatives to the ready availability of guns and their use against persons, to reliance on the death penalty, and to warfare. In the spirit of Jesus, we view violence with remorse and regret.

CHAPTER 15

Justice
The Moral Character of Society

Morality is not just about what we personally do that is right or wrong. Morality also concerns itself with what is right or wrong in our society. In recent years Church leaders have frequently addressed this social dimension of morality. By doing so, they have alerted us to take seriously underlying values as well as the commonly accepted ideas by which a society maintains itself. All dimensions of a particular community or society can help or hinder its members—not just the actions of particular individuals. In this chapter we will look at justice as the Christian virtue that applies morality to society and aims at creating fairness within that society.

Chapter Overview

- Justice expands moral discussion to include an investigation of society, its values and practices.

- Church teaching sees a strong link between justice and personal morality.

- Social analysis is a process for examining society in terms of justice.

- We can analyze social problems such as poverty and discrimination using core principles of justice.

- Through its teachings and its members, the Church is a strong voice for justice in the world today.

Let us pray . . .

Jesus, we praise you and thank you for taking on all the suffering of the world and making it your own. When we look around us—deeply, caringly, through your eyes—we discover people who are hurting in many ways. May we make your vision our vision, finding you in those who are hungry or alone or in those who are imprisoned, whether by the state or by poverty or by mental illness. As part of our moral quest, may we search for ways that we can transform our world so that it more closely resembles the vision you gave us. Amen.

Before we begin . . .

1. Make a list, as complete as possible, of what you consider to be major social problems that exist today.

2. Identify, as best you can, causes of these problems—both underlying, deep-seated causes as well as more immediate causes.

3. Name societal values that might contribute to any of these problems or that might stand in the way of our society overcoming them.

4. Identify ways that society might be changed so as to alleviate or minimize these problems.

Problems in Our Society

- Homelessness plagues our big cities. Today, many entire families need the services of shelters. Veterans, especially of the Vietnam War, make up a sizable portion of people living on the streets. Many homeless people are unable to work due to mental illness or other problems.

- Healthcare, income, and housing for the wealthiest people of the world are the best they have ever been. Meanwhile, adequate health care, employment opportunities, and affordable housing are often found lacking among poorer segments of society.

- The United States prides itself on guaranteeing education for all children. Nonetheless, illiteracy and insufficient education remain serious social problems in the country. Many unemployed persons or persons in low-paying, dead-end jobs do not have enough skills or education to help them move out of poverty. Many people in our prisons are either illiterate or poorly educated.

- In North America, hailed as the "breadbasket of the world," an alarming number of people suffer from malnutrition. Surprisingly, people who perform the essential task of harvesting crops are among the poorest paid and often work under the harshest conditions of any workers.

- Even though life expectancy has been increasing steadily in our country, life expectancy among African Americans, American Indians, and many Latino groups remains well below that for white Americans.

- In proportion to their numbers, women and minorities consistently have lower representation in Congress and other branches of government than white males have. Certainly, elected officials are supposed to work for the concerns of all the people they represent. Nonetheless, people can feel far removed from the centers of power when they see few government officials who are members of their particular minority group.

- Recycling and other anti-pollution measures have greatly increased in our communities, but waste and pollution remain serious problems. The problem is intensified by an attitude fostering excessive consuming of and then discarding of things. Neglect of the environment affects everyone, especially people living in poorer areas and, potentially, members of future generations.

Justice
Expanding Our Moral Imagination

The list on the previous page paints a bleak picture of our society. Certainly, the picture is not complete. Much could be said that would portray a positive image of our society. However, a quick look at any evening news broadcast reminds us that the picture painted in the list on page 282 is painfully realistic. Unfortunately, our society is not all that it could and should be.

The first thing we might notice about the list of statements is that it summarizes various ways that groups of people are suffering. As such, it is definitely a list of moral problems. However, if we view it solely from a personal morality perspective we might conclude that individually we are not responsible for this suffering. We might also feel that these problems are too overwhelming for us to tackle; anything we could do as individuals would make only a small dent toward solving them. To confront issues such as these, we need more than a personal morality approach. Christian teaching on justice expands our moral imagination beyond a focus on the behavior of individuals. Justice shifts our focus to identifying underlying causes and seeking long-term solutions to deep-seated social problems.

Wash yourselves; make yourselves clean;
remove the evil of your doings from before my eyes;
cease to do evil, learn to do good;
seek justice, rescue the oppressed,
defend the orphan, plead for the widow.

Isaiah 1:16–17

A Justice Perspective on Social Problems

Although it may seem obvious, it is actually a fact that can be easily overlooked: *Deep-seated social problems are problems affecting real people.* For instance, if the mother of a friend of yours loses her job, that would put a personal, human face on the social problem of unemployment. Sometimes when we hear about social problems such as factories shutting down and moving to other countries or people left to live homeless on city streets, we can forget that these news stories and statistics are about real people who are suffering. From a Christian perspective, these people are our brothers and sisters. **A**

Three qualities of a deep-seated social problem from a justice perspective

1. Those who are suffering are lumped together according to categories such as race, gender, income, age, and education.

2. Responsibility for these problems is not clearly designated. While victims are named, no clear villains are pinpointed. In each case, our society itself appears to be the "villain" causing these hardships.

3. Each personal problem relates to some value, policy, or commonly accepted practice pervading our entire society. In other words, *societal* problems are *personal* problems, only on a larger scale.

Activity A

1. Look over the editorial page of a newspaper from the past week or so. Cut out an article that deals with a particular social problem. Describe the article's point of view. State which viewpoint is emphasized: a personal morality (responsibility lies with individuals) or a social justice (deep-seated societal factors are at work) perspective on the problem. Explain your conclusion.

2. Select a social problem that you feel is causing suffering to people today. Write an editorial about that problem. Include suggestions about how justice might be applied to the problem. (You might consider submitting your editorial to your school or community newspaper.)

3. After you have finished, read over your editorial. Imagine that Jesus reads your editorial and decides to write a "letter to the editor" in response. Write this letter in the way you think Jesus would.

4. Name three problems that individuals might face. Describe possible ways that each personal problem could become a social justice issue as well.

5. Name three social justice issues. Describe possible ways that each justice issue might affect individuals as well.

All Morality Is Social Morality

Indeed, all morality is social morality. However, up until now our study of morality has focused mostly on our activities as individuals. We can't understand social problems such as poverty, illiteracy, and sexual discrimination if we look only at what individuals have done or not done to create these unjust conditions. Rather, these problems point to unfortunate and, at times, appalling characteristics of our society. If a concern of Christian morality is mending ways that people are hurting, then morality as solely the actions of individuals definitely proves inadequate to the task. Moral decision making is ineffective unless it also tries to analyze and solve deeply embedded social evils.

Here's an example: In certain communities plagued by poverty, a high percentage of children complete their schooling without education or training sufficient to succeed at anything other than low-paying, dead-end jobs that will never move them out of poverty. Surely this is a moral and social problem about which all of us should be concerned. Who would you say is to blame? Here are some possible culprits:

- The teachers in these communities are not living up to the standards of their profession compared to teachers in other communities.

- The parents are to blame for not supporting or pushing their children more.

- People who live in these communities are at fault because they do not make enough money to pay the taxes that would improve the schools.

- Leaders in these communities are not good role models.

- The children themselves are to blame. They are simply incapable of attaining, or are not motivated enough to achieve, educational success on a par with children born in other communities.

- Rather than concentrating on education, administrators at these schools are spending too much time monitoring whether or not the students are receiving adequate nourishment and are coming from homes that have sufficient heat and parental supervision.

- Federal, state, or local officials are not doing enough to help these children.

As you can see, a social problem, such as the effectiveness of education, is also a serious moral problem. However, responsibility for both the causes and the cure for the problem lies not simply with isolated individuals. A justice perspective looks at problems existing within a society and seeks to correct those problems in whatever ways possible. A justice perspective sees social problems as multi-faceted and therefore as requiring a multi-faceted approach to solutions. **B**

Activity B

Besides the actions of individuals, what social factors do you think might lead to schools in wealthier communities producing students who, on the average, achieve better test scores and end up in better jobs than do the students from schools in poorer neighborhoods? Based on your list of social factors, what changes would you recommend to improve schooling in poorer neighborhoods?

Common Good and Personal Good Are One

In earlier chapters we have already discussed the traditional Christian concept known as the common good. Christianity inherited this concept from classical sources, and it has since become an important principle of Catholic social teaching. The principle of common good proposes that society should be organized so that, as much as possible, the entire community, as well as individuals within that community, benefit from society's actions. Catholic social teaching sees the **common good** and the good of individuals as ultimately one and the same.

Here's an example to clarify this insight from traditional Catholic teaching. Imagine that you are in an algebra class grouped with a handful of students who are gifted in math and others who are much less mathematically gifted. Your teacher faces a dilemma. Does he aim his teaching at those students who are stronger or those who are weaker in math? If he directs his teaching to the poorer students, the better ones may feel cheated or bored or uninterested. If he directs his teaching toward the better students, the poorer ones will feel lost and left out. As a result, they may become disheartened and bored and also possibly disruptive. In either case the atmosphere of learning will be negatively affected. Even trying to maintain a medium-level pace would likely leave everyone dissatisfied.

In this classroom, unless the good of each student is addressed in some way, all the students will ultimately suffer. The teacher needs to be attentive to the first principle of the common good: The betterment of each community member leads to the betterment of all of its members. The teacher would also do well to put into practice two additional principles of this concept: Those who are more likely to be left out require special attention and all members of a community should have opportunities to contribute to the betterment of their community. In summary, then, concern for the common good seeks individual and society-wide development through increased equality and active participation of all members. **C**

common good— a long-standing Christian concept advocating that society should be organized so that, as much as possible, both individuals and the entire community are equally thriving

Principles of the Common Good

1. The betterment of each community member leads to the betterment of all its members.

2. Those who are more likely to be left out require special attention.

3. All members of a community should have opportunities to contribute to the betterment of their community.

Activity C

Imagine that you are an algebra teacher who has a class filled with students who have a wide range of math ability. How might you incorporate the three principles of the common good into your teaching of the class?

Common Good Applied to Social Problems

How is the common good played out in society at large? For instance, how can it be applied to poverty and homelessness? Surely, the presence of people who reach the depths of poverty and end up homeless has a negative impact on all members of a community. At the very least, the realization that some fellow community members are sleeping out in the cold should disturb the good sleep of all but the most heartless home-owners. A society in which there exists a wide gap between the fortunes of the very rich and the misfortunes of the very poor creates an increasingly unstable social and economic situation. When poor people feel hopeless, even wealthier people can feel their security threatened.

Common good asserts that everyone's life is enriched when each person's life is enriched. Most especially, common good reminds us that we are all in this together. Wherever we are going as a society, ultimately we are going together. The Christian concept known as the common good offers us an ideal that we can strive for as we ponder how best to help people. The common good calls for a strong sense of social responsibility and of mutual concern among all community members. Christian teaching on justice affirms that when the lot of the poorest members of society improves and the voiceless gain a voice, then all of society gains.

Complementary Approaches

Two things are complementary when one completes the other, like popcorn at a movie theater. To say that justice and morality are complementary means that we lack a complete picture of a problem unless we understand both the personal morality and the social justice aspects of that problem. If morality and justice are complementary, then all that we have learned so far about morality can be applied to the work of justice. For instance, the process for moral decision making described in chapter 8 can also be applied to justice. That is, if we can gain a clearer sense of what the problems are in a community or society, who is involved, and possible alternatives for responding, then we can begin to take conscientious steps toward overcoming these problems. **D**

For review . . .

1. What shift in perspective does justice bring to our moral imagination?

2. Name three qualities of a justice perspective on deep-seated social problems.

3. Give an example to illustrate why assigning responsibility to a particular individual is an inadequate way of dealing with deep-seated social problems.

4. Name the three principles of the concept common good.

5. What does it mean to say that justice and personal morality approaches to a problem are complementary?

Activity D

Look over again the process of moral decision making described in chapter 8. Choose a particular social problem and apply that process to the problem. What insights about the problem are uncovered by submitting it to the process?

- poverty in wealthy countries
- hate groups
- increases in the elderly population
- pressures experienced by single-parent families
- inadequate social and recreational activities for teens
- pressures experienced by disabled persons
- domestic abuse

The Process of Social Analysis

In recent decades Church leaders have frequently spoken out for social justice. They have called for analyzing our society from a justice perspective in order to eliminate problems and to bring about positive changes. They proposed a method of responding to social problems that addresses immediate concerns but that also looks at deeper issues. This method, the process of social analysis, provides a helpful companion to the more individualistic emphasis of personal morality. The social analysis process emphasizes looking for causes of social problems and seeking solutions based on these causes.

Essentially, the process includes four steps. Those who propose social analysis use a spiral rather than a straight line to illustrate it. In other words, in the process of identifying causes of a problem we discover additional social changes that might be called for. And if one solution proves ineffective, we try another.

Social Analysis Process

1. Identify root causes of problems.
2. Uncover harmful conditions.
3. Examine social institutions.
4. Recognize interdependence.

Identify Root Causes of Problems

symptoms—
a problem that is immediately apparent

social analysis—
a process for examining social problems that involves searching for underlying causes and long-term solutions to the problems

underlying causes—
underlying reasons why a problem exists; reasons that are not readily apparent

The first step in social analysis is to view problems—such as the ones mentioned at the beginning of this chapter—as **symptoms** of more deep-rooted problems. In this respect **social analysis** resembles good medical practice in which a physician does not simply treat symptoms of a health problem but also attends to its **underlying causes**. ("I can give you this cream for your acne, but you need to be careful about your diet as well. What you eat has a great impact on your complexion, you know." "I can give you medicine for your cold symptoms, but you're run down. Your body needs rest.")

One problem cited at the beginning of the chapter is that of the ever-increasing amount of waste that clutters our planet. Waste disposal is a serious problem, the resolution of which is necessary for human survival. A social analysis approach to this problem asks: Are there underlying causes for the great amount of waste that our society produces? Only when we address our fundamental attitude toward things—"Use things, then throw them away"—will we move toward achieving permanent solutions for this problem.

As with the environmental issue, attacking the symptoms of problems while ignoring the causes leads to frustration. Only by getting at the underlying causes of excessive waste can a true resolution occur. This way of handling things is also needed with other social problems. In the long run, root causes of a problem need to be addressed to reverse the symptoms that appear as problems in society. **E**

Activity E

A. Name five symptoms of our current environmental crisis. Then name five underlying causes of these symptoms. Write a proposal for a set of laws that would address environmental problems in our society.

B. For the following behaviors, rate yourself on a scale from one (environmentally faulty) to ten (environmentally friendly). What does your self-analysis indicate about your underlying attitude toward the environment?

_____ 1. When I go to a fast-food restaurant, I never take more napkins or other supplies than what I actually use.

_____ 2. I am always conscientious about recycling.

_____ 3. I am always thoughtful of the environmental impact of purchases that I make.

_____ 4. I make sure that clothes I no longer wear are given to a charitable organization.

_____ 5. I refuse to use products that pollute the environment.

_____ 6. I seek information about how to avoid pollution and how to help the environment.

_____ 7. I encourage others to be sensitive about environmental issues.

Uncover Harmful Conditions— Don't Cast Blame

Second, social analysis does not point a finger at individuals or groups and hold them alone responsible for social problems. (In the previous analogy, the wise doctor treating us for acne or a cold condition knows that our society's fast pace and its addiction to junk food are important factors contributing to our health problems.) Recall the earlier example of inadequate education in poor neighborhoods. In that example, it is clear that blame for the problem does not lie solely with individuals. Apply the same logic to another problem mentioned at the beginning of this chapter: Life expectancy among members of some racial groups is well below the national average. We cannot understand this phenomenon unless we search out deeply ingrained social conditions that create the problem.

Recognizing social conditions that cause or contribute to problems is not meant to eliminate personal responsibility but to focus it. (Our doctor wouldn't help us if she or he were to say, "Social factors have helped bring on your acne and your cold. Oh well, there's nothing you can do about it!") Only when we identify conditions leading up to a problem can we take effective steps to eliminate the problem. **F**

Examine Social Institutions

institution—
commonly accepted ways (structures, laws, rules, customs, and so on) that basic, essential functions are carried out within a society

Institution is a multi-leveled term for the commonly accepted way that basic, essential functions are carried out within a society—for instance, health care, punishment of wrongdoers, education of children, business dealings, and relational or behavioral patterns. An institution describes what is the "norm"—that is, what is considered normal—for a particular dimension of social life. For instance, when we refer to a particular school as an "academic institution," we really mean that it is one expression of the broader, more society-wide function of the expected norm for educating the populace. Reference to the "institution of marriage" points to the commonly accepted way that a couple would commit themselves to each other and to the care and raising of children and more importantly how they would live out that commitment.

Activity F

For each of the following, first list possible underlying causes and then potential long-term solutions to the problem.

- children and teen smoking
- teenagers drinking
- students experiencing excessive stress to succeed
- anorexia and bulimia
- excessive consumption
- vandalism

Examples of institutions in our society

- the education system
- housing
- investment, banking, and business
- employment and work
- the criminal justice system

- health care
- churches
- families
- media (advertising, television, films, magazines and newspapers)

Social analysis examines our society's institutions and the organizations that give expression to them in order to determine their role in increasing or diminishing problems. To continue our analogy of the doctor treating health problems, we recognize that junk food has become a normal, even though unhealthy, part of the diet of many people in our country. A number of institutions as they currently operate support and promote this trend. For instance, the numerous and varied activities of many family members often lead to eating separately and "on the road." A business climate that sharply reduces lunch breaks results in meals that have to be "fast service" or consumed while working. Thus, for people to avoid eating junk food would require going against accepted practices and some strong influences at work in our society.

Another example would be the social analysis of the problem of illiteracy that leads naturally to an investigation of the way the educational institution operates in our society. Social analysis asks about education:

- Is educating young people a primary concern in our society?

- Why aren't the children in our country the most well-educated in the world?

- Is teacher training adequate?

- Are teacher salaries sufficient to ensure that the best teachers are teaching?

- Does discussion of the quality of education in our society occupy a major portion of the time of committees of Congress, state legislatures, and local governments?

- Should parents' rights to choose their children's schools be blocked or be made virtually unattainable by their being refused government funds or tax breaks to send their children to non-government schools?

- Are measures taken to insure that the quality of education is first-rate for all segments of society?

- Is a large portion of our tax dollars spent on education or does education tend to lose out to other concerns?

- How are families and businesses being involved in curriculum preparation?

Applied to social institutions, justice suggests the following strategies: If we discover that the way a particular institution operates aggravates a problem, then in justice we should seek to change it. If we find that an institution has been effective but is currently under attack, then in justice we should seek to support and strengthen it or support an effective alternative. For instance, if we discover that schools receive inadequate assistance from various levels of government, then that information suggests types of activity justice calls for. Similarly, if we analyze trends in housing construction and discover that an emphasis on building luxury homes takes away from building homes affordable for people who have low incomes, then the work of justice would be to seek ways to alter this trend. **G**

Activity G

Societal institutions are so basic that they are rarely if ever all good or all bad, completely just or unjust. Nonetheless, it is important to examine the impact of our institutions in order to bring about greater justice. Choose an institution of our society and describe ways that it either does or could serve as an instrument of justice or injustice.

Work with Others in Community: Recognize Interdependence

Since men are members of the same human family, they are indissolubly linked with one another in the one destiny of the whole world, in the responsibility for which they all share.

SYNOD OF BISHOPS, *JUSTICE IN THE WORLD*, NUMBER 1.

interdependent— needing one another to survive and thrive

We have been shaped by the society in which we live; only together in community can we reshape our society. A social analysis approach to problems implies a spirit of community and a recognition that we need one another to survive and thrive. In other words, we are **interdependent**.

America is known as a land built upon a spirit of independence. Even today some rugged individualists try to live totally self-sufficient lives—growing their own food, using solar power for heating and light, and drinking water from their own wells. However, while such independence is honorable, it is misguided if it is built on the belief that we can ignore the people around us. Pollution from factories that are miles—even countries—away can poison the air we breathe. Dangerous chemicals seeping into the ground have a way of traveling to a neighbor's well. If vandalism is an accepted way of life in the surrounding area, then—no matter how isolated or fortified they are—all people should be concerned. Indeed, if warfare among nations is not curbed, ultimately the earth community and all its members are threatened.

Agriculture and food distribution represents an essential social institution that demonstrates interdependence. For example, the farming and food-distribution system in place in North America is the envy of the entire world. It exemplifies interdependence and the importance of a community approach to a social institution. Every link in the system's chain, from those who harvest crops to those who shelve food in supermarkets, is interdependent with every other link. If a "weak link" exists, the effects are felt all along the chain. If this delicate balance falls apart, everyone will suffer—beginning with those who have the least amount of financial, family, and other resources to fall back on. **H**

Activity H

Draw a picture, make a collage or chart, or write a song or poem illustrating interdependence as it relates to one area of society.

This Land Is Home to Me

The first official document issued by the North American Church that employs a social analysis approach to a problem is the pastoral letter *This Land Is Home to Me* (1975). In it the regional Catholic bishops address the problems of powerlessness and poverty in the Appalachian area of the United States. (The film "October Sky" offers a stirring portrait of the type of economic and social conditions that the bishops address.) Though a quarter of a century old, this pastoral letter, written in an unusual poetic style, is still worth reading to gain a sense of how social analysis can be applied to specific problems.

Here are portions of the document that reflect characteristics of social analysis as described in the text.

1. Identify root causes of problems that exist today

A long time ago in this country
when big industry just got started,
Appalachian coal played a big role.
It fed the furnaces of our first industrial giants,
like Pittsburgh and Buffalo.
The coal-based industry created many jobs,
and it brought other things, too,
among them oppression for the mountains.
Soon the mountain people
were dependent on the coal companies
and on the company towns that came with them.
(page 478)

2. Uncover harmful conditions but don't cast blame

We do not put ourselves in judgment of others.
The truth of Appalachia is judgment upon us all,
making hard demands on us bishops, as well as on
others. (pages 472–473)
Without judging anyone,
it has become clear to us
that the present economic order does not care for
its people.
In fact, profit and people frequently are contradictory.
(page 485)

3. Examine social institutions

An old song sings,
another day older and deeper in debt.
That was life for many people who lived in the shadow
of the mountain's coal. (page 478)
The mines in the hills began to close.
The industrial thunder of cities near the mines weakened.
The people from the mountains fled to the cities
looking for jobs.
But in the cities, the jobs were few.
It is a strange system which makes people suffer
both when they have work and when they don't have
work. (page 480)

4. Work with others in community; recognize interdependence

We know that there are many
–sincere business people,
–zealous reporters,
–truthful teachers,
–honest law enforcement officers,
–dedicated public officials,
–hard working lawyers and legislators who try to do
a good job. (page 489)
Together these groups struggle to achieve what must
become the foundation principle of our common life,
namely citizen involvement. (page 487)

PAGE NUMBERS REFER TO THE DOCUMENT FOUND IN *RENEWING THE EARTH: CATHOLIC DOCUMENTS ON PEACE, JUSTICE AND LIBERATION*, EDITED BY DAVID J. O'BRIEN AND THOMAS A. SHANNON [GARDEN CITY, NY: IMAGE BOOKS, 1977].

For review . . .

6. Define social analysis.
7. What is the difference between a symptom and an underlying cause of a problem?
8. What does recognizing social conditions underlying a problem add to personal responsibility?
9. What is an institution of a society?
10. Define interdependence.
11. What is a misguided understanding of independence?

Issues of Justice

The remainder of this chapter will deal in a brief manner with a number of justice issues faced by the people in our world today. Broader discussion of all these topics would be covered in a justice course.

Church leaders of the past century have recognized how central a role justice plays in carrying out the gospel message. A set of key principles of justice have emerged which run through Church teachings on justice. For instance, The U.S. Catholic bishops use these principles to begin their analysis of the U.S. economy in their pastoral letter, *Economic Justice for All* (1986). In addition to describing how justice should be done, these principles also hint at what a just world would look like.

These are lofty principles indeed. The question is what can we actually do to bring about a more just world?

Key Principles of a Just World

1. Creation is God's gift, meant for everyone.

2. All people possess inherent dignity, for they, too, are God's creation.

3. As a legacy of their dignity, all people deserve to have basic needs met.

4. All people have both rights and obligations aimed at creating fair distribution of the earth's goods. (That is, people are responsible, one for another.)

5. People who have special needs deserve special care and attention.

Applying Just World Principles

- Jorge spent most of his childhood and youth living on the streets of his small Mexican village. Recently, he has survived by making a small amount of money as a taxi driver. His "taxi" is really a bicycle fitted with a chair in the back that he pedals about town in search of passengers. In his village far too many young men try to make their living this way, and competition is fierce. Now that he is twenty, married, and with a young son, Jorge wants more than to survive. The only hope he sees is to join the thousands who make their way to Mexico City each day seeking some kind of work or to make the dangerous crossing into the United States.

- Since freshman year Sanghee and Kerry have been numbers one and two in their class academically. Now seniors, both have applied to and been accepted at prestigious Ivy League colleges. Sanghee's parents can afford to send him there, and he is looking forward to attending the school of his choice next year. Kerry's mother, however, tells her that

even with the scholarship and loan money promised her, the family cannot possibly afford to send her to the school of her choice. Instead, Kerry will join the large contingent of students from her school who will be attending the local state college next year.

- Darius and Sean, who are African American, have become friends with some classmates who are white. One day the pair wanders into a park in an all-white neighborhood, searching for their friends. Along the way they encounter suspicious

looks, and a park guard changes directions to follow them as they pass. When Darius and Sean finally meet up with their friends, they're asked, "Have any trouble getting here?" They just shrug their shoulders and say, "None at all," knowing how much race continues to be a dividing line in much of our society.

- When Alice's husband died, her sister Marie moved in with her. With the help of a local agency that brings them weekly meals, together they manage to maintain the house. However, both Alice and Marie are growing increasingly fearful of venturing outside of the house alone, even to the senior citizens' bus stop down the street. Neither wants to consider moving to a retirement home. None of the ones they have visited look much like "home" anyway— more like hospitals or warehouses to them. And so the two elderly women live more and more isolated lives and make do with less and less association with the world outside their home. ▮

Activity I

Apply one or more of the principles of justice to the above situations. Describe another situation in which each principle is violated. Describe a concrete way that each principle could be put into practice.

Poverty at Home and Abroad

One problem crying out for justice today is the amount of poverty that exists both here in North America and abroad. According to the United Nations, the richest one-fifth of the world's population receives over eighty percent of the world's income while the poorest one-fifth receives less than one percent. Again, without pointing blame at individuals, it is accurate to say that this statistic describes an injustice. That is, it violates every one of the principles of justice.

In large measure, poor people are not just poor; they are trapped in a **spiral of poverty**. That is, they are caught up in a system that makes breaking out of poverty extremely difficult. Jorge's story on the previous page illustrates the spiral of poverty. Since he needed to support himself even as a child, he attended school only sporadically. Thus he lacks marketable skills or even the basics of an education. He works all day driving his taxi, but he makes barely enough to live. He can put aside nothing for the future. His work is not leading up to any better paying job. If he follows the world-wide trend, he will surely make his way to a

big city. There he will find far too many people searching for far too few jobs.

The authors of a study on the worldwide phenomenon of urbanization, the growth of cities, describe the Jorge's of the world in these terms:

Cities draw displaced rural populations with the promise of jobs and by the lifestyles seen on television. But once they reach the city, most find no steady work. Or the work is offered only or mostly to women because they have been taught by their culture to expect less, to be more docile, and because they are more likely to be conveniently short-term workers who will eventually leave their jobs without pensions or benefits for marriage and childcare. Early in the morning women leave for work in factories where there is no job security, no worker safety, no union. Later, the children go to work—sometimes hustling in the streets. Men, finding no work, lose their place in the household economy

spiral of poverty— poor people being in a situation that makes overcoming poverty almost impossible

and often abandon their families. Or people are forced to consider options for survival that are offensive to their culture and their conscience. They steal, deal in drugs, or enter into prostitution. . . . Cities become the graveyards of what once was the functioning structure of traditional family life.

JOHN C. RAINES AND DONNA C. DAY-LOWER, *MODERN WORK AND HUMAN MEANING* [PHILADELPHIA, PA: THE WESTMINSTER PRESS, 1986].

urbanization— growth of cities worldwide

Urbanization encapsulates the spiral of poverty that operates on a global scale. Large numbers of people, especially in poorer countries, are both poor and powerless to make changes. Unfortunately, the call for "economic development" of poorer countries sometimes serves merely as a smoke screen for increasing the profits of those who are already wealthy. If economic development does not bring benefits such as living wages and job security to those who are poor, then such development does not serve justice. As the principles of justice remind us, the way to help poor people is not only to alleviate their poverty temporarily but to search for ways that they may increase their power so that poverty is less likely to occur long term.

The Archbishop of Cincinnati explains this principle of justice in these words:

When we say that we owe preferential respect and special attention to the poor, we are not saying that the poor should not be held accountable for their participation in society according to the same standards as everybody else. Rather, we are saying that they require respect and attention so as to be able to take their appropriate part in the social system and thus not only benefit from it but contribute to it.

When we think of our obligations to the poor, we must not allow ourselves to think in terms of "them" and "us." To one extent or another, we are all dependent, all disabled, all without power, and all underproductive. Ultimately, we all stand poor before the Lord. **J** **K**

ARCHBISHOP DANIEL E. PILARCZK, *BRINGING FORTH JUSTICE* [NEW YORK: PAULIST PRESS, 1997].

Activity J

1. Search around for someone who has visited or spent time in an economically poor country. Interview the person to find out his or her impression of conditions there. Report on your findings to the class.

2. The Catholic Campaign for Human Development is an agency of the Church dedicated to helping poor people help themselves. Send away for literature from this organization and report on a program that it has sponsored.

Activity K

Which do you think provides a better model for benefiting the common good of a country: Providing tax breaks and other incentives to the wealthiest individuals and companies as a way of providing jobs and other economic benefits for everyone, or raising taxes and supporting economic initiatives, such as low-income housing and public transportation that directly benefit people who are poor?

Environmental Injustice—the LULUs and the NIMBY Syndrome

environmental injustice—unequal distribution of environmental hazards based on racial and economic differences

In 1998, a Pennsylvania newspaper reported on a situation revealing that the association between poverty and lack of power exists in the United States as much as it does in Mexico and other poorer countries. One of the poorest cities in the U.S. is Chester, Pennsylvania. The paper reported that Chester, which already houses a trash incinerator, an infectious waste facility, and a contaminated soil treatment plant, had recently been chosen to have five new waste processing sites. As a result, all the solid and sewage waste of the wealthier nearby counties end up in Chester.

The United States Environmental Protection Agency has found such unequal exposure to pollution and toxic waste to be commonplace across the country. **Environmental injustice** refers to the unequal distribution of environmental hazards based on racial and economic factors. For example, if you are poor or a member of a particular minority group, there's an above average chance that you are living in a neighborhood exposed to hazardous material. Collectively, uncontrolled waste sites, hazardous landfills, and other contaminating land uses are called LULUs—Locally Undesirable Land Uses. Surely, if you had the time, the energy, the resources, and the political connections to keep a LULU out of your neighborhood, you would do what you could to do so. This understandable desire to keep obviously polluting plants and landfills out of one's own area reflects the NIMBY syndrome—the Not-In-My-Back-Yard syndrome. (" I don't care what they do with hazardous waste, just as long as it's not in my back yard.") Because of the economic, social, and political inequality that exists in our country, the NIMBY syndrome results in LULUs being placed in what are already depressed, deprived, and dangerous neighborhoods.

One of the principles of justice is fair distribution of the earth's goods. Environmental justice also calls for fair distribution of responsibility for pollution and environmental dangers. **L**

Activity L

1. Research the topic of hazardous waste. Find out whatever evidence you can that supports or refutes the existence of environmental injustice.

2. Why do you think that environmental hazards are more likely to be found in poorer communities such as on Native American reservations or in poor sections of the rural South?

Discrimination—Classism, Racism, Sexism, and Ageism

The Church's doctrine affirms . . . all racist theories are contrary to Christian faith and love. And yet, in sharp contrast to this growing awareness of human dignity, racism still exists and continually reappears in different forms. It is a wound in humanity's side that mysteriously remains open. Everyone, therefore, must make efforts to heal it with great firmness and patience . . . All forms of discrimination must be firmly opposed.

<small>PONTIFICAL COMMISSION ON JUSTICE AND PEACE, *THE CHURCH AND RACISM* [1988], CONCLUSION.</small>

classism—discrimination against people based on their socio-economic status

Justice concerns itself with how people are hurting in our communities, our country, and our world. The above quote points to one important way that groups of people are hurting today—discrimination. **Discrimination** exists when people suffer disadvantages simply because they are members of a particular group—for example, because they belong to a certain socio-economic class, or to a particular race, gender, or age. When it exists on a societal level, discrimination against members of these groups is termed *classism, racism, sexism*, and *ageism*.

discrimination— a situation in which people suffer disadvantages simply because they are members of a particular group (for example, age, race, gender)

Classism refers to the ways that people are penalized or lack privileges due to their socio-economic class within a particular society. Racism, sexism, and ageism apply the same criteria of a society to race, gender, and age respectively. In each case, these categories refer to deep-seated problems in a society and not simply to a few individuals who discriminate against others because of their socio-economic status or their race. Individuals who discriminate against others may be reflecting their society's point of view, but the most damaging expressions of discrimination are deeper and more pervasive than the actions of isolated individuals. Let's briefly examine each of these "isms" as possible patterns of discrimination in our society.

Classism

In our society, we like to downplay the importance of social class. We envision that anyone in the United States can grow up to become president, a millionaire, the head of a corporation, a world-renowned doctor, or a sports superstar. All it takes is talent, hard work, and the right amount of luck. We think that those who make it to the top deserve their rewards or simply happened to luck out, like winning the lottery. On the other hand, those at the bottom should accept the fact that they simply do not measure up to the successful. We look for inspiration to the story of Abraham Lincoln who made the leap from log cabin to White House. We recount stories of immigrants who arrived penniless in our country and later rose to wealth, fame, or power.

Some "rags to riches" stories are true. However, the great majority of poor people in our country are trapped in the same spiral of poverty at work worldwide. That is, the richest people in our country have a commanding head start in the competition for quality education, the best jobs, access to the finest health-care facilities, housing in safe and preferred neighborhoods, cultural enrichment, travel, and all other benefits that we equate with success in our society. On the other hand, a child born into a family living below the poverty line is unlikely to obtain a solid preparation for college, will receive inadequate or minimal health care and nutrition, and will not be exposed to much of the cultural enrichment that is commonplace for others. Only the most heroic of efforts and the best of luck will transport this child even into the mainstream of American social and economic life. Thus, the vast majority of poor people in our country currently make up an underclass who are trapped and powerless to make economic and cultural advances, at least by following conventional channels. **M**

Racism

Church leaders have called racism an open wound that still plagues our world. This wound is manifest in our country in ways such as inequality among racial groups in terms of life expectancy, infant mortality rates, unemployment statistics, representation in positions of power, and average income levels. Currently, even though the majority of poor people in the U.S. are white, a disproportionate percentage of the poor are American Indians, African Americans, and Latinos. Not surprisingly, members of these races also comprise a small percentage of those in positions of power in our society, such as politicians, lawyers, judges, college professors, business CEOs, and so forth.

Activity M

Defend your stance on this statement: In my country, class division exists though not openly.

racial prejudice—
strong dislike for members of a race other than one's own

racism—subordination of persons who belong to a particular race due to attitudes, actions, or institutional structures at work in a society

This last fact points to an important distinction that we need to make: Racism is different from racial prejudice. **Racial prejudice** is a strong dislike for members of another race simply because they are members of that race. On the other hand, **racism** is more than the racial prejudice of individuals. The U.S. Commission on Civil Rights defines racism as "any attitude, action or institutional structure which subordinates a person or group because of their color" *(Racism and How to Combat It,* 1970). In other words, racism means that in a society certain groups have more power and others less power because of race. Racism means that members of certain racial groups suffer disproportionately or lack benefits available to others. Like all justice concerns, racism describes society in general and not just individuals.

Racism can be direct, that is, when race is the obvious and intended criterion by which someone suffers injustice. Racism can also be indirect, in which case racial discrimination is not intentional but race is nonetheless a factor leading to injustice. An example of direct racism would be if a real estate company purposely refuses to sell homes in a designated neighborhood to members of a particular race. Indirect racism would be if all brokers of a particular real estate company are members of one race who seek out as prospective buyers only members of their race—not because it represents official policy but simply because that is the way they have always done business.

Sexism

Often when speaking about women, their lives and their needs, a member of the audience will confront me with the question, "How can you be concerned about women when there is so much suffering, so much poverty, so much starvation in the world?" That kind of question, I believe, comes from a habit of thinking of "the poor," "the homeless," or "the hungry" as abstractions. When we try to touch the human face of poverty, we will disproportionately discover a woman's face, often a minority woman's face. She will be young and she will be old. Statistically, she ranks among the "poorest of the poor." In the United States, two of three adults in poverty are women; worldwide that statistic climbs to over 70%.

MARIA RILEY OP, "WOMEN ARE THE POOR,"
IN *CENTER FOCUS* [NOVEMBER 1984],
WASHINGTON, DC: CENTER OF CONCERN.

sexism—attitudes, practices, and institutional structures that oppress people solely on the basis of gender

Sexism refers to attitudes, practices, and institutional structures that oppress people solely on the basis of their gender. In two important areas, income and public power, statistics show that women more than men suffer from sexism both in the U.S. and throughout the world. The vast majority of people who are poor are women and the children dependent upon them. Poor women tend to lack resources available to poor men; typically women carry added burdens that men do not. (For instance, a poor man is more likely to leave family behind to go in search of work or better living arrangements while a woman with children is more likely to place immediate needs of the children above her own economic betterment.)

Worldwide, to be born a girl and poor typically starts in motion a series of circumstances that keep women poor. Even apart from the numbers who are poor, women on average earn less than men do, even in the U.S.

To say that women suffer from sexism does not mean that men are free from pressures and problems because they are men. Our society presents stereotypes about what it means to be a woman and to be a man. As is equally true for women, men can experience great pressure to measure up to a particular image of society's ideal. Over against sexism, justice calls for setting people free to be themselves and providing equal opportunities for people to develop themselves.

The hour is coming, in fact has come, when the vocation of women is being acknowledged in its fullness, the hour in which women acquire in the world an influence, an effect and a power never hitherto achieved.

POPE JOHN PAUL II, *ON THE DIGNITY AND VOCATION OF WOMEN* [1988], INTRODUCTION.

Activity N

Use examples and find statistics to debate the following statement: In our society, women typically experience more disadvantages than men do.

Ageism

Growing old brings its pleasures and its pains. However, if difficulties experienced by older people are intensified by societal attitudes and practices, then ageism results. **Ageism**, discrimination based on age, can be a problem for people of any age. No doubt at some time in your life you have felt discriminated against because of your age. However, our society tends to glorify youth. Older people who wish to remain active and vital must fight against cultural stereotypes. Older people who find it more and more difficult to remain active and vital need special care from younger members of society.

As with every other "ism" we have named, justice applied to ageism asks: Are people hurting in any way because of societal values and practices related to age? In one culture, older people tend to be viewed more as a blessing than a burden. In another culture, the opposite attitude can be dominant. When social attitudes and commonly accepted practices add to rather than diminish the trials of biological aging, then injustice results.

ageism—discrimination against people solely on the basis of their age

For review . . .

12. Name the five key principles of Christian justice.

13. What does it mean to say that many people are trapped in a spiral of poverty?

14. Define urbanization. How is urbanization a symptom of worldwide poverty?

15. What is a just versus an unjust goal of economic development?

16. Define environmental injustice.

17. What do the acronyms LULU and NIMBY stand for?

18. Define classism.

19. What is the difference between racial prejudice and racism?

20. What is the difference between direct and indirect racism?

21. Define sexism.

22. Why is a discussion about the place of women in the world also a discussion about poverty?

23. How might men be negatively affected by sexism in our society?

24. What is ageism?

25. Name one way that our society contributes to the difficulties associated with old age.

Activity O

- How would you describe the dominant image of older people and of growing old that exists in our society?

- What is your image of older people and of growing old?

- Based on both of these images, are their societal attitudes and practices that you would like to see put into place? What are they?

Catholic Social Teaching
A Rich and Potent Tradition

From its beginning, the Christian community has considered justice to be an integral dimension of Jesus' message. Indeed, down to the present day many examples could be cited that illustrate concern for justice among Christians in word and in action. Words of Jesus recorded in the Gospels ring out with cries on behalf of poor and downtrodden members of society. Even more strikingly, the actions of Jesus demonstrate his concern for people who are suffering or overlooked. Numerous accounts from the first centuries indicate that the early Christians saw the work of justice as a hallmark of what it means to be a follower of Christ.

During the late Middle Ages, taking advantage of cheap labor and increased opportunities for trade, some people saw the possibility of amassing great wealth. In the midst of this fervor for wealth and possessions, Saint Francis of Assisi rejected the rich life into which he had been born and instead chose voluntarily to live like the poorest of the poor. Strangely enough, he gained many followers for his movement— women and men who felt drawn to live a simple life as the appropriate response to the call of the Gospels. The Franciscan movement was a radical living out of the Gospels and of the Christian principles of justice.

On the Condition of Workers—the 1891 encyclical of Pope Leo XIII voicing concern for industrial workers; the first of a series of documents comprising modern Catholic social teaching

Still later, industrialization brought with it big city poverty. Many holy women and men founded religious communities and Church organizations to care for homeless beggars, widows, orphans, the unschooled, and the physically and mentally ill. Perhaps your school itself represents part of the legacy of these Christian advocates of justice from the past.

The year 1891 marks an important date for modern Catholic teaching on justice. At the time in Europe, "the poor" meant especially factory workers. To call attention to their needs, Pope Leo XIII issued an encyclical letter called *On the Condition of Workers*. In this encyclical the pope made it clear that the Church intended to speak out on social and economic issues and to serve as an advocate for the poor, as Jesus himself was. This encyclical began a trend that continues today. It stands as the first of many official Church statements addressing issues of justice. Church leaders continue to speak out for justice today. Because of its many pronouncements, the Church counts itself as a strong voice calling for justice in the world. In response, Church members are challenged to think about how justice can be manifest in their living out of the moral life. **P**

Activity P

1. Read portions of a Church document that deals with justice. Select three short passages that you think contain key teachings about the topic. Write down each passage, then write a brief statement of your own about how this message could be applied to specific situations today.

2. Interview someone involved in a Church ministry directed toward helping people in need (for example, a nurse or chaplain in a Catholic hospital, a volunteer at a shelter for the poor, an aide at a convalescent home, or a reading tutor at a school or prison). Ask the person how this work is an expression of his or her Christian faith. Write a report on your interview.

26. What do the Gospels and accounts from the early centuries of Christianity indicate about the importance of justice to the Christian message?

27. What did Saint Francis of Assisi do in response to the emerging trend of his day?

28. What did many Christians do to respond to the side-effects of industrialization?

29. What two messages did Pope Leo XIII proclaim by issuing *On the Condition of Workers*?

30. What trend did Pope Leo's encyclical begin?

Conclusion
No Morality without Justice

As we have seen, justice is a key dimension of the gospel message and essential to a full application of Christian morality. Jesus wants us to do all that we can to alleviate suffering experienced by those around us—this is a basic component of his moral message. Justice takes this concern of Jesus and applies it to the entire social sphere. It recognizes that caring for those in need means attending to all the causes of their need, both individual and social. Justice adds an important and a necessary dimension to the Christian moral life.

Let us pray . . .

Christ our brother, you are the just one. You took on injustice in your own life, even unto death, and gave us the dream of a just world in which we all can share. Empower us with your Spirit. Guide us as we seek to uproot injustice. Grant us the courage to work with those who are poor and those who are discriminated against. Fill your people with hope. Amen.

A Review of Part II

Write down and discuss your thoughts on the following questions.

1. Look back over your notes and assignments for the last seven chapters. For each chapter name one insight that you gained from examining the topics covered in it.

2. What do you believe are the major moral issues facing our world today?

3. What are three or four action steps that you might take in response to these moral issues?

4. What changes would you like to see in the moral climate present in our society?

5. How can Christian moral principles help us in making these changes?

Glossary

abortion—deliberate cessation of prenatal life

acquaintance rape—forcing sex on someone known by the assailant

adultery—sex between two people at least one of whom is married to someone else

ageism—discrimination against people solely on the basis of their age

alienation—an experience of isolation and separateness resulting in uneasiness around others

almost-committed sex—the view that intimate sexual activity is acceptable when the two people have expressed a degree of commitment to each other, such as during engagement

apathy—an attitude of not getting involved, not caring, not acting when action is called for

appeal to authority—defending one's position by citing a respected source, such as the Constitution

artificial insemination by donor (AID)—mechanically introducing sperm from a man other than the woman's husband into a woman's uterus to bring about fertilization

artificial insemination by husband (AIH)—mechanically introducing a husband's sperm into his wife's uterus to bring about fertilization

Beatitude saints—people who take the Beatitude's message to heart and attempt to live it

Beatitudes—eight descriptions of early Christians as they struggled to live their life in Christ

bottom line—in business, realizing a profit

calumny—telling lies that could damage a person's reputation

capital punishment—death penalty; state-sanctioned execution of persons convicted of serious crimes

cardinal virtues—the four virtues that hold together the moral life—prudence, temperance, fortitude, and justice

Catechism of the Catholic Church—a document containing official Catholic teaching

character—the inclinations toward goodness or evil that are part of the fabric of a person's being

cheap grace—believing "God loves me no matter what; therefore I can do whatever I want"

Christian morality—the way that we live our lives in response to Jesus

classism—discrimination against people based on their socio-economic status

cloning—creating a plant, animal, or person asexually that is genetically identical with a donor plant, animal, or person

co-creators—people who help transform the world and the human community into what God intends them to be

common good—a long-standing Christian concept advocating that society should be organized so that, as much as possible, both individuals and the entire community are equally thriving

communal prayer—praying together with a group of people

communion of saints—people of the past, present, and future who were, are, and are to be inspired by the Holy Spirit to contribute to the world in some positive way

communities of support—a term affirming that everyone needs everyone else in making the Body of Christ effective

community of character—a community that exhibits an environment where virtue is the norm among its members

conscience—moral decision making involving awareness that there is right and wrong, a process of discernment, and finally judgment

conscientious objector—for moral or religious reasons one who is opposed to serving in the military

consciousness—awareness of oneself and one's surroundings

consequences—the outcome of actions

conventional level of morality—when a person's motive for behavior is fitting in and adhering to conventions of society

costly grace—a relationship with God that involves a challenge and a response on our part

covenant—in the ancient Middle East, an agreement between two parties; Israelites applied the concept to their relationship as a people with their God Yahweh.

critical thinking—using systematic thinking and analysis in our lives

date rape—rape that occurs in the context of a date or a dating relationship

designated decision maker—someone appointed to make medical decisions for a person who is incapacitated

deterrence—punishment or fear of punishment that can help prevent crime

discernment—investigating and analyzing the moral implications of choices we are faced with; taking whatever steps necessary to help make the best possible decision

discrimination—a situation in which people suffer disadvantages simply because they are members of a particular group (for example, age, race, gender)

DNA—the intricate interlocking chain of genetic material that makes up all living cells

domestic violence—violence that occurs in close relationships, such as husband-wife, parent-child, or boyfriend-girlfriend

dualistic view of the human condition—dividing the human into higher and lower components and labeling one evil

dynamic—developing, growing, changing

ecclesia—a Greek word for a "duly summoned assembly"; also means "Church"

Economic Justice for All—the U.S. Catholic bishops' 1986 pastoral letter on the economy

embryo—a fertilized egg possessing a unique genetic makeup

emotional-relationship sex—a view of sexual activity as being acceptable when the two people involved feel love for each other

empathy—identifying the joys and sorrows of others as our own

encyclical—an official letter from the pope, usually addressed to all Church members

environmental injustice—unequal distribution of environmental hazards based on racial and economic differences

erroneous conscience—when a person follows a process of conscientious decision making but unwittingly makes a wrong decision

euthanasia— deliberately taking steps to bring about a person's death for the purposes of eliminating suffering

explicit violence—a situation in which someone is physically harmed or killed by direct action

extraordinary means of life support—medical procedures that offer little hope of benefits or which cover undue or excessive burden to the patient or his or her family

fact finding—seeking information to help gain a better understanding of a problem

faith—belief in God; the theological virtue of seeking to know and to do God's will

footwashing—the activity Jesus performed prior to the Last Supper that becomes the model for all Christian service

fortitude—the virtue of acting courageously

general deterrence—the belief that fear of punishment will prevent people from committing crime

genetic engineering—changing inherited characteristics by changing genetic makeup of a plant, animal, or person

genetics—the study of characteristics inherited from one generation to another

genuine—not hiding behind a role or image; seeking honest communication with others

grace—God's love and life in us, God's help

guilt—doing wrong and recognizing one's wrongdoing

gun control—a variety of measures intended to cut down on gun accidents and gun violence

"hard sayings" of Jesus—teachings such as the Beatitudes and the Last Judgment that overturn commonly held values and priorities

hardness of heart—a biblical image for sin suggesting that sinful acts are a distortion of our true humanity

hero—someone who follows her or his conscience in the face of difficulties

heterosexuality—sexual attraction toward persons of the other sex

heterosexual activity—sexual activity engaged in by persons of different sexes

hidden violence—a situation in which someone is harmed or killed indirectly because of various social factors

homosexuality—sexual attraction toward persons of the same sex

homosexual activity—sexual activity engaged in by persons of the same sex

hope—trusting in God, in everything that Christ has promised, and in the help of the Holy Spirit

horizontal perspective on sin—viewing sin in terms of its effect on other people

hospice—an intense, multi-faceted, spiritually based approach to assisting people through the dying process

humility—admitting the truth about who you are, especially about limitations that you possess

idolatry—being all consumed with one thing and treating it as if it were more important than God

in vitro fertilization (IVF)—initiating the process of reproduction, or insemination, through laboratory procedures

inalienable rights—rights that all people possess because of their very nature as humans

infertility—an inability to bring about conception (for a man) or to conceive or bear a child (for a woman) through natural methods

informed conscience—a conscience that is educated and developed through constant use and examination

immoral decisions—choices that are deliberately harmful to ourselves or others

insemination—joining of egg and sperm, producing an entity that is genetically unique and distinct from the egg donor and the sperm donor

institution—commonly accepted ways (structures, laws, rules, customs, and so on) that basic, essential functions are carried out within a society

integrity—honesty, genuineness, and consistency in behavior patterns

interdependent—needing one another to survive and thrive

interdependence—the proposition that within a community all members depend upon one another

Internet etiquette—using the Internet in ways that do not cause harm to others

iron pipeline—the practice of buying large quantities of guns where gun-purchasing laws are lenient and re-selling them in high-crime areas

just wage—fair and adequate monetary compensation for one's work

justice—the virtue that states that all people have rights and deserve to have basic needs met

just-war principles—a set of principles first proposed in the fourth century outlining conditions when use of violence would be acceptable

kingdom of God—Jesus' vision of a world where God reigns—where people serve one another, share their goods with one another, and refuse to retaliate with violence against others

"The Last Judgment"—the story told in Matthew, chapter 25, where Jesus identifies himself with the needy of the world

lax conscience—when a person does not employ a process of conscientious decision making, therefore, a "lazy conscience"

legalism—an attitude of strict observance of laws, irregardless of circumstances and possible harm to people involved

lived values—qualities and concerns that we demonstrate as being important through our actions

living will—a declaration that a competent adult makes identifying the medical care desired if she or he becomes incapacitated

love—the theological virtue representing the core of the Christian moral life. Love is the virtue that places concern for God, manifest especially through concern for others, above everything else.

Luddites—English workers who, early in the industrial revolution, destroyed machines that were taking away their traditional means of livelihood

masochism—a psychological disorder marked by deliberately seeking out pain

mean world syndrome—the proposal that increased television viewing leads to a perception of the world as being a more hostile, dangerous place

medical ethics—moral decision making related to medical research and practice

minimalism—an attitude of doing only the bare minimum that is required by law in our moral life

ministry—work as serving others

missing the mark—a biblical image indicating that sin does not move us in the direction of our true goal, oneness with God

moral decisions—positive choices that promote human welfare

moral muscle—pushing ourselves to do more than the minimum in our moral life

moral principles—fundamental statements about right and wrong

morality—our decision-making capacity as it affects ourselves and others

mortal sin—an action so destructive that it mortally wounds our relationship with God; complete rejection of God

motives—why people do what they do

natural moral law—moral principles arrived at through rational investigation of human nature

nonmoral decisions—decisions that are morally neutral

nonviolence—conflict-resolving techniques that do not rely on physical or psychological injury of an opponent

nuclear deterrence—the proposition that if two nations possess the ability to inflict serious damage on each other, then neither nation is likely to use its nuclear weapons in the first place

nuclear proliferation—any increase in the number of nations that possess nuclear weapons or that have the capability to build them

obscene—literally means "off-stage." An insensitive, public portrayal of what should be kept private and intimate, such as sex and dying.

On the Condition of Workers—the 1891 encyclical of Pope Leo XIII voicing concern for industrial workers; the first of a series of documents comprising modern Catholic social teaching

ordinary means of life support—medical procedures that offer sufficient or reasonable benefits without excessive or undue burdens to the patient or his or her family

original sin—the human inclination toward evil

ovum—an egg cell

particular deterrence—preventing by imprisonment or execution someone who has committed a crime from committing crime again

pastoral letter—an official letter from a bishop to members of his diocese or from a conference of bishops in a particular country or area

physician-assisted suicide—a person who is incurably ill killing himself or herself with the help of a physician

playboy/playgirl philosophy—the belief that sex should be engaged in strictly for pleasure, with few if any restrictions

portfolio—the sum of someone's investments in various stocks

post-conventional level of morality—when a person's motive for behavior places universal good over self-good or the good of the group

pre-conventional level of morality—when a person's motive for behavior is fear of punishment or promise of reward

prime time—the evening hours when television viewing is heaviest

private confession—a practice introduced by Irish monks around the seventh century initially meant to assist people in their spiritual development. Eventually it became the standard form for the official Sacrament of Reconciliation.

procreative function of marriage— the life-giving dimension of a married relationship, including—but not exclusively—openness to children

prudence—the virtue of practical judgment

psychopath—a person lacking any sense of right and wrong

rabbi—Hebrew for "teacher," a term frequently applied to Jesus

racial prejudice—strong dislike for members of a race other than one's own

racism—subordination of persons who belong to a particular race due to attitudes, actions, or institutional structures at work in a society

rape—forcing sex on an unwilling partner

rash judgment—assuming as true negative comments made about another person

reconciliation—an experience of reuniting and reconnecting with others

recreational sex—a view of sexual activity as the pursuit of pleasure with no constraints other than mutual consent

rehabilitation—programs aimed at training and reforming wrongdoers so that they no longer commit crime

reproductive technology—scientific procedures related to procreation and the early stages of life

retribution—restoring the social order by punishing wrongdoers, thus declaring that certain behaviors are not tolerated in society

saboteurs—originally, French factory workers who temporarily dismantled industrial production by throwing their wooden shoes into machines

sacramental view of the human condition—affirming the fullness of the human reality as holy

scrutinize—examining various dimensions of a dilemma, especially so that overlooked aspects come to light

selective conscientious objector—one who is opposed for moral or religious reasons to serving in the military during a particular war

Sermon on the Mount—the account, for example, in Matthew, chapter 5–7, of Jesus' preaching important moral teachings beginning with the Beatitudes

sexism—attitudes, practices, and institutional structures that oppress people solely on the basis of gender

sexually transmitted diseases (STD)—diseases contracted primarily through sexual activity between people

shame—experiencing oneself as unworthy and unlovable

sin of commission—purposely doing an action that is harmful to oneself or another

sin of omission—not doing an action that is called for

sinful social structures—ways societies are structured resulting in unjust distribution of power, benefits, and privileges

sin—when people act contrary to their conscience and purposely choose to do wrong

skepticism—in general, a doubting and questioning attitude. As defined by Pope John Paul II, a lack of belief that there are fundamental truths, dismissing any sense of right or wrong.

slander—revealing information that could harm another person's reputation

social analysis—a process for examining social problems that involves searching for underlying causes and long-term solutions to the problems

social sin—recognition of the social dimension of sin, both in its causes and in its effects

Socrates—fifth-century B.C. Greek philosopher

Song of Solomon—a book of the Hebrew Scriptures; a love song between a man and a woman that also serves as an analogy for the love God has for people

spiral of poverty—poor people being in a situation that makes overcoming being poor almost impossible

stakeholders—people who are affected by a particular business

stated values—qualities and concerns that we claim are important to us

stewardship—biblical concept that humans represent God in caring for the earth's resources

stockholders—people who invest money in a company

surrogate mother—a woman who agrees to be artificially impregnated by a man married to another woman and to relinquish at birth legal custody of the child to the man and his wife

symptoms—a problem that is immediately apparent

talent— a unit of money in Jesus' time; in current usage it designates a natural endowment with which we are born

temperance—the virtue of self control

The Body of Christ—an image used by Saint Paul for all Christians working together to make the world a better place

The Challenge of Peace—1983 pastoral letter of U.S. Catholic bishops addressing issues of war and peace

The Gospel of Life—1985 encyclical by Pope John Paul II about the value and sacredness of human life

"the little way"—a "spirituality of the everyday," doing little things to reflect God's love in the world, as advocated by Saint Thérèse of Lisieux

The Splendor of Truth—Pope John Paul II's encyclical on morality

theological virtues—faith, hope, and love, the foundations of the Christian moral life

therapeutic—directed toward healing a disorder, disease, or illness

underlying causes—reasons why a problem exists; reasons that are not readily apparent

unitive function of marriage—the love-making and love-giving dimension of a married relationship

urbanization—growth of cities worldwide

Vatican Council II—a meeting of the world's bishops during which documents were published and commissions established to set an agenda for the Church (1962–1965)

venial sin—an action that turns us away from God in small degrees

vice—a pattern of behavior that is harmful to oneself or others

virtue—a character strength manifest on a consistent basis in decision making

whistle blower—an employee of a company who discovers illegal or immoral practices and makes that information public

youth culture—the belief that young people have values, interests, and activities distinct from those of other age groups

Photo List
AP/Wide World Photos—Jacqueline Arzt: 275; John Chadwick: 199; Dennis Cook: 143D, 157; Mark Duncan: 195, Eric Gay: 109; Allen Greth: 41; Dominique Mollard: 51; **Archive Photos**—Anne Frank Fonds, Basel/Anne Frank House, Amsterdam: 82; **Art Resource, NY**—SCALA 206A, 212; **James Baca**—260; **Catholic News Service**—55, Giordani: 91; Nancy Wiechec: 79C, 93, 237; *Company, A Jesuit Magazine*—Fr. Enrique Figaredo: 26; **Gene Plaisted/TheCrosiers**—6, 24, 63C, 73, 99, 119B, 124, 243D, 245A; **Nancy Dawe**—31B; **FPG International**—44; Josef Beck: 65; Ron Chapple: 68A, 221; Ken Chernus: 20A, 28; Jim Cummins: 63B, 64C; Rob Gage: 225C, 232; Keystone View Co.: 80; Harvey Lloyd: 7; Guy Marche: 153; Montes de Oca, ART 1990: 46; O'Brien & Mayor Photography: 64B; Hy Peshkin: 81; Chris Salvo: 138; Stephen Simpson: 132; Adam Smith: 67; Mike Smith 1972: 125A, Telegraph Colour Library: 23, 175; Arthur Tilley: 1E, 8; August Upitis: 103, VCG: 224A; **Robert Fried**—14, 50, 68B, 85; **The Image Works**—Bob Daemmrich: 225D, 239, 266; L. Dematteis: 296; Steven Rubin: 243C, 249, 270, 286; Tony Savino: 196, 273; Karim Shamsi-Basha: 281C, 301; Steve Skjold: 295; Charles Steiner: 186; UNEP/E.C. Tuyay: 79D, 86; Michael Wickes: 281D, 294; **Mary Messenger**—162;;**Monkmeyer**—R. Sidney 140; **National Portrait Gallery, London**—60; **North Wind Picture Archives**—210; **Chip and Rosa Maria de la Cueva Peterson**—75; **PhotoEdit**—112, 233; Bill Aron: 263; Jose Carillo: 256; Paul Conklin: 181; David K. Crow: 97B, 114; Mary Kate Denny: 147; Amy Etra: 243B, 253; Myrleen Ferguson: 89, 267; Tony Freeman: 79B, 87, 98; Spencer Grant: 113, 161; Jeff Greenberg: 53, 94; Richard Hutchings: 120, 285, 292B; Richard Lord: 40; Michael Newman: 122A, 148, 265, 288, 300; Alan Oddie: 1B, 281B, 283; Elena Rodraid: 225B, 235; David Young-Wolff: 72; **Photo Researchers, Inc.**—Deep Light Productions/SPL: 215; Phillip Hayson/SS: 192; Ken Lax: 191; Hank Morgan: 190; A. Sieveking/Petit Format: 207B, 216; **James L. Shaffer**—25, 31C, 42, 64A, 76, 78A, 104, 127, 130, 143C, 144, 146, 150, 151, 154, 170, 182, 183, 202, 207, 211, 214, 243, 245B, 250; **Tony Stone Images**—Bill Aron: 135; Bruce Ayres: 282; Christopher Bissell: 143B, 149; Bushnell/Soifer: 247; Michael Busselle: 118A; Peter Cade: 4, 155; Anthony Cassidy: viA, 15; Roger Charity: 200; Paul Chesley: 290; Lucien Clergue: 39B, 52; Richard Clintsman: 193; Philip Condit II: 262; Chris Craymer: 1D, 12; Robert E. Daemmrich: 1C, 17, 177; Reza Estakhrian: 38A, 48; Ken Fisher: 299; David R. Frazier: 272; Suzanne & Nick Geary: 100; Hulton Getty: 30, 83, 125B, 128; Paul Harris: 39, 59; Walter Hodges: 166, 302; Richard Hutchings: 292; Richard Kavlin: 169; Jerry Kobalenko: 289; Stuart McClymont: 139; Laurence Monneret: 201B; Jonathan Nourok: 71; Rosanne Olson: 39C, 43; Lori Adamski Peek: 164, 303; Joseph Poberskin: 227; Joe Polillio: 201C; Jon Riley: 47, 180; Andy Sacks: 21B, 31A, 292A; Chris Sanders: 173; Charles Thatcher: 217; Alan Thornton: 234; Terry Vine: 219; Lori Adamski Peek: 164, 303; Karl Weatherly: 142A, 158; Steven Weinberg: 96A, 116; David Young-Wolff: 21C, 35, 122B; **SuperStock**—32, 68C, 101, 119D, 134, 167, 168, 172, 178, 188, 201A, 229, 231, 242A, 244, 252, 274, 280A, 298; Tate Gallery, London/ET Archive, London: 62A; **Ullstein Bilderdienst**—11; **Whitman Photography**—2, 97C, 108, 137; **Jim Whitmer**—13, 16, 33, 106, 119C, 133

Index

CONTENTS

Part 1: Foundations for Christian Morality